D1558865

CAMBRIDGE STUDIES IN
MEDIEVAL LIFE AND THOUGHT

Edited by M. D. KNOWLES, Litt.D., F.B.A.
*Fellow of Peterhouse and Regius Professor of Modern History in the
University of Cambridge*

NEW SERIES, VOL. 6

MATTHEW PARIS

Virgin and Child. B.M. Roy. MS. 14 C vii, f. 6a.

MATTHEW PARIS

BY

RICHARD VAUGHAN

Fellow of Corpus Christi College
Cambridge

CAMBRIDGE
AT THE UNIVERSITY PRESS
1958

PUBLISHED BY
THE SYNDICS OF THE CAMBRIDGE UNIVERSITY PRESS

Bentley House, 200 Euston Road, London, N.W. 1
American Branch: 32 East 57th Street, New York 22, N.Y.

©

CAMBRIDGE UNIVERSITY PRESS
1958

Printed in Great Britain at the University Press, Cambridge
(Brooke Crutchley, University Printer)

CONTENTS

CONTENTS

LIST OF PLATES

Virgin and Child. British Museum Royal MS. 14 C
vii, f. 6 a. *frontispiece*

PREFACE

WHEN, in the summer of 1951, I was in a position to embark on research for a Ph.D. thesis, I found myself unable to decide on a suitable subject. It was Professor Knowles who suggested Matthew Paris to me, and who supervised my researches during the ensuing three years. The result was a study of the relationship and chronology of Matthew Paris's historical manuscripts which is incorporated—much altered, and, as I hope, improved—in the present work. My especial thanks are due to Professor Knowles, who, besides helping me as a supervisor and afterwards, has read the whole of this book in typescript and been kind enough to accept it for publication in the series of medieval studies which he edits. I must also thank Professor Galbraith, who has taken a lively interest in my work, and thereby been a constant source of encouragement and stimulation. Professor Cheney has provided help of a rather different kind, for which I must also record my thanks: he has read this book in typescript and proof and saved me from numerous errors, as well as making many suggestions which led to some important alterations in the text. For his encouragement since my undergraduate days, frequent loans and gifts of books, and much learned assistance, I must thank Professor Dickins. I would also like to thank Dr R. W. Hunt of the Bodleian Library, Dr C. E. Wright and Mrs Antonia Gransden of the British Museum, and Mr H. L. Pink of the University Library, Cambridge, for their help concerning manuscripts; Mr A. G. Woodhead for helping me with Matthew's Latin, and Dr M. H. Tweedy for helping me with his French; Dr T. E. Faber for advising me on some points concerning Matthew's scientific interests; and Professor Mynors, Dr Dorothy Whitelock, and Mr H. M. Adams. It is not perhaps inapposite here for me to record my obligations and thanks to my colleagues of Corpus Christi College for enabling me to complete this study by electing me into their Fellowship; and to my wife for her patience and forbearance during the many hours I have had to spend engrossed in Matthew Paris.

My thanks are due to the authorities of the following for allowing me to study manuscripts in their possession, and to the various librarians for their courtesy and help: the British Museum; the Public Record Office; the Bodleian Library; the University Library, Cambridge; the John Rylands Library; the Lambeth Palace Library; Chetham's Hospital, Manchester; Corpus Christi College, Oxford; Trinity College, Cambridge; my own College; and Eton College. I must also thank the Duke of Devonshire, Mr Francis Thompson and Mr T. E. Wragg for enabling me to see the manuscripts at Chatsworth; Lord Bute and Miss Catherine Armet for arranging for me to have Bute MS. 3 on loan in Cambridge, and Mr H. R. Creswick for allowing it to be deposited in the University Library here; Miss M. F. Austin, the Hertfordshire County Librarian, for lending me some extracts and off-prints concerning the history of St Albans; and Professor Arnould and Mr H. W. Parke of Trinity College, Dublin, for transcribing for me the marginalia in Trinity College, Dublin, MS. E i 40. Finally, I have to thank the authorities of the following libraries for giving me permission to reproduce portions of their manuscripts: the British Museum (frontispiece, Plates I, IV, V, IX (*a*), X (*a*), XI, XII, XIV (*c*) and (*d*), XV (*a*) and (*b*), XVIII (*a*), (*c*), and (*f*), and XIX); the Bodleian Library (Plates XIV (*f*) and XXI (*b*)); the University Library, Cambridge (Plate IX (*b*)); Trinity College, Dublin (Plate VIII); Corpus Christi College, Oxford (Plate XVII); and Corpus Christi College, Cambridge (Plates II, III, VI, VII, X (*b*), XII, XIV (*a*), (*b*), and (*e*), XV (*c*), XVI, XVIII (*b*), (*d*), and (*e*), XX, and XXI (*a*)).

R. V.

CORPUS CHRISTI COLLEGE
CAMBRIDGE
3 April 1956

ABBREVIATIONS

A	Corpus Christi College, Cambridge, MS. 26.
B	Corpus Christi College, Cambridge, MS. 16.
C	British Museum Cotton MS. Nero D v, Part II.
Ch	Chetham's Library, Manchester, MS. 6712.
E	Eton College, MS. 123.
LA	British Museum Cotton MS. Nero D i.
O	British Museum Cotton MS. Otho B v.
R	British Museum Royal MS. 14 C vii.
V	British Museum Cotton MS. Vitellius A xx.
W	Bodleian Library Douce MS. 207.
CM.	*Chronica Majora* (ed. Luard).
HA.	*Historia Anglorum* (ed. Madden).
FH.	*Flores Historiarum* (ed. Luard).
AC.	*Abbreviatio Chronicorum* (ed. Madden).
Wats	*Gesta Abbatum* and *Vitae Offarum* (ed. Wats).
GA.	*Gesta Abbatum* (ed. Riley).
MGH,SS.	*Monumenta Germaniae Historica, Scriptores.*
EHR.	*English Historical Review.*

CHAPTER I

THE LIFE OF MATTHEW PARIS

THE writings of Matthew Paris, monk of St Albans and historian, seem to have come down to us almost intact, and it is from them that our very fragmentary knowledge of his life is derived. In the last century two great scholars, Madden and Liebermann, brought this information together,[1] and, since their work, not a scrap of new material concerning the events of Matthew's life has come to light. We have no knowledge of his family or even nationality. His name, which he usually wrote 'Parisiensis', but sometimes 'de Parisius', was formerly taken to refer either to this, or to his university education; and it was surmised in consequence either that Matthew was French, or that he was educated at Paris University. But Parisiensis was a common enough patronymic in thirteenth-century England, and, on the whole, it seems probable that Matthew was English, and that he did not receive his education at Paris, or indeed any other, university. His interests are not those of a university educated clerk, and his outlook is characteristically English. The phrase 'which in common speech we call Hoke Day' in his *Chronica Majora* (v, p. 281) shows that he thought of English as his own language; and his English feelings are displayed in his account of Henry III's campaign in Poitou in 1242, when he uses the phrase 'our men' ('nostri anglici') in reference to the English troops.[2]

The date of Matthew's birth also remains in doubt. He himself tells us that he took the religious habit (that is, became a monk) at St Albans on 21 January 1217.[3] It was customary at this time for a novice to take the habit when he entered the house, instead of waiting until he made his profession,[4] so that it is probable that Matthew entered St Albans as a novice in

[1] *HA.* III, pp. vii–xxii (Madden), and Liebermann, *MGH,SS.* XXVIII, pp. 74 ff.   [2] *CM.* IV, pp. 210, 219.   [3] *HA.* III, p. ix.
[4] That this was true for St Albans is shown by a statute of Abbot Warin; Wats, pp. 101–2. It was also the custom in Lanfranc's time: see his *Monastic Constitutions* (ed. M. D. Knowles), pp. 105–6.

1217, and made his profession a year or two later. At this time, the minimum age of admission for a novice could hardly have been under fifteen, so that the date of Matthew's birth cannot be placed much after 1200. It is unlikely, too, that he was born much before this, since he lived until 1259, and sixty must have been a ripe old age for a medieval monk. Some remarks of Matthew himself which might be taken as evidence for an earlier date than 1200 are in fact of very doubtful significance. In the *Chronica Majora*, for instance, he tells under the year 1195 the story of Vitalis the Venetian, with the following marginal note: 'King Richard's Apologue, which he related to Warin, abbot of St Albans; and which he (Warin) passed on to us' (*Apologus Ricardi regis quem abbati Sancti Albani Guarino et ipse nobis enarravit*).[1] If the word 'nobis' here means 'to me', then Matthew must have been born some years before the death of Abbot Warin in 1195; but in fact it probably only means 'to us', that is 'to the community'. Under the year 1213[2] Matthew inserts another story, which he says was related in his hearing (p. 564: 'audiente Mathaeo qui et haec scripsit') to various St Albans monks by Robert of London, the secular custodian of the abbey. Robert of London was secular 'custos' of St Albans in 1208,[3] but he may easily have visited the abbey on some later occasion. A third statement of Matthew's, this time in the *Gesta Abbatum*, is equally inconclusive: he says, in reference to Abbot John de Cella's extraordinary feats of memory:[4] 'Hoc enim quasi in confusionem nesciorum fecisse ipsum, profecto meminimus.' The word 'meminimus' here need not necessarily mean 'we remember', it may only mean 'we have recorded'; and so we are by no means compelled to conclude from this statement that Matthew Paris actually knew Abbot John, who died in 1214. It seems likely, therefore, that Matthew was born about the year 1200: at any rate there is no reliable evidence that he was born before this date.

We know nothing certain about Matthew between 1217 and 1247, but from the language of his chronicle it seems probable that he was present at Canterbury for the translation of St Thomas Becket on 7 July 1220; that he was at St Albans in 1228 when

[1] II, pp. 413–14.   [2] *CM*. II, pp. 559–64.
[2] *HA*. III, p. xi.   [4] Wats, p. 108.

the abbey was visited by an Armenian archbishop; and that he attended the marriage of Henry III and Eleanor at Westminster in January 1236.[1] His account of each of these events seems to be that of an eye-witness. Our lack of knowledge of Matthew Paris during these years is probably due to the life he was leading as a cloistered monk at St Albans; and we may assume that throughout this time, as well as during most of the rest of his life, it was only occasionally that he interrupted his historical writing (in which he was probably more or less continually engaged from *c.* 1245 onwards) and the service of God in his house, to witness some great event either at Westminster, Canterbury, Winchester, or some other centre. How he was enabled to leave the abbey from time to time in this way, we do not know. It is possible, as Professor Cheney has suggested to me, that he held some such office as chaplain to the abbot; but there is, so far as I have been able to discover, no evidence in contemporary records of any monastic official at St Albans at this time by the name of Matthew. On 13 October 1247 Matthew Paris was present at Westminster for the feast of St Edward the Confessor, and his account shows that Henry III knew by this time that he was writing a chronicle, and had already met him, perhaps during one of his many visits to St Albans.[2] Matthew's account of his meeting with the king on this occasion is as follows:[3]

And while...the king was seated on his throne, noticing the writer of this work, he called him to him, made him sit down on a step between the throne and the rest of the hall, and said to him: 'You have noticed all these things, and they are firmly impressed on your mind.' To which he answered: 'Yes, my Lord, for the splendid doings of this day are worthy of record.' The king then went on: '...I entreat you...therefore...to write an accurate and full account of all these events...lest in the future their memory be in any way lost to posterity'; and he invited the person with whom he was speaking to dinner, together with his three companions.

Under the year 1250[4] Matthew has recorded another of his conversations with the king, which perhaps occurred in April

---

[1] *HA.* II, pp. 241–2; *CM.* III, pp. 161–4; and *CM.* III, pp. 336 ff.
[2] For these see below, pp. 12–13.
[3] *CM.* IV, pp. 644–5.　　　　[4] *CM.* V, pp. 129–30.

　　　　　　　　　　　　　　　　　　1-2

1251, when the king was at St Albans.[1] On this occasion, he tells us, he remonstrated with the king for granting rights of free warren contrary to the privileges of St Albans. In July 1251 Matthew was with the king again, this time at Winchester, and he there heard and noted down at length Thomas of Sherborne's account of the Pastoureaux in France.[2] In November 1251 he may have been present at the dedication of the church of Hayles in Gloucestershire, and at Christmas at York for the marriage of Henry III's daughter Margaret to Alexander II of Scotland; for his accounts of these events seem to be those of an eye-witness.[3] Finally, we hear of him again with Henry III at St Albans in March 1257,[4] when he spent some time in the king's company both at table and in the royal lodgings. On this occasion the king imparted to him some historical information, including a list of the canonized kings of England (which Matthew inserted into his chronicle) and the names of two hundred and fifty English baronies. During the week which the king spent at St Albans at this time, Matthew had an opportunity of putting in a good word to him on behalf of the University of Oxford, whose M.A.'s had sent a deputation to complain of the oppression of the bishop of Lincoln.

Matthew's life as a monk of St Albans was on one occasion disturbed much more seriously than by the occasional visits to Westminster or elsewhere which we have hitherto noted. It seems that in the year 1246, as a result of the disappearance of its abbot with the convent's seal, the abbey of St Benet Holm on the island of Nidarholm in Norway got into serious financial difficulties with the London Cahorsins.[5] King Haakon of Norway sent the prior to England with a letter to Matthew Paris, requesting his help; and, through his good offices, an agreement was reached with the money-lenders which enabled the monks of St Benet Holm to free themselves from debt. In 1247 or 1248, however, they were in trouble again; this time because of a quarrel with their archbishop, and they were advised by the papal legate then in Norway to apply to the

[1] CM. v, pp. 233–4. [2] CM. v, pp. 246–54.
[3] CM. v, pp. 262 and 266–7. [4] CM. v, pp. 617–18.
[5] CM. v, pp. 42–5. I have also used the narrative in Knowles, *Religious Orders*, I, pp. 294–5.

pope for someone to visit and reform their house. Innocent IV allowed them to choose whom they liked, and they decided on Matthew Paris, probably because of his previous services to them. The papal mandate to the abbot of St Albans instructing him to send Matthew to Norway to reform the monastery of St Benet Holm is copied out by Matthew Paris in four of his manuscripts. Although by it Matthew is only appointed to instruct and advise the abbot and monks of St Benet Holm 'in regularibus disciplinis et statutis' pertaining to the Benedictine Order, he copied it into his collection of additional documents with this heading: [1]

The original papal document (*Auctenticum papale*) by which Dom Matthew Paris, who wrote these things, was appointed, though unwillingly, reformer of the Benedictine observance and Visitor of the Benedictine abbeys and their monks in the kingdom of Norway.

In his *Historia Anglorum* [2] he introduces the same document with similar words:

...Brother Matthew, the author of this work, was sent by order of the pope to Norway, to restore Benedictine observance in the monasteries of the Black monks (*ad reformandum Ordinem Sancti Benedicti in coenobiis monachorum Nigri Ordinis*).

It looks very much as if Matthew's natural pride in his appointment caused him to magnify the importance of this mission and to consider himself Visitor to the whole of the Benedictine Order in Norway. Be this as it may, his visit there poses an interesting problem. No doubt the monks of St Benet Holm chose Matthew as their Visitor on account of the services he had previously rendered them; but why did King Haakon write to him, in 1246, asking him to negotiate with the Cahorsin money-lenders in London on behalf of the monks of St Benet Holm? H. G. Leach [3] suggested that Matthew's visit to Norway in 1248 was perhaps not his first, and that he had met Haakon on a previous visit there. Matthew, however, tells us nothing of this, and it is most unlikely that, had such an event taken place, he would have passed over it in silence. The mystery of Haakon's selection of Matthew as his financial agent in this

---

[1] *LA*, f. 92b; for the heading, see *CM.* v, p. 244, note 4.
[2] III, p. 40.   [3] *Angevin Britain and Scandinavia*, p. 105.

affair is perhaps partly elucidated, however, by his appointment, in 1238, of a certain Richard of St Albans to look after his affairs in England,[1] for it is possible that this Richard, relinquishing his post, recommended Matthew to Haakon as a suitable successor. Nevertheless, however we try to explain the choice of Matthew in this matter, we still do not know why he was considered suitable; and we can only hazard the guess that the interest in and knowledge of financial matters which he displays throughout his writings[2] reflect a considerable experience in practical affairs, which he had perhaps already obtained before 1246, and which qualified him to undertake these transactions.

The papal mandate sending Matthew to Norway is dated 27 November 1247, and it probably arrived at St Albans early in 1248; but it was not until the early summer that Matthew finally set out for Norway. He arrived at the port of Bergen *c.* 10 June,[3] at the very moment when a great fire was raging in the city. Both Matthew and the author of Haakon's Saga give a vivid description of this fire, which was followed by a violent thunderstorm over the town.[4] Haakon's Saga describes how the lightning struck the mast of a ship in the harbour and dashed it into small pieces, and how only one person on the ship was hurt— a citizen of Bergen who had gone on board from the town to buy finery. Matthew, who was ashore at the time celebrating mass in a neighbouring church, and thanking God for his safe passage through the perils of the sea, also describes how the mast of his ship was shivered into pieces, but he, with the pardonable hyperbole of a passenger, claims that, besides one man killed, all those on the ship were either wounded or hurt in some way. He goes on to record how, when Haakon heard of this accident, he provided the ship with a new and bigger and better ('praestantiorem...et majorem') mast. Haakon was in Bergen at the time,[5] and Matthew delivered to him letters from King Louis IX of France seeking Haakon's company on his projected crusade,

---

[1] Rymer (ed.), *Foedera*, I, p. 236.
[2] See below, pp. 145–6.
[3] Leach, *Angevin Britain and Scandinavia*, p. 105.
[4] *CM.* v, pp. 35–6, and Dasent (ed.), *Saga of Hacon*, pp. 266–7.
[5] Dasent (ed.), *Saga of Hacon*, p. 266: he organized attempts to extinguish the fire with 'kettles' full of sea-water.

and giving him permission to land in French territory on his way. Haakon received Matthew kindly and rewarded him with sumptuous gifts.[1] It would be interesting to know how Matthew Paris came to be the bearer of these important letters from Louis IX. Was it mere chance? Or did that monarch have personal knowledge of the monk of St Albans? There is no hint, in Matthew's writings, of the answer to these questions; nor indeed does he give us any further information about his visit to Norway and his reformation of the monks of St Benet Holm. He does not even mention his return journey, which probably took place in 1249.

We have now passed in review the few known facts about the life of Matthew Paris. The last of these, his death in 1259, was once undisputed; but recently Sir Maurice Powicke has cast doubts on this, and has argued that Matthew may have lived 'for some little time after 1259'.[2] The belief that Matthew died in this year is based on the colophon which closes the text of his *Chronica Majora*, and which is illustrated in Plate I. The text of this, as translated by Professor Galbraith,[3] reads:

Thus far wrote (*perscripsit*) the venerable man, brother Matthew Paris: and though the hand on the pen may vary, nevertheless, as the same method of composition is maintained throughout, the whole is ascribed to him. What has been added and continued from this point onwards may be ascribed to another brother, who presuming to approach the works of so great a predecessor, and unworthy to continue them, as he is unworthy to undo the latchet of his shoe, has not deserved to have even his name mentioned on the page.

Below these words is a drawing of Matthew on his death-bed, with his 'book of chronicles' on the desk by him, and with the words 'Hic obit Matheus Parisiensis' written above. Professor Galbraith, in his criticism of Sir Maurice Powicke's theory, produced other evidence for the date of Matthew's death. He pointed out that the continuator of Matthew's *Gesta Abbatum* states that Matthew Paris lived and died in the time of Abbot

---

[1] See below, p. 18.

[2] Powicke, 'Compilation of the *Chronica Majora*', *Proceedings of the British Academy*, XXX (1944), pp. 157–8.

[3] Galbraith, *Roger Wendover and Matthew Paris*, p. 12.

John of Hertford.[1] Now H. T. Riley, in his edition of the *Gesta Abbatum*, claims that Abbot John ruled from 1235 to 1260, and suggests that the text of the *Gesta Abbatum* from about the year 1255 to 1308 was written by a monk who lived in the early years of the fourteenth century.[2] If Riley were right on these two points, the statement about Matthew referred to by Professor Galbraith would constitute evidence that he died before 1260. In fact, however, Abbot John of Hertford did not die in 1260, but in 1263. The date 1260 is found only in the latest manuscript of the *Gesta Abbatum* (written by Walsingham), and is due to a copying error. The true date, 1263, is given in the Bute manuscript of the *Gesta Abbatum* and in the *Flores Historiarum*, and it can also be inferred from the record evidence.[3] Furthermore there is evidence that the statement that Matthew Paris lived and died in the time of Abbot John occurs in a passage added to the *Gesta Abbatum* by Thomas Walsingham, and that it did not form part of the so-called 'Second Continuation' of the *Gesta Abbatum* which Riley thought was written in the first half of the fourteenth century. It is found only in Walsingham's manuscript of the *Gesta*, where it follows a series of extracts from the *Chronica Majora* which are likewise only in the Walsingham manuscript. It seems that Walsingham, having extracted a considerable amount of material from Matthew Paris's *Chronica Majora*, inserted this statement into his description of the rule of Abbot John as a memorial to his famous predecessor, and on exactly the same evidence as modern historical opinion has supposed Matthew to have died in 1259, namely, the colophon at the end of the text of the *Chronica Majora*.

Sir Maurice Powicke had no positive evidence that Matthew lived after 1259, but he considered that the evidence from the colophon and picture at the end of Matthew's chronicle was inconclusive, and he further remarked that 'in the course of original composition, a time-lag [i.e. between the events and

---

[1] Galbraith, *Roger Wendover and Matthew Paris*, p. 30.

[2] Perhaps William Rishanger: *GA.* II, pp. ix–xiii, and I, p. xvii.

[3] Bute MS. 3, p. 278 (the manuscript called by Wats the 'Spelman MS.'; it was not known to Riley; its text ends in 1308, and it was written independently of the Walsingham MS., *c.* 1400); *FH.* II, p. 478; *Cal. Pat. Rolls, 1258–66*, p. 256 (23 April 1263): grant of abbey to prior and convent during vacancy for 600 marks.

the recording of them] of a year or more was almost inevitable',
and he showed that the annal for 1252 in the *Chronica Majora*
was not written before November 1253.[1] Powicke's conclusion
is, on the face of it, eminently reasonable. One would not expect
an author to bring the text of his chronicle right up to the time
of his death, and the inference from the colophon might very
well only be that Matthew died (perhaps in 1260 or 1261 or
even later) at a time when the text of his chronicle had arrived
at the point, during the annal for 1259, where it is inserted. In
spite of this, however, I think it far more likely that Matthew
was overtaken by death very soon after the occurrence of the
last event recorded in his chronicle. In a work of the scope and
size of the *Chronica Majora*, the author must surely have recorded
events in a first rough draft almost as soon as news of them
reached him. In the course of the annal for 1256[2] Matthew
records the departure abroad of certain people, and adds that he
does not know why they went: a confession of ignorance which
is understandable only if it was included inadvertently in
the final text from a rough draft made very soon after their
departure—especially as they were back in England again in
January 1257.[3] There is more evidence for the use of rough
drafts in the course of the annal for 1257, where a number of
entries are repeated, apparently because they were carelessly
copied twice from a series of rough drafts written perhaps on
loose sheets and scraps of parchment. There is, in fact, every
reason to believe that Matthew wrote out rough drafts immediately on receipt of the information he wished to record,
and that these were later used for writing up the final text of the
chronicle in the existing manuscripts (*B* and *R*). If this is so,
it by no means follows that, because there was a time-lag of a
year or two between events and the recording of them in the
manuscript of the *Chronica Majora*, Matthew died perhaps a
year or more after the date of the last event recorded in his
chronicle. On the contrary, there was probably no such time-
lag between the events and the composition of his drafts, and
these latter no doubt continued right up to the time of his death.
Composed and probably written out by Matthew himself, and

---

[1] Powicke, 'Compilation of the *Chronica Majora*', *loc. cit.* pp. 157–8.
[2] *CM.* v, p. 560.   [3] *CM.* v, p. 618.

kept up to date, as I suppose, these would have been ready at hand for Matthew's scribe to copy out into the *Chronica Majora* after his death, thus bringing its text up to the last event recorded by Matthew in draft.

The obvious implication of the picture which accompanies the colophon at the end of Matthew's *Chronica Majora* (Plate 1) is that he died while still at work on it, and there is in fact much evidence to show that Matthew continued to write out his own manuscripts until failing powers forced him to employ a scribe. In the *Liber Additamentorum*, for instance, there is a series of documents in just the rough chronological order we should expect to find had they been copied as their texts became available to Matthew. These documents extend from f. 71 to f. 82; they are all in Matthew's own handwriting; and they extend in date from 1255 to 1259.[1] The last, a document of March 1259, is the latest piece of writing that has survived in Matthew's own hand, and it is clearly the work of a person of failing powers.[2] It is followed by some documents of 1258 copied into the book by the scribe who helped Matthew to complete the texts of his historical manuscripts, and who wrote the colophon we have been discussing.[3] This, I think, shows that Matthew's powers failed in the spring or early summer of 1259. Had he lived beyond the summer of this year, we should expect to find at any rate some signs of his continued use of the *Liber Additamentorum*, of all his manuscripts the most intimate and personal. The scribe of the colophon at the end of Matthew's *Chronica Majora* distinguishes carefully between that work and his own continuation of it, and if, as I have suggested, Matthew died shortly after the end of the text ascribed to him, we may assume also that he did so before the earliest event recorded in the continuation. The original version of this continuation is no longer extant, but, as Madden has shown,[4] a transcript of it was

[1] See pp. 82–3 below.

[2] See Vaughan, 'The handwriting of Matthew Paris', *Trans. Camb. Bibliog. Soc.* I (1953), Plate XVII (*d*) and p. 388.

[3] *HA.* I, p. li and note 1. Besides these documents in the *Liber Additamentorum*, this scribe wrote the last part of the texts of Matthew's *Chronica Majora* (R, ff. 210a–218b); *Historia Anglorum* (R, ff. 154b–156b); and *Abbreviatio Chronicorum* (B.M. Cotton MS. Claudius D vi, ff. 87b–94b).

[4] *HA.* I, p. xxiii, note 2. See also Galbraith (ed.), *St Albans Chronicle, 1406–1420* (1937), p. xxviii.

made in the Chetham manuscript of the *Flores Historiarum*. Now the first entry of this continuation refers to 26 June 1259, and the last entry in Matthew's *Chronica Majora* to the week following 25 May.[1] It seems therefore reasonable to conclude that Matthew Paris died in June 1259.

It may well be asked how it was that a monk of St Albans, who apparently left the seclusion of the cloister only from time to time, and who only once left this country, and then only for a short period, could have kept himself well enough informed of current events in all parts of Europe to write one of the fullest and most elaborate of all medieval chronicles. The answer is that the cloister at St Albans was by no means secluded, and that Matthew could count many of the leading men of his day among his acquaintances. Contacts of various kinds with the outside world were kept up so continually that one wonders if it is right to use the term 'the outside world' in reference to a monastery like St Albans, which was in many ways at the very heart of affairs. The abbey was situated one day's journey from London on the main route to the north, and it is probable that the guests' stables, which Matthew tells us held 300 horses,[2] were by no means unnecessarily large. Between 1220 and 1259 the king visited St Albans at least nine times, sometimes staying as long as a week, and, had a visitors' book been kept in these years, and preserved for posterity, we might reasonably expect to find in it the names of most of the great men in the kingdom, as well as those of a number of important foreigners. The list printed here is far from complete, for it includes only those guests mentioned by Roger Wendover and Matthew Paris. How useful these visitors were, as a source of information for the chronicler, may be judged from the number who appear also in the list of Matthew's informants which follows. This list not only shows how Matthew obtained much of his information and from whom, but also the variety of circles in which he moved, the extent of his acquaintance, and the fame and influence which he enjoyed in his lifetime.

[1] *FH.* II, p. 426 and *CM.* v, p. 747.   [2] *CM.* v, p. 344.

VISITORS TO ST ALBANS MENTIONED BY ROGER WENDOVER AND MATTHEW PARIS, 1220–59

	CM.	
1223	III, p. 80	A chaplain of the Emperor Baldwin
1225, Easter	V, p. 320	Henry III stayed for five days
1228	III, p. 161	An Armenian archbishop who told the monks about the Wandering Jew
1239	III, p. 568	Otho, the papal legate
1240	IV, p. 43	Richard, earl of Cornwall
1241	IV, p. 172	The prior of Coventry and some of his monks stayed more than a year
1244, 11 June	IV, p. 358	Henry III stayed for three days
1244	IV, p. 378	Thomas of Savoy, count of Flanders; his brother, Boniface, archbishop-elect of Canterbury; and Walter Suffield, bishop-elect of Norwich
1244, 21 Dec.	IV, p. 402	Henry III stayed for three days
1247	IV, p. 600	John and Alexander, Franciscans and papal emissaries
1248	V, p. 2	Richard, bishop of Bangor
1251, 2 April	V, p. 233	Henry III stayed for three days
1251, 15 Sept.	V, pp. 257–8	Henry III stayed for three or four days
1251, 29 Sept.	V, p. 258	Visitation by the prior of Hurley and the sub-prior of St Augustine's, Canterbury
1252	V, p. 288	Alan de la Zouche, a royal administrator returning from Wales
1252	V, p. 288	Richard, bishop of Bangor
1252, 23 Aug.	V, pp. 319–20	Henry III stayed five days, together with his son Edward and his half-brother Geoffrey of Lusignan (*CM.* v, pp. 344–5). Philip Luvel and John Mansel, royal councillors, were also probably with the king
1252	V, pp. 340–1	Certain Armenians
1253, Nov.	V, pp. 413 ff.	Archbishop Boniface, on his way from Lincoln to London; he left on 11 November
1254, 11 July	V, p. 451	Walter Suffield, bishop of Norwich and royal tax collector
1254, Dec.	V, p. 468	Some Winchester monks
1255, 9 Mar.	V, p. 489	Henry III stayed for six days
1256, Aug.	V, p. 574	Henry III
1257, 2 Jan.	V, p. 608	Richard, bishop of Bangor; Philip de Eia, a councillor of Earl Richard of Cornwall; and some nobles from the household of William of Valence

CM.

1257, 3 March	v, pp. 617–18	Henry III stayed a week, during which time a deputation of M.A.'s from the University of Oxford arrived to see him
1257	v, p. 630	The prior of St Thomas of Acre
1257, 8 Oct.	v, pp. 653–4	Queen Eleanor, Eleanor of Castile, and other noble ladies
1258	v, p. 684	Simon Passelewe, a royal administrator
1258	v, p. 719	Archbishop Boniface

LIST OF MATTHEW'S KNOWN FRIENDS AND INFORMANTS

(1) *Nobility and knights of the British Isles*

King Henry III. Matthew knew him well, and he must have given the chronicler much useful information. For instance, he told Matthew the cost of the new feretory for St Edward's remains,[1] and of the homage done to him by Count Amadeus of Savoy.[2]

Queen Eleanor. Gave Matthew some cloth.[3]

Richard, earl of Cornwall, brother of Henry III. Evidently one of Matthew's chief informants. For instance, he told Matthew of his expenses at Hayles,[4] and Matthew's account of his crusade is certainly based on information given him by Richard himself.[5]

Hubert de Burgh, earl of Kent. Told Matthew about his escape from Devizes in 1233;[6] and many of Matthew's additions to Roger Wendover seem to be based on his information.[7]

Richard of Clare, earl of Gloucester. Told Matthew about some mounted knights seen in the sky in 1236.[8]

Isabella, countess of Arundel, widow of Hugh of Albini. Must have told Matthew about her interview with the king in 1252.[9] Matthew lent her one of his books.[10]

Richard of Argenton, knight. Witnessed to the truth of the statements of the archbishop of Armenia.[11]

[1] *HA.* II, p. 455. [2] *HA.* III, p. 8.
[3] *CM.* VI, p. 391. [4] *CM.* V, p. 262.
[5] *CM.* IV, pp. 43–7, 71, 144–8, 166–7. [6] *HA.* II, p. 359, note 1.
[7] See *CM.* III, pp. 3–4, 28–9, 121, 199 ff., 290–1, etc.
[8] *CM.* III, p. 368. [9] *CM.* V, pp. 336–7.
[10] See below, p. 170. [11] *CM.* III, p. 164.

13

Baldwin de Vere, knight; Henry III's messenger to the emperor in 1236. He almost certainly told Matthew about this embassy.[1]

John of Gaddesden, knight. Gave Matthew information about the family of Raymond-Berenger V.[2] Evidently a useful contact for Matthew since he was sent on at least two important diplomatic missions.[3]

The master of the Temple in Scotland. Probably gave Matthew information about Louis IX's crusade.[4]

(2) *Royal administrators*

John Mansel, councillor of Henry III. Matthew had almost certainly met him, and he figures largely in the *Chronica Majora*. He seems to have lent Matthew a book, for in the margin of the manuscript of Matthew's life of St Alban[5] we find an alternative reading headed by Matthew: 'de libro Johannis Mansel'.[6]

John of Lexinton, councillor of Henry III. Told Matthew of the miracles at the tomb of the archdeacon of Northumberland.[7]

Roger Thurkelby, judge de Banco. Conversed with Matthew at dinner on one occasion.[8]

Alexander Swereford, baron of the Exchequer. Gave Matthew some information about King Offa.[9] He was evidently Matthew's main contact at the Exchequer, and he allowed Matthew to inspect the Exchequer records.[10]

Robert of London, a clerk employed by King John; in 1208 he was the secular 'custos' of St Albans. It was he who told Matthew the story of John's embassy to Morocco.[11]

Edward, a councillor of Henry III, and Nicholas, moneyer to Henry III. These two were among Matthew's informants about the theft of the relics of St Alban by the Danes.[12]

(3) *Bishops of the British Isles*

Alexander Stavensby, bishop of Coventry and Lichfield. Told Matthew about the repentance of Fawkes de Breauté.[13]

---

[1] *CM.* III, pp. 376–8. [2] *CM.* III, p. 335.
[3] *CM.* V, pp. 585 and 611. [4] *CM.* VI, p. 521.
[5] Trinity College, Dublin, MS. E i 40, f. 22a.
[6] See below, p. 196. [7] *CM.* V, p. 384.
[8] *CM.* V, p. 317; see also V, p. 211.
[9] *CM.* VI, p. 519, note 1. [10] See below, pp. 17–18.
[11] *CM.* II, pp. 559–64. [12] *GA.* I, p. 19.
[13] *HA.* II, p. 265; see also *CM.* III, pp. 169, 172, 268.

Eustace de Fauconberg, bishop of London. Told Matthew about his conversation with Fawkes de Breauté in 1224.[1]

Peter des Roches, bishop of Winchester. Matthew obtained from him a book on the marvels of the East which he had brought back from Palestine in 1231.[2]

Nicholas of Farnham, bishop of Durham. Told Matthew the story of Simon of Tournay.[3]

Robert Grosseteste, bishop of Lincoln. In the colophon to the tract on the virginity of the Blessed Virgin Mary in B.M. Royal MS. 4 D vii (f. 248a), Matthew says that he had obtained his exemplar from Grosseteste himself. He was with Grosseteste at Westminster in October 1247.[4]

William Button, bishop of Bath. Told Matthew about an earthquake in 1248.[5]

Richard Wych, bishop of Chichester. Gave Matthew information about St Edmund of Abingdon.[6]

John, bishop of Ardfert. Died at St Albans in 1245 after a long period of residence there.[7]

Richard, bishop of Bangor. Resided at St Albans between 1248 and 1256. He repeated, to Matthew, Richard of Cornwall's words on accepting the German crown.[8]

(4) *Other English ecclesiastics*

Ranulph Besace, canon of St Paul's; formerly physician to King Richard I. Told Matthew about the murder of the prince of Antioch by Saladin.[9]

Thomas of St Albans, physician to the earl of Arundel and prior of Wymondham. Probably told Matthew of the earl's anger with the papal legate in 1219.[10]

John of Basingstoke, archdeacon of Leicester and a friend of Robert Grosseteste. Told Matthew the stories of the deacon who apostatized[11] and the beautiful Athenian girl;[12] and showed him the Greek numerals which he copied into his chronicle.[13]

---

[1] *HA.* II, p. 266. [2] *HA.* I, p. 163, note 4.
[3] *CM.* II, pp. 476–7 and *HA.* II, p. 90.
[4] *CM.* IV, pp. 643–4. [5] *CM.* V, p. 46 and *HA.* III, p. 42.
[6] *CM.* V, p. 369 and *HA.* III, p. 135.
[7] *HA.* II, p. 511 etc. [8] *CM.* V, p. 602.
[9] *CM.* II, p. 391; V, p. 221, and *HA.* II, p. 37.
[10] *HA.* II, pp. 237 and note 3, 249. [11] *HA.* II, pp. 254–5.
[12] *CM.* V, pp. 286–7. [13] *CM.* V, p. 285.

John Crakehall, archdeacon of Bedford. Told Matthew of the bells which rang miraculously on the death of Grosseteste.[1]

Ralph, abbot of Ramsey. Gave Matthew a silk cloth.[2]

The prior of Westacre. Told Matthew of various gifts made to the pope at the Council of Lyons.[3]

Walter of St Martin, a Dominican, and confessor of Cecilia de Sanford. Told Matthew of her pious death;[4] and probably gave Matthew copies of the letters he received from Palestine.[5]

John of St Giles, a Dominican. He confessed William de Marisco before his execution and probably gave Matthew an account of this.[6]

Robert Bacon, a Dominican. Gave Matthew information about St Edmund of Abingdon.[7]

Thomas, a monk of Sherborne. Matthew met him when he was with the king at Winchester in 1251, and copied down his account of the Pastoureaux.[8]

William, a Franciscan. Matthew drew a picture of him in the margin of his chronicle,[9] and inserted his picture of Christ in the *Liber Additamentorum* (f. 155).[10]

Gervase of Melkeley, perhaps a clerk of Archbishop Stephen Langton. Probably gave Matthew information about Langton, as he is cited as a source in Matthew's Life of Langton.[11] There are some verses of his in the *Chronica Majora*.[12]

(5) *Foreign informants and acquaintances*

King Haakon IV of Norway. Told Matthew how he had refused the pope's offer of the imperial crown.[13]

Waleran, bishop of Beirut. Probably told Matthew of the difficulties of the journey to Palestine.[14] He was apparently in England in the summer of 1245.[15]

---

[1] *CM.* v, p. 408. [2] Below, p. 18. [3] *CM.* iv, p. 428.
[4] *CM.* v, pp. 235–6. [5] *CM.* vi, pp. 203 ff.
[6] *CM.* iv, pp. 196–7; see also *CM.* iii, pp. 324 and 627, and v, p. 705.
[7] *CM.* v, p. 369. [8] *CM.* v, pp. 246–54.
[9] James, 'Drawings of Matthew Paris', *Walpole Society*, xiv (1925–6), no. 52.
[10] See Little, 'Brother William of England', *Franciscan Papers*, pp. 16–24.
[11] Liebermann (ed.), *Ungedruckte anglo-normannische Geschichtsquellen*, p. 327. [12] iii, p. 43, and note 5; and iv, p. 493.
[13] *CM.* v, p. 201; see also above, pp. 4–6.
[14] *CM.* iv, p. 345, and *HA.* ii, p. 483. [15] *CM.* iv, pp. 488–9.

Peter, proctor of Philip of Savoy, archbishop-elect of Lyons. Told Matthew of the archbishop's expenses at a feast.[1]

Thomas, chaplain of Cardinal Raynier Cappochi, incarcerated with him at Naples in 1241. Told Matthew about their imprisonment.[2]

A messenger of Ferdinand III of Castile. Told Matthew about his king.[3]

(6) *Other persons*

Geoffrey Hackesalt, a servant of Abbot Warin of St Albans. Told Matthew about Warin's gifts to King Richard I in 1194.[4]

John of St Albans, a goldsmith; and Odo, former moneyer to King Waldemar III of Denmark. These two were among Matthew's informants about the theft of the relics of St Alban by the Danes.[5]

Aaron, a Jew of York. Told Matthew how much money the king had taken from him.[6]

A Cahorsin money-lender. Told Matthew how the London Cahorsins were being despoiled.[7]

A note ought to be included here on Matthew's connexion with the royal Exchequer. He evidently knew Alexander Swereford, a baron of the Exchequer, personally, and was in the habit of collecting information about matters of state from the Exchequer clerks. He certainly had access to the Exchequer records, and well understood their value.[8] Fourteen of the documents copied into his manuscripts are also to be found in the *Red Book of the Exchequer*. The most important of these are a group of four letters between Pope Gregory IX and the patriarch of Constantinople, Germanus, of the year 1232; and a group of six imperial letters. In his *Chronica Majora* Matthew refers his readers to the 'consuetudinario scaccarii' for a fuller account of the coronation of Henry III and Eleanor in 1236.[9] A comparison of the two accounts shows that Matthew did not use the existing *Red Book*, but probably its exemplar; and this

---

[1] *CM.* vi, p. 444. [2] *CM.* iv, p. 130. [3] *CM.* v, pp. 231–2.
[4] *HA.* ii, p. 47. [5] *GA.* i, p. 19. [6] *CM.* v, p. 136.
[7] *CM.* v, pp. 245–6.
[8] Hall (ed.), *Red Book of the Exchequer*, i, pp. xxix–xxx; Liebermann (ed.), in *MGH,SS.* xxviii, p. 82.
[9] Hall (ed.), *Red Book*, i, p. xix.

is borne out by collation of the documents in Matthew with those in the *Red Book*. On the basis of this evidence, it is reasonable to suppose that Matthew obtained from the Exchequer a great deal of information and documentary material; it may indeed have been his main source of the latter. It is worth noting, too, that the system of *signa* which Matthew uses in referring to documents is very similar to that used in the Exchequer, and was probably copied from it.[1]

As a result of his wide connexions, Matthew Paris received a number of gifts which he later passed on to his house. A list of some of these, written by himself, has survived at the end of a short tract which he included in his *Liber Additamentorum*, headed 'De pannis sericis huius ecclesiae'.[2] Henry III gave him some silk material from which he made a set of vestments for use in the chapel of St Matthias; and Matthew also presented to his house a choir-cope he had made out of some cloth given him by Queen Eleanor, and ornamented with a fine orphrey given him by his friend King Haakon of Norway. The abbot of Ramsey, too, gave him some ornamental silk material which he afterwards gave to St Albans. It seems likely that the gifts recorded in the late-fourteenth-century *Book of Benefactors of St Albans* as from Matthew Paris[3] had likewise been given to him by friends of his; except perhaps the last item mentioned, a silver cup, which he may have made himself.[4] The other gifts recorded are two silver basins, which Matthew perhaps acquired in Norway, since it appears from the text of the *Book of Benefactors* that he gave them on his return thence, and a pendent reliquary of gold. While on the subject of his gifts to St Albans we ought to note Matthew's gifts of books. Of his surviving autograph manuscripts, four still contain inscriptions in his own hand recording his gift of them 'to God and St Albans'.[5]

[1] Palgrave (ed.), *Ancient Kalendars*, I, pp. xxvi–xxvii, describes the system used in Bishop Stapleton's Calendar.   [2] *CM*. VI, pp. 389–92.

[3] B.M. Cotton MS. Nero D vii, ff. 50b–51a.

[4] Oman, 'Goldsmiths at St Albans Abbey', *Trans. St Albans and Herts Archit. and Archaeol. Soc.* (1932), p. 230.

[5] They are B.M. Cotton MS. Nero D i (the *Liber Additamentorum*); B.M. Royal MS. 14 C vii (*R*); Corpus Christi College, Cambridge, MS. 16 (*B*); and University Library, Cambridge, MS. Dd xi 78 (poems of Henry of Avranches, etc.).

It was no doubt largely because of his gifts that Matthew found his way into the *Book of Benefactors*, compiled 150 years after his death.[1] But Thomas Walsingham does not limit himself to them; he says:[2]

Matthew Paris, a religious monk, an incomparable chronicler and an excellent painter, was sent by Pope Innocent to reform the monastery of Holm in Norway, which was under the jurisdiction of the archbishop of Nidaros. Owing to the idleness of the monks of this place, its religion had disappeared, its fame had dwindled away, and its goods had been dissipated. He caused its religion to flourish again; advanced its fame for sanctity; and carefully added to its possessions, so that, among the monasteries of that region, it was reputed inferior to none.

He then goes on to describe the gifts to St Albans which we have mentioned above. Elsewhere, in a tract 'On the foundation and merits of the monastery of St Albans',[3] Thomas Walsingham includes Matthew in his list of the historians of his house with the following remarks:[4]

Afterwards flourished Matthew Paris, who ably enlarged (*necessarie ampliavit*) the aforesaid Roger's chronicles; who wrote and most elegantly illustrated (*depinxit*) the Lives of Saints Alban and Amphibalus, and of the archbishops of Canterbury Thomas and Edmund; and who provided many books for the church. Were I to try to sing all his praises, the task would be interminable.

The only other notice of Matthew Paris in a later St Albans source is the well-known eulogy of him in the *Gesta Abbatum*, which, as we have seen, is also probably from the pen of Thomas Walsingham:[5]

At this time, too, flourished and died Dom Matthew Paris; monk of St Albans, and an eloquent and famous man full of innumerable virtues; a magnificent historian and chronicler; an excellent author

[1] See Galbraith (ed.), *St Albans Chronicle*, pp. xxxvi–xxxvii.
[2] B.M. Cotton MS. Nero D vii, ff. 50b–51a.
[3] B.M. Cotton MS. Claudius E iv, f. 331b; printed in Riley (ed.), *Johannis Amundesham Annales*, II, pp. 296–306.
[4] Riley (ed.), *Amundesham*, p. 303. The phrase 'ably enlarged' in the first line of my translation of this passage is taken from Galbraith's translation, *Roger Wendover and Matthew Paris*, p. 22.
[5] See above, pp. 7–8. Printed, *GA.* I, pp. 394–5. I am again indebted to Galbraith, *Roger Wendover and Matthew Paris*, p. 30, for parts of my translation of this passage.

(*dictator*), who frequently revolved in his heart the saying: 'Laziness is the enemy of the soul', and whom widespread fame commended in remote parts where he had never been. Diligently compiling his chronicle from the earliest times up to the end of his life, he fully recorded the deeds of magnates, both lay and ecclesiastical, as well as various and wonderful events; and left for the notice of posterity a marvellous record of the past. He had such skill in the working (*sculpendo*) of gold and silver and other metal, and in painting pictures, that it is thought that there has been no equal to him since in the Latin world.

Outside St Albans Matthew is mentioned, so far as I have been able to discover, by only three later chroniclers.[1] Of these, the most interesting is an anonymous monk of Ramsey, who wrote, before 1267, a little treatise in prose and verse on the struggle between Henry III and the barons. For the history of the period up to the start of the war, he refers his readers to Matthew Paris with the following words:[2]

If anyone wishes to know about his [i.e. Henry III's] deeds up to the forty-second year of his reign [1258], he should consult the chronicle of Master Matthew, a monk of St Albans; there the diligent reader can find out how he [Henry III] captured Bedford castle, how he exiled Archbishop St Edmund, how he behaved in general (*qualiter duxerit*); and many other things concerning England in his time.

The other two notices of Matthew are the barest mentions: Thomas Wykes includes his name, together with those of Bede and William of Newburgh, among his predecessors in the writing of history;[3] and the author of the *Book of Hyde* cites him by name: 'ut scribit Matheus Parisiacensis'.[4] A number of later chroniclers copied from Matthew Paris without mentioning his name, but the use thus made of his historical writings will be examined in a later chapter.

[1] The mention of Matthew Paris in John of Oxenedes's chronicle (Ellis (ed.), *Chronica J. de Oxenedes*, p. 184) has been copied, together with most of the rest of the text, from John of Wallingford's chronicle in B.M. Cotton MS. Julius D vii, ff. 61–110, copied in its turn from Matthew's own writings.

[2] Halliwell (ed.), *William Rishanger*, p. xxi note; the Ramsey monk's use of the title 'magister', in reference to Matthew Paris, is doubtless an error, for it is not used elsewhere.

[3] Luard (ed.), *Annales monastici*, IV, p. 7.

[4] See below, pp. 40–1.

CHAPTER II

MATTHEW PARIS AND
ROGER WENDOVER

M ATTHEW PARIS was the most distinguished of a succession of historical writers at St Albans, and his most important work, the *Chronica Majora*, takes the form of a revised edition and continuation of the *Flores Historiarum* of his predecessor Roger Wendover, who died on 6 May 1236,[1] twenty-three years before Matthew. It is thus essential, before we examine Matthew's historical writings, to discuss their relationship to the work of his predecessor. Our knowledge of Roger Wendover and of his chronicle is extremely scanty, and, in spite of the fact that Roger's work formed the basis of his own, Matthew tells us nothing about it. Two manuscripts of Roger's *Flores Historiarum* survive, both of them late copies, one written *c*. 1300, and the other *c*. 1350.[2] These, following Luard's terminology,[3] I shall call respectively *W* and *O*; and the text which they share in common, *OW*. Fortunately, the original manuscript of Matthew's *Chronica Majora* survives in three parts: *A*, Corpus Christi College, Cambridge, MS. 26, containing the text up to 1188; *B*, Corpus Christi College, Cambridge, MS. 16, with the text from 1189 to 1253; *R*, British Museum Royal MS. 14 C vii, containing the text from 1254 to the end, as well as the whole of Matthew's *Historia Anglorum*. *A* was produced under the supervision of Matthew Paris, and *B* and *R* are almost entirely autograph.[4] In this chapter we shall be concerned only with *A* and *B*, since it is in them that the text of Roger's *Flores Historiarum* was incorporated by Matthew; and, since they were written originally as one book,[5] I shall refer

---

[1] *CM*. VI, p. 274.

[2] *W*, Oxford, Bodleian Library, Douce MS. 207; and *O*, B.M. Cotton MS. Otho B v. Corpus Christi College, Cambridge, MS. 264, ff. 1–64, is a series of extracts from *O* extending from 1199 to 1234 and written in the fourteenth century, before 1352.   [3] *CM*. I, p. lxxxv.

[4] Vaughan, 'Handwriting of M. Paris', *Trans. Camb. Bibliog. Soc.* I (1953), pp. 390–1.   [5] See below, pp. 56–7.

to them with the symbol *AB* except when it is necessary to distinguish between them.

Until recently historians disputed Madden's belief[1] that Roger Wendover was the founder of the St Albans historical school. Hardy supposed that Roger had based his *Flores Historiarum* on an earlier, twelfth-century, 'St Albans compilation' perhaps written by Walter of St Albans, and extending to 1154 or even to 1188.[2] Luard put forward the theory that this 'St Albans compilation' was written by Abbot John de Cella (1195–1214); that its text extended to 1188; and that it formed the basis of Roger's chronicle.[3] Liebermann, in the introduction to his edition of excerpts from Roger's chronicle, did not deny the possibility that Roger used the work of a predecessor extending to 1188, and he claimed as evidence for this that, up to the annal for 1188 in the *Flores Historiarum*, the compiler refers to himself in the plural, and after it in the singular.[4] But this is not in fact true, for in at least two places in the early part of the text the compiler refers to himself in the singular.[5] Liebermann, however, showed that if there were a compilation lying behind the text of Roger's chronicle, it was probably not written until after *c.* 1204.[6] This did not rule out the possibility that Abbot John de Cella was the author of the compilation, and in 1904 Miss Rickert restated this theory, and argued that Abbot John also wrote the *Vitae Offarum* and the chronicle attributed to John of Wallingford in British Museum Cotton MS. Julius D vii —which she took to be a sort of rough draft of the 'St Albans compilation'.[7] In 1922 Professor Claude Jenkins revived the theory of a twelfth-century compilation at St Albans, and suggested that the original compilation perhaps ended in 1154, and that Abbot John continued it thence up to 1188.[8] The basis of the theory of Abbot John's authorship of a compilation extending

[1] *HA.* I, p. xiii.
[2] Hardy, *A Descriptive Catalogue of Materials relating to the History of Great Britain and Ireland,* III, p. xxxvi and note 3.
[3] *CM.* II, pp. x–xii and VII, pp. ix–xi.
[4] Liebermann (ed.), in *MGH,SS.* XXVIII, p. 8.
[5] *CM.* I, pp. 270, note 2, and 509.
[6] Liebermann (ed.), in *MGH,SS.* XXVIII, pp. 7–8.
[7] Rickert, 'Old English Offa Saga', *Modern Philol.* II (1904–5), pp. 29–39.
[8] Jenkins, *Monastic Chronicler and the Early School of St Albans,* pp. 32 ff. and 40–1.

to 1188 was a marginal note in one of the manuscripts of Roger Wendover's *Flores Historiarum* opposite the annal for 1188:[1] 'huc usque in lib. cronic. Johannis abbatis'; but Sir Maurice Powicke showed that this note, far from referring to a compilation written by Abbot John de Cella, merely meant that, when it was written, *c.* 1300, the Abbot John of the time was in possession of another manuscript of the chronicle (probably *A*), the text of which ended at that point. Powicke went on to state that there was in fact no evidence of the existence of a 'St Albans compilation' previous to Roger Wendover; and Professor Galbraith agreed with him.[2]

I do not propose here to attempt to examine in detail the complex question of the sources of Roger Wendover's *Flores Historiarum*, but it should be remarked that, in spite of the statements of Powicke and Galbraith, the possibility remains that he may have used an earlier compilation of some kind. The existing manuscripts *O* and *W* are evidently both copies of Roger's chronicle, for in both the text ends with the words: 'Huc usque scripsit cronica Dominus Rogerus de Wendovre';[3] and we may assume from this that *OW* (as I call the common source of *O* and *W*) was likewise a copy of Roger's chronicle. But we cannot overlook the possibility that the opening words of *O* and *W*, 'Incipit prologus in librum qui Flores Historiarum intitulatur',[4] refer to a compilation called *Flores Historiarum*, on which Roger based the *cronica* referred to at the end of these manuscripts. No doubt Madden, Powicke, and Galbraith are right in considering Roger Wendover as the founder of the St Albans historical school so far as original historical writing is concerned, but nobody has yet proved that he did not make use of a historical compilation written by some unknown monk of the twelfth or early thirteenth century.

While we are on the subject of Roger Wendover, there is one small point which we ought to note. Both Sir Maurice Powicke and Professor Galbraith assumed that Roger Wendover begins to be original about the year 1201, when 'the great histories of

---

[1] *W*, f. 135a.
[2] Powicke, 'Compilation of the *Chronica Majora*', *Proc. Brit. Acad.* XXX (1944), pp. 148–9; Galbraith, *Roger Wendover and Matthew Paris*, p. 16, and note 1.   [3] *CM.* III, p. 327, note 2.   [4] *CM.* I, p. 1.

Hoveden and Diceto, his main standby, stopped'.[1] Liebermann, however, had long before pointed out that Roger used a book of annals (called by Liebermann *ew*) for the reign of King John which were used later by Taxster, and which had already been used by the author of the *Annales Sancti Edmundi*.[2] The manuscript of these latter ends abruptly in 1212, but Liebermann suggests that their source, *ew*, continued at least until 1214, and possibly for the rest of the reign of John; and that many of the passages which are in Roger Wendover but not in the *Annales Sancti Edmundi* were in *ew* but were omitted by the annalist of St Edmunds. Roger Wendover also used some annals added at the end of the St Albans copy of Ralph de Diceto for his account of John's reign,[3] and it seems, in fact, that there may be little original material in Roger's chronicle before his account of Henry III's reign.

The text of the existing manuscripts of Roger's *Flores Historiarum* (*OW*) is by no means identical with that of Matthew's manuscript of the *Chronica Majora*, *AB*. Two main types of variant occur in the latter, both of which must be examined here. In the first place, the text of *AB*, as originally written by Matthew's scribes, differs in places from that of Roger; and, secondly, many variations occur in *AB* which are due to Matthew Paris himself, both in those parts of the text which he wrote out himself, and in the margins or between the lines. Let us take first those variations in the *text* of *AB* which are not due to Matthew himself. Luard discovered that, up to the annal for 231, and again between the annals for 1012 and 1065, the variations of this kind between *OW* and *AB* were such that they could not rightly be called copies of the same book. Between 231 and 1012, however, he found that these two texts were identical 'with only such variations as will always exist between two copies of the same work'.[4] Luard noticed, too, that, up to

---

[1] Powicke, 'Roger Wendover and the Coggeshall Chronicle', *EHR.* xxi (1906), p. 287; Galbraith, *Roger Wendover and Matthew Paris*, p. 15, whence the quotation.

[2] Liebermann (ed.), *Ungedruckte anglo-normannische Geschichtsquellen*, pp. 101 ff.

[3] B.M. Royal MS. 13 E vi, ff. 136–7; they are printed in Liebermann (ed.), *Ungedruckte anglo-norm. Geschichtsquellen*, pp. 167–72.

[4] *CM.* I, pp. xiii and xxx; the quotation is from p. xiii. Powicke has misrepresented Luard when he states ('Compilation of the *Chronica Majora*',

231, *OW* is fuller than *AB*, and he thought that this was due to the fact that, while *AB* had been *copied* from an earlier compilation, *OW* had been *enlarged* from it.[1] He concluded that Matthew Paris, in supervising the writing of his *Chronica Majora* in *AB*, had used a manuscript of an earlier compilation which had been used independently by Roger Wendover; and that, while *AB* was throughout an accurate copy of this compilation, the text of *OW* had been altered from it up to 231, and again

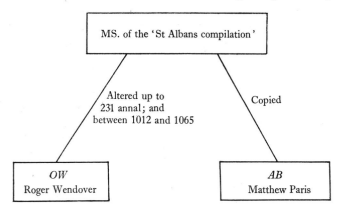

Fig. 1. Diagram to show Luard's theory of the relationship between *OW* and *AB* up to 1066.

between 1012 and 1065 (see fig. 1). Powicke disagreed with Luard, and thought that the differences between *AB* and *OW* were due either to Matthew himself, or to the use by his scribes in *AB* of a different compilation up to the annal for 231.[2] The only way to resolve this problem is to compare carefully a passage as it is in *OW*, *AB*, and the original source whence it was derived. Here, first, is an example from before the annal for 231:

The source, Geoffrey of Monmouth's *Historia regum Britanniae*.[3]

Nec mora concurrentes undique nationum populi exemplum regis

pp. 149–50): 'Luard...assumed that the whole of *A* was independent of Wendover. He did not point out, what can be inferred from his own footnotes, that in fact there is no such independence except for the period from the Creation to the year A.D. 231, and the period from 1013 to 1065.'

[1] *CM.* I, pp. xxx–xxxi.

[2] Powicke, 'Compilation of the *Chronica Majora*', *Proc. Brit. Acad.* xxx (1944), p. 150.   [3] A. Griscom (ed.), p. 329 (Bern MS.).

insequntur, eodemque lauacro mundati, celesti regno restituuntur. Beati igitur doctores cum per totam fere insulam paganismum deleuissent, templa que in honore plurimorum deorum fundata fuerant uni deo eiusque sanctis dedicauerunt, diuersisque cetibus ordinatorum repleuerunt.

AB. Part of the annal for 185.[1]

...concurrerunt ad baptismum nationes diversae, *exemplum regis sequentes, ita ut in brevi nullus inveniretur infidelis. Beati igitur doctores, cum per totam* Britanniam *paganismum delevissent, templa, quae in honore plurimorum deorum fundata fuerant, uni Deo* ejusdemque *sanctis dedicaverunt, diversisque ordinatorum coetibus* expleverunt.

OW. The same passage, but under the year 183.[2]

...concurrebant ad baptismum sacramentum nationes diuerse *regis exemplum sequentes, ita ut in breui nullus infidelis remaneret. Beati igitur doctores* Christi, *cum per totam* Britanniam *paganismum deleuissent, templi* [sic] *que* ob honorem *deorum* gentilium *fundata fuerant* [in *W* the 'n' is expunct] *uni Deo* eius *sanctis* dedicantes, *diuersis ordinatorum cetibus* inpleuerunt.

I have italicized those words in *AB* and *OW* which are taken directly from the source. It will be seen that *AB* and *OW* share a text in common which is different from the source, though obviously based on it; they are, in fact, clearly versions of one and the same compilation. It will also be seen that, where the texts of *AB* and *OW* differ, *AB* is nearer the original source; a fact which shows that, while the scribe of *AB* has copied his exemplar more or less accurately, the scribe of *OW* has made alterations from it in the course of writing. A similar comparison between *AB*, *OW* and their source may be made for part of the text between 1012 and 1065:

The source, Florence of Worcester's *Chronicon ex chronicis.*[3]

Rex Walanorum Griffinus non. Augusti a suis interficitur, et caput eius caputque navis ipsius cum ornatura comiti Haroldo mittitur, quae mox ille regi detulit Eadwardo. Quibus gestis, suis fratribus Blethgento et Rithwalano, rex terram Walanorum dedit; cui et

---

[1] *CM.* I, p. 129.

[2] *W*, f. 29a and *O*, f. 26a. *O* is unfortunately badly damaged by fire, and could therefore only be partially collated here.

[3] B. Thorpe (ed.), I, p. 222.

Haroldo comiti, fidelitatem illi juraverunt, et ad imperium illorum... obedienter se pensuros spoponderunt.

AB. The annal for 1064.[1]

Gens *Walanorum, nonas Augusti,* interfecto rege suo Griffino, *caput ejus* duci *Haroldo* miserunt, quod *mox* Haroldus ad regem Eadwardum transmittens, alium Walensibus regem praefecit. Qui Eadwardo regi *fidelitatem* praestito faciens juramento, omnia, quae regibus Anglorum solvi consueverant, ipse fideliter *se pensurum* spopondit.

OW. The annal for 1064.[2]

Gens Wallensium *nonas Augusti,* rege Griffino perempto, *caput* suum duci *Haroldo* miserunt, quod *mox* Haroldus ad regem Eadwardum transmittens, alium Wallensibus regem praefecit; qui, Anglorum regi *fidelitatem* faciens, omnia, quae regibus Anglicis solvi debebantur, ipse fideliter se redditurum spopondit.

Here, again, *AB* and *OW* were clearly taken from a common exemplar, which was, in its turn, taken from the original source; and, here again, where *AB* and *OW* differ, *AB* is almost invariably nearer the source than *OW.* Thus the differences between *AB* and *OW* are again due to the scribe of *OW,* who is making free with the exemplar while that of *AB* keeps strictly to it. In this part of the text, however, the scribe of *OW* has usually abridged his exemplar, instead of amplifying it, as he did before the annal for 231. Luard, then, was right in supposing that the differences between *AB* and *OW* are due to alterations made by the scribe of *OW* from an exemplar which was copied more or less accurately by the scribe of *AB.*

If we take the whole text of the chronicle up to 1066, and compare it carefully in *AB, O* and *W,* the relationship of the manuscripts can be established with some degree of certainty. *O* and *W,* for instance, were certainly copied from a single exemplar, *OW: W* could not have been copied from *O,* since it is earlier than that manuscript, nor could *O* have been copied from *W,* since in *W* four different lines are omitted through homoeoteleuton,[3] yet in each case the missing line is in *O.* On

---

[1] *CM.* I, p. 531.　　　　[2] H. O. Coxe (ed.), I, p. 504.

[3] At *CM.* I, pp. 252, note 3; 328, note 1; 400, note 1; and 487, note 16. The possibility of an intermediate manuscript between *OW* and *O* is not considered here, since its existence would not affect the argument.

the other hand the readings which O and W have in common show that they shared a common exemplar;[1] and, since in both manuscripts the text is attributed to Roger Wendover, it is certain that their common exemplar, OW, was likewise a text of Roger Wendover. OW was undoubtedly copied from another manuscript, which I shall call b, for errors and omissions common to O and W, which can only have been due to the carelessness of the scribe of OW in copying, occur frequently.[2] Since these errors are not found in AB, that manuscript cannot have been copied from OW, and the virtual identity of much of the text of AB and OW can only be explained on the hypothesis that AB, like OW, was copied from b (see fig. 2).

This same relationship is found after the annal for 1066. For instance, in the course of the annals for 1098 and 1228, there are cases of the loss of a line through homoeoteleuton in both O and W,[3] which show that they still derive from the common exemplar OW; and the fact that in each case AB has the missing line shows that it is still not copied from OW (the scribe of which must have omitted these lines in order that they should be missing in both O and W) but from OW's exemplar, b. All the manuscripts carelessly omit several lines of the text of Magna Carta,[4] a fact which shows that at this point, too, they all derive from a single manuscript, b. The fact that the text of b continued at any rate up to the annal for 1228 is of some significance; for Luard believed that the exemplar of OW and AB, that is b, was a manuscript of a compilation written at St Albans before Roger Wendover's time.[5] But the text of any such compilation would certainly not have extended up to the year 1228, within eight years of Roger's death; and in fact b must surely have been an early copy or recension of Roger's own chronicle, and not an earlier 'St Albans compilation'.[6] There is some evidence that Roger's *Flores Historiarum* did in fact exist in two recensions. In both O and W the text is attributed to Roger Wendover and ends at a point about half-way through the annal for 1235, the last date mentioned being that of the

[1] See Luard's remarks on this, *CM.* I, p. xiv.
[2] See, for instance, *CM.* I, pp. 297, note 1, 340, note 1, and 448, note 2.
[3] *CM.* II, p. 83, note 3, and III, p. 149, note 3.
[4] *CM.* II, p. 591, note 5.   [5] *CM.* I, pp. xxx–xxxi.
[6] For a discussion of the manuscript lying behind b, see below, pp. 96–7.

marriage of Frederick II and Isabella on 20 July.[1] On the
other hand a rubric in *O* at the beginning of book two of Roger's
chronicle (f. 3 a) states that the text continues 'up to the year of
Our Lord 1234'; and in the fair copy of part two of Matthew's
Chronica Majora (*C*) the rubricator has written a note referring
to a point in the text between April and May 1234 which says:[2]
'Dom Roger Wendover, one time prior of Belvoir, completed

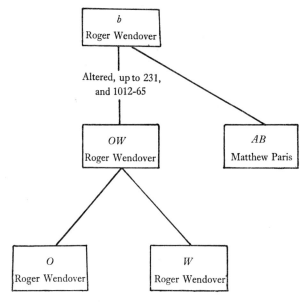

Fig. 2. Diagram to show the relationship of the manuscripts of
Roger Wendover and Matthew Paris.

(*digessit*) his chronicle up to this point. Brother Matthew Paris
begins [here].' This note must have been written in or soon
after 1250, and it seems to be the earliest surviving evidence for
the termination of Roger Wendover's *Flores Historiarum*. It
was copied, *c.* 1300, into the margin of Matthew's autograph
manuscript of the *Chronica Majora* (*B*), but here it refers, not
to a point in the annal for 1234, as in *C*, but to the point where
the text of *O* and *W* ends. Its writer, presumably, had seen
a copy of Roger Wendover's chronicle which ended at this point

---

[1] *CM.* III, p. 324.   [2] *CM.* III, p. 290, note 8.

in 1235, and assumed that the note in *C* was misplaced. A possible explanation of the discrepancy in this evidence concerning the termination of Roger's *Flores Historiarum* is that Roger finished one recension of his chronicle up to 1234, and that he then produced a second recension of it, in which the text was continued into 1235. If this is so, it seems possible that *b* represented Roger's first recension, and *OW* his second; though on the other hand it is perhaps unlikely that Matthew Paris would have been content to use the first recension of his predecessor's work, when a more up to date version was available to him.

Before we go on to discuss those variations in *AB* which are due to Matthew Paris, we ought to note that there are a few cases where a passage in *OW* does not occur in *AB*. It is, however, impossible to ascertain whether these passages were omitted on purpose by Matthew, or whether they were only added by Roger in the second recension of his chronicle, that is in *OW*, and were consequently omitted in *AB* simply because they did not occur in its exemplar *b*.[1]

By no means all the variations from *OW* which occur in the original text of *AB* have so far been discussed, for a large number occur in those parts of *AB* which were written by Matthew himself, not to mention those which are due to his subsequent additions and alterations in that manuscript. Matthew himself wrote the annals for 619 and 620 in *A*, and nearly all the text of *B* from the annal for 1213 onwards, and throughout both manuscripts he has rewritten passages on erasures and made corrections and additions in the margins. If we look first at those sections of the *text* written by Matthew himself, we find that verbal variations from *OW* (apart from those already discussed) occur in them, and very seldom elsewhere. Thus, a number occur in the annal for 620, but very few are to be found elsewhere in this part of *A*.[2] Again, when Matthew himself begins writing the text of *B* during the annal

---

[1] The most important of these passages are mentioned by Luard in his notes to the *Chronica Majora*, and printed in Hewlett's edition of Roger Wendover's *Flores Historiarum*, I, pp. 225–6; and II, pp. 356–8 and 369–72. See *CM*. II, p. 398, note 4; III, p. 165, note 2; and III, p. 176, note 3.

[2] Purely *scribal* variations are, of course, found throughout the text, but these differ in character from the deliberate *verbal* alterations made by Matthew Paris.

for 1213, a large number of variations from *OW* occur; but they cease (except for two small additions)[1] when Matthew hands the quill back to his scribe for ff. 46b–50a of *B*. Unfortunately Luard's edition of the *Chronica Majora* is extremely confusing here, because he frequently does not point out whether or not a passage added in *AB* to the text of *OW*—and consequently printed by him in large type—was in the *original text* of the manuscript, or only added subsequently. Owing to this, and to Luard's uncertainty about the identity of Matthew's hand-writing, the striking coincidence between the occurrence of variations in the text of *AB* and the sections of this text written by Matthew Paris himself is not at all apparent in his edition. A careful comparison of the manuscripts, however, shows that Matthew was at first content merely to supervise the writing of *AB*; to insert many of the rubrics in his own hand; and occasionally to write out a piece of its text himself; while his scribes made a close copy of the exemplar, *b*. But when the text reached his own lifetime he took over the writing of it himself, so that he could incorporate directly into it his own version of the chronicle of his predecessor. Later he went through the manuscript making further additions and alterations, both to the sections of text written by himself, and to those written by his scribes. These facts are of the utmost importance, for they show that *AB* is the actual manuscript into which Matthew Paris first made his revisions of Roger Wendover: it is, in fact, *the earliest and original complete manuscript* of his *Chronica Majora*.[2] Were this not so, we should not find variations from *OW* occurring in just those parts of the text of *AB* which were written by Matthew Paris himself.

Matthew evidently at first intended to go carefully through the whole of *AB* in order to correct the errors of his scribes. But this good intention was carried out systematically only up to about p. 75 (about the annal for 500). At this point he evidently grew tired of the work of correction, and in the rest of *A* he was active only at a few scattered points. Thus, between the beginning of the book and p. 75 he made over 100 corrections; but from here on until the annal for 1066 there are only about

---

[1] *CM.* II, pp. 653 and 669.
[2] For more on this, see below, pp. 50 ff.

thirty, twenty-two of which occur between the annals for 1006 and 1066. After the annal for 1066 corrections again become frequent, and it is clear that Matthew went through this part of the text of *A* with much more care. Matthew's work of correction was not, on the whole, very satisfactory. Sometimes he fails to correct in one place an error which he had avoided elsewhere. Thus he spoils the sense of one passage which he misunderstood because the scribe had omitted the initial letter for illumination; yet he wrote the same passage out correctly in the *Vitae Offarum*.[1] Sometimes he makes blundering attempts at correction which entirely spoil the sense of the passage; as, for instance, where, mistaking *an'* (= 'annis') for *ante*, he alters Roger Wendover's 'Francorum [rex] Marcomirus annis triginta quatuor' to 'Francorum [rex] Marcomirus an[te] triginta quatuor dies obiit'.[2] Sometimes, however, his corrections are successful: he supplies a missing verb or corrects a scribal blunder, and, on one occasion, provides a missing line in the margin.[3] Occasionally he corrects a historical mistake of Roger's: for instance, where Roger wrongly had 'Walone', Matthew corrects to 'Pandulpho'.[4] On the whole, however, Matthew's corrections of Roger are inadequate and few in number, and they hardly make up for the numerous new blunders and inaccuracies which were introduced into the chronicle through his own or his scribe's carelessness in *AB*.

Apart from correction or attempted correction, Matthew's revision of Roger's *Flores Historiarum* consists of 'improvements', in part stylistic and literary, and in part historical. His literary alterations often take the form of the addition of words and phrases, usually colourful and tendentious, to give vigour and picturesqueness to the narrative, and frequently he substitutes his own phrases for Roger's more prosaic ones. For instance, he alters Roger's 'subridens' (in reference to King John) to 'subsannans'; and 'cerebro perforato' (speaking of Eustace de Vescy's death from a head wound) to 'cerebro

---

[1] *CM*. I, p. 359, note 4; Wats, p. 29.
[2] *CM*. I, p. 171, note 1; see also *CM*. I, p. 141, note 2, and II, pp. xxx–xxxi.
[3] *CM*. I, p. 203. Luard does not point out that the words 'Vae tibi... lacerabuntur' are omitted through homoeoteleuton in all the MSS., but added in the margin of *A* by Matthew himself.
[4] *CM*. III, p. 61, note 5.

terebrato'; and elsewhere he adds to Roger's phrase 'cum juramento' the word 'horribili'.[1] Many other examples of this kind of 'improvement' could be cited.[2] Matthew's love of playing on words is often reflected in the addition in the margin of the manuscript of a word similar in form to that used by Roger, usually preceded with a *vel*: thus we find 'vel indicio' in reference to the word 'editio', and 'vel fir.' in reference to 'conformari'.[3] Frequently Roger's narrative is 'improved' by the provision of an apt quotation, some illustrative verses, or an epitaph.[4] Other characteristic literary alterations are the introduction of direct speech,[5] and the insertion of epithets or short character sketches, usually bestowing praise or blame, where Roger Wendover only mentions a name. Here is a passage containing a number of examples of this kind of 'improvement':[6]

Fawkes, *lacking the bowels of compassion; the warlike and bloodthirsty* Savari de Mauléon with *his* Poitevins; William Brewer, *bellicose and experienced*, with his men; Walter Buc, *an assassin and man of blood*, with *his filthy ignoble Flemings and* Brabanters, *stained with every kind of crime....*

This passage exemplifies another of Matthew's favourite 'improvements' to the text of his predecessor: the introduction of his own opinions, feelings, and prejudices. When Roger records Henry III's return from Poitou in 1230 without any comment, Matthew supplies it thus:[7] '[He returned...] having wasted an infinite amount of money, and having caused the death of innumerable nobles; weakened them with sickness and hunger; or reduced them to extreme poverty....' Again, when Roger records John of Brienne's flight to France in 1230, Matthew adds:[8] '[He fled...] with his mercenaries, whom the pope enriched with ecclesiastical plunder and honoured with goods taken whencesoever from the poor....'
Many of these colourful, partisan comments and statements

---

[1] *CM.* II, pp. 586, note 3, and 666, note 2; III, p. 21.
[2] See *CM.* II, p. xxxii, and pp. 622–3, 639–40 etc.
[3] *CM.* I, pp. 174, note 3, and 130, note 2.
[4] E.g. at *CM.* II, pp. 452 and 669; III, pp. 43, 57, 105, 112, 186, note 5, etc.
[5] E.g. at *CM.* II, pp. 624, 637, 645; and III, p. 161.
[6] *CM.* II, pp. 635–6; I have italicized Matthew's additions to the text of Roger.   [7] *CM.* III, p. 199.   [8] *CM.* III, p. 194.

added by Matthew enliven the narrative of Roger Wendover; and we must, I think, regard them as literary, rather than historical, 'improvements'. Of these latter, however, there are many examples. A number of small factual details, such as the insertion of a name or a date,[1] and a large number of short annalistic entries, sometimes from sources not used by Roger, are added.[2] Besides these, Matthew added a good many documents to Roger's text,[3] and on one occasion he inserted in the margin of *AB* a more accurate version of a document given by Roger in the text.[4] Another important type of historical 'improvement' is the addition of a number of fairly long pieces describing an event or relating a story, such as the description of William Rufus's death and the account of Henry I's speech to the nobles in 1106.[5] As the text approaches his own time, Matthew contributes more and more of these insertions, usually on the basis of information given him by people he knew. The story of Simon of Tournay, for instance, was told to Matthew by Nicholas of Farnham, bishop of Durham,[6] and much seems to have been added on the information of Hubert de Burgh.[7] Sometimes Matthew has a different account of an event from that of Roger, and he adds his own account into the margin of *AB* without any attempt to integrate it with Roger's.[8]

We have examined, in some detail, the actual relationship of the chronicles of Roger Wendover and Matthew Paris. Although it is true that Matthew's *Chronica Majora* is more than a mere continuation of Roger's *Flores Historiarum*, it is also true that Matthew owed much more to Roger than a mere source for the first part of his chronicle, for, besides the content, which, up to the annal for 1236, is almost wholly Roger's, the form, scope, and technique of Matthew's *Chronica Majora* are all based on Roger's work. As to the relationship of the two men, we know nothing certain, except, what is clear from a study of their chronicles, that Matthew learnt his profession, as a historian, from Roger Wendover.

---

[1] E.g. at *CM*. III, pp. 1 and 112; II, p. 495.
[2] For these, see below, pp. 103 ff.
[3] E.g. at *CM*. II, pp. 607–10 and III, p. 34.
[4] *CM*. I, p. 348, note 2.   [5] *CM*. II, pp. 112–13 and 130–1.
[6] *CM*. II, pp. 476–7.   [7] See above, p. 13.
[8] E.g. *CM*. III, pp. 28 ff.

CHAPTER III

THE HANDWRITING AND AUTHORSHIP OF
THE HISTORICAL MANUSCRIPTS

I T is only recently that the problem of Matthew Paris's handwriting has been thoroughly investigated, and a definite conclusion reached.[1] It is unnecessary, here, to recapitulate the detailed evidence, but it ought, perhaps, to be pointed out that my study of Matthew's handwriting led me to the conclusion that Sir Frederick Madden identified it correctly, and that Sir Thomas Duffus Hardy did not. Since this paper was published, I have come across a further piece of evidence which I had previously overlooked, that the Corpus Christi College, Cambridge, manuscript of the *Chronica Majora* (*B*) is Matthew's autograph. In one place[2] Matthew describes himself as 'scriptor huius libri', but the scribe of the fair copy, British Museum Cotton MS. Nero D v (*C*), normally an accurate copyist, has altered this to 'confector huius libri'. At another point, too,[3] Matthew's reference to himself as 'huius paginae scriptori' has been altered by the scribe of *C* to 'compositori'. It appears from this that the word *scriptor* (and presumably the verb *scribo*) had the definite meaning of 'writer' or 'scribe'; and that when Matthew refers to himself in this way, as he frequently does,[4] he means that he is actually writing.

The *Historia Anglorum* has always been accepted as Matthew's autograph; to this, unless the evidence and conclusion of my paper on Matthew Paris's handwriting be discredited, must now be added the text of the *Chronica Majora* from 1213 onwards; the text of the *Flores Historiarum* from 1241 to 1249; the *Liber Additamentorum*; and the *Abbreviatio Chronicorum*—in fact all the more important historical works usually attributed to Matthew Paris. As we shall have occasion to mention these

[1] In my paper 'The Handwriting of Matthew Paris', *Trans. Camb. Bibl. Soc.* I (1953).   [2] *CM.* v, p. 129 and note 3.

[3] *CM.* v, p. 136 and note 3.

[4] See Vaughan, 'Handwriting of M. Paris', *loc. cit.* p. 385, and *CM.* v, pp. 201 and 317. Sometimes he refers to himself as *compositor*, as at *HA.* III, p. 40.

3-2

works frequently in the pages which follow, a brief description of some of them will not be out of place here.

(1) *Chronica Majora*: see above, p. 21.

(2) *Historia Anglorum*: in B.M. Royal MS. 14 C vii (*R*); the text extends from 1066 to 1253 and is based on that of the *Chronica Majora*.

(3) *Flores Historiarum* up to the annal for 1249: the earliest existing manuscript is number 6712 in the Chetham Library, Manchester (*Ch*). This is the work previously ascribed to 'Matthew of Westminster', and is not to be confused with the *Flores Historiarum* of Roger Wendover. It has been edited by Luard for the Rolls Series, and I refer to this edition with the letters *FH*.

(4) *Abbreviatio Chronicorum*: in B.M. Cotton MS. Claudius D vi; based for the most part on the *Historia Anglorum*. The text extends from 1000 to 1255. It was edited by Madden in the third volume of his *Historia Anglorum*, but, to avoid confusion, I shall refer to this edition with the letters *AC*.

We may now turn to examine the evidence for the authorship of these works. Matthew's authorship of the *Chronica Majora* from 1236 to 1253 has never been doubted; nor has it ever been suggested that he did not write the *Historia Anglorum*; but there has been no unanimous agreement about his authorship of the *Chronica Majora* from 1254 to 1259, the *Abbreviatio Chronicorum*, and the *Flores Historiarum*. The question of the authorship of the last part of the *Chronica Majora* need not detain us long. Only Hardy has raised a voice against Matthew's authorship of it,[1] and his view was refuted by Liebermann, who pointed out that he had misunderstood the meaning of the word *ascribere* in the colophon,[2] and went on to show convincingly that Matthew was indeed the author of the final section of the *Chronica Majora*. A suggestion put forward recently by Denholm-Young takes a modified view of the theory that Matthew did not himself write this part of the *Chronica Majora*.[3]

[1] Hardy, *A Descriptive Catalogue of Materials relating to the History of Great Britain and Ireland*, III, pp. 154-5.
[2] Liebermann (ed.), *MGH,SS.* xxviii, p. 78; and 'Bericht über Arbeiten in England...' in *Neues Archiv der Gesellschaft für ältere deutsche Geschichtskunde*, IV (1879), p. 21.
[3] Denholm-Young, *Handwriting in England and Wales*, p. 52.

He suggested that the colophon to the *Chronica Majora* (Plate I, and above p. 7), linked to the fact that the last eight leaves of the manuscript are not in Matthew's hand, might lead to the conclusion that the author of these eight leaves was not Matthew himself, but his scribe, who perhaps wrote them up from Matthew's notes. But this theory appears to misinterpret the colophon in much the same way as did Hardy, and to ignore the explicit words 'up to this point wrote the venerable man, brother Matthew Paris': 'hucusque perscripsit venerabilis vir frater Matheus Parisiensis.'

Matthew's authorship of the other two historical works mentioned above, the *Abbreviatio Chronicorum* and the *Flores Historiarum*, has been questioned by Liebermann and Luard respectively.[1] The objections of both are based on the assumption that these works contain too many absurd blunders to have been written by Matthew Paris. In fact, however, many blunders occur in the *Chronica Majora* and the *Historia Anglorum*, which show that Matthew, both when composing and when copying or abridging, frequently makes careless mistakes of just the kind that Luard and Liebermann supposed him incapable of. Many examples could be cited from the *Historia Anglorum* of faulty constructions;[2] omissions of a verb or other important word;[3] copying blunders such as 'navigavit' for 'negavit' and 'Oxoniam' for 'Exoniam';[4] and the omission of a line through homoeoteleuton in the exemplar.[5] More serious mistakes also occur; for instance, Matthew summarizes a bull of Gregory IX with the words[6] 'Summa: de discordia Templi et Hospitalis'; yet the bull contains no mention of any dissension between the two Orders. In the *Chronica Majora*, too, errors are frequent, as, for instance, when Matthew writes 'comitis pontificis', apparently for 'comitis Pontivi'.[7] Elsewhere, he makes the king of Navarre and count of Champagne two different people, and in

---

[1] Liebermann (ed.), *MGH,SS.* xxviii, pp. 101–2 and Luard (ed.), *FH.* I, pp. xxxviii–xxxix.

[2] E.g. at *HA.* I, pp. 38, note 3, and 129, note 1.

[3] E.g. at *HA.* I, p. 229, note 3; III, pp. 21, note 1, and 128, note 1.

[4] *HA.* I, pp. 14, note 3, and 254, note 3.

[5] *HA.* I, p. 323, note 4.   [6] *HA.* II, p. 368.

[7] *CM.* III, p. 328; see Powicke, *King Henry III and the Lord Edward*, I, p. 160, note 2.

another place he treats the count of Louvain and duke of Brabant in the same way.[1] Sometimes a verb is carelessly omitted; on one occasion a passage is *repeated* through homoeoteleuton; Aragon is written for Navarre; and the bishop of Carlisle is said to have been consecrated 'on St Agatha's day', when 'in St Agatha's church' is meant.[2] But it would be most unfair to begin a study of Matthew Paris's works with a list of his errors: I cite these few merely to show that he was quite capable of making them, and that, if the *Abbreviatio Chronicorum* and the *Flores Historiarum* are to be excluded from the Parisian corpus, some other objection to them will have to be found.

There is much positive evidence, quite apart from the fact that the *Abbreviatio Chronicorum* is mainly, and the *Flores Historiarum* partly, autograph, that Matthew was the author of both these works. In the *Abbreviatio*, for instance, he refers to himself as 'huius opusculi compositor'.[3] This is in fact copied from the *Historia Anglorum*,[4] but it seems unlikely that it would have been retained in the *Abbreviatio* had Matthew not also been the *compositor* of that work. The system of *signa*, which he uses in the *Chronica Majora* and the *Historia Anglorum* in reference to documents transcribed elsewhere,[5] is also used in the *Abbreviatio*—a fact which affords further evidence that he was its author. Again, several quotations used elsewhere by Matthew occur in the *Abbreviatio*: for instance, a line from Geoffrey of Vinsauf's *Nova Poetria*[6] which is used twice in the *Historia Anglorum*,[7] and a line of Ovid[8] which occurs in both the *Historia Anglorum*[9] and the *Chronica Majora*.[10] The play on words, which is so characteristic a feature of Matthew's other historical works,[11] is common also in the *Abbreviatio*: we find, for instance, 'molliti et melliti';[12] 'duris ac diris';[13] 'plures et

---

[1] *CM.* III, p. 335 (see note 4) and IV, p. 21, note 2.
[2] *CM.* IV, pp. 13, note 1, 79, note 1, and 645, note 1.
[3] *AC.*, p. 304.   [4] III, p. 40.
[5] See below, pp. 65 ff. and 211.   [6] *AC.*, p. 244.
[7] II, p. 276, and III, p. 83.   [8] *AC.*, p. 228.
[9] I, p. 454.   [10] IV, p. 611.
[11] See below, p. 127.
[12] *AC.*, p. 232; they occur together elsewhere at *CM.* III, p. 331; IV, pp. 61, 221, 374; V, p. 14; *HA.* I, p. 15.
[13] *AC.*, p. 233; they occur together elsewhere at *CM.* IV, pp. 238, 400; *HA.* I, p. 369.

pluries';[1] 'reticere quam recitare'.[2] Even more significant is the occurrence in the *Abbreviatio Chronicorum* of some of Matthew's favourite allusions, such as 'nodum quaerentes in [s]cirpo'[3] and 'in arcum pravum';[4] as well as phrases which he very frequently uses, such as: 'novit Ille qui nihil ignorat'; 'in arcto positus'; 'patulis rictibus inhiantes'; 'minus quam deceret aut expediret'; 'haec iccirco dixerim'; 'tractatus exigit speciales'; and 'inter duas molas contriti':[5] all of which occur frequently in the *Chronica Majora* and the *Historia Anglorum*. Many of these phrases are, of course, common enough in other medieval writers, but the appearance of so many of them in the *Abbreviatio Chronicorum* is very good evidence for Matthew's authorship of this work; and, if we take into account the other evidence mentioned above, we must surely conclude that Matthew Paris was its author as well as its scribe.

Professor Galbraith was the first to put forward evidence to show that Matthew was the author of the *Flores Historiarum* up to the annal for 1249, and his evidence is all the more important in that it is wholly drawn from the printed text, and is therefore independent of Madden's attribution of the *Flores Historiarum* to Matthew Paris, which was based on the handwriting of the Chetham manuscript. Galbraith cites two instances in the *Chronica Majora* where a quotation is used by Matthew, and shows that each of these quotations is used in the *Flores* in reference to quite different events, but under an identical mental stimulus.[6] As he puts it: 'The same kind of stimulus extracts the same quotation'; and he adds in his Appendix a number of other instances of the use of an identical expression in a different context, but under a similar mental stimulus, in the *Chronica Majora* or the *Historia Anglorum* and the *Flores*

---

[1] *AC.*, p. 224; they occur together elsewhere at *CM.* III, pp. 407, 532; IV, p. 211.

[2] *AC.*, p. 278; it also occurs at *HA.* II, p. 240.

[3] *AC.*, p. 256; cf. Terence, *Andr.* v, iv, 38; it occurs in the *Chronica Majora* at IV, p. 246 and v, pp. 277, 371 and 635.

[4] *AC.*, p. 169; see Ps. lxxvii, 57; it occurs in the *Chronica Majora* at III, p. 409; IV, pp. 69, 171, 479; v, pp. 52, 128 and 183.

[5] At p. 202, pp. 208 and 267, p. 229, p. 310, pp. 229 and 260, p. 199, and p. 234, respectively.

[6] Galbraith, *Roger Wendover and Matthew Paris*, pp. 32–3; the quotation which follows is from p. 33. For his Appendix, see pp. 45–6.

Historiarum. Galbraith's evidence can easily be amplified: one of the quotations which he mentions, from Ovid, occurs three times in the *Chronica Majora* and once in the *Historia Anglorum*, and is, indeed, one of Matthew's favourites.[1] Again, a note on the word Friday, which Matthew adds in two places in the *Chronica Majora* to the text of Roger Wendover, occurs in a different context, but almost identical words, in the *Flores Historiarum*.[2] The play on words, which we have already noticed in connexion with the *Abbreviatio Chronicorum*, is a feature, too, of the *Flores Historiarum*. Thus we find 'valeo' and 'volo'[3] and 'exaudire' and 'audire'[4] used together, as frequently also in the *Chronica Majora*.[5] Moreover in the *Flores Historiarum* we find some of the very same phrases and allusions which we noted in the *Abbreviatio*, such as: 'versus in arcum pravum';[6] 'in arcto positus';[7] 'secus quam deceret aut expediret';[8] 'haec iccirco dixerim';[9] and 'tractatus exigere(n)t speciales',[10] all of which occur frequently in the *Chronica Majora* and the *Historia Anglorum*; as well as 'rationis trutina ponderabat',[11] 'felix suscepit incrementum',[12] 'etsi de aliis taceamus',[13] 'trahunt ab alto [*or* immo] suspiria',[14] and 'luce clarius',[15] which are all characteristic of Matthew Paris. Another remark which occurs in the *Flores* is: 'ne laeta impermixta tristibus in hoc mundo eveniant',[16] which appears in slightly different words on a number of occasions in Matthew's historical writings; for example, in the *Chronica Majora*:[17] 'ne laetitia huius mundi eveniat mortalibus impermixta.'

There is one important piece of external evidence for Matthew's authorship of the *Flores Historiarum*. The anonymous Winchester monk of the late fourteenth century who wrote the chronicle in the *Book of Hyde* cites Matthew Paris as his source with the words: 'ut scribit Mattheus Parisiacensis',[18] and he

---

[1] Ovid, *Metam.* IV, 472; it occurs at *CM.* IV, pp. 61, 122; V, p. 55; *HA.* I, p. 189.   [2] *CM.* I, pp. 343, note 1, and 403; *FH.* I, p. 217.
[3] II, pp. 292, 350.   [4] II, p. 293.
[5] For instance, 'volo' and 'valeo', at *CM.* IV, pp. 210, 423, 486, 559 and 636; 'exaudire' and 'audire', for instance, at *CM.* III, p. 482; IV, p. 99; V, p. 4.
[6] II, pp. 36, 103.   [7] II, p. 4.   [8] II, p. 180.
[9] II, p. 279.   [10] II, pp. 48, 72, 133, 259.   [11] II, p. 350.
[12] II, p. 311.   [13] II, p. 353.   [14] II, pp. 14, 278.   [15] II, p. 277.
[16] *FH.* II, p. 48. Cf. *FH.* II, p. 187, *HA.* I, p. 230, and below, p. 189 note 1.
[17] *CM.* V, p. 731.   [18] Edwards (ed.), *Liber monasterii de Hyda*, p. 261.

also cites the *Flores Historiarum*: 'Haec omnia habentur in Flores Historiarum',[1] in reference to some passages of which the editor of the *Book of Hyde*, misled perhaps by the phrase 'Flores Historiarum', points out Roger Wendover as the source. We might indeed easily suppose that they derive either from Roger's *Flores Historiarum* or from Matthew's *Chronica Majora*, but a careful comparison of these extracts with the manuscripts of Roger Wendover and Matthew Paris shows that they are taken from the work under discussion, that is from the *Flores Historiarum* formerly attributed to 'Matthew of Westminster' and found in the Chetham manuscript number 6712, and not from the *Flores Historiarum* of Roger Wendover. The author of the chronicle in the *Book of Hyde* uses this work, calls it the *Flores Historiarum*, and attributes it to Matthew Paris. Although he probably wrote more than a century after Matthew's death, his testimony is quite explicit, and, when the internal evidence is also taken into account, we can surely no longer remain in doubt as to the authorship of the *Flores Historiarum* up to the annal for 1249: it was written by Matthew Paris.

There is another work of general historical interest which ought to be included in the Parisian corpus; for, though it is not possible to prove that Matthew composed it himself, it was certainly written under his supervision. This is the short chronicle in B.M. Cotton MS. Vitellius A xx,[2] which is headed by Matthew Paris: 'Cronica excerpta a magnis cronicis S. Albani a conquestu Anglie usque deinceps'. Matthew wrote some of the text at the beginning of the chronicle, as well as a number of corrections and additions in the margins or between the lines. It extends from 1066 to 1246, and the manuscript in which it is written was given to Tynemouth Priory by Ralph of Dunham, prior from 1252 to 1265.

So far we have discussed the authorship of works of general historical interest; but we must turn now to two works of domestic interest to the abbey of St Albans: the *Vitae duorum*

---

[1] Edwards (ed.), *Liber monasterii de Hyda*, p. 265.
[2] Ff. 77a–108b; see Vaughan, 'Handwriting of M. Paris', *Trans. Camb. Bibl. Soc.* I (1953), p. 391, and the references to Madden given there. See also below, pp. 115–16 ff.

Offarum and the *Gesta Abbatum*. The first of these consists of
two separate Lives, that of Offa I, a fourth-century ruler of the
Angles, and that of Offa II, king of Mercia in the latter part of
the eighth century. The Lives are linked together by the promise
of Offa I to found a monastery, which remained unfulfilled until
his descendant Offa II founded St Albans.[1] Luard thought that
the *Vitae Offarum* could not have been written by Matthew
Paris, but that it was the work of a St Albans monk writing,
probably, towards the end of the twelfth century.[2] Both
Chambers and Rickert agreed with him,[3] and indeed this
theory as to the date and authorship of the *Vitae Offarum* has
been generally accepted ever since. Professor Wilson, for
instance, in his little work *The Lost Literature of Medieval
England*, refers to the *Vitae Offarum* as written by an anonymous
twelfth-century St Albans monk.[4] In the very same year,
however, as the publication of Luard's first volume of Matthew
Paris's *Chronica Majora* (1872), containing his view that the
Vitae Offarum was the work of a twelfth-century St Albans
monk, there appeared a doctoral dissertation by Ludwig
Theopold, on the sources for the history of eighth-century
England, in which the theory was advanced that the *Vitae
Offarum* was written by Matthew Paris.[5] Unfortunately, however, Theopold's work has been ignored by later students of the
Vitae Offarum. I propose here to examine, first, Luard's argu-
ments against Matthew's authorship of this work, and to show
that they are without foundation; and then to put forward
evidence, based partly on that of Theopold, to show that the
Vitae Offarum was in fact written by Matthew Paris.

In support of his theory that the *Vitae Offarum* was written
by a twelfth-century monk of St Albans, Luard cites what he
took to be conclusive evidence that the *Vitae Offarum* was not
written by Matthew Paris. In the course of the description of

[1] For a fuller discussion of the *Vitae Offarum*, see below, pp. 189 ff.

[2] *CM.* I, pp. lxxix–lxxx and xxxii–xxxiii.

[3] Chambers, *Beowulf*, p. 34, note 3; Rickert, 'Old English Offa Saga',
Mod. Philol. II (1904–5), p. 30, and note 5.

[4] Wilson, *Lost Literature*, pp. 10–11.

[5] *Kritische Untersuchungen über die Quellen zur angelsächsischen Geschichte
des achten Jahrhunderts*, pp. 112 ff. Liebermann (ed.), *MGH,SS.* XXVIII,
pp. 97–8, also supposed Matthew to have been the author of the *Vitae
Offarum*.

Offa's visit to Rome, the *Vitae Offarum* begins a paragraph with the words: 'Dinumerata denique pro distractione pratorum pecunia, a loco rex progreditur.'[1] This passage also occurs in Roger Wendover. In manuscript *A* of the *Chronica Majora* the 'D' of 'Dinumerata' was originally omitted in order that an illuminated initial could be inserted,[2] but this was in fact never carried out, and Matthew, going through the manuscript, corrected the word to 'Innumerata', and added 'soluta' to make up the sense, not realizing that the true reading was 'Dinumerata'. This, thought Luard, affords 'a proof that Paris could not have been the author of the Life of Offa'.[3] But the text of the *Vitae Offarum* in Matthew's *Liber Additamentorum* is written out in his own hand, so that, at one time at any rate, he was perfectly well acquainted with the correct reading of this passage, and Luard's argument from this blundering attempt at correction, that Matthew was ignorant of the text of the *Vitae Offarum* and therefore could not himself have written it, loses all its force. Moreover, in other manuscripts Matthew frequently makes blunders very similar to this one, even when he is copying or abridging from a manuscript written and composed by himself.[4] Although the invalidity of this piece of evidence allows us to reconsider Matthew as a possible author of the *Vitae Offarum*, Luard's other evidence, if valid, rules him out altogether, for he maintained that the *Vitae Offarum* was used by Roger Wendover, and, if this is so, it could hardly have been written by Matthew Paris.

The *Vitae Offarum* and Roger Wendover's *Flores Historiarum* have a certain amount of matter in very similar words, which, if neither has copied from the other, must have been derived from a source common to them both. This matter consists in the main of a detailed account of the invention and translation of St Alban by Offa; the consequent foundation of St Albans and Offa's journey to Rome; and the martyrdom of St Aethelbert. In Roger Wendover's version of the story of the murder of St Aethelbert, Aethelbert travels to Mercia on his own account to seek the hand of Offa's daughter in marriage, whereas in the *Vitae Offarum* Aethelbert is summoned to Mercia by Offa,

---

[1] Wats, p. 29.   [2] *CM.* I, p. 359, and note 4.
[3] *CM.* I, p. lxxx.   [4] See above, pp. 37–8.

against the wishes of his queen, Quendrida, with the object of a matrimonial alliance.[1] While Roger's version of this story agrees closely with both the lives of St Aethelbert printed by M. R. James,[2] the *Vitae Offarum* differs considerably from them: a fact which shows that Roger's version could not have been derived from that in the *Vitae Offarum*. Immediately after his account of the murder of Aethelbert the author of the *Vitae Offarum* describes Offa's grief and the exile of his wicked queen to a remote spot where, after some years, she was robbed and thrown into her own well by some thieves. We are then told of the burial of Aethelbert at Lichfield, of the neglect of his body, and of its subsequent translation to Hereford. The writer then explains that, since Aethelbert had no children, his kingdom of East Anglia fell into Offa's hands; and goes on to describe the Council of Chelsea.[3] Roger Wendover describes Offa's grief in words different from those used in the *Vitae Offarum*; mentions that he did not eat for three days in exactly the same words as the *Vitae Offarum*; and then, passing over the next two paragraphs in the *Vitae Offarum*, concludes his sentence with a mention of Offa's expedition to East Anglia, partly in the same words as the *Vitae Offarum*. He then returns to the account of Aethelbert with a description of his burial, after some neglect, at Hereford, in words almost identical with those of the *Vitae Offarum*, though beginning half-way through a paragraph of that work. Had Roger been using the *Vitae Offarum* itself, he would surely not have deviated from its text in this extraordinary manner. So far as the account of St Aethelbert is concerned, we can indeed be sure that Roger has not, in fact, used the *Vitae Offarum* at all.

The account of Offa's journey to Rome is often verbally identical in Roger Wendover and the *Vitae Offarum*,[4] but, here again, Roger is evidently not using the *Vitae*. Both Roger and the author of the *Vitae*, for instance, have the chapter-heading: 'Ut rex Offa Romam pergens pratum emerit peregrinis', yet whereas Roger describes this in his text, the author of the *Vitae*

---

[1] *CM.* I, pp. 354–5, and Wats, p. 23.

[2] James, 'Two Lives of St Aethelbert', *EHR.* XXXII (1917), pp. 222–44.

[3] Wats, p. 25. Roger Wendover describes the same events at *CM.* I, p. 355.　　　　[4] *CM.* I, pp. 358–9, and Wats, pp. 28–9.

Offarum does not mention Offa's gift of the land to pilgrims. A comparison of the accounts of the invention of St Alban and the foundation of St Albans in the *Vitae Offarum* and in Roger's *Flores Historiarum* yields no evidence that Roger is using the *Vitae*;[1] and indeed it seems much more probable that the *Vitae* is here taken from Roger Wendover, for the account in the *Vitae* is altogether fuller and more elaborate. Further evidence that Roger did not use the *Vitae* is afforded by the fact that, while they both include a list of bishops with their sees, originally taken from William of Malmesbury, Roger has 'Halardus Helmhamensis et Tidfert Domucensis' nearly correctly, but the *Vitae Offarum* has 'Haraldus Helmamensis et Tedfordensis'.[2] Had Roger Wendover really had the text of the *Vitae Offarum* before him, he would surely have made full use of it. Yet he does not mention Offa I, nor any of the legends concerning Offa II, except the obviously local tradition of his burial by the Ouse. Nor does he use the detailed description in the *Vitae* of the first Danish attack on England, which turns the story into an encomium of Offa: instead he scrapes together a meagre account of this from Henry of Huntingdon and William of Malmesbury.[3]

There is, indeed, every indication that Roger Wendover did not use the *Vitae Offarum*; and consequently it seems likely that it did not even exist when he wrote his *Flores Historiarum*. This conclusion allows us to reconsider the whole question of the authorship of the *Vitae Offarum*, for we need no longer attribute it to a contemporary or even precursor of Roger Wendover. It also reopens the question of the sources of the *Vitae*, which will be discussed in a later chapter,[4] where I hope to show that the historical material in the *Vitae Offarum* is derived from Roger Wendover's *Flores Historiarum*, but was actually taken from Matthew Paris's own manuscript of the *Chronica Majora* (*A*). Here we are concerned only with the problem of the authorship of the *Vitae*, but, before we go on to examine Matthew Paris's claims, we must consider an alternative possibility that has been put forward.

Miss Rickert, agreeing with Luard that the *Vitae Offarum* was

---

[1] Wats, pp. 26–30, and *CM*. I, pp. 356–61.
[2] *CM*. I, p. 345, and Wats, p. 22.
[3] *CM*. I, p. 353; cf. Wats, p. 22.　　　　[4] Below, pp. 191 ff.

written before Matthew Paris's time, advanced the theory that it was written by the author of the chronicle attributed to John of Wallingford.[1] It is true that this writer states that he knows more about Offa than he describes in his chronicle, and promises to recount it at a later date when he has investigated the truth of the matter.[2] This perhaps refers to Offa's part in the murder of Aethelbert, about which the anonymous author confesses his ignorance. That he could not have been the author of the *Vitae Offarum* has been shown by Theopold, who pointed out that he knew far more about the historical Offa and his place in history than the author of the *Vitae*;[3] and it may be added that the critical outlook of the anonymous chronicler is quite different from the rather credulous tone of the *Vitae*.

Before we discuss the evidence for Matthew's authorship of the *Vitae Offarum*, it is worth noting that there is nothing inherently improbable about this attribution. Indeed we know that Matthew was keenly interested in Offa of Mercia;[4] that much of the material used in the *Vitae Offarum* was available to him; and that some of it, such as Charlemagne's letter to Offa,[5] was used elsewhere by him. Furthermore, the earliest text of the *Vitae* is written into the *Liber Additamentorum* in Matthew's own hand, and there is a reference, before the close of its text, to other material in this manuscript.

We have already noticed, in our discussion of the authorship of the *Flores Historiarum* and the *Abbreviatio Chronicorum*, that Matthew frequently uses certain characteristic phrases. Now although the *Vitae Offarum* is a very short work, several of these phrases, such as 'felix suscepit incrementum',[6] 'tractatus exigit speciales',[7] 'ex immo (*or* alto) trahens suspiria'[8] and 'ut decuit et expedivit',[9] occur in it, and their presence goes some way towards proving that Matthew wrote it. Furthermore, in the *Vitae Offarum*, we find exactly the same play on words as we

[1] Rickert, 'Old English Offa Saga', *Mod. Philol.* II (1904–5), pp. 29–39.

[2] Gale (ed.), *Historiae...Scriptores XV*, p. 530; see p. 194 below.

[3] Theopold, *Kritische Untersuchungen*, p. 113.

[4] Theopold, *Kritische Untersuchungen*, p. 114. Matthew has written notes about Offa on odd leaves in *A* and the *Liber Additamentorum*.

[5] Copied by Matthew into the margin of his *Chronica Majora* (*A*) from B.M. Royal MS. 13 D v (text of William of Malmesbury), whence, too, the copy in the *Vitae Offarum* was taken.   [6] Wats, pp. 5, 10, 20.

[7] *Idem*, pp. 5, 14.   [8] *Idem*, pp. 6, 26.   [9] *Idem*, p. 22.

noted above in the *Abbreviatio* and the *Flores*; and sometimes even the same pairs of words, such as 'volo' and 'valeo'[1] and 'mellitus' and 'mollitus',[2] as well as other pairs of words used in an identical way, such as 'potenter' and 'prudenter'[3] and 'subactis' and 'subtractis'.[4] Other phrases commonly used by Matthew Paris which occur in the *Vitae Offarum* are 'infausto sidere', 'quamvis mulier non tamen muliebriter', 'parvipendentes immo vilipendentes', 'singultibus sermonem prorumpentibus', 'in arcto constituti', 'in ore gladii' and 'nec censeo praetereundum'. We find, too, in the *Vitae Offarum*, some of Matthew's favourite colourful words, such as 'formidolosus', 'truculenter', and 'muscipula', as well as one of his most frequently used quotations from Ovid, introduced with his usual words 'juxta illud poeticum'.[5]

Besides these stylistic and literary parallels between the *Vitae Offarum* and Matthew's accepted works, there are some striking parallels in the accounts of battles. Indeed in this respect Matthew's descriptive powers seem to have been rather stereotyped, as the following examples show.

Account of a battle from the *Vitae Offarum*.[6]

Et congressu inito cruentissimo...perstrepunt...tubae cum lituis, et clamor exhortantium, equorum hinnitus, morientium et vulneratorum gemitus, fragor lancearum, gladiorum tinnitus, ictuum tumultus, aera perturbare videbantur...irruit [Offa] truculenter, gladium suum cruore hostili inebriando...[Brutum] sub equinis pedibus potenter praecipitavit.

Account of a battle from the *Historia Anglorum*.[7]

...congressum ineunt cruentissimum. Incipit igitur jam conflictus, extrahuntur gladii sanguine hinc indeque inebriandi, resonabant aeneae cassides malleis ferreis.... Fragor hastarum, tinnitus gladiorum, gemitus percussorum, equorum tumultus compressorum ...aera usque ad nubes commoverunt.... Nonnulli...sub equorum pedibus conculcantur....

Account of a battle from the *Chronica Majora*.[8]

...et initum certamen in cruentissimum bellum suscitarunt.... Clamor congredientium bellatorum, gemitus morientium, tinnitus

---

[1] Wats, pp. 4, 19.   [2] *Idem*, p. 17.   [3] *Idem*, pp. 11, 17, 22.
[4] *Idem*, p. 5.   [5] *Metam.* IV, 472, see above, p. 40 and note 1.
[6] Wats, p. 3.   [7] I, p. 124.   [8] III, p. 408.

armorum, hinnitus equorum...ictuum fulgurantium frequens malleatio ipsum aera tumultibus repleverunt. Tandem post multa hinc inde cruenta certamina....

If this evidence has not convinced the reader of Matthew's authorship of the *Vitae Offarum*, more can be found, of which the most conclusive is, perhaps, the expression in it of Matthew's characteristic outlook and prejudices, and the way in which the text of its main source is amplified in a manner identical with Matthew's treatment of the text of Roger Wendover in his *Chronica Majora*. Thus of Offa I it is said that, like the best princes, he did not wish to resist the desires of his nobles; and of Offa II that he sent gifts to Pope Adrian because he knew of the greed of the Romans.[1] We find, too, that the author of the *Vitae Offarum* adds to the text of his source an etymological note or a remark glorifying St Albans, in just the way that Matthew added to Roger's *Flores Historiarum* in his *Chronica Majora*.[2] If we add to this evidence the fact mentioned above, and discussed in a later chapter, that the historical material in the *Vitae* was taken from Matthew's own manuscript of the *Chronica Majora*, we can hardly doubt that the *Vitae Offarum* ought to be added to the corpus of historical works written by Matthew Paris.

The *Gesta Abbatum* has been generally accepted as the work of Matthew Paris, and there is no need to put forward the evidence for his authorship in detail. His own manuscript, written by himself, with many corrections and marginal additions, is to be found in his *Liber Additamentorum* (ff. 30 on). Its text abounds with phrases characteristic of him, and with expressions of his feelings about Rome and other matters, and it contains several references to his other manuscripts. Like the *Chronica Majora*, it incorporates the work of a predecessor, but we may conveniently defer our discussion of the relationship of Matthew Paris and Adam the Cellarer until we review Matthew's work in the field of domestic history.

---

[1] Wats, pp. 6 and 21.

[2] For instance, at Wats, p. 30, he has added the words 'quod interpretatur volens bonum' to the source's mention of Abbot Willegod; and at p. 28 we find the source interpolated as follows: 'Tractarent de conventu monachorum...atque coenobio *constituendo et magnifice ac regaliter* privilegiando; ubi protomartyris regni sui, *imo totius Britanniae vel Angliae*...' (cf. *CM*. I, p. 358).

CHAPTER IV

THE RELATIONSHIP AND CHRONOLOGY OF THE 'CHRONICA MAJORA', THE 'HISTORIA ANGLORUM', AND THE 'LIBER ADDITAMENTORUM'

IN this chapter we shall be concerned with the three most important of Matthew Paris's historical productions: the *Chronica Majora*, the *Historia Anglorum* and the *Liber Additamentorum*. These are now divided between four manuscripts: *A* and *B*, containing the text of the *Chronica Majora* up to the annal for 1253; *R*, containing the last part of the text of the *Chronica Majora* and the whole of the *Historia Anglorum*; and British Museum Cotton MS. Nero D i, the miscellaneous collection of documentary and other material generally known as the *Liber Additamentorum*.[1] The problem of the relationship and chronology of these manuscripts is an important one, and its solution is made possible only by the work of H. R. Luard and Sir Frederick Madden, each of whom, besides their excellent editions of the *Chronica Majora* and the *Historia Anglorum* respectively, provided in their prefaces detailed and illuminating studies of Matthew Paris's historical manuscripts. Neither of them, however, tried to explain exactly how these manuscripts were related to each other, though they assumed that the *Historia Anglorum* was abridged by Matthew Paris from the text of his *Chronica Majora* in *A* and *B*. In 1941, however, Sir Maurice Powicke published a paper on the compilation of Matthew's *Chronica Majora*, in which for the first time an attempt was made to establish the relationship of the existing manuscripts of the *Chronica Majora*, the *Historia Anglorum* and the *Liber Additamentorum*. Powicke maintained that the text of the *Historia Anglorum* up to the annal for 1249 was written before *AB*, and that *B* itself, at any rate from the annal for 1235

---

[1] For the *Chronica Majora*, see above, pp. 21–2; and, for the *Historia Anglorum*, above, p. 36.

onwards, was a fair copy of the *Chronica* written in or after 1257.[1] Three years later, in a lecture delivered at Glasgow, Professor Galbraith showed that Powicke's evidence that *B* was written as late as 1257 was unsound, and he gave reasons for supposing that Madden was right in thinking that the *Historia Anglorum* was derived directly from the actual manuscript *B*.[2] In the same year, Powicke published a revised version of his paper,[3] in which he accepted Galbraith's criticism of his theory as to the date of *B*, but still maintained that it was a late transcript of the *Chronica Majora* made about the year 1255. Needless to say, this modern controversy concerning the relationship of Matthew's historical manuscripts has been of great help in the present study. Although my conclusions differ greatly from those of Powicke, his arguments and evidence have been of as much assistance to me as Galbraith's criticism of his conclusions; and, without the help of the work of these two scholars, the present study would probably not have been possible.

It was unfortunate that, when Sir Maurice Powicke wrote his paper on the compilation of the *Chronica Majora*, the problem of Matthew's handwriting had not been solved, nor, I believe, were the manuscripts available to him at that time. In my study of Matthew's handwriting, I came to the conclusion that Madden was right in believing that almost the whole of *B* is autograph;[4] but Powicke believed it to be a transcript written by a scribe. Furthermore he states: '*A*, and the first part of *B*, to the middle of the year 1213, are in the same hand...';[5] but had the manuscripts been available he would surely have seen at once that Madden and James were right in attributing this part of the *Chronica Majora* to several scribes (one of whom, as Madden pointed out, was Matthew Paris

[1] This first version of Powicke's paper was published in *Modern Philology*, xxxviii (1940–1), pp. 305 ff.
[2] Galbraith, *Roger Wendover and Matthew Paris*, pp. 26–9; *HA*. I, p. liii.
[3] In Volume xxx (1944) of the *Proceedings of the British Academy*, pp. 147–60.
[4] Vaughan, 'Handwriting of M. Paris', *Trans. Camb. Bibliog. Soc.* I (1953), p. 390; see *HA*. I, p. lvii.
[5] Powicke, 'Compilation of the *Chronica Majora*', *Proc. Brit. Acad.* xxx (1944), p. 151.

himself).[1] Powicke was likewise mistaken in his statement about *B* that 'The continuation [that is, *B* from the annal for 1213 onwards] in another hand, proceeds from the middle of a sentence without a break, and continues smoothly to the end'; and he goes on to say that this part of the manuscript 'announces itself as a copy made in the course of a short period'.[2] In fact, from the point in the annal for 1213 where the handwriting changes, onwards, the text by no means proceeds smoothly in the way we should expect of a fair copy, but as follows:

    ff. 35a–46a, written by Matthew Paris;
    ff. 46a–49a, written by a scribe;
    ff. 49b–50a, written by another scribe;
    ff. 50b–54b, written by Matthew Paris;
    ff. 55a–61b, written by the first scribe mentioned above;
    ff. 61b–111b, written by Matthew Paris;
    f. 112a–b, written by a third scribe;
    f. 112b to the end, written by Matthew Paris.

Speaking of this manuscript, Sir Frederick Madden says:[3] 'These pages exhibit the variations in the hand of the author at different periods, neater and closer at first, and looser and more irregular towards the close'; and I think there can be no doubt that this is so. Far from being a copy executed in a single short period, *B* is an autograph manuscript over the writing of which Matthew must have spent a number of years. A glance at Plates II and III shows the contrast between his writing in the early part of *B*, and in the later part; indeed the difference is so great as to make it seem possible, until a close examination reveals the similarities, that the handwriting of these folios is the work of different scribes. The general palaeographical features of the manuscript show that its writing covered a period of years. There are frequent changes of ink, marginal additions and drawings, erasures and alterations in the text, added pages (for instance ff. 11, 12 and 34) and so on; all of which give the impression that the book was at Matthew's side for a long period, and that it was added to and worked at by the author during several years.

[1] *HA.* I, pp. liv, lvii–lviii; James, *Catalogue of C.C.C.C. MSS.*, I, pp. 51, 54.
[2] Powicke, 'Compilation of the *Chronica Majora*', *loc. cit.* p. 152.
[3] *HA.* I, p. lviii.

4-2

The structure of the manuscript is too complex to be ascertained exactly, but I have tried to show all that I have been able to discover about it in the accompanying diagram (fig. 3). An examination of this diagram shows, I think, that the manuscript is much more likely to be the result of several years' work by the author than a fair copy written at one time. It should be noted, too, that there is a striking variation in the size of the leaves of the manuscript, which would scarcely be likely to occur in a fair copy. From about the beginning of quire 12 onwards the leaves become steadily shorter until those of quires 15 and 16, which are a full quarter of an inch shorter than the leaves of the first eleven quires. Ff. 212–15 are longer, but the succeeding leaves are again short, up to quire 21, when they revert to their former size, and remain so to near the end.

Matthew, we know, at first intended to finish his chronicle at the end of the annal for 1250, and at this point in the *Chronica Majora*[1] he takes leave of the reader with an elaborate termination which includes these verses:

> Terminantur hic Matthaei
> Cronica: nam jubilaei
>   Anni dispensatio
> Tempus spondet requiei.
> Detur ergo quies ei,
>   Hic, et caeli solio.

And the couplet:

> Siste tui metas studii, Matthaee, quietas,
> Nec ventura petas quae postera proferet aetas.

The text in *B*, however, continues beyond this point without an obvious break, and without any further comment, to the end of the annal for 1253. Now if *B* really is the autograph and original manuscript of the *Chronica Majora*, written by Matthew Paris over a period of years, we should naturally expect to find some sign of a break in the writing of the manuscript at the point where he himself tells us that he at first laid down his pen. Powicke found no sign of such a break, and he says:

If it [that is *B*] were not a fair copy of the whole chronicle up to the year 1253, a break at 1250, where Matthew brings his work to

[1] v, pp. 197–8.

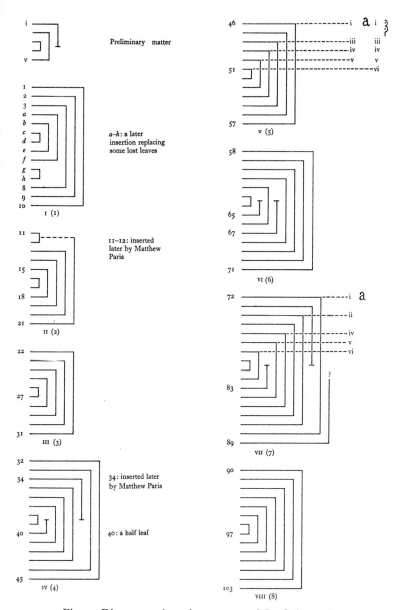

Fig. 3. Diagram to show the structure of *B*. Quires 1–8.

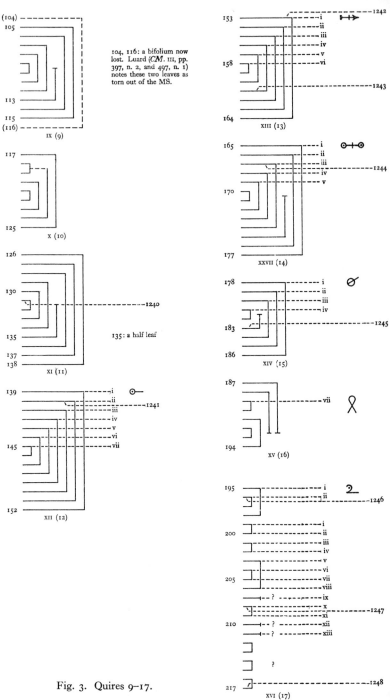

Fig. 3. Quires 9–17.

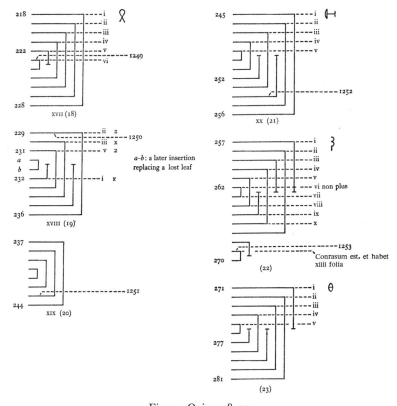

Fig. 3. Quires 18–23.

Fig. 3. The arrangement of the leaves in each quire is shown diagrammatically, with the folio numbers on the left. Matthew's quire numbers are given below the diagram of each quire, in the place where they occur in the manuscript; and his numbering of the leaves, together with the symbols he uses to distinguish the different quires, is given on the right. It will be seen that this numbering is neither consistent nor methodical, and the leaves of many of the quires are not numbered at all. I have not always been able to determine the exact arrangement of the leaves—especially in the case of quire 17. I have marked the leaves added after Matthew Paris's time, *a*, *b*, etc. All the quire and leaf numbers, as well as the symbols, seem to have been executed by Matthew himself; and the comments in quire 22 are in his hand. The numbers vii–x, in this quire, are written in plummet in the inner, lower corners of the verso of each leaf, not, as elsewhere, in ink in the centre of the lower margin. The only annal which begins at the beginning of a new leaf is that for 1252.

a stately close, would have been inevitable, but in the manuscript this conclusion is written by the scribe *currente calamo* on his way to the actual termination at the year 1253.[1]

In fact, however, a careful examination of the manuscript shows that there *was* a break in the writing at the end of the annal for 1250, although it is by no means obvious.

The quires of *A* are numbered throughout the manuscript on the last leaf of each quire, in red, and almost certainly by Matthew himself. Those in *B* are numbered in a similar way, in red, but with blue ornamentation surrounding the figures. A careful examination shows that these quire numbers in *B* are not the original ones, for in almost every case up to and including quire number XVIII, traces of an earlier numbering, in red, are visible, either under or near them. A magnifying glass reveals that the vermilion, which was used for these numbers, cracks and peels off the parchment very easily, and does not stain it in the same way as ink, so that the task of erasing the first set of numbers must have been an easy one; and it is hardly surprising that in the case of two of the quires (VI and VIII), no trace of the original number has survived. Sometimes, however, the remains of the earlier number are quite easily visible, as with quires II and III. Fortunately for us, Matthew, when he was renumbering the quires in this manuscript, inadvertently omitted to alter the number of the fourteenth quire, which, consequently, retains its original number, XXVII, and disturbs the sequence of quire numbers, which run XIII, XXVII, XIV. This number XXVII is quite unlike the other numbers in *B*, all of which have blue ornamentation round them, but it is identical with those in *A*. Furthermore, if we count the quires from the start of *A*, the fourteenth quire of *B* is the twenty-seventh in all, a fact which proves conclusively that Matthew originally wrote *A* and *B* as one book, *AB*. The original set of quire numbers in *AB* extended, so far as can be judged, only up to and including number XVIII in *B*; for there is no sign that numbers XIX and XX have been written over earlier, erased numbers; and the last two quires are not numbered at all. The quires in *B*, then, were probably renumbered before quires XIX and XX had been numbered, and before

[1] Powicke, 'Compilation of the *Chronica Majora*', *Proc. Brit. Acad.* XXX (1944), p. 152.

the last two quires were added. Now the text of the annal for 1250 ends on the penultimate leaf of quire XIX (f. 243 a), and it seems, therefore, very likely that Matthew originally ended *AB* with the annal for 1250, leaving the last leaf of the last quire blank, and unnumbered. He then apparently decided to divide this bulky volume in two, renumbered the quires in *B*, and, as he proceeded with his continuation of the text over the remaining blank leaf and on to an additional quire, numbered these last two quires XIX and XX.

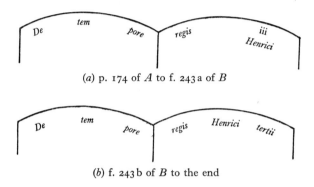

(*a*) p. 174 of *A* to f. 243 a of *B*

(*b*) f. 243 b of *B* to the end

Fig. 4. Diagram to show the change in the arrangement of the page heads in *AB* at the end of the annal for 1250.

There is, however, some much more direct evidence of a break in the writing of *B* at the end of the annal for 1250. From p. 174 of *A* up to f. 243 a of *B* (the page on which the text of the annal for 1250 ends), the rubric headings at the top of each page are decorated with blue coil and line work; but from f. 243 b to the end of *B* these headings have no blue decoration, and are arranged differently across the openings (see fig. 4). The identity of the ornamentation in the two books shows that it was executed when they still formed one volume: it is just the kind of decoration which an author would add (it was executed by Matthew himself) as a finishing touch to a completed manuscript.[1] The

---

[1] It should be noted that this decoration begins on the same page (174 of *A*) as the annal for 1066; the explanation probably being that it was carried out at the time (in 1250) when Matthew began to abridge the *Historia Anglorum*, the text of which begins in 1066, from *AB*.

fact that it ends on the very same page as the annal for 1250 shows that, when it was carried out, the text of *AB* ended at that point, and that Matthew at first intended to leave it thus. It was only later, when he had continued his chronicle beyond the year 1250, that he added the second set of rubric headings from f. 243 b onwards.

A further piece of evidence for a break in the writing of *AB* at the end of the annal for 1250 ought to be mentioned, though its value is doubtful. On the fly-leaf at the end of what is now *A*, there is a note in Matthew's hand which reads: 'Cronica ab origine mundi usque ad annum domini millesimum... ...simum; videlicet usque ad mortem henrici ii regis anglie.' Between 'millesimum' and 'videlicet' the original reading of the note has been erased, and Matthew has rewritten some words on slips of vellum stuck over the erasure. In the first part of this erasure there is room for about eight letters, but unfortunately the first reading is illegible and the slip of vellum on which the second was written has disappeared. In the second part of the erasure, however, both readings appear to have been *-simum*. What is the significance of this altered note? When was it written, and why did Matthew find it necessary to alter it? Certainly the date of the termination of the chronicle has been altered, and the words 'videlicet usque ad mortem henrici ii' appear to have been added when the alteration was made, and to refer to the second, rewritten date. It is hard to explain why this second date should end with the letters *-simum*. *A* in fact ends at the end of the annal for 1188, and Henry's death is recorded at the beginning of *B*, under the year 1189. Neither of these dates ends with the letters *-simum*, but Matthew perhaps wrote the approximate date 1190, and then qualified it with the remark about Henry II's death. Be this as it may, the second version of this note certainly refers to *A*; and the most plausible explanation of the alteration of the date is that what is now the fly-leaf of *A* was at one time the fly-leaf of the combined manuscript *AB*, and that the note originally referred to the chronicle in this combined manuscript. If this was so, the original date could hardly have been 1253, since it ended with the letters *-simum*. The words 'ducentesimum quinquagesimum', however, would fit in, and it therefore seems probable that this note

58

originally read: 'Cronica ab origine mundi usque ad annum millesimum ducentesimum quinquagesimum', and referred to *AB* as originally finished by Matthew up to the annal for 1250. Evidently, when *AB* was divided, the leaf on which this note was written was removed to the end of *A*, and the note altered accordingly.

A more convincing piece of evidence for a break in the writing of *B* at the end of the annal for 1250 is the fact that the text of *C* ends at this point.[1] There is no doubt that *C* was copied from the actual manuscript *B*, and, since it was copied by a scribe, there is no reason why its text should have broken off at the end of the annal for 1250, unless the text of its exemplar likewise ended at that point. The text of *C* extends from 1189 to 1250, and it was evidently designed by Matthew as a fair copy of the second part of his *Chronica Majora* as he at first intended to leave it. It is thus very probable that, when it was copied, the text of its exemplar extended over the same years. *AB* was no doubt divided soon after its text up to 1250 was completed, and *C* copied before Matthew had begun to continue *B* beyond the annal for 1250.

This rather prolonged discussion has led us to the conclusion that Matthew wrote *A* and *B* as one book, and that this book, *AB*, was the earliest and original manuscript of his *Chronica Majora*, the text of which at first ended with the annal for 1250. The evidence just advanced, for a break after the annal for 1250 in the writing of the present manuscript *B*, clinches this point, and confirms the conclusion reached in Chapter II, that *AB* was the actual manuscript in which Matthew first made his revisions of the chronicle of his predecessor, Roger Wendover.

We may now approach the difficult problem of the date of *AB*. Plehn pointed out that, under the year 1239,[2] Matthew alludes to the unfortunate deaths of the brothers Gilbert and Walter Marshal, and that the latter did not in fact die until November 1245. From this he concluded that the annal for 1239 in *B* was

---

[1] *C* is what I call B.M. Cotton MS. Nero D v, Part II. See below, p. 110.

[2] *CM*. III, p. 524.

written after November 1245.[1] This gives us a *terminus a quo* for the writing of Matthew's original section of the *Chronica Majora* in *B* (1236 on): it could hardly have been begun much before 1245. There is no evidence as to the date of the writing of the earlier part of the *Chronica Majora*, adapted from Roger Wendover (Creation to 1236). Up to the annal for 1213 this was carried out, as we have seen, by scribes under the direction of Matthew Paris, and it may well have been written in a comparatively short time; so that it seems possible that *AB* was not begun until about 1240 or even later.

In the annals after 1245 Matthew frequently lagged, in *B*, a year or more behind the occurrence of the events he describes; for instance, the annal for 1248 was written in or after 1249, and in the course of the annal for 1249 there are references to events which took place in 1250.[2] It was perhaps Matthew's visit to Norway in 1248–9 which made him so behindhand, but, if this is so, he must have worked extremely hard during 1249–50, for we have conclusive evidence that he had brought the text of his chronicle right up to date by the end of 1250 or early in 1251. The Emperor Frederick II died on 13 December 1250, and Matthew mentions this event three times in the *Chronica Majora*.[3] It is significant that the death of the famous emperor, who figures so largely in the pages of the *Chronica Majora*, is not recorded in the text of the annal for 1250, but only in the margin. It is noticed again in the text of the annal for 1251 among entries recording the events of February 1251, in words which show that the news of it did not reach Matthew until late January or early February of that year. The third mention of Frederick's death is at the end of Matthew's description of the marvellous events of the last half century with which he originally concluded his *Chronica Majora*, and which follows the end of the annal for 1250. Here we find the laconic statement:[4] 'Obiit insuper stupor mundi Frethericus, die Sanctae Luciae, in Apulia.' These words are clearly out of place in the

---

[1] Plehn, 'Der politische Charakter von Matheus Parisiensis', in *Staats- und socialwissenschaftliche Forschungen*, XIV (1897), p. 135; he gives other evidence for this conclusion, pp. 134–5.

[2] See *CM*. v, pp. 77 and 88.

[3] *CM*. v, pp. 190 (margin of 1250 annal), 196, and 216 (1251 annal).

[4] v, p. 196.

context, and a glance at the manuscript shows that they are written over an erasure. They occupy one line at the top of column two on f. 243 a of *B*, and the line which was erased in order to make way for them has been rewritten at the foot of the preceding column. The explanation of their curious position in the text of the *Chronica Majora* is, simply, the convenience of insertion here. It is inconceivable that Matthew would have omitted this important piece of news from the text of his chronicle, had it been available to him at the time of writing, and we must conclude that he had already completed the annal for 1250 and brought his chronicle to its elaborate close in *B*, before the news of the emperor's death reached him, that is to say, before January or early February 1251. It is not possible to ascertain when exactly Matthew took up his pen to continue the text of *B* beyond f. 243 a; but in the course of the annal for 1251 there are two allusions which show that it was not before 1252.[1] In the rest of *B*, and in *R*, Matthew seems again to have been writing a year or two after the events he records.

Our conclusions about *B* show that Sir Maurice Powicke was mistaken in his belief that it was a copy of the *Chronica Majora* written about the year 1255. His theory, too, that the *Historia Anglorum* was, in the main, written before *B* is likewise mistaken, for we know that it was not begun until 1250:[2] the year in which Matthew was busy completing the text of *AB*. How long Matthew took to write the *Historia Anglorum* we do not know, but it is probable that the penultimate annal, that for the year 1252, was not written before 1255, since in copying from *B* an allusion to Innocent IV as 'iste papa praesens'[3] Matthew, in the annal for 1252 in the *Historia Anglorum*, omits the word 'praesens', which suggests that, by the time he wrote these words into the *Historia Anglorum*, Innocent IV was no longer 'the present Pope' (he died in December 1254). The writing of the *Historia Anglorum*, then, probably extended over the years 1250–5.

There can be no doubt that the *Historia Anglorum* was almost

---

[1] *CM.* v, pp. 236 and 239.

[2] On the first page of the *Historia Anglorum* (I, p. 9) Matthew remarks: 'Nec usque ad tempora haec scribentis, videlicet annum gratiae MCCL est inventus rex Angliae titulo sanctitatis insignitus.'

[3] *CM.* v, p. 355, *HA.* III, p. 128.

entirely copied, or rather abridged, from the actual manuscripts *A* and *B*; but, as this is an important conclusion, and one directly contrary to Powicke's thesis, I must, at the risk of being tedious, give some detailed evidence of its accuracy.

(1) In *A*, between the annal for 1066 and the end, Matthew has made many small alterations to the text, which are followed in the *Historia Anglorum*. Thus:

Original reading of *A*	Matthew's altered reading of *A*	Reading of the *Historia Anglorum*
Normanniam	Northanhumbriam	Northambriam[1]
inter	praeter	praeter[2]
continentiam	abstinentiam	abstinentiam[3]
castellis	catallis	catallis[4]

In *B*, too, Matthew has made similar alterations, which are followed in the *Historia Anglorum*. On f. 51 b, for instance, he has altered 'balistarios' to 'regales', and 'urbem' to 'urbi': the *Historia Anglorum* has 'regales' and 'urbi'.[5]

(2) In the annal for 1200[6] a line is omitted in *B* through homoeoteleuton in the exemplar, a mistake which was not due to Matthew himself, since he did not write this section of the text of *B*. In copying this passage into the *Historia Anglorum* Matthew noticed that there was an error and added some words in order to make up the sense:[7] he did not write in the missing line. It is clear that, in the exemplar of *B* (*b*), two lines must have ended with the same syllables (in this case, of the words 'monasterium' and 'ministerium'). The line must have been present in this manuscript, for it occurs in *O* and *W*.[8] If the *Historia Anglorum* had been copied from *b*, Matthew would surely either not have made the error of omitting the line, or he would have omitted it without realizing that he had done so. The fact that he made up the sense proves that he noticed that the line was missing in his exemplar; and *B* is the only manuscript in which this line is omitted.

---

[1] 1094; *CM.* II, p. 35, note 2; *HA.* I, p. 47.

[2] 1135; *CM.* II, p. 161, note 7; *HA.* I, p. 249.

[3] 1178; *CM.* II, p. 305, note 1; *HA.* I, p. 406.

[4] 1188; *CM.* II, p. 330, note 5; *HA.* I, p. 446, and note 1.

[5] *HA.* II, pp. 213 and 211.   [6] *CM.* II, p. 467.

[7] *HA.* II, p. 88; see also *CM.* II, p. 467, note 6.

[8] See fig. 2 above, p. 29.

(3) In the course of the annal for 1217 in *B*, Matthew inserts the word 'nisi' into a sentence (f. 50b), because his scribe had mistakenly omitted the word 'cum'; and this correction is found in the text of the *Historia Anglorum*.[1] The *nisi* reading is peculiar to *B*, and was due to a scribal error in it; the other manuscripts have the reading *cum*.[2]

(4) In the annal for 1222 a piece of direct speech is added by Matthew in the margin of *B* (f. 58a), and marked to be inserted in the text. In the *Historia Anglorum*[3] it is incorporated into the text in the exact place pointed out in *B*. Many other examples of this could be cited.

Although the *Historia Anglorum* is for the most part derived from *AB*, up to the annal for 1191 Matthew sometimes used another manuscript for it (possibly *b*), perhaps at times when *A* or *B* was being copied by the scribe of *C* or the *Flores Historiarum*. Here are some examples of the *Historia Anglorum* following the manuscripts of Roger Wendover against *A* and *B*, which make it clear that some other manuscript was in use:

(1) Annal for 1151.[4] The source (Robert de Monte), *O*, and *W* all have 'etiam hi'; as also the *Historia Anglorum*. But *A* has 'quidem'.

(2) Annal for 1162.[5] A line omitted in *A* through homoeoteleuton is in *O*, *W*, and the *Historia Anglorum*, in identical words.

(3) Annal for 1191.[6] Ralph de Diceto the source, *O*, and *W* all have 'quasi'; as also the *Historia Anglorum*; but this is omitted in *B*.

These examples show that Matthew sometimes used one of the manuscripts of Roger Wendover (either *OW* or *b*) for the *Historia Anglorum*; he also occasionally used *C*, for Madden notices an entry in the *Historia* which was certainly taken from this manuscript,[7] and there are probably other examples of its use. In general, however, it is quite certain that Matthew abridged the *Historia Anglorum* from the text of his *Chronica Majora* in *A* and *B*.

---

[1] II, p. 206.   [2] *CM*. III, p. 15, note 8.   [3] II, p. 251.
[4] *CM*. II, p. 186, note 6; and *HA*. I, p. 289.
[5] *CM*. II, p. 220, note 2; and *HA*. I, p. 319.
[6] *CM*. II, p. 373, note 2; *HA*. II, p. 22.   [7] *HA*. II, p. 119, note 5.

Another problem concerning the relationship of *B* (as well as *C*) and the *Historia Anglorum* now demands our attention. Throughout *B* there are marginal notices in Matthew's hand, consisting usually of a short phrase or single word such as *vacat*, *offendiculum* or *impertinens*, pointing out passages in the text which ought to be omitted, or which, at any rate, Matthew evidently considered offensive or unnecessary. Powicke maintained that these directions do not refer to the *Historia Anglorum*, but, in so far as they are genuine instructions and not mere comments, to *C*. He says:[1]

Occasionally a marginal note added later in *B* and followed by a sign reads 'impertinens Anglorum historiae usque huc', suggesting that it was intended as a direction to omit certain passages from the shorter history. Investigation shows, however, that notes of this kind were added in a most capricious way and also that the writer was not thinking of any particular book, for he wrote in other places 'pertinens historiae Wallensium, indirecte tamen Anglorum usque ad hoc signum', and 'pertinet historiae Scotorum'. Moreover the variant 'impertinens Anglis usque huc' also appears.... In so far as (these marginalia)...are directions, they were intended for the guidance of the scribe who made Nero D v, the copy of *A* and *B*.

Professor Galbraith took an opposite view. He says: '...the plain inference is that these notes were made on the Corpus MS. [*B*] as a guide in the compilation of the *Historia Anglorum*.'[2]

Apart from rather vague comments, often in a single word, these directions in the margins of *B* fall into two groups. In one group the wording is usually 'vacat quia offendiculum', 'offendiculum vacat', or 'cave quia offendiculum', and the letters are usually written in red and spaced out vertically in the margin against the offending passage of text.[3] In the other group the marginal directions always contain the word 'impertinens', frequently followed by the phrase 'Anglorum historiae', and the limits of the passage thus referred to are defined by means of signs. The passages referred to in the first group are invariably offensive either to the king (usually), or to the pope (occasionally);

[1] Powicke, 'Compilation of the *Chronica Majora*', in *Proc. Brit. Acad.* xxx (1944), pp. 156–7.
[2] Galbraith, *Roger Wendover and Matthew Paris*, p. 29.
[3] Other passages are marked, simply, *offendiculum*, but these directions seem to have no especial significance.

whereas those referred to in the second group of marginal directions are inoffensive, and are usually concerned with affairs on the Continent or in Wales or Scotland; or with legendary matter, prodigies and visions. I have counted thirty-three marginal directions of the first group between the annals for 1199 and 1247 in *B*, and twenty of the passages thus indicated are either omitted, or written in the margin, in *C*. The scribe of *C*, therefore, evidently took some notice of these directions. Sometimes he began to copy out the offending passage in his text, then crossed out what he had written and wrote the whole passage in the margin. In one place in *B*[1] a passage beginning in the middle of a sentence is marked in the margin 'vacat, non quia falsum sed provocans'; and the text of *C* breaks off abruptly at this point. Of the forty-seven passages in *B* marked with the other type of marginal direction—that having the word *impertinens* and a sign to delimit the impertinent passage—which I have counted, thirty-nine are entirely omitted in the *Historia Anglorum*, and the other eight severely abridged. Furthermore, not a single one of these passages is omitted by the scribe of *C*. It is thus evident that, while the first type of marginal direction (*vacat quia offendiculum* etc.) was designed for the scribe of *C*, the second type (*impertinens* etc.) was written into the margins of *B* by Matthew to remind him of certain passages in the main chronicle which could well be omitted from the *Historia Anglorum* on the grounds of irrelevance.

So far we have found nothing to make us alter our conclusion that *AB* is the earliest manuscript of the *Chronica Majora*; that it was completed up to 1250 early in 1251; and that the *Historia Anglorum* was taken from it. The latter point has been confirmed by our examination of the marginal directions in *B*. Sir Maurice Powicke, however, based his conclusions about the relationship of *B* and the *Historia Anglorum* partly on the evidence from Matthew's references to documents in these manuscripts. Throughout the latter part of the *Chronica Majora*, both in *B* and in *R* (B.M. Royal MS. 14 C vii), there are numerous references to documents as being in the *Liber Additamentorum*. The earliest of these in the *text* of *B* is on f. 212b,[2] in the course

---

[1] *CM.* III, p. 381.
[2] *CM.* IV, p. 619. The reference is actually to the 'liber literarum' (*sic*).

of the annal for 1247. From here onwards references to the *Liber Additamentorum* in the text are of frequent occurrence, and, as most of them are provided with a *signum* which is usually still to be found in the *Liber Additamentorum* next to the document referred to, there can be little doubt that these references are to the existing leaves of the *Liber Additamentorum*. In one case this is certain, for, under the year 1252,[1] a document is said in *B* to be in the *Liber Additamentorum* 'in cedulis margini insitis'; and it is still to be found there, on a strip of parchment attached to one of the leaves.

Why did Matthew copy out his documents in full into *B* until he reached the annal for 1247, and then suddenly begin to keep them separate as a kind of supplement to his chronicle? The answer to this question seems to be that he grew tired of the work of transcription, and perhaps also found that the texts of the documents in *B* were adding unnecessarily to the length of that manuscript. The diagram facing this page (fig. 5) shows the number of references to the *Liber Additamentorum* in the text of each annal of the *Chronica Majora*, and the number of documents copied out in full, between the annals for 1235 and 1259. Now in the five annals 1242–6 Matthew copied out fifty-nine documents in full into *B*, whereas in the five annals 1248–52, out of a total of thirty-nine documents, only eighteen are copied out in *B*, and the remainder are referred to as being in the *Liber Additamentorum*. This, I think, shows that Matthew thought of creating the *Liber Additamentorum*, probably as a labour-saving device as well as to shorten *B*, while he was actually writing that manuscript. The *Liber Additamentorum*, in fact, seems to have originated as a gradually growing collection of documents which Matthew had omitted from *B*; and not, as Powicke thought, as a collection of documents which gradually dwindled as its contents were copied into *B*.[2] This conclusion is confirmed by the presence, in *B*, before the annal for 1247, of a number of *marginal* references to the *Liber Additamentorum*. Had the *Liber Additamentorum* already been in existence while Matthew was writing the earlier part of *B* (up to the annal for 1247),

---

[1] *CM.* v, p. 312. The reference is in the margin of *B*.

[2] Powicke, 'Compilation of the *Chronica Majora*', *Proc. Brit. Acad.* xxx (1944), p. 153.

he would surely have inserted his references to it in the text. No doubt the documents concerned were at first omitted from *B* because Matthew thought he could dispense with them; but when, later, he conceived the idea of a special supplement of documents, he would naturally include them in it, and go back in *B* writing references to them in the margin in the appropriate places.

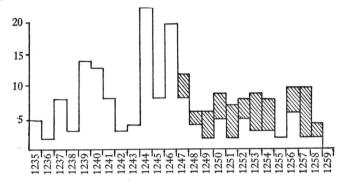

Fig. 5. Diagram to show the number of documents per annal written out in full in *B* (white); and the number of references to documents as being in the *Liber Additamentorum* (shaded).

Seven documents are referred to in the margins of *B* before the textual references to the *Liber Additamentorum* begin during the annal for 1247. In the case of three of these documents, the reference is a straightforward one to the *Liber Additamentorum*, and requires no further discussion, but the references to the other four documents need detailed examination. The first of these documents is said in one place to be 'at the end of the book'; but later on in *B* it is referred to as being 'in the *Liber Additamentorum*'.[1] In the case of the second document, there are again two references in the margins of *B*. In the first the document is said to be 'at the end of the book', but these words have been partially erased; and in the second the document is said to be 'in the book which is a continuation of this one' ('qui huic est continuandus').[2] The third document is said to be 'in the book

---

[1] *CM.* III, pp. 233, note 5, and 620.
[2] *CM.* IV, pp. 400, note 4, and 427.

of letters' and also 'in the *Liber Additamentorum*', but the words
'in the book of letters' are on an erasure, and the words 'in the
Liber Additamentorum' have been added to the reference later.[1]
In the case of the last of these documents the reference is to 'the
end of the book', and has been run through with a pen.[2] The
only possible conclusion from these altered references seems to
be that the documents they refer to were at one time at the end
of *B*, and that they were later removed from that manuscript
and kept in a separate volume called the *Liber Additamentorum*.
We seem to be arriving at a complicated situation. Apparently
Matthew started a supplement of documents while he was
writing the annal for 1247 in *B*, and yet, later, when he wrote
these marginal references into *B*, he seems to have given up the
Liber Additamentorum and to be keeping his documents at the
end of *B*. Later still, it appears that he resuscitated the *Liber
Additamentorum* and had to alter his references to the 'end of
the book' into references to the *Liber Additamentorum*.

The *Liber Additamentorum* still exists, and we cannot do better
at this juncture than to turn to it to see what light it throws on
the meaning of these references, and, consequently, on its own
origins. The first document in our group of four is written out
on an independent bifolium bound up near the end of the *Liber
Additamentorum* with some odd leaves and matter not originally
belonging to it. It has perhaps been misplaced. The other three
documents now occupy ff. 87–88 b of the *Liber Additamentorum*,
where they follow each other in the order they are referred to
in *B*, near the beginning of a homogeneous group of documents
extending over two separate quires of the *Liber Additamentorum*
(12 and part of what is now 13), from f. 85 to 100 b.[3] The
documents extend continuously over these leaves, except for
a break between ff. 97 and 98, where a new quire now begins,
and where the continuity of the text is also interrupted. But
a note on f. 94 a, in which Matthew directs the reader to a
document on f. 99 with the words 'verte v folia sequentia',
shows that all the documents now on ff. 85–100 b of the *Liber
Additamentorum* are probably in the same order in which they
were originally written by Matthew. This whole group of docu-

---

[1] *CM.* iv, p. 518, and notes 3 and 4.　　[2] *CM.* iv, p. 586, note 2.
[3] For this group of documents, see below, pp. 83–4.

68

ments might therefore easily have been removed from the end of *B* and inserted in the *Liber Additamentorum*. It comprises every document referred to in *B* up to (and including) the annal for 1250 as being in the *Liber Additamentorum*, with the exception of the first document in our group with altered references which, as we saw, is now at the end of the *Liber Additamentorum* and evidently misplaced; one document which is no longer to be found in the *Liber Additamentorum*; and three referred to in the margins of *B*, the references to which were evidently inserted after 1250. The documents in this group are written into the *Liber Additamentorum* in roughly chronological order and extend in date from 1242 to 1250; there is not a single document in the group of later date than 1250. Furthermore, these documents were evidently written out either in or before 1250, as the following statement in Matthew's hand on f. 99 shows.[1]

It can therefore be gathered from this and other letters that, by the grace of God, the most christian King of the French, Louis...in the year of our Lord 1250 has become (*factus est*) lord of Damietta, Babylon, Cairo, Alexandria and the transmarine shores. Those who persevered in this most glorious battle and in the hardship of the journey are universally considered fortunate; and the prayers for him which were offered up to the Lord are believed to have had a glorious outcome.

This passage must have been written before the news of the disastrous failure of Louis's expedition had reached Matthew Paris, and soon after the arrival of the letters which announced his success, that is in 1249–50;[2] and, since it forms part of the text of f. 99 of the *Liber Additamentorum*, near the end of our group of documents, we can be sure that they were written out in or before 1250. This conclusion points to the probability that the present ff. 85–100 of the *Liber Additamentorum* were originally at the end of *B*, and it is not surprising, therefore, to find on the lower margin of the verso of f. 100 an erased quire number written in exactly the same style as those now in *B*, with the number in red, surrounded with blue decoration, which might well have been xx. Now if these documents had been added to *B* when that manuscript was completed up to the end

---

[1] *CM.* vi, p. 169.   [2] See *CM.* v, pp. 118 and 138; and 147.

of the annal for 1250, they probably would have been given the quire number xx, since, as we have seen, the annal for 1250 ends on the penultimate leaf of quire xix. It seems, therefore, that when Matthew had completed *AB* up to this point, and divided it into two, he attached this quire of documents to the end of *B*; and presumably it remained there until he decided to continue the text of his *Chronica Majora* beyond the annal for 1250.

We are now in a position to attempt to describe the writing of *B* and the early history of the *Liber Additamentorum*. While he was writing the annal for 1247 in *B*, Matthew evidently decided to keep a separate appendix of documents. In his first reference to this appendix, he called it the *liber literarum*;[1] but after this it is invariably called the *Liber Additamentorum*. When he had finished *AB* up to 1250, the point where he intended to bring his *Chronica Majora* to a close, Matthew added his ornamental rubrication at the top of the pages, from 1066 up to the end (1250). Soon after this, however, he decided that the single volume *AB* was too bulky. He therefore separated it into two; renumbered the quires in *B*; and added his appendix of documents after the last quire of *B*. Among these documents were several dating from before 1247, which he had not referred to in the text of *B*; and it must have been at this time that Matthew went back and added references to them in the margins of *B* before the annal for 1247.[2] Since he had just added them to the end of *B*, it is only natural that, instead of referring to them as being in the *Liber Additamentorum* in the same way as the references to documents in the text of *B* from 1247 onwards, he referred to them as being 'at the end of the book'. It is natural, too, that he should not trouble to alter the textual references to the *Liber Additamentorum*, since, though the documents were now at the end of *B*, he probably still thought of them as constituting a *Liber Additamentorum*. When he decided to take up his pen and continue *B* after 1250, Matthew had to remove the documents from it; and it was this removal which, no doubt, caused him to alter the marginal references to

---

[1] *Sic*; *CM.* iv, p. 619.

[2] See above, pp. 66–7. While the textual references to the *Liber Additamentorum*, 1247–50, are copied into *C*, those in the margin before 1247 are not, no doubt because they were inserted after the transcription of *C* in *c.* 1250.

documents at the end of the book into references to the *Liber Additamentorum*, and in two cases to add new references to this effect.[1] To this removal, too, was due the final appearance of the *Liber Additamentorum* as a separate, independent volume. When he wrote the annal for 1251 into *B*, and had finally removed his appendix of documents from it, Matthew could well refer to the *Liber Additamentorum*, as he does during this annal, with the words: 'sed ea in libro Additamentorum, ut hoc volumen deoneretur, annotantur.'[2]

We must now take leave of *B*, and turn our attention again to the *Historia Anglorum*, which contains a number of references to documents both 'in libro Additamentorum' and 'in cronicis majoribus S. Albani', though without the signs which are used so extensively in *B*. Sir Maurice Powicke supposed that none of the references in the *Historia Anglorum* before the annal for 1249 referred to the actual manuscript *B*. He was led to this conclusion by the fact that, in the course of the annal for 1249 in the *Historia Anglorum*, a document is said to be in the *Chronica Majora* at a certain sign; and the sign and the document are still to be found there, while none of the earlier references in the *Historia Anglorum* to documents in the *Chronica Majora* is provided with signs.[3] Powicke also noticed that a number of documents said in the *Historia Anglorum* to be in the *Liber Additamentorum* are no longer to be found there, but are in the text of *B*; and he concluded from this that the documents were in the *Liber Additamentorum* when the *Historia Anglorum* was written, but were removed thence later when Matthew copied them into *B*. But, as we have seen, Powicke was wrong in supposing that most of the *Historia Anglorum* was written before *B*, and we must find some other explanation of these apparently erroneous references. Owing to the fact that very many of the references in the *Historia Anglorum* to documents elsewhere have been erased and altered by Matthew, an analysis of them is bound to be incomplete. Wherever possible, however, Madden made out the original reference, as well as the subsequent one which Matthew frequently added on a piece of vellum

---

[1] See above, pp. 67–8.   [2] *CM.* v, p. 229.
[3] For this and what follows, see Powicke, 'Compilation of the *Chronica Majora*', *Proc. Brit. Acad.* xxx (1944), pp. 153–5.

stuck down over its predecessor. Out of a probable total of eighty explicit references to other manuscripts in the text of the *Historia Anglorum*, sixty-six have been altered into vague general references of the type 'in libris plurimorum', 'in libris multorum', 'in libris religiosorum', 'in multis locis Angliae', 'in aliquibus Aquilonarium rotulis', 'in originali', 'in rotulis scaccarii', 'in rotulis vicecomitum', 'in autentico papae', etc. Of these altered references, ten were originally to the *Chronica Majora*: namely, 'in majoribus cronicis S. Albani', 'in historia magna huius opusculi', 'in magnis cronicis S. Albani', etc.; and twenty-seven to the *Liber Additamentorum*, namely, 'in libro additamentorum', 'in libro suplementorum vel additamentorum', etc.[1]

It is impossible to explain this wholesale alteration of specific references to the *Chronica Majora* and the *Liber Additamentorum* on the grounds that the references were correct when first made, but became incorrect when the documents referred to were transferred by Matthew from the *Liber Additamentorum* into *B*, because (quite apart from the fact that *B* was written before the *Historia Anglorum*) among those so altered were at least ten correct references to documents as being in the *Chronica Majora*, and at least six correct references to documents in the *Liber Additamentorum* which are still there. This alteration of references to documents in the *Historia Anglorum* extends only to the annal for 1251. Before it Matthew referred the reader to the *Liber Additamentorum* or the *Chronica Majora* for a document whenever he had an opportunity; after this annal many documents are mentioned in the *Historia Anglorum* but without any reference to where they can be found, and some are referred to in terms as vague as those used in the second set of references mentioned above. Matthew evidently changed his method of referring to documents before he had finished writing the *Historia Anglorum*,

---

[1] According to Powicke ('Compilation of the *Chronica Majora*', *Proc. Brit. Acad.* xxx (1944), p. 153), Matthew referred to the *Liber Additamentorum* as 'the book of many things, the book of very many things (*liber plurimorum*) and so on'. But in fact the *Liber Additamentorum* is always referred to as the *liber additamentorum*, the *liber suplementorum*, or the *liber literarum*. Perhaps Powicke mistook the phrases 'in libris plurimorum' and 'in libris multorum' for references to the *Liber Additamentorum*, though they clearly mean 'in most people's books' and 'in the books of many people'.

and probably while he was writing the annal for 1251. At this point he for some reason decided to give up referring explicitly to documents as being in the *Chronica Majora* or the *Liber Additamentorum*, and took the trouble to go back through his text erasing the explicit references wherever he found them. (He overlooked fourteen.) In this way he brought the *Historia Anglorum* into line with the *Flores Historiarum*, in Matthew's section of which there are some vague references to documents as being elsewhere ('apud S. Albanum', 'in regio thesauro', etc.), but no explicit ones. It is worth noting, too, that just the same kind of vague reference occurs in the *Abbreviatio Chronicorum*. The alteration of these references in the *Historia Anglorum*, then, is of no significance in our discussion of the relationship of that work to *B* and the *Liber Additamentorum*; it was carried out with the immediate object of expunging from the *Historia Anglorum* all the explicit references to Matthew's other manuscripts. What the ultimate object was it is difficult to say, but it may not be mere coincidence that Matthew's expurgation of the *Historia Anglorum*, that is to say his erasure of many offensive passages and their replacement with milder or harmless ones, likewise ends in the course of the annal for 1251.[1] If, as is possible, these two series of alterations were made at the same time, then it seems likely that they were made for the same reason, and that Matthew intended to make the manuscript fit for someone outside St Albans,[2] for whom references to documents in his other manuscripts would be useless.

We may now proceed with our discussion of the original set of references to documents in the *Historia Anglorum*. The text of fifty of these can be ascertained with a reasonable degree of certainty, thirty-eight of which referred to the *Liber Additamentorum*, and twelve to the *Chronica Majora*. Of the thirty-eight referring to the *Liber Additamentorum* (or *liber suplementorum*), about thirty refer to documents which are in fact in *B*, and which were undoubtedly in *B* when the *Historia Anglorum* was copied from it. What is the explanation of this curious fact? Either, it seems, Matthew intended, when he wrote the *Historia Anglorum*, to collect all these documents into the *Liber Addita-*

---

[1] See below, pp. 121–4.
[2] Madden (*HA*. III, p. xxxii) suggested the king.

mentorum at some later date, or the references to the *Liber Additamentorum* do not refer to the separate *Liber Additamentorum* as we know it now, but to the actual manuscript *B*, of which, as we have seen, the *Liber Additamentorum* formed part at the time when the *Historia Anglorum* was copied from it. Now the first of these explanations seems most unlikely, for it implies that Matthew planned to make the *Liber Additamentorum* an independent work: a great collection of all his documentary material. Yet all the evidence points to its continued use as an appendix of documents only, and certainly, if such an intention ever existed, it can only have been a momentary one, for Matthew continued using the *Liber Additamentorum* as an appendix to his main chronicle until shortly before his death, and there is no sign at all that he ever attempted to turn it into a grand collection of all his documents. On the other hand, the second possible explanation, that, at the time when he was writing the *Historia Anglorum*, Matthew thought of *B*, since the documents were then at the end of it, as his *Liber Additamentorum*, although *prima facie* equally fantastic, is supported by some quite substantial evidence. In the early part of the *Historia Anglorum*, up to the annal for 1188, all the references are to documents as being 'in cronicis S. Albani', 'in magnis cronicis', etc., and there is not one to the *Liber Additamentorum*.[1] The documents thus referred to are all in *A*, the manuscript from which Matthew was copying, and which at this time was probably still joined to *B*; and we may assume from these references that he thought of the undivided *AB* as 'the great St Albans chronicle'. If we look at the *Historia Anglorum* from 1189 onwards, we find that all the recoverable references to documents in the *text*, between the annals for 1189 and 1246 inclusive, are to the *Liber Additamentorum*: there is not a single one to the *magna cronica*. Yet all the documents thus referred to are in *B*—the very manuscript from which Matthew was copying when he wrote these references in the *Historia Anglorum*. It can hardly be a coincidence that, in the early part of the *Historia* (up to 1188), the references are to the 'Chronica Majora'; and in the part taken from *B*, to the 'Liber Additamentorum', while the documents referred to are all in *A* and *B* respectively, and it seems that we

---

[1] One is possibly to the *liber epistolarum*; see *HA.* I, p. 345, note 6.

74

must conclude that Matthew split *AB* into two while he was writing the *Historia Anglorum*, and that after this operation, *B*, since it contained his own continuation (1235–50) of the 'St Albans chronicle', as well as his appendix of additional documents, to which he had already often referred as the *Liber Additamentorum*, was regarded as constituting the additional book itself.

We have seen that, when Matthew decided to continue the text of *B* after 1250, he removed his additional documents from it, and made them into a separate *Liber Additamentorum*. Now this change is reflected in a change in the character of the references to documents in the *Historia Anglorum*. Let us imagine, for a moment, the actual process of writing the *Historia*. Matthew has before him the text of *B*, to which he refers the reader from time to time as he abridges the *Historia Anglorum* from it, for documents which he does not trouble to copy out in full. Let us suppose, as we have given some grounds for supposing, that he is in the habit of referring to *B* as the 'Liber Additamentorum'. Now when he arrives at the annal for 1247, he comes across, first of all, a marginal reference in *B* to a document as being in the *Liber Additamentorum*,[1] and, soon afterwards, he meets with the earliest references in the text of *B* to the *Liber Additamentorum*. He copied these references more or less word for word into the *Historia Anglorum*.[2] They could be left unaltered, as references to the *Liber Additamentorum*, since the documents to which they referred were still in the end of *B*; and in the course of the annal for 1248 in the *Historia Anglorum* Matthew still refers to documents in *B* as being in the *Liber Additamentorum*. Soon after this, however, he must have decided to continue the text of his *Chronica Majora* in *B*, and he was forced to remove the additional documents from it, and to reconstitute them finally as a separate *Liber Additamentorum*. This entailed a radical change in his terminology, for he had to give up calling *B* the *Liber Additamentorum*. It is no doubt for this reason that, in the course of the annal for 1249 in the *Historia Anglorum*, we find a reference in the text (the first since before the annal for 1188 when *A* was the exemplar) 'majoribus cronicis S. Albani'; and a sign is drawn in the

---

[1] *CM.* IV, p. 609.   [2] III, pp. 22, note 7; and 27, note 3.

margin which is also found in the margin of *B* next to the document concerned.[1] But Matthew evidently had difficulty in remembering his new distinction between *B* and the *Liber Additamentorum*, for on two occasions in this same annal in the *Historia Anglorum* he mistakenly reverts to the old terminology, and calls *B* the *Liber Additamentorum*.[2] In the second of these references his memory slipped badly, for it is to the very same document which he had already correctly said, earlier in this annal,[3] to be 'in cronicis majoribus', which we know, from the sign, to have meant the actual manuscript *B*. The remaining references in the *Historia Anglorum* are 'correct'; that is, those to the *Liber Additamentorum* refer to documents in the existing *Liber* (there are four or five in all), and the only reference to the *Chronica Majora* is to a document in *B*. To this last we ought to add two marginal references, no doubt inserted into the *Historia* after Matthew's change of terminology, in both of which a document in *B* is said to be in the *Chronica Majora*.[4]

Although this supposed change of terminology by Matthew appears perhaps rather far-fetched, it does seem to be the only hypothesis which fits all the evidence. It is borne out, too, by the fact that, in the case of one of the references to a document as being in the *Liber Additamentorum* when it was actually in *B*, Matthew has later added the words 'vel in magnis cronicis'; and in the case of another, he afterwards inserted the words 'et cronicorum S. Albani' under the words 'libro Additamentorum' of the original reference: 'in the book of Additamenta and St Albans chronicles'.[5]

The rather detailed discussions of this chapter may now be briefly summarized. Matthew first wrote out the *Chronica Majora* in *AB*, finishing its text at the end of the annal for 1250, early in 1251. During the writing of the last four annals, he had omitted a number of documents from the text, and referred to them as being in the *Liber Additamentorum*. When *AB* had been completed to the year 1250, he split it into two, altered the quire numbers in *B*, and added the documents, to which he had been

---

[1] *HA.* III, p. 45, note 8.   [2] III, pp. 47, note 5, and 53.
[3] *HA.* III, p. 45.   [4] II, pp. 440 and 494, note 4.
[5] *HA.* II, p. 500, note 5; and III, p. 16, note 1.

referring as the *Liber Additamentorum*, at the end of *B*. It must have been at about this time that *C* was copied, by a scribe, from *B*. Work on the *Historia Anglorum* had been started in 1250, and probably proceeded slowly, as it was written by Matthew himself. Meanwhile some further references to documents had been added to the margins of *B* before the annal for 1247, and, since the *Liber Additamentorum* now formed part of *B*, these references were at first to 'the end of the book'; but they were altered to references to the *Liber Additamentorum* after Matthew had removed his documents from the end of *B*, to make room for his continuation of the text of the *Chronica Majora* (1251 onwards) in that manuscript. When this happened we do not exactly know, but it was probably in the years 1252–3, and not before the writing of the *Historia Anglorum* had reached the annal for 1249, for, up to then, in the *Historia*, *B* is referred to as the *Liber Additamentorum*. The most important conclusion that emerges is that the writing of the *Chronica Majora* in *B* and *R*, from about the annal for 1245 to the end, was throughout only a year or two behind events. Far from being a late copy, made at the end of Matthew's life, *B* is, at any rate from the annal for 1245 onwards, the author's original, autograph account of contemporary events.

CHAPTER V

THE 'LIBER ADDITAMENTORUM'

IN the course of the preceding chapter much reference has been made to Matthew's *Liber Additamentorum*, and we have seen that it began its life as a small group of documents at the end of *B*. The existing *Liber Additamentorum* contains many of the documents referred to by Matthew in his historical manuscripts, as well as others which he does not mention elsewhere. It contains, too, a collection of St Albans charters and papal privileges; Matthew's *Gesta Abbatum* and *Vitae Offarum*; and much miscellaneous material. Owing to the fact that many of the leaves are no longer in their original quires, it presents a difficult problem for the palaeographer; but its structure is important because of the evidence it affords of the way in which this unique collection of historical material was gathered together, and, consequently, I have tried to set it out in diagrammatic form (see fig. 6).

If we are to reconstruct this manuscript in anything like its original form, the first stage must be to rearrange the contents according to the late medieval foliation which still in part survives. We know that this earlier foliation goes back to the fourteenth or early fifteenth century, because there are several references in British Museum Cotton MS. Tiberius E vi (the St Albans *Liber Memorandorum*) to a *Liber de Gestis Abbatum*, which give the correct folio number for the earlier foliation of our *Liber Additamentorum*; and these references occur on ff. 260–63 of the *Liber Memorandorum*, a section of the manuscript written *c*. 1400. We can omit, from our reconstruction, the group of folios 161–6 inclusive, since these were probably added to the manuscript in modern times. This quire certainly once belonged to some other book, for on f. 161 we have the signature of Sir Robert Cotton, which suggests that in his time this leaf prefaced some other manuscript in his possession; and in any case these leaves differ from those in the rest of the book in size and lay-out, and are foliated 2–6 in an early hand. Here, then,

78

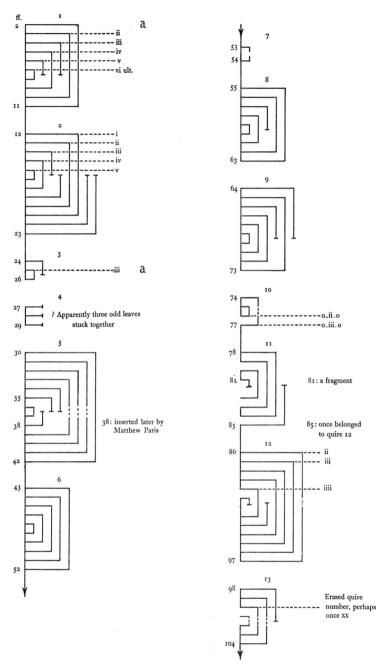

Fig. 6. Diagram to show the structure of the *Liber Additamentorum*. Quires 1–13.

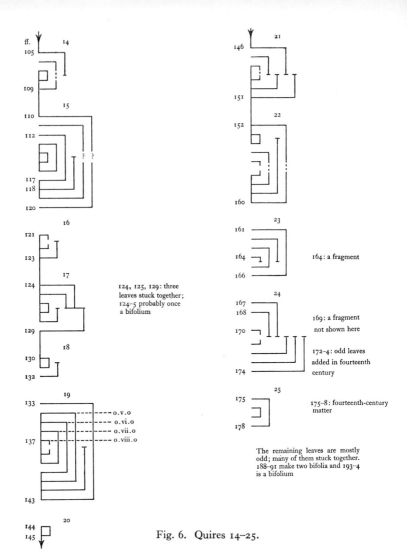

The remaining leaves are mostly odd; many of them stuck together. 188–91 make two bifolia and 193–4 is a bifolium

Fig. 6. Quires 14–25.

Fig. 6. The foliation used in this diagram is that of Luard (*CM.* vi). The original arrangement of the quires has been much disturbed by subsequent rebinding, and in the diagram I have followed the present division into quires, though for the sake of clarity I have made more divisions than are really necessary: for instance, quires 16, 17, and 18 in the diagram might well be regarded as forming a single gathering. Up to f. 160, leaves over which the text runs continuously are linked by a vertical line running down the left of each quire diagram. In cases where two leaves have been stuck together to make a bifolium, the line representing the sheet of parchment in the manuscript is broken by dots. In many cases leaves stuck together in this way probably originally formed bifolia, which later came apart and then had to be repaired. Quire 23 did not originally belong to this manuscript (see above, p. 78).

is a rough list of the contents of the *Liber Additamentorum* as it probably was in the fourteenth century, within a hundred years of Matthew's death. Luard's foliation, used in his edition of the *Liber Additamentorum* in volume VI of the *Chronica Majora*, is placed in brackets after the fourteenth-century foliation.[1]

1–25 (2–26)	*Vitae Offarum*, with a short tract *Cum Danorum rabies*.
27–39 (148–60)	St Albans charters and papal privileges.
40–73 (30–63)	Part I of the *Gesta Abbatum*, with some documents written on spare leaves at the end of the last quire.
74–83 (64–73)	Part II of the *Gesta Abbatum*, with documents of 1255–7.
84–115 (74–106)	Documents of 1242–59.
116–19 (171–4)	Fourteenth-century matter.
120–33 (107–20)	Documents of 1252–4.
134–41 (121–8)	Miscellaneous documents, many of 1254.
142–50 (175–83)	Mostly fourteenth-century matter, with some odd leaves.
151–3 (27–9)	Tracts on St Alban etc.
154–74 (129–47)	Miscellaneous, including Matthew's tract on the St Albans gems etc.
176–7 (167–8)	The charges against Hubert de Burgh (1239).
178 on (184 on)	Miscellaneous.

The next stage in our reconstruction of the original *Liber Additamentorum* is to omit all the fourteenth-century matter, as well as the odd leaves which have only fragmentary material, and which contribute nothing towards our knowledge of the structure and history of the manuscript. We may omit, too, the tracts on St Alban (ff. 27–9 of Luard's foliation), and divide the documentary material into more homogeneous groups. The *Liber Additamentorum* must have been arranged roughly as follows when Matthew died.

Luard's foliation	
2–26	*Vitae Offarum* and *Cum Danorum rabies*.
148–60	St Albans charters and papal privileges.
30–63	Part I of the *Gesta Abbatum*, with attached documents.

---

[1] Luard (ed.), *CM.* VI, pp. 491–523, published a full description of this manuscript, and, in all the references to it in this book, his foliation, given there, is used.

Luard's
foliation

64–73 Part II of the *Gesta Abbatum*, written in 1255, followed
by documents in rough chronological order of 1255–7.

74–84 Documents of 1256–9.

85–100 Documents of 1242–50, written out in or before 1250.
Ff. 167–8 perhaps once preceded f. 85.

101–5 Miscellaneous documents of 1250 and 1256–7.

107–20 Documents, mostly of 1252–4. A study of the references
in the *Chronica Majora* shows that these documents
were thus arranged when the text of the annal for
1254 was written into *R*.

121–8 Miscellaneous documents, including a number of 1254.

129–36 Miscellaneous material of 1257, together with some later
material added after Matthew's death.

144–6 Matthew's tract on the gems etc. Once followed f. 63;
moved when Part II of the *Gesta Abbatum* was inserted
into its present position.

167–8 The charges against Hubert de Burgh.

We are now in a position to try to describe the way in which
the documentary material in the *Liber Additamentorum* was put
together. The *Gesta Abbatum* was written in two parts, the first
of which extends from the beginning to the death of Abbot
William in 1235. After this there follow some documents,
written on the spare leaves remaining at the end of quire 8.
The second part of the *Gesta Abbatum* begins on the first leaf of
the next quire (f. 64). It consists of a short description of the
abbacy of John of Hertford (1235–63), and the continuous text
breaks down on f. 68b, at a point where Matthew says:[1]

Moreover this Abbot John...has never, I say, since the time of his
creation up to the twentieth year of his rule (in which year this page
was written by Brother Matthew Paris, who does not presume to lay
down the law (*diffinire*) concerning the future), alienated the possessions of his church.

The text of part two of the *Gesta Abbatum* continues beyond
this point in the form of short paragraphs recording isolated
events, but it soon gives way to documents; at first of domestic
interest only, but, from f. 71 onwards, of general interest as well.
These continue until f. 84, but in Matthew's hand only to f. 82.

---

[1] Wats, p. 145.

The dates of the documents on these leaves, which follow straight on from the St Albans documents of various dates with which the second part of the *Gesta Abbatum* closes, are significant. They begin with the year 1255, and continue in rough chronological order to f. 82, where the last of this group in Matthew's hand is the latest document written by him into the *Liber Additamentorum*, dated March 1259. The last two leaves of the quire (f. 85 belongs to the next quire) have been used for some documents of 1258 not written by Matthew. Now these documents, dating from 1255 to 1259, form a homogeneous group collected and written into the *Liber Additamentorum* by Matthew between 1255 and his death; for they carry straight on from the concluding section of the second part of the *Gesta Abbatum*, which we know, from Matthew's statement translated above, was written in 1255. The only interloper in this series of documents is one of 1252 on f. 70b; but an examination of the manuscript shows that this was inserted after the main series was written, and not by Matthew Paris. To this group of documents we must add those on ff. 129–39. These consist of a number in Matthew's hand, of 1257, and some others written into the book by his assistant, shortly after his death. As can be seen from fig. 6, Matthew's numbering of ff. 134–7 follows on from that of ff. 76–7 (though the leaf numbered o. iiii. o is not now to be found); and indeed it appears that the whole quire, ff. 129–43 (some blank leaves, filled up in the fourteenth century, originally followed the documents on ff. 129–39), was once connected with ff. 74–84. The group of documents, then, which Matthew wrote into the *Liber Additamentorum* between 1255 and his death, extends over ff. 71–82 and 129–36; while the documents added to this group shortly after his death extend over ff. 83–4 and 136–9. Although, owing to subsequent rearrangement of the manuscript, it is impossible to ascertain exactly how ff. 129–39 were connected with ff. 74–84, it is very probable that all the documents in this group were originally in rough chronological order.

A second easily identifiable group of documents, extending over ff. 85–100, follows the one just described. The handwriting of this group looks earlier than that of most of the rest of the book; it is tidier and more controlled. The earliest document in this group dates from 1242, the latest from 1250, and most of the documents in it are of 1247–50. The arrangement is again roughly chronological. On the verso of the last leaf of the group (f. 100) is the erased quire number which has already been mentioned[1] as being apparently identical with those in *B*, and, as we have seen, this group of documents contains almost all those referred to in *B* up to the annal for 1250 as being in the *Liber Additamentorum*. It is, in fact, the group of documents added by Matthew to the end of *B*, which was later removed to form the documentary nucleus of the *Liber Additamentorum*.

So far we have identified the first group of documents which went to make up the *Liber Additamentorum*, and the last. The documents of the intermediate years, 1250–4, are rather more difficult to arrange into well-ordered groups. One group seems to extend over ff. 101–5, but the documents are not in any particular order, for the first few date from 1250, with one of 1251, while there follow documents of various dates (1247–54) which are repeated elsewhere in the book, and then a series of documents of the years 1255–6, with one at the end dating from 1257 which appears to have been added some time later. Following these, however, is a better defined group extending over ff. 107–20, mostly of 1252–4. Apart from one or two documents of earlier date, the chronological order of this group is only seriously disturbed by a document of 1255, but this has almost certainly been inserted later, and was not written by Matthew himself. Lastly, there is another group of documents on ff. 121–8, of rather miscellaneous date, though about half of them belong to 1254.

The identification of these groups of documents shows that the *Liber Additamentorum* was not compiled in an entirely haphazard fashion, but that Matthew collected his documents more or less in chronological order, probably as he obtained them; and, apart from the group of documents written in or before 1250,[2] which was originally at the end of *B*, there is every indication that the documentary material in the *Liber Additamentorum* dates from after 1250. On the verso of f. 63, in the lower margin, is a pencil note in Matthew's hand which is now partly illegible; but it is still possible to make out the words: '. . . abbatis Johannis'. This could be taken to imply that the second part of

---

[1] See above, p. 69.　　　　[2] See pp. 68–70 above.

the *Gesta Abbatum*, which now begins on the next page, was not originally in this position. Indeed we know from other evidence that at one time the tract on the St Albans gems, etc., followed f. 63; for on f. 62a Matthew says that some verses on Abbot William are written out three leaves further on, but they are now to be found on f. 145, where the tract on the gems begins. It is therefore very probable that the second part of the *Gesta Abbatum*, which Matthew was writing in 1255, together with the documents which he added to it dating from 1255 to 1259, had its original place in the book after the last group of documents mentioned above (ff. 121–8), which includes a number of 1254, and immediately before the other documents of 1257–9 on ff. 129–39. It seems likely that the '1254' group originally followed, as it still does, the group of documents dating from 1252–4. The arrangement of the bulk of the documentary material, before Matthew moved the second part of the *Gesta Abbatum* and the documents attached to it, would thus have been as follows:

ff. 85–100	Documents of 1242–50, originally at the end of *B*.
ff. 107–20	Documents of 1252–4.
ff. 121–8	Miscellaneous documents, about half of 1254.
ff. 64–84 and 129–39	Documents of 1255–9, preceded by Part II of the *Gesta Abbatum*.

The *Liber Additamentorum*, then, was evidently a reasonably well-ordered collection of documents and extracts dating from *c.* 1244–59, which Matthew put together in the first place at the end of *B*, and which, after *c.* 1251–3, constituted a separate book which was added to steadily until his death; the documents being copied into it more or less in the order in which he obtained them.

Besides documentary material, the *Liber Additamentorum* contains two historical works of domestic importance, the *Gesta Abbatum* and the *Vitae Offarum*. Although I shall postpone a general discussion of these until a later chapter, something ought to be said here about their date and relationship to Matthew's other manuscripts. In view of the fact that the *Gesta Abbatum* is nowhere mentioned in the *Chronica Majora*, yet is referred to on a number of occasions in the *Historia Anglorum*, it would seem probable that, when *AB* was written, Matthew had not yet begun the *Gesta Abbatum*. This is confirmed when the text of the *Gesta Abbatum* is compared with that of *AB*, for we find a number of cases where it seems to be taken from *AB*, and occasionally one of Matthew's additions to Roger Wendover in *AB* has found its way into the text of the *Gesta Abbatum*. In the two following examples I have italicized Matthew's additions in *AB*.[1]

(1) *Chronica Majora*; part of the annal for 1214:[2] 'Eodem tempore Johannes abbas ecclesiae sancti Albani, in die beati Kenelmi regis et martyris, decimo nono anno praelationis suae, *plenus dierum, sanctitate et religione insignis*, scientia ad plenum eruditus....'

The *Gesta Abbatum*:[3] 'Transit igitur ab hoc mundo praenominatus abbas Johannes, de exilio videlicet ad patriam, de naufragio ad portum, anno domini MCCXIIII die beati Kenelmi regis et martyris...anno vero praelationis suae XIX, sanctitate et religione insignis, dierum plenus....'

(2) *Chronica Majora*; part of the annal for 1217:[4] 'Quibus ita gestis dictus Falcasius cum suis praedonibus excommunicatis et spoliis nimis dampnosis, *et captivis tractis* turpiterque vinctis....'

The *Gesta Abbatum*:[5] 'Et sic ipse Falco et sui complices cum captivorum numerositate quam secum trahebant, diversis praediis onerati....'

These parallels show that the first part of the *Gesta Abbatum* was not written until after the early part of *AB*. On the other hand, it was certainly concluded by 1250, for Matthew refers to the *Gesta* on a number of occasions in the *Historia Anglorum*,[6] which he began in 1250; and a comparison of the two shows that the first part of the *Gesta Abbatum* was sometimes used in the writing of the *Historia Anglorum*. The second part of the *Gesta Abbatum* was, as we shall see, written in 1255. Again, there are striking parallels with *AB*, especially in the account of the election of Abbot John in 1235,[7] which make it clear that the second part of the *Gesta* was also based in part on Matthew's *Chronica Majora* in *AB*.

---

[1] These were made while he was writing the text; see pp. 30–1 above.
[2] II, p. 576.   [3] Wats, p. 112.   [4] III, p. 12.   [5] Wats, p. 119.
[6] *HA*. I, pp. 23, 228, 276, 291; II, p. 55.
[7] *CM*. III, pp. 307–8; Wats, pp. 135–8.

In the *Liber Additamentorum*, the text of the first part of the *Gesta Abbatum* extends from ff. 30 to 62 a, and it appears to have been written more or less *currente calamo*, apart from one leaf probably inserted later (f. 38), and a number of marginal additions and corrections. On f. 62 the text breaks down into a number of isolated passages and transcripts of documents, which continue on to the next leaf. The character of the handwriting bears out our conclusion about the date of this part of the *Gesta*, for it appears to have been written before most of the rest of the *Liber Additamentorum*, that is, before 1250. The documents on ff. 62–63 b date from 1219 to 1251, and have been written on the spare leaves which remained at the end of the quire. Powicke says that the *Gesta Abbatum* was finished in 1255,[1] but this statement needs some qualification, for, judging from the presence of the documents just mentioned, some of which have no connexion with St Albans, the first part of the *Gesta* seems originally to have been planned and written as a work complete in itself, ending at the end of the abbacy of William of Trumpington (1235); and, as we have seen, it was finished before 1250. It would not even be quite accurate to say that the second part of the *Gesta Abbatum* was finished in 1255, for the text, in the *Liber Additamentorum*, continues beyond Matthew's statement, already quoted, to the effect that he was writing in 1255. Judging from its brevity, however, and from the way in which it precedes documents of the years 1255 on, and probably once followed those of 1254, the whole of the second part of the *Gesta* would seem to have been written in the year 1255.

In the course of the *Gesta Abbatum* Matthew on several occasions refers the reader to material elsewhere in the *Liber Additamentorum*, or in one of his other manuscripts. In his account of Warin's abbacy, for instance, he says that the papal bull *Religiosam vitam eligentibus* 'is written out above, in the present volume';[2] and it is in fact still to be found in the *Liber Additamentorum* among the other papal documents, which, as can be seen from our reconstruction of the original arrangement of the book,[3] were once between the *Vitae Offarum* and the *Gesta Abbatum*. There is a curious reference in the text of the

---

[1] Powicke, 'Compilation of the *Chronica Majora*', *Proc. Brit. Acad.* XXX (1944), p. 155.   [2] Wats, p. 95.   [3] Above, pp. 81–2.

Gesta on f. 49 b, where the description of the invention of St Amphibalus is said by Matthew to be in a chronicle 'in this book'.[1] Powicke supposed that the chronicle in question was the *Historia Anglorum*,[2] but this is impossible, since this reference occurs in the first part of the *Gesta*, which was written before the *Historia Anglorum*. It is probable, in fact, that the chronicle 'in this book' was either a copy of Roger Wendover's *Flores Historiarum*, or *AB* itself; and, as it seems unlikely that Matthew would have kept his *Gesta* together with a manuscript of Roger Wendover's chronicle, we may conclude that the reference is probably to *AB*. In the years leading up to 1250, evidently, Matthew kept his general and domestic histories together, or at least intended to do so, for this reference might represent an intention rather than a fact.

The most puzzling reference in the *Gesta Abbatum* to another manuscript of Matthew's occurs in the text of the second part of the *Gesta*. In his account of the election of Abbot John of Hertford, Matthew refers us to some letters concerning it as being 'in hoc volumine ubi scilicet pingitur avicula'. The letters thus referred to are not now to be found in the *Liber Additamentorum*, but they have been copied out by Matthew into the text of *B*, though there is no sign there of an *avicula*.[3] Powicke thought that when this reference was written, *B* had not yet been begun, and the documents referred to were in the *Liber Additamentorum*, but were removed some time later when they were copied into *B*.[4] But we have seen that the second part of the *Gesta* was probably written in 1255, when the text of *B* up to 1250 had long been finished; and, in any case, this part of the *Gesta* can be shown to be based in part on the text of *AB*.[5] I can only suggest that the documents referred to were in the *Liber Additamentorum* when Matthew made this reference to them, together with the sign of the 'little bird', but that they have since been lost; like the copy of the agreement between St Albans and Westminster which we know was in the *Liber Additamentorum* until after Matthew's death, though there is no sign of

[1] Wats, p. 93.
[2] Powicke, 'Compilation of the *Chronica Majora*', *loc. cit.* p. 156.
[3] Wats, p. 139, and *CM*. III, pp. 313–18.
[4] Powicke, 'Compilation of the *Chronica Majora*', *loc. cit.* pp. 153–6.
[5] See p. 86 above.

it there now.[1] There is another rather puzzling reference in the text of the first part of the *Gesta Abbatum*, in which Matthew says that the story of the recovery by Egwin of the bones of St Alban, which had been stolen by the Danes and removed by them to Denmark, is told above in the course of the history of Abbot Wlnoth.[2] If we turn back to f. 30b,[3] we find no mention of this story in the text, but Matthew has added a few lines in the margin, directing the reader to the tract *Cum Danorum rabies*, where it is set out in full on ff. 25b–26b. It is curious that the reference to this should be in the text, while the story itself was obviously added later, but an examination of the manuscript shows that the leaf on which this reference occurs (f. 38) has been inserted later by Matthew into the text of the *Gesta*. Two other references in the *Gesta Abbatum* ought to be mentioned, though I have not discovered to what they in fact refer. They are:

(1) Concerning the knights of the Swan, 'sed haec suo loco plenius conscribentur'.[4]

(2) Concerning the Cross of Josaphath, 'quae quadam prolixa narratione continetur in fine huius libri'.[5]

The only evidence for the date of the *Vitae Offarum* is Matthew's own statement near the end of its text. He says:[6]

…in quantum licet alicui abbati habere pontificalem dignitatem, prout tam nova quam vetera instrumenta inde obtenta manifeste protestantur, quae in hoc libro, videlicet in sequentibus, annotantur. Gesta quoque abbatum omnium qui a tempore regis Offani fundatoris ecclesiae Sancti Albani in eadem ecclesia extiterunt, usque ad annum gratiae millesimum ducentesimum quinquagesimum, similiter in praesenti volumine denotantur.

The text of the first part of the *Gesta Abbatum* extends to 1235, and that of the second part to 1255, so that this statement can hardly refer to either of them, and Matthew is evidently here thinking rather of the year in which he was writing than of his book on the abbots. The translation should therefore probably be '…the deeds of all the abbots from Offa until now [i.e. 1250] are described in this book'; and we may therefore tenta-

---

[1] It was copied thence by the continuator of the *Gesta Abbatum*, and is printed in *GA*. I, pp. 363–6.   [2] Wats, p. 60.   [3] Wats, p. 38.
[4] Wats, p. 46.   [5] Wats, p. 126.   [6] Wats, p. 31.

tively conclude that the *Vitae Offarum* was completed in 1250, and added, in that year, to a book which already contained the papal privileges referred to by Matthew (which originally preceded the *Gesta*), as well as the first part of the *Gesta Abbatum*. Now was this book originally (that is, in or before 1250) a part of the *Liber Additamentorum*, or was it only added later into the *Liber Additamentorum*? This is a difficult question to answer with any degree of certainty, but, from the reference to a 'chronicle in this book' which we discussed above,[1] it seems likely that the *Gesta Abbatum* was originally at the end of *AB*, and, if this were so, it is possible that the *Vitae Offarum* and the papal privileges (together no doubt with the charters that go with them) formed with it part of the collection of documents which, as we have seen, were kept at the end of *B* until Matthew conceived the idea of a separate *Liber Additamentorum*.

It seems not unreasonable to suppose that, in the year 1250, when Matthew drew the text of the *Chronica Majora* to its intended close, he purposed at the same time to complete his other historical labours, and to combine the whole in a single manuscript, *AB*, containing the full text of his *Chronica Majora*, the additional documents referred to in its text but not copied out there, as well as his domestic histories and the documents concerning them. The references to the *Gesta Abbatum* in the *Historia Anglorum* do not cast serious doubts on this theory, for the words 'cuius beneficia in libro de Gestis Abbatum, apud Sanctum Albanum habito, plenius describuntur' (I, p. 228), for instance, do not necessarily mean that the *Gesta Abbatum* was at this time a separate book, all on its own. In or before 1250, then, Matthew had probably gathered the material that was later to become his *Liber Additamentorum* at the end of his *Chronica Majora* in *AB*. To this original nucleus the documentary material was evidently added by Matthew more or less continually from 1250 onwards until his death, during which time, probably *c.* 1252, it was finally separated from *B*, to become the *Liber Additamentorum* as we know it now. This book became the repository for all kinds of rough notes, jottings, and even drawings, as well as much miscellaneous material; all of which reflect Matthew's catholic interests and inquisitive mind.

[1] P. 88.

Among other things, we find in the *Liber Additamentorum* a drawing of an elephant (f. 168b); an itinerary from London to Apulia (ff. 182b–183a); a page of coloured shields (f. 170b); a list of 'farms' belonging to St Albans (ff. 180b–181a); a drawing of a parhelion seen in the sky in 1233 (f. 185a); and an outline map of Great Britain (f. 186b): all of them executed by Matthew himself. More material was added to the *Liber Additamentorum* after Matthew's death, and indeed from its origins until recent times it has been constantly added to and rearranged; and its present chaotic and haphazard appearance is by no means due entirely to Matthew Paris. As it was built up and used by him, the *Liber Additamentorum* was a reasonably well organized appendix to his main chronicle, consisting in the main of a collection of texts of domestic interest, followed by the documentary material of general interest which he gathered together during the last ten or twelve years of his life.[1]

---

[1] In the whole of the *Liber Additamentorum* there are less than half a dozen documents of general interest dating from before 1247.

CHAPTER VI

THE 'FLORES HISTORIARUM': SOME MANUSCRIPT PROBLEMS

MATTHEW PARIS'S *Flores Historiarum* presents us with yet another series of intricate manuscript problems, which we must try to unravel.[1] Though many manuscripts of this work are extant, only two concern us here, for all the others have been shown to derive from them.[2] These are the manuscript in Chetham's Library, Manchester, number 6712 (which, following Luard, I shall call *Ch*), and manuscript number 123 in the Library of Eton College (*E*). Up to the annal for 1294 *E* is a fair copy of the *Flores Historiarum* written by one scribe of *c*. 1300, and after this it has been continued by various scribes up to 1306. *Ch*, on the other hand, must be regarded as original, at least in part. Up to the annal for 1241 it was written by two St Albans scribes of *c*. 1250. From 1241 to near the end of the annal for 1249 it was written by Matthew Paris himself; and from 1249 to 1265 by other St Albans scribes of the mid-thirteenth century. From the annal for 1265 onwards it was written at Westminster.[3] In all the manuscripts of the *Flores Historiarum* the text is divided into two books, the first of which ends with the annal for 1066. Here we shall be concerned only with Book I, and Book II up to the annal for 1249, this being the part of the *Flores* for which Matthew Paris was responsible. Although both books are based on Matthew's *Chronica Majora*, they differ very much in character, for, while Book I is for the most part a full and exact copy of the *Chronica Majora*, Book II has been very much abridged and altered from it, although it includes a considerable amount of additional matter. Unfortunately Luard, in his edition of the *Flores Historiarum*, only very inadequately carried out the task, which he set himself in his preface,[4] of distinguishing by means of large and small type

[1] For the authorship of the *Flores*, see above, pp. 39–41.
[2] *FH*. I, pp. xxxiii–xxxiv, and xvii.
[3] For *Ch*, see *FH*. I, pp. xii ff.; and for *E*, I, pp. xv ff.
[4] *FH*. I, p. xlix.

between the text of the *Chronica Majora*, as copied into the *Flores*, and the additional matter in the *Flores* which was not taken from the *Chronica*. This unfortunate failure has necessitated a complete collation of the printed texts of the *Flores* and the *Chronica Majora*, and it is on this collation, and not on the differences of type in Luard's edition of the *Flores*, that the discussion which follows is based.

The two books of the *Flores Historiarum* are so different in character that a separate discussion is demanded for each of them. Let us look first at Book I, which extends from the Creation up to 1066. A problem that confronts us immediately is the relationship of *Ch* and *E*. The text which these two manuscripts share in common varies sufficiently from that of the *Chronica Majora* for us to be sure that they cannot have been taken independently from that work.[1] Either, then, they shared a common exemplar, in its turn derived from the *Chronica Majora*, or one of them was copied from the other. *Ch* could not have been copied from *E*, because *E* was written fifty years after *Ch*; nor could *E* have been copied from *Ch*, for there are four separate lines missing in *Ch* through homoeoteleuton in the exemplar, all of which are present in *E*.[2] Both Luard and Liebermann agreed that neither of these manuscripts could have been copied from the other,[3] and we must therefore conclude that they shared a common exemplar, which I shall call *ChE*.[4]

Having established the existence of a manuscript, *ChE*, lying behind *Ch* and *E*, we are now in a position to examine the relationship of *ChE* and the early part of Matthew's *Chronica Majora* in *A*. There are considerable differences, in Book I, between *ChE* and *A*, although they occur only in certain parts of the text. Up to about the annal for 231, *ChE* is a reasonably accurate copy of *A*, but with a number of additional passages, and a few small alterations. From about the annal for 231 to that for 567, and again between 619 and 633, there are many verbal

[1] As Luard apparently supposed; *FH.* I, p. xxxiv.
[2] At *FH.* I, pp. 157, note 4; 264, note 4; 281, and 544, note 2.
[3] *FH.* I, pp. xxxiii–xxxiv.
[4] It should be noted that there was probably an intermediate manuscript between *ChE* and *E* (see below, pp. 101–2). Its existence, however, would not affect the present discussion.

differences between *A* and *ChE*, but only two material additions to *ChE*. One of these, the story of the miraculous appearance of the chrism at the baptism of Clovis, is inserted into the annal for 476, and the other, an abridgement of an entry in Roger Wendover omitted from *A*, under the year 352.[1] Between the annals for 633 and 1065 the texts of *ChE* and *A* are identical, apart from the usual scribal variations, but after the beginning of the annal for 1065, until the end of Book I, *ChE* is very much altered from the text of *A*. The character of the variations between *ChE* and *A* in the annals 231–567 and 619–33 is well shown when their texts are compared with that of their ultimate source. In the example which follows, I have italicized the alterations from *A* in *ChE*.

The source, Geoffrey of Monmonth's *Historia regum Britanniae*.[2]

Et si omnes istum liberare niterentur, ego eum in frusta conscinderem. Insequerer namque prophetam Samuelem, qui cum Agag regem Amalech in potestatem tenuisset, conscidit illum in frusta, dicens: sicut fecisti matres sine liberis, sic faciam hodie matrem tuam sine liberis inter mulieres: sic igitur facite de isto, qui alter Agag consistit.

A. Part of the annal for 489.[3]

Etsi omnes istum liberare vellent, ego eum in frusta conciderem. Samuel namque propheta, cum Agag regem Amalech in bello cepisset, mactavit illum in frusta, dicens, 'Sicut fecisti matres sine liberis, sic faciam matrem tuam hodie sine liberis inter mulieres; similiter facite de isto qui alter Agag existit.'

ChE. Part of the annal for 489.[4]

...*et ait, frendens prae ira*, 'Etsi omnes istum liberare vellent, ego eum in frusta concid*am. Quid haesitatis, effeminati? Nonne* Samuel propheta, cum regem Amalech in bello *captum membratim concidisset, ait*, Sicut fecisti matres sine liberis, sic faciam matrem tuam *esse* sine liberis hodie inter mulieres; similiter facite de isto *altero* Agag, *qui multas matres suis orbavit filiis*.'

A comparison of these passages shows that, while the compiler of *A* has made a sober and more or less accurate paraphrase of

[1] See *FH*. I, pp. 240 and 188; for the latter, see also *CM*. I, p. 164, note 3.
[2] A. Griscom (ed.), p. 406.
[3] *CM*. I, p. 221. [4] *FH*. I, p. 244.

his source, the author of *ChE* has produced, in the process of copying from *A*, a rather highly coloured and greatly 'improved' version of this speech. The author of *ChE* was, of course, Matthew Paris. The way in which *ChE* has been altered from *A* in this part of Book I of the *Flores Historiarum* is characteristic of him, and is paralleled exactly by his treatment of Roger Wendover in the *Chronica Majora*, which we discussed in Chapter II.[1] Sometimes a minute alteration in *ChE* is identical with one made by Matthew to the text of Roger Wendover in *A*. For instance, in one place where the text of *A* had 'exulatus', Matthew has written 'vel exul' above the line.[2] In another place, where the word 'exulatusque' occurred in *A*, this has been altered, in *ChE*, into 'exulque';[3] and elsewhere, the word 'exiliatus' in *A* has been altered, in *ChE*, into 'exul'.[4] All the variations from *A*, in *ChE*, seem to be due to Matthew Paris, and it is likely that their curious distribution in Book I of the *Flores Historiarum* (231–567; 619–33; 1065–6) is due to the fact that Matthew himself wrote out these parts of the text of *ChE*, while the rest was left to a scribe.

The excerpts printed above show that *A* and *ChE* are, in spite of their variations, versions of one and the same compilation; and the fact that some of the errors which are common to them both occur also in *O* and *W* demonstrates the dependence of *A*, *OW* and *ChE* on a single ultimate exemplar. In one place, for instance, a passage is omitted, because of homoeoteleuton, in all these manuscripts;[5] and elsewhere they all have 'Orencestriam' for 'Cirencestriam', and 'Cnutoni' erroneously for 'Tovio'.[6] Up to the annal for 1066, then, *A*, *OW* and *ChE* are merely different versions of Roger Wendover's *Flores Historiarum*.

Let us look a little more closely at the relationship of these manuscripts. Book I of *ChE* is certainly derived from the actual manuscript *A*, for some of Matthew's alterations in *A* are copied into *ChE*. For example, in the annal for 261 *ChE* copies an

---

[1] See pp. 32 ff., above. [2] *CM*. I, p. 17, note 1.
[3] In the annal for 241; *CM*. I, p. 138, and *FH*. I, p. 155.
[4] In the annal for 519; *CM*. I, p. 235, and *FH*. I, p. 260.
[5] *CM*. I, p. 203; see above, p. 32, note 3.
[6] *CM*. I, p. 502, note 1; *FH*. I, p. 549, note 1 (Luard does not point out that *W* also reads 'Orencestriam'), and *CM*. I, p. 516, note 3; *FH*. I, p. 564.

alteration wrongly made by Matthew in *A* because he misread that manuscript;[1] and again, in the annal for 386, another of Matthew's blundering attempts at correction is copied into *ChE* from *A*.[2] Throughout the text of Book I, *ChE* and *A* have a number of errors, variants and omissions in common, which show that the scribe of *ChE* had *A* before him while he wrote, and copied largely from it. But it is easy to show that he was not wholly dependent on *A*; and, indeed, it is clear that he had access to a manuscript lying behind both *A* and *OW*. In the annal for 885, for instance, *ChE* has correctly, with William of Malmesbury (the source), 'in imperio Romanorum', while *A* and *OW* have 'in paganorum imperio'.[3] Again, in the annal for 490, *A* and *OW* have 'grandi' wrongly for 'grandes', which *ChE* has.[4] In *A*, three separate lines are lost at different points through careless copying; but none of these is missing in *ChE*.[5] There is one example, too, of a line lost through homoeoteleuton in manuscripts *A*, *O* and *W*, which is present in *ChE*.[6] Besides making use of *A*, then, the scribe of *ChE* used a manuscript lying behind all the others. This manuscript cannot have been the exemplar of *A* and *OW*, which we have called *b*,[7] for *ChE* avoids mistakes common to *A* and *OW*, which they must have copied from *b*. We have, therefore, to postulate another manuscript, the exemplar of *b* and part-exemplar of *ChE*, which I shall call *a*. In Book I of the *Flores Historiarum* the manuscripts are thus related as shown in fig. 7.

We saw in Chapter II that *b*, since its text extended at least to the annal for 1228, was probably a manuscript of Roger Wendover's *Flores Historiarum*, and not an earlier compilation. But what of *a*? This, it seems, could have been a manuscript of some early compilation called the *Flores Historiarum* and perhaps extending only to 1066, which was used by Roger Wendover as the basis for the early part of his chronicle, and used again by

[1] *CM.* I, p. 141, note 2; *FH.* I, p. 159, note 4.
[2] *CM.* I, p. 171, note 1; *FH.* I, p. 195.
[3] *CM.* I, p. 420, note 1, and *FH.* I, p. 462.
[4] *CM.* I, p. 222, note 5, and *FH.* I, p. 245.
[5] *CM.* I, pp. 232, 315 and 477; *FH.* I, pp. 257, 352 and 524.
[6] *CM.* I, p. 300 and *FH.* I, p. 334. The line, not noticed by Luard, is 'diebus tribus, et cessavit sedes anno uno, mensibus sex'.
[7] See p. 28 above.

Matthew Paris in the preparation of *ChE*. But we cannot embark here on an examination of the sources of Roger Wendover. What is important for us is to note that Matthew made two

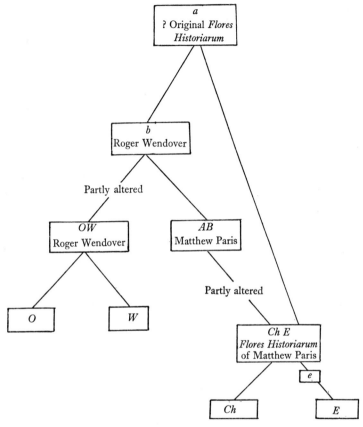

Fig. 7. Diagram to show the relationship of the manuscripts of Book I of Matthew's *Flores Historiarum* to those of Matthew's *Chronica Majora* and Roger Wendover's *Flores Historiarum*.

separate versions of the compilation used by Roger, one in *AB*, and the other in Book I of *ChE*.

So far we have limited our discussion to Book I of the *Flores Historiarum*, the text of which extends from the Creation to 1066. Book II presents a very different series of problems, for its text is quite different in character from that of Book I, which follows the *Chronica Majora* more or less closely. In Book II, however, as in Book I, *Ch* and *E* continue to share, in the main, the same text, and it is clear that their relationship remains the same: they are derived from a common exemplar, *ChE*. As with Book I, so with Book II, it is certain that *Ch* was not copied from *E*, for the latter was written fifty years after the former. Nor can *E* be derived from *Ch*, for, in the course of the annal for 1212,[1] *E* has the date 'quinto', correctly, while *Ch* has 'septimo'; and, elsewhere, *Ch* has a passage taken word for word from the *Southwark Annals*, except for the last word 'intimaverunt', while *E* ends the same sentence, as does the *Southwark Annals*, with the word 'nunciaverunt'.[2] Again, in the course of the annal for 1217 a long passage is omitted in *Ch* through homoeoteleuton, but it is present in *E*.[3] Many more examples could be cited to show that *E* is not derived from *Ch*, and there is thus no doubt as to the continued existence, in Book II, of their common exemplar. I shall continue to call this *ChE*, although it is by no means clear that it formed part of the manuscript containing Book I of *ChE*. It is difficult to be sure how far the text of this exemplar extended. It seems very likely, however, that from the annal for 1241, when Matthew takes up the pen in *Ch*,[4] that manuscript is no longer copied accurately from an exemplar, and the fact that *E* follows Matthew's text very closely until the annal for 1244 seems to show that it is here derived from *Ch*. At one point there is a marginal addition in *Ch* which is in the text of *E*, and, elsewhere, *Ch* has 'vi' interlined, and this also occurs in the text of *E*.[5] Although the evidence is slight, then, it seems likely that the text of *ChE* extended only to the point in *Ch* where Matthew took up his pen near the end of the annal for 1241.

In Book II of the *Flores Historiarum* there is no sign of the use of the manuscript which I have called *a*, but, owing to the very abbreviated nature of the excerpts from the *Chronica Majora* in this part of the *Flores*, we cannot be sure that it was

---

[1] *FH*. II, p. 142.
[2] *FH*. II, p. 106, note 3; B.M. Cotton MS. Faustina A viii, f. 135b.
[3] *FH*. II, pp. 164–5; see p. 164, note 4.   [4] *FH*. II, p. 250, note 1.
[5] *FH*. II, pp. 266, note 4, and 272, note 2.

not used. Certainly *AB* was used, and indeed it is clear that
Book II of *ChE*, like Book I, is mainly derived from Matthew's
Chronica Majora in *AB*. In one place, for instance, while *O*
and *W* have 'Ivo' correctly, *A* has 'suo', and *ChE* 'suho';[1]
and, elsewhere, *O* and *W* have 'capiuntur' while *A* and *ChE*
have 'capti sunt'.[2] Furthermore, in the course of Book II, *ChE*
often, though by no means always, incorporates Matthew's
corrections in *AB* into its text. Besides *AB*, the fair copy of *B*,
which I have called *C*, seems to have been used in the preparation of *ChE*, perhaps at times when *B* was not available for
copying. Thus, in one place, *C* and *ChE* have 'Cisterciensem'
against all the other manuscripts, which read correctly 'Certes-
iensem';[3] and, in another place, Luard was able to show that
C was the exemplar of *ChE*.[4] But, even in the part of the text of
ChE where *C* was used, *B* was not abandoned for long, for,
while the examples just cited, of the use of *C*, occur in the
annals for 1198 and 1209, it is certain that *B* was used in the
annals for 1204 and 1205, and again in the annal for 1221.[5] In
the section of *Ch* which Matthew himself wrote the exemplar
was *B*, as may be seen in the course of the annal for 1242,[6] where
the phrase 'de scuto xx solidis', which is not in *C*, is introduced
into the text of *Ch* from the margin of *B*.

Much use has been made, in the preceding pages, of the
symbol *ChE*, to denote the common exemplar of *Ch* and *E*.
These two manuscripts, however, are by no means identical,
and we must turn now to consider their differences. In Book I,
Ch has two entries concerning Westminster which are not in *E*,[7]
and *E* has some passages from the *Historia Miscella* and other
sources,[8] as well as some corrections, which are not found in *Ch*.
In Book II, the differences between these two manuscripts are
more extensive. There are a few passages which are in *E* but
not in *Ch*, and these seem to be additions in *E* rather than

---

[1] *CM.* II, p. 34, note 1, and *FH.* II, p. 25, note 8.
[2] *CM.* II, p. 328, note 4, and *FH.* II, p. 98.
[3] *FH.* II, p. 120, note 1; *CM.* II, p. 450, note 1.
[4] *FH.* II, p. 138, note 5.
[5] See *FH.* II, pp. 129, 130 and 172, where evidence to this effect is found.
[6] *FH.* II, p. 258.   [7] *FH.* I, pp. 566–7 and 579–80.
[8] For instance, *FH.* I, pp. 47–53 and 111–13.

omissions in *Ch*. The copy of King John's charter of submission in *E* appears to be one of them.[1] A number of variations between *Ch* and *E* occur, in which *E* appears to have a shortened version of the corresponding passage in *Ch*; but it is difficult to ascertain whether these variations are due to amplification from the text of *ChE* by the scribe of *Ch*, or to abridgement in *E*. The former, however, seems more probable, in view of the interesting fact that on a number of occasions the version in *E* is found in identical words in the short chronicle in British Museum Cotton MS. Vitellius A xx, which I have already mentioned,[2] and which I shall here call *V*. Owing to the damaged state of *V*, it is often difficult to collate these passages, but the version of part of the annal for 1119 in *E* is certainly the same as that in *V*, and part of the annal for 1128, which is not from *AB*, is given in the same words in *E* and *V*.[3] After the annal for 1134 the text of *V* is no longer similar to that of the *Flores Historiarum*, and no more parallels are found. The explanation of these passages common to *E* and *V* seems to be that they were in the text of *ChE*, but that *Ch* has been amplified in the process of copying, while *E* has not. This certainly seems to have happened in the annals 1220–2,[4] where there are a number of passages in *Ch* which are neither in *E* nor *AB*, and which were therefore probably added in the course of writing by the scribe of *Ch*, no doubt under the supervision of Matthew Paris.

Ch, as we have seen, contains a number of entries relating to Westminster which are not taken from *AB*, and which, since they do not appear in *E*, were probably not in *ChE*. Besides the two Westminster entries in Book I of *Ch*, there are a number in Book II.[5] Now *Ch* was sent to Westminster in or soon after 1265,[6] and the fact that it actually went there removes any doubts which might have been entertained about these Westminster entries: Matthew must have had the book especially written for Westminster. It is probable that he intended to

---

[1] *FH*. II, pp. 145–6.

[2] Above, p. 41. See also below, pp. 115–16 ff.

[3] *FH*. II, pp. 47, note 5 (1119), and 53, notes 3, 4 and 6 (1128). See v, f. 80a–b.

[4] *FH*. II, pp. 170–5.

[5] *FH*. II, pp. 106, 122, 231, 289, 314 and 321.

[6] *FH*. I, p. xiii.

finish the manuscript near the end of the annal for 1249, for he closes his section of the text at this point with the couplet:[1]

Cernis completas hic nostro tempore metas,
Si plus forte petas, tibi postera nunciet aetas.

For some reason, however, it was not sent at once to Westminster, but kept at St Albans. Later two scribes finished the annal for 1249, and started that for 1250, abridging from *B*. This part of the text of *Ch* was evidently written some years after that written by Matthew, for, whereas in the preceding annals the original text of *B* is copied into *Ch*, here Matthew's edited text of *B* has been followed, and, as we shall see, it was probably not until 1257 or later that Matthew carried out his large-scale editing of the text of *B*.[2] Later still another scribe, the last who wrote at St Albans, copied into *Ch* the text of Matthew's *Abbreviatio Chronicorum* until its close in the middle of the annal for 1255. He then abridged the annals 1256–9 from the *Chronica Majora*; and continued up to 1265 from the original continuation of Matthew's *Chronica Majora*, which was once at the end of the third volume, *R*.[3] This last block of annals seems to have been written *currente calamo* by a scribe who was perhaps instructed to bring the manuscript up to date ready for its dispatch to Westminster, where the text from 1265 onwards was written, and where the manuscript remained for the rest of the Middle Ages.

Luard called *E* the 'Merton manuscript' because it contains a series of marginal entries concerning the priors of that house.[4] But none of these is in the text, and, out of four entries concerning Merton in the text of *Ch*, all of which were presumably in the text of the exemplar *ChE*, only two have been copied into *E*,[5] so that it seems unlikely, in fact, that *E* was originally a Merton manuscript. So far, in this chapter, we have assumed that the actual manuscripts *Ch* and *E* derived from a common exemplar, *ChE*. But there are reasons for supposing that an

[1] *FH.* II, p. 361.
[2] For the annals 1249–50, see *FH.* II, pp. 361 ff. Luard shows that the edited text of *B* was used for these annals, *FH.* II, p. 361, note 1. For the editing of *B*, see below, pp. 117 ff.   [3] See pp. 10–11 above.
[4] *FH.* I, pp. xv–xvi.
[5] *FH.* II, pp. 46 and 51. Those omitted are at *FH.* II, pp. 81 and 88.

intermediate manuscript, *e*, existed, between *ChE* and *E*.[1] *E* is
a fair copy written by one scribe *c*. 1300, and we can hardly
suppose that this scribe, writing at that time, would have taken
his text up to 1241 from *ChE*; for the annals 1241–4 from *Ch*;
and for the annals 1244–59 from Matthew's *Chronica Majora* in
AB and *R*—work which must surely have been carried out at
St Albans—and then gone to Westminster to copy the annals
from 1265 onwards from the later parts of *Ch*. It is far more
likely that a manuscript *e* was written at St Albans in the middle
years of the thirteenth century, and that the scribe of *E* took the
first part of his text (probably up to 1264) from this manuscript,
and the later part, from 1265 onwards, from *Ch* or a manuscript
related to it. If we suppose this to have been the case, it is
possible to explain the sudden abandonment of *Ch*, by the scribe
of *e*, during the annal for 1244, on the supposition that he was
working at St Albans just at the time (*c*. 1265) when *Ch* was
sent to Westminster. However, this is not the place to pursue
the intricate problems presented by the post-Parisian section of
the *Flores Historiarum*, and it should be noted that the presence
or absence of *e*, intermediate between *ChE* and *E*, cannot affect
the argument of this chapter that *Ch* and *E* (at any rate up to
1241) are derived from a common exemplar, taken, in its turn,
from Matthew's *Chronica Majora*.

We showed, in Chapter III, that Matthew was the author of
the *Flores Historiarum* up to 1249; and we have now examined
the relationship of the manuscripts of the *Flores* and Matthew's
other historical manuscripts. One problem, however, remains:
when was the *Flores Historiarum* written? Book I of *ChE* incorporates only a few of Matthew's corrections and alterations in *A*,
and none of his longer additions, so that we may be sure that
it was copied soon after the early part of *A*, up to 1066, was
written. Unfortunately we know little or nothing about the date
of this part of *A*, but it was probably not begun until *c*. 1240,[2]
and we may therefore perhaps date Book I of the *Flores Historiarum* to *c*. 1240–5. Book II of the *Flores*, on the other hand,
could hardly have been written before 1250, since it occasionally
has readings from *C*, the fair copy of the *Chronica Majora* made
in or soon after 1250;[3] and it was probably completed by 1257,

[1] See fig. 7, above, p. 97.   [2] See pp. 59–60 above.   [3] See p. 59 above.

when, as we shall see in the next chapter, Matthew seems to have made his expurgatory alterations to the text of *B*, for these are not followed in the *Flores Historiarum*. Book II (up to the end of the annal for 1249), therefore, probably dates from *c.* 1250–5. The two books of the *Flores Historiarum* thus differ considerably in date, as well as in character, and it seems possible that the *Flores*, as we know it now, was built up out of two quite separate works: a version of the main chronicle of Roger and Matthew extending to 1066; and a severe abridgement of Matthew's *Chronica Majora*, together with much additional material, made some time later, and extending from 1066 to 1249.

There is one text which, owing to its close connexion with Book II of the *Flores Historiarum*, may conveniently be discussed here. This is a series of short entries of an annalistic nature, which occurs in the *Chronica Majora*, the *Flores Historiarum*, and in the short chronicle *V*; and which I shall call Matthew's 'new material'. In the *Chronica Majora*, much of it has been added by Matthew in the margins of *AB* between the annals for 1066 and 1223, and many of these entries are written in a pale brown ink and a cursive hand, giving the impression of having been written more or less at one time. Most of the new material is incorporated into the text of Book II of the *Flores Historiarum*, but, on the whole, this is done very clumsily, and in a way that allows it to be readily distinguished from the rest of the text, for the most part abridged from *AB*. Sometimes it is inserted at the start of the annal, as in 1196, where Matthew begins the entry with some excerpts from the new material, and, when these are finished, goes back to *AB* and copies thence, so that the phrase 'Rex Anglorum fuit ad Natale apud...', which normally begins the annal in *AB*, appears half-way through it in the *Flores*.[1] Elsewhere the process is altered, and the new material is inserted in a block at the end of the annal, or, sometimes, during the course of it. The new material is also found in part of the short chronicle *V*, between the annals for 1066 and 1134. It occurs, too, in the *Historia Anglorum* and in *C*, but in these manuscripts it can be shown to be derived directly from the margins of *AB*.

[1] *FH.* II, p. 114.

The sources of the new material are difficult to identify accurately, except where well-known works such as William of Malmesbury's *Historia Novella* and Ralph de Diceto's *Abbreviatio Chronicorum* are used. Part of the new material is taken from these, as well as from Robert de Monte and perhaps Henry of Huntingdon, but much of it was taken from monastic annals which are no longer extant in their original form. From the number of entries concerning Reading, for instance, Luard deduced that a manuscript from that house was used; but this manuscript is not now known to exist.[1] Again, Luard noticed that a Southwark manuscript had been used, which he thought was that actually existing in the Cottonian collection under the press-mark Faustina A viii. This contains a thirteenth-century chronicle, apparently written contemporaneously by the canons of Southwark, the text of which ends in 1240, and which is generally known as the *Southwark Annals*.[2] In fact, however, the Southwark manuscript which was used in the compilation of Matthew's new material was evidently not Faustina A viii itself, but a source of the chronicle in that manuscript, as a comparison of these two extracts shows:

The annal for 1113 in Faustina A viii, f. 132.

Tamisia exiccata et maxim' [*sic*] miliaria duobus diebus. Cometa mense. Radulphus archiepiscopus factus.

Part of the new material added in the margin of *A*.[3]

Quarto kalendas Aprilis Tamisia exiccata est et mare [per] duodecim miliaria, per duos dies. Radulfus episcopus Rofensis eligitur ad archiepiscopatum Cantuariensem, sexto kalendas Maii...cometa quoque apparuit mense Maii....

A similar situation is found when the text of the Coggeshall chronicle is compared with the new material: all the evidence points to the independent use of a common source rather than the derivation of one from the other. As Powicke long ago pointed out, 'it is impossible to prove that even Matthew Paris knew Coggeshall after 1195'.[4]

---

[1] *CM.* II, p. xxix; the Southwark manuscript is noticed on the same page.

[2] On this see Tyson, 'Annals of Southwark and Merton', *Surrey Arch. Coll.* XXXVI (1925), pp. 24–57.   [3] *CM.* II, p. 141.

[4] Powicke, 'Roger Wendover and the Coggeshall Chronicle', *EHR.* XXI (1906), pp. 292–3, note 25.

We cannot, however, pursue here the problem of the origins of Matthew's new material, for there is much research still to be done on the thirteenth-century monastic annals, and a number of texts (including the *Southwark Annals*) still need editing. But from whatever sources it was compiled, it seems clear that the new material was used independently by Matthew in *AB* and *ChE*. That is to say, even though, as we have shown, *ChE* was undoubtedly abridged from *AB*, the new material, which is written into the margins of *AB*, was not copied thence into *ChE*. In the course of the annal for 1106, for example, Matthew wrote into the margin of *A* an entry concerning the institution of canons at Southwark, but he mistakenly wrote 'Salisbury' for 'Southwark': yet *ChE* and the *Southwark Annals* give 'Southwark' correctly.[1] Again, in the course of the annal for 1179, Matthew has 'Wudestoc' wrongly for 'Wenloc' in the margin of *A*; but *ChE* and the *Southwark Annals* give 'Wenloc' correctly.[2] Moreover, there are some entries from the new material in the margins of *AB*, which do not appear at all in *ChE*: for instance, those added to the annal for 1198, which occur also in the *Southwark Annals*.[3] If we examine the new material in the chronicle *V*, we find a similar situation, for it was apparently not copied into *V* from the margins of *AB*, nor from *ChE*; nor is the new material in *AB* or *ChE* taken from that in *V*. For the year 1091, for instance, the *Southwark Annals* record a strong wind; and the entry, though not in *A*, is in *ChE*, in similar words, but without the date, and embroidered in Matthew's usual fashion. This entry is also in *V*, which gives the date correctly, as in the *Southwark Annals*.[4] In another place *V* has phrases from Diceto which are neither in *A* nor in *ChE*,[5] and in the course of the annal for 1070, where both *ChE* and *V* have a description of the plundering of the monasteries by William the Conqueror, taken from Diceto, the account in *V* includes two lines or more *ad verbum* with Diceto, which are not in *ChE*.[6] Furthermore, errors in *ChE* are often avoided in *V*: for instance in the annal for 1120, where *A* and *V* have 'Maii'

---

[1] *CM.* II, p. 133, note 3; *FH.* II, p. 39; Faustina A viii, f. 132.
[2] *CM.* II, p. 309; *FH.* II, p. 91; Faustina A viii, f. 134.
[3] *CM.* II, pp. 450–1.
[4] *V*, f. 78b; Faustina A viii, f. 131b; *FH.* II, p. 22.
[5] In the annal for 1067, *V*, f. 77a.   [6] *V*, f. 77a; *FH.* II, p. 4.

and *ChE* has, wrongly, 'Aprilis'.[1] That the new material in *ChE* cannot have been taken from *V* is evident from the annal for 1073, where *V* has 'presente' for 'presidente' of *AB* and *ChE*, and 'detrudi' for *ChE*'s 'intrudi'.[2]

We must conclude, then, that the new material was copied independently, but from a common exemplar, into *V*, *ChE* and *AB*. There is some evidence that this common exemplar was written in a continuous chronicle form, and that the *Flores Historiarum* of Roger Wendover, rather than the *Chronica Majora* of Matthew Paris, was used in its compilation. The annal for 1104, for instance, is composed of some extracts altered from Roger Wendover, a sentence from the *Southwark Annals*, and another from an unidentified source; and it occurs in almost identical words, and with the separate entries in the same order, in *V* and *ChE*.[3] It seems, in fact, to have been copied directly, in both these manuscripts, from the new material. As for the use of Roger Wendover in the new material, we find that in *V*, between the annals for 1066 and 1134, there is only one point where the text seems to incorporate a reading from *A*, but there are several examples of *V* reading with *OW* against *A*: for instance, in the annal for 1112, where *V* and *OW* have the word 'suorum', which is omitted in *A*.[4]

If the new material really was compiled in part from Roger Wendover, it was probably written at St Albans; and we cannot preclude the possibility that it was written by Matthew Paris, and that, since it was based in part on Roger Wendover instead of on his *Chronica Majora*, it represents Matthew's earliest historical activity. Be this as it may, he certainly made use of the new material, though he failed to integrate it fully into any one of his chronicles. He seems to have used it first as a basis for *V*; but it was abandoned when the writing of that manuscript reached the annal for 1134. In the *Flores Historiarum* not all of it was used, and it is incorporated in a rather clumsy fashion; and in *AB* it is incomplete, and only added in the margins. This muddled use of his material reflects a certain lack of system in

---

[1] *V*, f. 80a; *FH*. II, p. 48; *CM*. II, p. 149, and note 1.
[2] *V*, f. 77a; *FH*. II, p. 6; *CM*. II, p. 11. *A* has 'retrudi'.
[3] *V*, f. 79a; *FH*. II, p. 37; *CM*. II, p. 126.
[4] *V*, f. 79b; *FH*. II, p. 42; *CM*. II, p. 140, note 1.

Matthew Paris, but we must remember that some of these manuscripts were evidently written contemporaneously. If this were not so, it would be virtually impossible to explain the curious fact that, while the new material is copied independently into *ChE* and the margins of *AB*, both *AB* itself and *C*, the fair copy of *B*, were used in the writing of *ChE*. In fig. 8 I have tried to

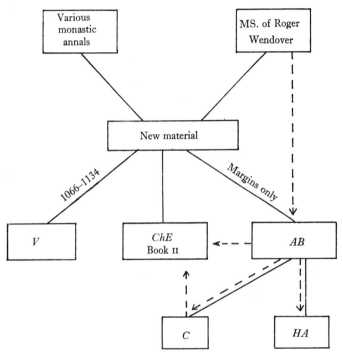

Fig. 8. Diagram to show Matthew's use of the new material in his historical manuscripts. The dotted lines indicate the relationship of the texts; the continuous lines show the derivation and use of the new material.

show how the new material was used in Matthew's historical manuscripts. This diagram no doubt appears complicated; but we are dealing with a complicated situation. It is quite possible, for instance, that while Matthew was copying the text of *ChE* from *AB*, he had the new material before him, and copied it into *ChE*, at the same time adding it to the margins of his exemplar *AB*.

Although our discussion, in this chapter, of Matthew's *Flores Historiarum* and his new material cannot be regarded as exhaustive, we are now in a position to try to describe his activities in connexion with these two works, and to fit them into our picture of the writing of the *Chronica Majora*, the *Historia Anglorum*, and the *Liber Additamentorum*. Matthew's historical activities seem to have reached a peak in 1251, at about the time when he brought his *Chronica Majora* to its intended close in *AB* with the annal for 1250. He had already begun work, in 1250, on the *Historia Anglorum*, which he wrote out himself; and it must have been at this time, that is in 1250–1, that his scribe made the fair copy of *B* which I have called *C*. While this work was in progress, a new book, the *Flores Historiarum*, evidently began to take shape. This was probably a composite work, Book I of which—a version of the Paris-Wendover compilation extending only to 1066—was apparently already in existence by 1250. To this, probably in or soon after 1250, Matthew began to add Book II, which was in the main abridged from *AB*, though much additional matter was incorporated into it. The bulk of this additional matter in Book II of the *Flores Historiarum* was apparently copied from the collection of monastic annals which I have called the new material, part of which (1066–1134) had probably already been used in the short chronicle *V*. We do not know exactly when Matthew decided to add most of this new material into the margins of *AB*, but it must have been soon after the completion of *AB* to 1250, for it has been copied thence into both *C* and the *Historia Anglorum*. It seems that Matthew must have gone ahead, writing the new material into the margins of *AB*, while work on Book II of *ChE* was still in progress, for, by the time the writing of *ChE* had reached the annal for 1198, *C* was sometimes being used as its exemplar, instead of *AB*. Book II of the *Flores Historiarum* (in *ChE*) was perhaps not written out by Matthew himself, but he must have supervised its compilation. Its text seems to have ended in the annal for 1241, and it seems possible that it was left unfinished until Matthew had *Ch* copied from it. *Ch* was written specially for Westminster, and Matthew himself continued its text from 1241 to near the end of the annal for 1249.

It must be admitted that this theory, as to the writing of

Matthew's historical manuscripts, is an extremely tentative one, and, in particular, it should be noted that the chronology of some of them is uncertain. Matthew's scribe, for instance, may have finished copying *C* from *B* very soon after *AB* was completed to 1250. If this was the case, Book II of *ChE* could be dated earlier: indeed it might even be possible to claim that it was finished, and much of *Ch* copied from it, by 1251–2. Different interpretations, too, can be put on our evidence concerning Matthew's use of the new material. Our conclusions, then, must remain provisional ones; but it is hoped that the discussions of this chapter have thrown some light on the relationship of Matthew's historical manuscripts and on his methods as a historian, even if only to illuminate their complexity.

CHAPTER VII

MATTHEW PARIS'S HISTORICAL WORKS: ABRIDGEMENT AND EXPURGATION

MATTHEW'S various historical works are perhaps best regarded as editions of his main chronicle: the *Historia Anglorum* and Book II of the *Flores Historiarum* are abridged editions of the *Chronica Majora*, and the *Abbreviatio Chronicorum* is an abridged edition of the *Historia Anglorum*. Even the *Chronica Majora* itself can be regarded merely as a 'new edition' of Roger Wendover's chronicle. In each of these abridgements Matthew introduced alterations and additional material, so that each of them has some independent value of its own. Before we review these different works, however, it is worth looking for a moment at the *Chronica Majora* itself. There is no evidence that Matthew ever produced a fair copy of the early part of its text (up to 1188), for the first part of British Museum Cotton MS. Nero D v (a copy of *A*) dates from about fifty years after his death. He did, however, produce a fair copy of the text of the *Chronica Majora* from 1189 to 1250, which is now the second part of Nero D v, and which I have called *C*. *C* was copied by a scribe from *B*, probably in or shortly after 1250, and many of Matthew's marginalia in *B* are incorporated in its text. Some of the errors and inconsistencies of *B* are avoided in *C*: for instance, a passage inadvertently repeated in *B* is only copied once into *C*.[1] On the other hand, many of *B*'s errors are transcribed unaltered into *C*, and its scribe made no serious or systematic attempt at correction.[2] Matthew wrote very few marginalia into *C*, and he seems to have lost interest in it once it was copied, so that it remains to this day a more or less untouched copy of his *Chronica Majora* as he originally intended to leave it. If we are thinking in terms of editions, *C* was the first edition of the *Chronica Majora*. *B*, on the other hand, was Matthew's actual working manuscript, into the margins of which

---

[1] *CM.* II, p. 351, note 1.
[2] See Luard's remarks on the scribe of *C*, *CM.* I, p. xii.

he added new information, alternative readings and corrections; and to the text of which he went on adding until the end of the annal for 1253, after which he embarked on the third volume of the *Chronica Majora*, which I have called *R*.

We must not be too ready to assume, from its title, that the *Historia Anglorum* was designed as an 'English History' in contrast to the general European history in the *Chronica Majora*. In fact, Matthew himself refers to the *Chronica Majora* as the 'historia anglorum', and, in writing it, he evidently thought of himself as writing what was essentially a history of England, even though it contained a great deal of Continental history. In the course of the annal for 1244 in the *Chronica Majora* he begins his paragraph describing the pope's attempts to get David, prince of North Wales, into his power, with the words:[1] 'Nor do I think it irrelevant to my matter, or inapposite (*impertinens*), or indeed wholly unconnected with the history of England (*historiae regni Angliae penitus inutile*), to elucidate for our posterity....' And, in the course of the 1249 annal,[2] he says that an enumeration of all the crusaders killed in Cyprus would be 'historiae Anglorum impertinens'. Further on in the *Chronica Majora*[3] he excuses himself for including an account of the battle of Walcheren, with the words: 'Nec haec in cronicis Anglorum collocassem...nisi...'; and, shortly afterwards,[4] he explains that he is confining himself 'ad ea quae Anglicam contingunt historiam'. Matthew, then, evidently thought of his *Chronica Majora* as a history of England, and we need not therefore attach any special significance to the phrase 'historia anglorum' in the prologue to the *Historia Anglorum*, nor to its occurrence in several places in the text, where it, or something similar, is evidently used in the same sense as in the passages quoted above from the *Chronica Majora*. Thus, in the *Historia Anglorum* Matthew justifies his account of the siege of Nicaea with the words:[5] 'Nec mihi videtur a materia cronicorum et historiarum super eventibus Angliae confectarum alienum, si...'; and he leaves the subject of the crusade and returns to Henry I, with the phrase: 'Redeuntes autem ad Anglorum historiam'.[6] In one place in the *Historia Anglorum*[7]

---

[1] *CM*. IV, p. 316. [2] *V*, p. 92. [3] *V*, p. 438. [4] *V*, p. 440.
[5] I, p. 79. [6] *HA*. I, p. 188. [7] I, p. 342.

he omits some letters (which are given in the *Chronica Majora*), 'ut difficile et diffusum foret in hiis cronicis, quae tantum statum regni Angliae debent describendo manifestare, plenius enucleare'; and in the course of the annal for 1249 he excuses himself for omitting the names of the crusaders killed in Cyprus with the same words as in the *Chronica Majora*, 'Anglorum historiae impertinens'.[1]

It appears probable that Matthew, in the course of writing his *Chronica Majora*, found it hard not to include every item of news which came to hand, and that he was aware of the irrelevance, to English history, of much of his material. It was, it seems from the passages quoted above, his intention all along to confine himself to English affairs, or at least to matters connected with England. But in the *Chronica Majora* he had failed to do this, and it may well be that he embarked on the *Historia Anglorum* with the idea of trying to rectify this failing by drastic abridgement, especially of material which, on reflexion, he considered irrelevant to English history. The marginal directions which he wrote into *AB* for his own use in writing the *Historia Anglorum* bear this out:[2] the description of the Albigensian crusade is marked in the margin of *B*,[3] 'Utile, sed impertinens historiae Anglorum'; and the accounts of the council at Bourges and the siege of Avignon in 1226 are marked in the margin of *B*,[4] 'Impertinens ad Anglicam historiam'. These passages are drastically abridged in the *Historia Anglorum*, and there are many others like them, marked in *AB* in a similar way (usually with signs to delimit them), and omitted or much abridged in the *Historia Anglorum*. The formula varies, and sometimes throws more light on Matthew's intentions. We find, for instance: 'Haec plus pertinent ad imperatorem quam ad historiam Anglorum'; and 'Pertinens historiae Walensium, indirecte tamen Anglorum'.[5]

But if Matthew was determined, in writing the *Historia Anglorum*, to omit a great deal of the material in the *Chronica Majora* which was irrelevant to the history of England, he was also determined to abridge throughout; and the *Historia Anglorum* shows a marked desire for brevity. Of the 160 docu-

---

[1] III, p. 66.   [2] See above, pp. 64–5.   [3] *CM.* II, p. 554, note 4.
[4] *CM.* III, pp. 105 and 114.   [5] *CM.* III, p. 145 and IV, p. 316.

ments written out in full in *B*, only five are copied into the *Historia Anglorum*. One document, Matthew confesses, is copied into the *Historia* because it is short: '. . . in haec verba. Quae, quia sunt brevia, hic duximus ea annotanda';[1] and another, on the double excuse of brevity and relevance: 'Quae, quia breves et multum operantur ad praesentem materiam, hic notantur';[2] but the lengthy account of the Evesham monk's vision in the *Chronica Majora* is omitted in the *Historia* 'quia narratio prolixa est'.[3] The *Historia Anglorum*, then, is an abridgement of the *Chronica Majora* designed to be confined more particularly to English affairs. It is successful as an abridgement, but contains a great deal of matter not strictly relevant to English history. As in the *Chronica*, so in the *Historia*, Matthew evidently found it impossible to confine himself purely to the affairs of his own country.

The *Historia Anglorum*, especially in its earlier part,[4] contains a certain amount of matter not in the *Chronica Majora*, and it incorporates in its text a considerable part, though by no means all, of the new material which Matthew added into the margins of *AB*. Towards the end, and especially during the last few annals, the *Historia Anglorum* is very much abridged, and, in comparison with the *Chronica Majora*, it is lifeless and dull. In parts its text degenerates into a mere series of laconic entries, of the type familiar in the lesser monastic chronicles of the time,[5] and there is very little of the lively descriptive narrative so characteristic of the *Chronica Majora*. There are, however, some signs of an attempt, on Matthew's part, to arrange his material more systematically, for he has tried to collect all the obituary notices of each annal together at the end,[6] and sometimes the entries are rearranged in the *Historia Anglorum* in a more logical order. The text of the *Historia* ends with the annal for 1253, and it seems that Matthew must have lost interest in it some time before it was finished, no doubt because he was still engrossed in the recording of contemporary events.

Some time after 1250 (very likely after 1255), Matthew com-

---

[1] I, p. 347.   [2] I, p. 355.   [3] II, p. 60.
[4] See *HA*. III, pp. xxxv ff.
[5] See, for instance, *HA*. III, pp. 119 and 126.
[6] I.e. in the annals for 1242, 1245, 1246 and 1247.

piled the *Abbreviatio Chronicorum*. The text of this short work extends from 1000 to 1255, and remains unfinished. Up to the annal for 1066 it is derived from Roger Wendover or the *Chronica Majora*, with some additional material from Henry of Huntingdon and others.[1] From 1066 to 1250 it is abridged from the *Historia Anglorum*, but with occasional passages from the *Chronica Majora*;[2] and from 1251 onwards it is abridged partly from the *Chronica Majora* and partly from the *Historia Anglorum*, the last two annals being taken wholly from the *Chronica*. Matthew seems to have made no effort, in the *Abbreviatio Chronicorum*, to confine himself to English history, and it is difficult to know with exactly what motive it was written. It is headed simply: 'Haec est Abbreviatio compendiosa Cronicorum Angliae',[3] and perhaps it should be regarded as just another attempt on Matthew's part to produce an abridged version of his main chronicle. There is little new material in the *Abbreviatio*, and many of the passages in it which are not derived from the *Historia Anglorum* or the *Chronica Majora* are mere expressions of opinion, adding nothing new of a factual nature. Minor alterations from the text of the *Historia Anglorum* are not infrequent in the *Abbreviatio*: for instance the papal legate is blamed for fomenting the quarrel between Archbishop Edmund and his monks, while in the *Historia Anglorum* this is said to have been due to the devil.[4]

Although we have already discussed Book II of the *Flores Historiarum* at some length in the previous chapter, it ought, for the sake of completeness, to be mentioned here. Owing to the additional material it contains, the *Flores* is, apart from the *Chronica Majora*, probably the most interesting of Matthew's historical works. It seems to have been designed as a popular edition of the main chronicle: one manuscript of it (*Ch*) was certainly written especially for Westminster. The tone of Book II of the *Flores* is vigorous and colourful, and much of it is characteristic of Matthew's best writing. It is markedly anti-papal, and it is interesting to note that, although it seems to have been written with a view to general publication, it is the only one of

---

[1] See *HA*. III, pp. 156–7.
[2] For instance, at *AC*. pp. 253, note 5, 304, note 6, and 313.
[3] *AC*. p. 159.   [4] *AC*. p. 277, and *HA*. II, p. 411.

Matthew's more important historical works which has not been expurgated by him after it was written.

The shortest of Matthew's abridged editions of the *Chronica Majora* is the chronicle in British Museum Cotton MS. Vitellius A xx, which I have called *V*.[1] Its text extends from 1066 to 1246, and, up to the annal for 1134, it is, as we have seen, compiled from Matthew's new material. The next section of the text of *V*, from 1135 to 1214, is in part abridged from Matthew's *Chronica Majora* in *AB*, and some of Matthew's additions and alterations in the margins of *AB* are copied into it; but there are some variants which show that a manuscript of Roger Wendover was also used. The annal for 1215, in *V*, consists of a series of documents which together take up nine pages— a large proportion of the chronicle's total length of thirty-one pages.[2] The first of these documents is Magna Carta. Up to chapter 25, *V*'s text of this document is similar to that of Matthew Paris in *B*, and it is vitiated in the same way by the omission of some passages (which have, however, been supplied in the margins of *B*, and also of *V*; all those in *B* and some of those in *V* being in Matthew's hand) and by the introduction of other passages from the 1225 re-issue of Magna Carta. From chapter 25 onwards, however, *V* has the text of the 1215 charter correctly, instead of the garbled version found in Roger Wendover and Matthew Paris. Innocent III's grant of free elections to the church follows Magna Carta in *V*; and, after it, the list of barons who swore to support the charter.[3] Both these documents occur also in *B* and the *Liber Additamentorum*, and the text of the former in *V* seems to have been taken from the same source as was used by Matthew for his other copies of it. Next follows a complete text of 'John's Forest Charter', which is in fact Henry III's Forest Charter of 1225; this document is corrupt and incomplete in *B* and in the manuscripts of Roger Wendover.[4] After this Forest Charter, *V* continues with a complete and uncorrupt copy of the 1225 reissue of Magna Carta,[5] the only copy of this document in any of Matthew's manu-

---

[1] See p. 41 above, where I have printed the title.
[2] The documents take up ff. 93 b–102 a of *V*.
[3] *V*, ff. 97–8.   [4] *V*, ff. 98–9; *CM*. ii, pp. 598–602.
[5] *V*, ff. 99–101 b.

scripts; and this is followed by a copy of the Coronation Charter of Henry I,[1] which is given twice in Matthew's *Chronica Majora*. It is noteworthy, in connexion with these documents in *V*, that they are less corrupt than any other copies given by Matthew Paris, and that they are independent of those in *B*. From 1216 to the end of *V* in 1246 the text seems to have been abridged from *B*, but there is some evidence that a manuscript of Roger Wendover was also used up to the annal for 1235. *V*, therefore, though a work of minute size when compared to the others so far reviewed, is of considerable interest, both for the copies of documents which it contains, and on account of its variety of sources; for this little chronicle has been compiled not only from the *Chronica Majora*, but also from Roger Wendover's *Flores Historiarum*, Matthew's new material, and at least one other source.

There is one work, quite different in character from any of those so far discussed, which we ought to mention: this is Matthew's genealogical chronicle, which he calls in *A* (f. ivb): 'Cronica sub conpendio abreuiata a fratre M. Parisiensi'. It is not an abridgement of any particular manuscript, but a brief chronicle of the kings of England from Alfred onwards. The names of the kings, sometimes accompanied by drawings of them, are written in central medallions, and their children are shown in small medallions below. In general scheme it is very like the illustrated versions of Peter of Poitier's universal chronicle, and indeed Matthew may well have based it on manuscript number 96 in the Library of Eton College, which was probably executed at St Albans during his lifetime.[2] The subject-matter of Matthew's genealogical chronicle of the kings of England is brief and unimportant. He wrote several different versions of it, for that in *A* (f. ivb and p. 285) differs considerably from that in *B* (ff. iiia–b); and that in the *Abbreviatio Chronicorum*[3] differs from them both. Copies and versions of this chronicle are very numerous, and it was evidently a popular work. John of Wallingford included it in his collection of historical material,[4] and another nearly contemporary copy has

[1] *V*, ff. 101b–102.   [2] See below, p. 225.
[3] Brit. Mus. Cotton MS. Claudius D vi, ff. 6b–8a.
[4] Brit. Mus. Cotton MS. Julius D vii, ff. 56b–59b.

been preserved in the form of a separate parchment roll, with Merlin's prophecies written out on the verso.[1]

It cannot be denied that Matthew Paris was an extremely unsystematic worker, and he seems to have been constantly striving to improve on what he had written. Besides producing a number of shorter versions of his main chronicle, he frequently went back over his manuscripts, making additions and corrections, and, especially towards the end of his life, erasures and alterations. These latter represent an attempt at a systematic expurgation of his manuscripts on a far larger scale than that carried out, for instance, by William of Malmesbury. Matthew is a remarkably outspoken writer, and he seems to have realized, as early as 1250, that many of the offensive comments, scandalous reports and bitter complaints, in reference especially to the king, which adorned the text of his *Chronica Majora*, ought not to be reproduced in a fair copy. He therefore went through *B*, pointing out in the margins with the word *vacat*, or something similar, the passages to be omitted by the scribe of the fair copy.[2] He did not, however, go through *B* very systematically, and many passages just as offensive as those marked *vacat* were left unnoticed. Moreover the scribe of *C*, the existing fair copy of *B*, frequently included passages marked *vacat* in his text, and most of those he noticed are only relegated to the margin, instead of being omitted altogether. All but three of the twenty passages either omitted from, or written into the margin of, *C*, because they are marked *vacat* in *B*, cast aspersions on King Henry III. It is difficult to understand the object of this partial expurgation, unless Matthew was planning to produce an expurgated version of his *Chronica Majora*, perhaps for the king himself, which was to have been copied from *C*, the scribe being instructed to omit the marginalia in that manuscript. Be this as it may, it was not for several years that Matthew again resorted to expurgation, and this time it was *B* itself which suffered.

In the *Chronica Majora* the expurgation extends in *B* and *R* from the annal for 1241 up to that for 1257. Up to 1250 the text of all the passages either erased or altered in *B* is preserved

---

[1] Gerould, 'A text of Merlin's prophecies', *Speculum*, XXIII (1948), pp. 102–3.   [2] See pp. 64–5 above.

for us in C; but after this annal the original reading is lost, and consequently we cannot always be sure of the nature of the offending remarks. The work of expurgation is neither systematically, nor very thoroughly, carried out. There is none at all, for instance, in the annals for 1251 and 1252, nor before the annal for 1241. Even between 1241 and 1250 the expurgation was far from thorough, and Matthew seems to have worked at it patchily and more or less at random. If we take Luard's fourth volume of the *Chronica Majora*, which includes the annals 1240–7, we find that passages either rewritten or simply erased occur (apart from a few solitary ones) in well-defined groups;[1] and that, outside these groups, many passages are left which are just as offensive as some of those expurgated.[2] Even in those parts of B in which these groups of expurgated passages occur, where we might expect to find the work of expurgation efficiently carried out, it is not. Had Matthew set about his work more thoroughly, for instance, he would surely not have left the words 'and the papal Charybdis devoured all his goods' untouched, at the end of a paragraph whence the words 'inspired by manifest avarice', in reference to the pope, have been expunged as offensive.[3] Although this work of expurgation is evidently due to Matthew himself, his scribe rewrote a number of passages for him.[4] In B (1241–53), nineteen passages of more than a line in length are erased with nothing substituted, and thirteen have been erased and rewritten, four by Matthew and nine by his scribe. In British Museum Royal MS. 14 C vii (R; 1254–9), where not a single passage has been merely erased, three passages of more than a line in length have been rewritten by Matthew, and nineteen by his scribe. The largest number of such passages expurgated in any one annal occurs in that for 1254 (twelve), and the second largest in 1255 (four). Towards the end of B the editing diminishes in frequency, so that in the last five annals (1249–53) only three passages of more than a line have been erased, and only one of these is rewritten. The scribe who helped Matthew with the rewriting of these passages is the

---

[1] At pp. 101–5, 206–11, 254–65, 396–410, 509–14, 553–65 and 604–19. For some of the solitary passages, see pp. 279, 360, 425 and 639.

[2] See pp. 9, 137, 547 and 577–8 etc.   [3] *CM.* IV, pp. 604–5.

[4] For instance at *CM.* IV, pp. 360, 509 and 510.

same as the one who finished for him the texts of the *Chronica Majora*, the *Historia Anglorum* and the *Abbreviatio Chronicorum*, and he appears to have been called in to help only towards the end of Matthew's life.[1] This suggests a late date for the expurgation of the *Chronica Majora*, and the fact that it extends up to the annal for 1257, and that there is no noticeable change in the tone of the *Chronica Majora* right up to its close, supports this suggestion. A comparison of the *Historia Anglorum* and the *Chronica Majora* shows that the former was copied before the editing had been carried out in the latter, and this fact, too, points to a late date for the expurgation of *B* and *R*. Moreover, the presence of a number of passages erased (as well as the tearing out of a whole leaf at one point),[2] but with nothing substituted, makes it probable that the work of editing has been left unfinished. It seems, in fact, to have been carried out at the end of Matthew's life (1258-9), and to have been begun with the annals after 1253, in *R*. Matthew seems to have expurgated this part of his *Chronica Majora* first, and then to have turned to the earlier part of its text, in *B*, beginning at the annal for 1241, and working unsystematically through the succeeding annals, until death overtook him in the midst of his labours.

An analysis of those expurgated passages whose original reading is ascertainable shows that they included both abusive words and phrases, and factual material presented in a scurrilous or tendentious manner. Apart from a few erasures of single words and phrases, and omitting also the erased chapter-headings, I have counted sixty-one edited passages in the *Chronica Majora*. Of forty-three of these it is possible to be certain of the nature of the offence in the original version: fifteen were offensive to the papacy; twelve to Archbishop Boniface; nine to the king; three to the friars; and one each to Richard of Cornwall, Robert Grosseteste, the papal legate in Norway, and the king's mother. It seems likely, as pointed out above, that Matthew intended to rewrite most of the passages which have been merely erased. No doubt, for instance, the leaf describing Archbishop Boniface's activities on Visitation, which he tore out altogether, would have been replaced by another with a milder account of this; and the same is probably

---

[1] See above, p. 10, and note 3.   [2] See *CM.* v, pp. xii–xiii.

true of the offensive passage against the friars, which he erased, but did not rewrite.[1] But in some cases single words, such as 'turpiter', 'enormiter', 'indecens', 'falsum', etc., or offensive chapter-headings, such as 'Fratres Predicatores et Minores fiunt theolonarii papae',[2] have been erased apparently without any intention of substituting milder ones. Where a passage has been erased, and another substituted, a comparison of the two versions is often illuminating. Sometimes the second reading is a toned-down version of the first, as in the following example:[3]

First reading: But the king, realizing the hidden snares and detesting the greed of the Roman court....

Second reading: But the king, realizing that a thing of this kind was harmful to that church, and likewise to others....

But frequently the second, edited reading has a quite different emphasis from the first. For instance, in one place in the *Chronica Majora*[4] Matthew at first described Archbishop Boniface as 'a man...insufficient for such a dignity, when compared to his predecessors the archbishops of Canterbury, in learning, manners, and years...'; but he later erased this, and wrote instead: 'a man of tall stature and elegant body, the uncle of the lady Eleanor, the illustrious Queen of England...'.

Sometimes the second passage contradicts what was said in the first. For instance, Matthew originally put into the mouth of a French noble the statement that King Henry III unjustly hanged Constantine FitzAthulf;[5] but this has been erased, and in the passage substituted for it the noble is made to state explicitly that the king knew nothing about it! On several occasions, too, the second passage has no connexion whatsoever with the first: thus Matthew's description of Boniface's oppression of the Canterbury monks in 1244[6] is altered into an account of the bishop of Winchester's reception by the king.

Matthew's expurgation of the *Historia Anglorum* was much more thorough and effective than that of the *Chronica Majora*. It begins with the early thirteenth-century annals, and continues

---

[1] For the torn-out leaf, see above, p. 119, note 2. For the attack on the friars: *CM.* IV, pp. 279–80. [2] *CM.* V, p. 73. [3] *CM.* IV, p. 102.
[4] IV, p. 104. [5] *CM.* IV, p. 206. [6] *CM.* IV, p. 360.

nearly up to the end. There are some passages, mostly in the margin, which have been erased, and nothing substituted; but, apart from these few, the expunged passages in the *Historia Anglorum* have been replaced with milder ones, written either on the erasure itself, or on a piece of vellum pasted down over the original passage. All the expurgation in the *Historia Anglorum*, save for one passage in the annal for 1252 which was rewritten by his scribe,[1] was carried out by Matthew himself. As in the *Chronica Majora*, most of the expurgated passages were of a kind calculated to give offence to pope, king, or archbishop, but the editing in the *Historia Anglorum* is on a bigger scale altogether than that in the *Chronica Majora*. The account of John's reign, for instance, is altered slightly in tone by a large number of minute alterations, as when 'collectioni' is substituted for 'extorsioni', or 'iracundiam' for 'tyrannidem'.[2] In the annals for 1244–50 so many passages have been expurgated and others substituted, that the whole character of this part of the *Historia Anglorum* has been altered and toned down. The alterations are often minute, but subtle; and Matthew seems to have gone through the whole manuscript very carefully. In every case Madden did his best, usually with success, to read the earlier, expunged passage, but in cases of simple erasure and rewriting over the erasure this was often impossible; and we have to guess at the nature of the alteration when we find, for instance, William of Valence described, on an erasure, as 'vir elegans et generosus'.[3] Often a comparison with the *Chronica Majora* will help to establish the original reading in the *Historia Anglorum*. In his account, for instance, of the baptism of Edward, the eldest son of Henry III, Matthew records that Otho, the papal legate, baptized the child, and continues, a little clumsily: 'ubi praesens extitit archiepiscopus Cantuariensis Edmundus'. In the *Historia Anglorum*, where this sentence occurs, the words 'ubi' and 'extitit' are on erasures, and the original reading must have been, as in the *Chronica Majora*, 'licet praesens esset archiepiscopus': a subtle piece of editing![4]

The scope and technique of Matthew's expurgation of the *Historia Anglorum* are noteworthy, and throw a great deal of

---

[1] *HA.* III, p. 127. [2] *HA.* II, pp. 102, note 1, and 108, note 3.
[3] *HA.* II, p. 421. [4] *HA.* II, p. 422, and *CM.* III, p. 540.

light on his mentality. Here is an example, where the second passage was pasted down over the first on a slip of vellum, so that Madden was able to print them both, which shows him at work in a way characteristic of the expurgation in both the *Historia Anglorum* and the *Chronica Majora*.

First version:[1] At this time the Dominicans and Franciscans diligently busied themselves in their now lucrative preaching, and, working hard on behalf of the crusade to the extent of making themselves hoarse with vociferation and preaching, they bestowed the Cross on people of every age, sex, and condition, including invalids. But on the following day, or even immediately afterwards, receiving back the Cross for whatever price, they absolved those who had taken it from their vow of pilgrimage, and collected the money into the treasury of some powerful person. To simple people this seemed unseemly and ridiculous, and the devotion of many was cooled, for it was being sold like sheep for their fleeces; and out of this no small scandal arose.

Second version:[2] At this time the Dominicans and Franciscans, as well as others expert and learned in the art of preaching, busied themselves with their sermons, and, sowing useful seed in God's field, they produced manifold fruit. And in order that Christ's faithful should not be deprived of the advantage of the indulgence which they promised to those who took the Cross for the crusade, they courteously received a redemption according to the means of each, so that, with the help of God's great munificence, a ready will might be reckoned as good as the deed. For it was considered that women, children, and invalids, as well as poor and unarmed people, would be of little use against the armed multitude of infidels.

In some cases the substituted passage describes something quite different from what was at first related. One passage casting aspersions on Archbishop Boniface,[3] for instance, is pasted over with a vellum slip, on which Matthew wrote some innocuous remarks describing Henry III's request for prayers to be made for a male heir, suggested, no doubt, by the next entry in the *Historia Anglorum*, which recorded the birth of his son. Covering up his many attacks on Boniface seems to have taxed Matthew's ingenuity, for another of them is pasted over with a harmless but apparently entirely fictitious meteorological entry![4]

[1] *HA.* III, pp. 51 and 52, note 3.   [2] *HA.* III, pp. 51–2.
[3] *HA.* II, p. 499.   [4] *HA.* II, pp. 489–90.

The editing of the *Historia Anglorum* was evidently not carried out in a hurry, and one passage at least has been rewritten twice: first, on an erasure (and also with a plummet in the lower margin), and afterwards on a slip of vellum stuck down over the text.[1] After the middle of the annal for 1251 in the *Historia Anglorum* there is no further editing,[2] though there are one or two harsh passages which perhaps ought to have been edited.[3] The cessation of the expurgation during the annal for 1251 makes it likely that it was carried out before Matthew finished writing the *Historia Anglorum*. Unfortunately, however, there is very little evidence as to its date, and we can only conclude, tentatively, that it was carried out towards the end of Matthew's life, and probably during the years 1256–9.

A number of passages in the *Historia Anglorum* are marked with red letters in the margin *vacat*, or *vacat quia offendiculum*, in just the same way as passages in *B* were pointed out for omission in *C*;[4] and it seems probable that these notices were intended as a guide to Matthew (or a possible scribe) in the writing of the *Abbreviatio Chronicorum*, for a number of passages marked in this way are omitted in that work. A careful comparison of the texts of the *Historia Anglorum* and the *Abbreviatio Chronicorum* shows that, up to about the annal for 1243, the *Abbreviatio* was abridged from the original, unaltered text of the *Historia*, while from this point onwards it seems to derive from the expurgated, altered text.

Why did Matthew Paris expurgate his works in this way? In the case of his fair copy of the *Chronica Majora* in *C*, the expurgation was, in the main, limited to passages offensive to the king. It was carried out while that manuscript was being written, probably *c.* 1250, and we have suggested that its object was perhaps to produce a fair copy of the *Chronica* suitable for presentation to the king.[5] Now Madden thought that the expurgation of the *Historia Anglorum* was perhaps carried out with this object in view.[6] It is a fact that the sudden cessation of the expurgation during the annal for 1251 in the *Historia Anglorum*

---

[1] *HA.* II, p. 455, note 4.
[2] Save for one passage rewritten by Matthew's scribe at III, p. 127.
[3] See e.g. *HA.* III, pp. 125–9. [4] See above, pp. 64–5 and 117.
[5] Above, p. 117. [6] *HA.* III, p. xxxii.

coincides with the cessation of a series of explicit references to documents in Matthew's other manuscripts. Up to the annal for 1251, these references have nearly all been altered into vague, general ones, while, after the 1251 annal, vague general references occur in the text. It does seem possible, as we suggested above,[1] that the expurgation and the alteration of the references to documents were undertaken with the same end: to make the book suitable for someone outside St Albans, perhaps the king. If so, the intention was certainly never carried out, for, on f. 6b of the *Historia Anglorum*, there is an inscription in Matthew's own hand recording his gift of the book to St Albans. Luard suggested that the editing of the *Chronica Majora* may have been carried out by Matthew for fear of giving offence to the king: for Henry III was a frequent visitor to St Albans.[2] But this is hardly an adequate explanation, for Matthew was already well known to the king in 1247, and Henry visited St Albans at least five times between 1250 and 1256; yet the *Chronica Majora* was probably not expurgated until 1258–9. It seems much more likely that the expurgation of the *Chronica Majora* was a product of advancing years: the result of a resolve, on Matthew's part, to try to correct some of his extravagances, many of which he must have realized were unjust and undeserved. The thought of approaching death perhaps led him to soften his animosity towards old friends like the king and public figures like Archbishop Boniface; and he may have been impelled, by a fear of Divine Judgement, to expunge or tone down his most violent attacks on the papacy. Qualms of conscience may well have afflicted a Benedictine monk who had recorded that 'the papal court stinks to the high heavens',[3] and who had cast so many aspersions on his king and archbishop. Be this as it may, it is certainly fortunate for us that this expurgation was unsystematically carried out, and, at any rate in the *Chronica Majora*, never finished; for, had it been more thorough and complete, Matthew might never have earned his well-deserved reputation for outspokenness, nor left some of his more vigorous and colourful prejudices on record for posterity.

[1] P. 73.   [2] *CM.* IV, pp. xii–xiii.   [3] *CM.* IV, p. 410.

CHAPTER VIII

MATTHEW PARIS THE CHRONICLER

THE large corpus of historical material which Matthew Paris has left us includes five works of general interest: the *Chronica Majora*, *Historia Anglorum*, *Abbreviatio Chronicorum*, *Flores Historiarum* and the *Liber Additamentorum*; but the last of these is in effect only an appendix or supplement to the *Chronica Majora*. Compared to the *Chronica Majora*, their source, the *Historia Anglorum*, *Abbreviatio Chronicorum* and the *Flores Historiarum* are of only incidental value, and our study of Matthew Paris as a writer and chronicler will therefore be based on the *Chronica Majora*. As a historian, in the sense of one who studies the past, Matthew is of little significance, for his efforts at historical research were limited to the collection of some annalistic material, and the composition of the *Vitae Offarum*, a work which contains a number of absurd historical blunders—as, for instance, the statement that the first St Albans monks came from the abbey of Bec in Normandy[1]—and which betrays, on the part of its author, a very slight knowledge of the historical Offa of Mercia. The real importance of Matthew's writing lies in his detailed account of the events of his own lifetime. He drew the *Chronica Majora* to its intended close in 1250 with these words:[2] 'Here ends the chronicle of Brother Matthew Paris, monk of St Albans, which he has written down for the use of posterity and for the love of God and St Alban, lest age or oblivion efface the memory of modern events.'

Evidently his primary object was the recording of contemporary events, and he did this in fuller detail than almost any other medieval writer. His own section of the *Chronica Majora* extends from 1236 to 1259, and almost the whole of this, amounting to some 300,000 words, has survived in autograph. It includes accounts of events in England, Wales, Scotland, France, Germany, Italy, the Iberian peninsula, Denmark,

---

[1] Wats, p. 30. Bec was founded in 1039, some 250 years after St Albans.
[2] v, p. 197.

Norway, and the East; indeed, it seems that Matthew considered no information irrelevant, in spite of the fact that he thought of his chronicle, primarily, as a history of England. He well understood the importance of supporting and amplifying his narrative with documentary material, and he has preserved copies, in the *Chronica Majora* and the *Liber Additamentorum*, of some 350 documents of all kinds. Of these, about 100 are of domestic (St Albans) interest only. Among those of general interest are about forty royal letters and writs; some twenty letters of Frederick II; and about sixty papal documents. Matthew Paris, on account of the scope and size of his chronicle alone, is unique among medieval English chroniclers.

Matthew's Latin style is vigorous, forceful, and direct: there is no artificial elegance about it, and little conscious artistry. It is blunt and straightforward, yet often lively and colourful. Although it is the rough, unpolished, downright writing of a man of limited intelligence and fixed ideas, yet it is always vivid and expressive. It is individual enough to be easily recognizable, and N. Denholm-Young noted the interesting fact that, even in his use of the *cursus*, Matthew is peculiar.[1] His style is rather stereotyped, and he tends to be repetitive in his use of certain phrases, biblical and classical allusions, descriptive epithets, and the like. Some of these recur over and over again, so that their presence can be used to demonstrate his authorship of doubtful works.[2] Here are some of the phrases and allusions of which he was particularly fond:

seminarium discordiae	felix suscepit incrementum
zelo justitiae	novit Ipse qui nihil ignorat
in ore gladii	quorum numerum longum foret
quod est inauditum	explicare
secus quam deceret	ab alto (*or* immo) trahens
dignum duximus huic libro	suspirium
inserere	sicut sequens sermo declarabit
versus in arcum pravum	nec censeo praetereundum
patulis rictibus inhiantes	immo potius
in magna cordis amaritudine	haec iccirco dixerim

[1] Denholm-Young, *Handwriting in England and Wales*, p. 52. See also Browne, *British Latin Selections*, pp. xxxvii–xxxviii.
[2] See Chapter III above, pp. 38 ff.

nimis moleste ferens	ne mundus iste prospera sine
in triste praesagium	adversis impermixta
tractatus exigeret speciales	negotium martis
libra rationis trutinare	torvo vultu (*or* oculo)
infausto sidere	pedibus equinis
ut plura paucis perstringamus	parvipendendo immo potius
in arcto positus	vilipendendo
factus de rege tirannus	nodum in scirpo quaerere
ut viderentur Apostolorum	si scriberentur taedium audien-
tempora renovari	tibus generarent
quasi a servis ultimae conditionis	

In vocabulary, too, Matthew tends to be repetitive, and to use the same, often rather colourful, words over and over again, such as:

cruentus	saginari	quisquiliae
inhiare	ridiculosus	truculenter
subsannare	procaciter	vindemiare (pecuniam)
vispilio	muscipulum	impudenter

Neologisms and unusual words or phrases also occur, for instance: 'Romipedes'; 'clericulus'; and 'Fretherizare'.

A characteristic feature of Matthew's style is his love of play on words, frequently expressed by the use of pairs of words of similar form but different meaning. Some of the commonest of these are: 'mellitus' and 'mollitus'; 'misertus' and 'miseratus'; 'durus' and 'dirus'; 'doto' and 'dito'; 'plures' and 'pluries'; 'volo' and 'valeo'.

As with vocabulary, so with imagery Matthew tends to be limited in resources and repetitive; and the following metaphors occur many times:

> like birds in a net
> like a thorn in the eye
> as if between two millstones
> clearer than light
> like sand without lime
> like a mountain torrent

The metaphor from Isaiah, of the splintering staff which pierces the hand, is very frequently used; as well as that from the

Psalms of the vineyard without a wall, pillaged by passers-by.[1] England is often likened to an inexhaustible well; and when one thing or person is superior to another, the relationship is compared to the superiority of St Albans over the other English abbeys, or of St Alban over the other English saints. Matthew's imagery often reflects his interest in natural phenomena of all kinds. In this connexion, the following metaphors are among the most striking:

> like blind men feeling along a wall[2]
> like throwing a bone to a crowd of dogs[3]
> like bees coming out of a hive[4]
> like a cuckoo supplanting its foster-parent[5]
> like a mouse in a sack[6]
> like a bladder in frosty weather[7]
> like pouring cold water into a boiling cauldron[8]

Matthew has the usual medieval repertory of biblical and classical quotations; the latter perhaps taken from a *Florilegium*. He delights in misquoting a line from a Latin poet to suit his own purposes; for instance he quotes Lucan:[9]

> ...omnisque potestas
> Impatiens consortis erit...

and gives an alternative version with 'superbus' instead of 'potestas'. He seems to have been much pleased with this emendation, for he uses it on three more occasions in the *Chronica Majora*, and once in the *Historia Anglorum*. Some of the classical quotations are repeated up to six times. Ovid is the most frequently cited author, with thirty-two quotations in all; Horace comes next, with eleven; Juvenal follows with six; and Lucan, Claudian and Virgil are each quoted three times. Of late classical and medieval authors Matthew quotes from Justinian; Abdias's apocryphal *Acta Apostolorum*; Bernard Sylvester's *Cosmographia*; Geoffrey of Vinsauf's *Nova Poetria* (four times); and Henry of Avranches and Gervase of Melkeley.

---

[1] Isa. xxxvi. 6, and Ps. lxxix. 13.   [2] *CM.* v, p. 532.
[3] *CM.* v, p. 357.   [4] *FH.* ii, p. 281.
[5] *AC.* p. 322.   [6] *FH.* ii, p. 283.
[7] *CM.* v, p. 31.   [8] *HA.* ii, p. 405.
[9] Lucan, *Phars.* i, 93–4; *CM.* v, p. 77.

He was interested in verse, and is particularly fond of epitaphs and topical verses. About ten of the former are given in the *Chronica Majora*, some, perhaps, taken from his own collection of verse in University Library, Cambridge, MS. Dd xi 38.[1] Biblical quotations are frequent in all Matthew's historical writings, but they are unevenly distributed through the Bible, and an analysis of them would probably reflect Matthew's biblical interest and knowledge. Thus, Luard notices thirty-eight quotations from Psalms; twenty-four from Matthew; seventeen from Luke; nine from Isaiah; five each from Acts, Kings, Proverbs and Galatians; and four each from Peter, Job, Exodus and Timothy. Of historians, Matthew knew and used the great twelfth-century writers William of Malmesbury, Henry of Huntingdon, Florence of Worcester, Robert de Monte, Geoffrey of Monmouth, and Ralph de Diceto;[2] and he made use of later monastic annals from Southwark, Reading, Coggeshall, Caen and probably Ramsey. Other twelfth-century works mentioned in the *Chronica Majora* are Peter Lombard's *Sentences*; Peter Comestor's *Historia Scholastica*;[3] and a work by William of Tyre on the marvels of the East, which included an account of the capture of Antioch and Jerusalem.[4]

As a writer, Matthew is endowed with considerable descriptive and anecdotal powers; with a talent for recording conversation in direct speech; and with a remarkable flair for the observation and description of incidental details. Furthermore, he has an interest in human beings and in the ordinary episodes of daily life, which is a rare and valuable quality among medieval chroniclers. Notices of curious and interesting detail, which show his eager curiosity in everything about him, as well as his powers of observation, are very common in Matthew's writings. We are given a detailed account of the metal point used at the

[1] See below, p. 260.
[2] The copies of Malmesbury, Geoffrey of Monmouth, and Diceto used by Matthew still exist: the former two in B.M. Royal MS. 13 D v, and the latter in Royal 13 E vi. See Vaughan, 'Handwriting of M. Paris', *Trans. Camb. Bibliog. Soc.* I (1953), p. 391.
[3] The MS. used by Matthew was, presumably, B.M. Royal MS. 4 D vii, which contains examples of his handwriting: see Vaughan, *ibid*.
[4] *HA.* I, p. 163. On Matthew's knowledge of historians and classical literature see Marshall, 'Thirteenth-century culture as illustrated by Matthew Paris', *Speculum*, XIV (1939), pp. 466–71.

end of a lance, in connexion with the accidental killing of a knight during a tournament; the monks' practice of examining the stars in order to discover the right time for Matins is mentioned incidentally; and an invasion of curious birds which broke open the apples in the abbey orchard in order to eat the pips is recorded in 1251.[1] The details provided in the account of the latter leave no doubt that the birds were crossbills, a species which periodically invades the British Isles in large numbers from north-east Europe. Matthew's writings are by no means devoid of human interest and sentiment. For instance, after his account of the king's departure for Gascony in 1253, he continues:[2] 'The boy Edward, who had been kissed and embraced repeatedly by his weeping father, stood on the beach crying and sobbing, for he would not go away while the billowing (*sinuosa*) sails of the ships were still in sight.'

Of Matthew's failings, as a chronicler, one of the most obvious is his carelessness. Many errors, some of language, some due to faulty copying, and some of a historical nature, are to be found in his writings. A characteristic error of language, due to carelessness, occurs in the annal for 1253 of the *Chronica Majora*,[3] where he has forgotten, half-way through a sentence, how he had begun it, so that the construction is altered and nonsense made of the whole passage. A common mistake of this kind is the inadvertent omission of the verb,[4] or some other vital part of a sentence. Matthew is just as careless when copying as he is when composing. Lines are frequently lost through homoeoteleuton, and single words are often copied wrongly, as 'venerabilem' for 'verbalem', 'specialiter' for 'spiritualiter', and 'cotidie' for 'custodie'.[5] Of the many historical blunders which are due to carelessness, we may note the writing of 'Aragon' for 'Navarre', 'Henricus' for 'Ensius', 'tertio' for 'quarto', and 'Maii' for 'Martii'.[6] If Matthew's work is careless, it is also undisciplined and unsystematic. Not one of his manuscripts is a final fair copy: in all of them, marginal additions and corrections show that he went back constantly to re-read,

---

[1] *CM.* v, pp. 319, 422–3, and 254–5.
[2] *CM.* v, p. 383.   [3] v, p. 367, note 1.
[4] See, for instance, *CM.* iv, p. 550, and v, p. 100.
[5] *CM.* vi, p. 486; p. 478; iv, p. 413, note 2.
[6] *CM.* iv, p. 79, note 1; p. 124, note 1; and v, pp. 638, note 2; 431, note 3.

revise and amplify what he had already written. Additional information, not in the *Chronica Majora*, is to be found in the *Historia Anglorum, Flores Historiarum*, and even the *Abbreviatio Chronicorum*. A fault common to all these works, which demonstrates Matthew's lack of order and control, is the frequent repetition, whether of isolated entries,[1] or of a whole series of entries;[2] and sometimes an entry is made in the margin, as if to remedy an omission in the text, when it has already been entered there.[3]

Matthew's carelessness makes him an inaccurate, and therefore frequently unreliable, writer, but his reliability can only be properly assessed by an examination of his veracity. He himself was certainly conscious on occasions of his duty to record the truth, for in one place he expatiates on the difficulty of doing this: 'The lot of historians is hard indeed, for, if they speak the truth, they provoke man, and if they record falsehoods they offend God.'[4] Elsewhere in the *Chronica Majora* we find the incidental remark 'lest I should insert something false in this book', which shows, at any rate, that he recognized his obligations in this respect.[5] There is, too, a note written with a plummet in the margin of f. 244 of *B*, which reflects his regard for accuracy; for, in reference to a certain Guido, mentioned in the text, he writes: 'Dubium si Guido vel Galfridus.' On the other hand, Matthew's pious statements about his intentions cannot be accepted at their face value. In reference to the pope, for instance, he makes a thoroughly hypocritical remark: 'The Lord, Judge of all judges, will judge if he has done well...for it is not my business to judge papal actions.'[6] In the very next annal, however, we find, in reference to a papal letter obtained by the bishop of Hereford, the exclamation: 'Alas! For shame and grief! These and other detestable things emanated at this time from the sulphurous fountain of the Roman church.'[7]

In fact, Matthew certainly sometimes allows himself considerable licence in the reporting of facts. We have seen how, when he went through his manuscripts striking out the offensive

---

[1] E.g. at *CM.* IV, pp. 8 and 47–8.
[2] Six entries are repeated in the 1257 annal in the *Chronica Majora*.
[3] E.g. at *CM.* IV, p. 207, and note 3.
[4] *CM.* v, pp. 469–70.   [5] *CM.* v, p. 262.
[6] *CM.* v, p. 459.   [7] *CM.* v, p. 524.

passages and substituting milder ones, he sometimes concocted an apparently fictitious entry to replace the erased passage.[1] A careful examination of his copies of documents convicts him of occasionally tampering with their texts, even to the extent of deliberate falsification, although he evidently understood the importance of documents as historical evidence, and had a great deal of respect for them. In one place, for instance, he goes out of his way to point out that he was copying from an original letter, to which twelve seals were appended.[2] But the possibility of tampering with the texts of the documents he was copying was always there; and to this standing temptation Matthew from time to time unfortunately succumbed. In the *Chronica Majora*, for instance, he copied from Roger Wendover the text of an imperial letter written from Jerusalem, describing Frederick's recovery of that city. But when he came to transcribe this letter into the *Florès Historiarum*, he could not resist the temptation of adding to it the following fictitious report of the emperor's troubles on his return:[3]

But, because in this world bitter things are invariably mixed with sweet, when we were returning to our Empire—the way being with difficulty open—we crushed our enemies, who were supported to our detriment by our father the pope, and managed to put a stop to their sedition. Had not this business recalled us in great haste, the state of the church would, by the grace of God, have been consolidated and wonderfully improved.

At the end of the annal for 1237 in the *Chronica Majora* a group of four letters has been inserted, written in fact in 1232, which passed between Pope Gregory IX and the patriarch, Germanus, of Constantinople; and there are a number of material additions to the texts of the patriarch's two letters, though those of the pope are left untouched.[4] Matthew begins with the insertion into the patriarch's first letter of a long

---

[1] See above, p. 122.   [2] *CM.* IV, p. 344.
[3] *CM.* III, pp. 173–6; *FH.* II, pp. 197–8; the passage translated is from *FH.* II, p. 198.
[4] These letters are at *CM.* III, pp. 448–69; Luard collates them with the copies in the Vatican, VI, pp. 482–5; and I have collated them with the copies in the *Red Book of the Exchequer*, ff. 184 ff. The passage translated is from *CM.* IV, p. 452, and I have used the translation of Giles, *Matthew Paris's English History*, I, p. 102.

passage aimed at the pope, part of which runs thus: 'And, that we may arrive at the very pith of the truth, many powerful and noble men would obey you, if they did not fear the unjust oppressions, the wanton extortion of money which you practise, and the undue services which you demand of those subject to you.' Having taken the plunge, so to speak, with this long interpolation, Matthew proceeds to make some minor literary improvements to the text of his exemplar; and, warming to his task, he inserts more than a (printed) page of additional matter into the patriarch's second letter, nearly all of which is directed against the Roman church. The patriarch is made to address the cardinals thus:[1] 'It has given rise to offence in our minds, that you gape after earthly possessions whencesoever you can scrape them together, and collect gold and silver...you compel kingdoms to be tributary to you...you multiply money by traffic....'

This unscrupulous tampering with the texts of documents leads us to suspect Matthew of wilful falsification on occasions when we should find a scribe guilty only of carelessness: for instance, at the beginning of his text of Innocent III's famous letter to the English prelates Matthew omits the words 'in Christo filius' from the phrase 'carissimus in Christo filius J(ohannes) rex'.[2] We must be careful, however, not to go too far in accusing Matthew of faking his documentary material, for in fact his texts of documents, though marred by frequent errors, are only occasionally embellished with fanciful 'improvements' of his own, and material interpolations of more than a few words are even rarer. In his Ford lectures, A. L. Smith claimed that the glaring inconsistencies in Matthew's version of Grosseteste's letter complaining of papal abuses are matched by similar inconsistencies in letters circulated 'as from the pen of' the Emperor Frederick II.[3] He implied that Matthew had either fabricated or very seriously tampered with the text of the Grosseteste letter, and that many of his texts of imperial letters had been treated in the same way, though not perhaps by

---

[1] *CM.* III, p. 459. I have again used Giles's translation, *Matthew Paris's English History,* I, p. 107.

[2] 30 March 1215; *CM.* II, p. 607, note 6.

[3] Smith, *Church and State in the Middle Ages,* pp. 103 ff. The authenticity of this letter was first questioned by Jourdain in *Excursions historiques,* pp. 155–7 and 170. For Matthew's copy of it, see *CM.* V, pp. 389–92.

Matthew himself. This, however, is not the case, for Matthew's text of Grosseteste's letter is almost identical with that in the *Red Book of the Exchequer*, and Professor Thomson has demonstrated its authenticity;[1] and there are actually very few interpolations or alterations in the texts of his copies of imperial letters.[2]

Owing to his occasional indulgence in unscrupulous falsification Matthew can never be relied on in his treatment of historical material. When he repeats a good story, the second version often differs considerably from the first. Thus his account of an unnamed cardinal's vision of Innocent IV's judgement is greatly improved and elaborated when it is retailed on the second occasion, and definitely attributed to Alexander IV.[3] Professor Galbraith has shown how Matthew sometimes went so far as to use the same story twice in reference to two different people.[4] Perhaps the most blatant example of his abuse of historical material is his account, during the annal for 1244 in the *Chronica Majora*, of the demands of Master Martin, the papal emissary, and the English prelates' reply to them; for a long passage is taken word for word from Roger Wendover's description of the legate Otho's demands and the prelates' resistance to them, in 1226, the only serious alteration being the substitution of 'Master Martin' for Roger's 'Master Otho'.[5]

Matthew, then, has something of the forger in him. He is neither systematic nor thorough in his fraudulence, but his sporadic tampering with documentary sources, and misuse of historical material, as well as his many errors, make him basically unreliable as a historical source. In his inaccuracy and occasional deceit or wilful misrepresentation Matthew is by no means exceptional. He may be a little more fraudulent than most other medieval chroniclers, but I doubt if he can be singled out as

---

[1] *Writings of R. Grosseteste*, pp. 212–13; see the *Red Book of the Exchequer*, ff. 196 b–197 a.

[2] The only material interpolation I have discovered is that printed above, p. 132. For Matthew's treatment of the text of Magna Carta in his *Chronica Majora*, see *CM.* II, pp. xxxiii–xxxvi.

[3] *CM.* V, pp. 471–2 and 491–3.

[4] *Roger Wendover and Matthew Paris*, p. 36, note 1. See also Smith, *Church and State in the Middle Ages*, p. 177, where he points out that Matthew puts identical words about the pope into the mouths of two different people.   [5] *CM.* III, p. 103, and IV, pp. 374–5.

either more or less careless: certainly he should not be described, as he has been, as 'the most careful writer of his age'.[1]

Before we go on to examine Matthew's outlook and prejudices, there are one or two small points affecting his general veracity which may conveniently be mentioned here. Although he is well known for his habitual outspokenness, and frequently expresses his own opinions directly, his attacks on king and pope are more often put into the mouths of others. Thus it is certain 'holy and religious men' who are disgusted with the pope; and 'many discerning men' are said to have feared that the spread of the Dominican Order would upset the ancient equilibrium of the Church.[2] In this way Matthew conceals his own opinion and at the same time pays himself a discreet compliment; though sometimes, no doubt, these opinions did represent a section of contemporary 'public opinion'. Current rumours are often explicitly reported, some of which, like that of an imminent Danish invasion of England or the conversion of the Mongol Khan to Christianity, turned out later to be false.[3] It is evident that Matthew, in his eagerness to collect information of all kinds, tended to be uncritical in recording it, and this no doubt accounts for a number of the strange tales and curious anecdotes which adorn his chronicle. A large part of the *Chronica Majora* was probably written down more or less directly from oral reports,[4] and some of Matthew's acquaintances seem to have been only too willing to contribute matter redounding to their own merit to the famous chronicle. Professor Knowles points out that 'public men...realized that their share in events could best be preserved for posterity by judicious conversations at St Albans'.[5] The most prominent of these, apart from the king, was Earl Richard of Cornwall, who took the trouble, for example, to inform Matthew of the cost of his religious foundation at Hayles, and to add a pious aspiration

[1] Collins, 'Documents of the Great Charter', *Proc. Brit. Acad.* xxxiv (1948), p. 259. German historians of the thirteenth century have noted Matthew's unreliability, especially in Continental affairs: see, in particular, Felten, *Papst Gregor IX*, pp. 6 and 363, and notes; and Kempf, *Geschichte des deutschen Reiches während des grossen Interregnums*, pp. 269–73.

[2] *CM.* iii, p. 574, and iv, p. 511.   [3] *CM.* iv, p. 9, and v, p. 87.

[4] A list of Matthew's informants is given above, pp. 13–17.

[5] Knowles, *Religious Orders*, i, p. 294. See also Hunt, *Dict. Nat. Biog.* xv, p. 207.

which the chronicler duly noted down.[1] When we consider the worth and reliability of the *Chronica Majora*, it is important to remember that some of it, at least, was contributed in this way by the leading men of the time, who no doubt often exaggerated their own part in affairs.

On the whole, Matthew is careful with chronology, and few events and documents are badly misdated. Information seems to have been entered up on rough drafts more or less as he received it, and copied thence into the *Chronica Majora*, so that an approximate chronological order was usually achieved. Professor Cheney has recently shown that there is no reason to suppose that the famous 'Paper Constitution' of 1244, which Denholm-Young had attributed to 1238, is misplaced in the *Chronica Majora*;[2] and in fact it is only very occasionally that an event or document is inserted under the wrong year.[3] In the dating of events within the year, however, the *Chronica Majora* is often unreliable. Thus the Dominican Chapter of 1250 is described as meeting 'about the Feast of the Nativity of St John the Baptist', that is, *c.* 24 June; but later in the same paragraph it is said to have met 'about Pentecost', *c.* 15 May, in 1250.[4] It is worth noting that Matthew's numbers are no more reliable than those of most medieval chroniclers. On f. 170a of the *Liber Additamentorum*, for instance, he says that in the campaign of 1244 the king of Scotland had 500 knights and 60,000 foot-soldiers; but in the *Chronica Majora* this is altered to 1,000 knights and 100,000 foot-soldiers.[5]

If, when considering Matthew's trustworthiness and veracity as a chronicler, we have to make extensive allowances for his frequent acceptance of verbal reports, for his inclusion of rumours and current opinion, as well as for his periodic disregard for historical accuracy, we must make even larger allowances for his grievances, beliefs, and prejudices; for these

---

[1] *CM.* v, p. 262.

[2] Cheney, 'The Paper Constitution preserved by Matthew Paris', *EHR.* LXV (1950), pp. 213–31, and Denholm-Young, 'The Paper Constitution of 1244', *ibid.* LVIII (1943), pp. 401–23.

[3] For instance, *CM.* IV, pp. 386–9 should be under the year 1245. See also p. 132 above. One document in *LA* is misdated by ten years through careless copying: see Powicke, 'Writ for enforcing watch and ward, 1242', in *EHR.* LVII (1942), p. 469.

[4] *CM.* v, p. 127.   [5] *CM.* VI, p. 518, note 1; IV, p. 380.

colour his whole work. Among English writers, Matthew stands out in front of the curtain of medieval anonymity as a real person, and in his *Chronica Majora* his outlook on life, prejudices, and interests, as well as his personality, are all revealed in a manner unusual among chroniclers of his age. He refers to himself by name on six occasions in the *Chronica Majora*, either as 'Brother Matthew Paris',[1] or simply 'Matthew, the writer of this',[2] or even on one occasion as 'dominus Matthaeus Parisiensis monachus ecclesiae Sancti Albani'.[3] The words 'monachus ecclesiae Sancti Albani' provide a key to the understanding of his whole outlook on life, for this was in a large measure based on his own material interests as a monk, and on those of the small aristocratic community of which he was proud to be a member.[4] In the *Gesta Abbatum* the convent is invariably supported against its abbot; and the apparent moral judgement of each abbot is in reality a purely material one, based on the abbot's treatment of, and value to, the convent; he is praised, for instance, if he gives a rent to the convent for the improvement of its beer or kitchen.[5] In sympathy with his own position, Matthew always supports aristocratic corporations similar to his own against those exercising power over them: he takes the side of the canons of Lincoln against their bishop, the monks of Canterbury against their archbishop,[6] and even the barons against the king. This, of course, is a question of sentiment rather than of political theory, but it affects his habits of mind in just the same way as his zealous devotion to and enthusiasm for his own Order. The extravagant praises he bestows on Hugh Northwold, bishop of Ely—the only bishop at the time who was a Benedictine monk[7]—and his sympathy for the abbots of Westminster and Bardney in their quarrels with Grosseteste,[8] are due, in the main, to his patriotic feelings as a Benedictine. In the *Chronica Majora* the Cistercian monks of Pontigny are

---

[1] v, pp. 129–30.   [2] v, p. 201.   [3] v, p. 369.
[4] See Plehn, 'Der politische Charakter von Matheus Parisiensis', *Staats- und socialwissenschaftliche Forschungen*, XIV (1897), pp. 42–5. In the whole of what follows I am much indebted to this work.
[5] See, on this, Coulton, *Five Centuries of Religion*, III, p. 192.
[6] *CM.* III, pp. 527 ff.
[7] *CM.* v, pp. 454–5; see Gibbs and Lang, *Bishops and Reform, 1215–1272*, pp. 9–10.   [8] *CM.* IV, pp. 151 and 246.

criticized for cutting off the arm of St Edmund, and it is implied that the Benedictines would never have done such a thing:[1] 'Many people, considering how carefully the bodies of saints are venerated in the churches of the Black monks, deplored the fact that the body of so respected a saint should repose in a Cistercian church.'

Apart from the Augustinian canons, who perhaps escaped his diatribes on account of their early foundation, Matthew disapproves of all religious orders other than his own. The Dominicans and Franciscans are often bitterly attacked,[2] and the appearance of new orders of friars like the *cruciferi* and the Bethlehemites calls forth a derogatory remark on the confusion caused by new and unknown orders.[3] Matthew, incidentally, is more favourably disposed towards the Hospitallers than towards the Templars, whom he considered proud, ambitious, and worldly.[4]

Matthew's material interests are paramount, too, in his attitude towards the important contemporary movements for Church reform. He does not understand the significance of the efforts of men like Archbishop Boniface and Robert Grosseteste, and he frequently criticizes their visitations, especially of Benedictine houses, for their thoroughness and efficiency.[5] Matthew, indeed, though he is prepared to admire the sanctity of the monks of earlier days,[6] is against any attempt at interference with the privileged social existence of the monks of his own day, and his idea of what a visitation ought to be must have been similar to that which took place at St Albans in 1251;[7] which seems to have been little more than a social visit, with ample warning, by the prior of Hurley, the sub-prior of St Augustine's, Canterbury, and a papal chaplain. In spite of his habitual support of chapters against royal interference in the election of bishops, Matthew was quite out of touch with the ideas of some of the leading churchmen of his day on the subject of the independence of the Church from secular interference. Here, again, it is sentiment and prejudice which mould his

---

[1] *CM.* v, p. 113.
[2] For instance, at *CM.* iv, pp. 279–80, 511–12, 599–600, etc.
[3] *CM.* iv, pp. 393–4, and v, p. 631.
[4] *CM.* iv, pp. 167–8.   [5] See for example *CM.* v, pp. 226–7.
[6] *CM.* v, pp. 243–4.   [7] *CM.* v, pp. 258–9.

attitude rather than informed opinion. He seems to approve of Henry III's prohibition of Grosseteste's proposed inquisition into the morals of his diocese;[1] and he does not complain of the king's interference in Grosseteste's dispute with his chapter.[2] His opposition to royal interference in episcopal elections is arbitrary and conventional, and often bears little relation to the realities of the situation. Sometimes his indignation is aroused because a foreigner is appointed, or a religious rejected; more often it is due to the appointment by the king of a *curialis*; and when the monks or canons themselves elect one of the latter, Matthew adds a conventional surmise that this was because they feared the king would oppose any other person.[3]

Matthew's view of the State, often referred to as his 'constitutional' attitude, seems also to be based on his own material interests and those of his house. All forms of taxation are violently opposed and invariably regarded as mere royal extortion, even when the tax has been agreed to by the *universitas regni*. For instance, we are told that Henry III 'extorted' (*fecit extorqueri*) a scutage in 1242, whereas in fact this had been agreed to by the barons.[4] Matthew's hatred of taxation leads him to oppose other aspects of government as mere tyrannical interference on the part of the king, and both forest inquisitions and itinerant justices are bitterly complained of. The latter are regarded merely as royal financial agents,[5] and Matthew refers to a sum of money raised by Henry III in 1254 with the words '...whatever he could extract from the rapines of the itinerant justices'.[6] He complains, too, of the royal administration of vacant bishoprics, and regards the government's inquiry into weights and measures in 1256 purely as a device for raising money.[7] From this ingenuous disapproval of almost all forms of governmental activity Matthew no doubt derived his view of a monarch chosen and controlled by his barons: the royal extortions must somehow be checked. His political outlook was evidently in some respects extremely superficial. His most profound thought on the constitutional struggle of his day is the

[1] *CM.* IV, pp. 579–80. [2] *CM.* IV, p. 156.
[3] See Gibbs and Lang, *Bishops and Reform*, p. 89.
[4] *CM.* IV, p. 227; Plehn, 'Der politische Charakter von Matheus Parisiensis', *loc. cit.* pp. 62–3.
[5] *CM.* IV, p. 34 [6] *CM.* V, p. 458. [7] *CM.* V, pp. 594–5.

precept which, having once got hold of, he blindly adheres to, that the king should take the advice of his natural counsellors. He did not understand the significance of the struggle for power which was going on during his lifetime between the barons and the king. His account of the events of 1258, for instance, shows that he was neither so well informed, nor so conscious of the significance of what was going on, as the Burton annalist.[1] So far as one can judge from his description of the 'Parliament' at Oxford, its only interest for him was in the successful expulsion of Henry III's Poitevin councillors, and the appointment of Hugh Bigod as justiciar.[2] Elsewhere Matthew describes how the corrupt practices and illegal extortions of the sheriffs were to be heavily punished, but he does not connect this with the baronial plan of reform.[3] Indeed it is clear that Matthew understood very little of the nature and significance of the baronial reform movement, and still less of the events of 1258. On the other hand, his interest in political issues cannot be denied, and he evidently had some idea of what constituted a community, and what was meant by representation. In one place he quotes the well-known maxim 'what touches all should be approved by all';[4] and elsewhere he claims that, if the bishops had united together and sent a representative to Rome, all would have been well.[5] It is interesting to find that he seems to regard the monarchy as elective, a belief which demonstrates a certain grasp of political theory. Thus he alters Roger Wendover's statement that the barons 'crowned' Henry III to 'raised him up';[6] and he makes Hubert Walter state, at the coronation of King John, that he had been made king as the result of popular choice.[7]

Matthew's view of the Church in general, and of the papacy in particular, is similar to, and apparently based on the same feelings as, his view of the State.[8] All methods of raising money on behalf of the pope are considered extortionate; and almost all forms of papal interference in England are condemned as

---

[1] But it is fair to note that Matthew was at this time an old man, no doubt with failing powers.

[2] *CM.* v, pp. 697–8.   [3] *CM.* v, p. 720.   [4] *CM.* v, p. 225.

[5] *CM.* v, p. 532.   [6] *CM.* III, p. 1, 'exaltant'.   [7] *CM.* II, pp. 454 ff.

[8] For what follows see Plehn, 'Der politische Charakter von Matheus Parisiensis', *loc. cit.* pp. 94 ff.

obnoxious and oppressive. Matthew is bitterly hostile to papal provisions; he thinks it disgraceful that England should be a papal fief; and he maintains that, just as the barons should resist royal demands, so the bishops should resist those of the pope. His hostility to the papacy is neither the result of rational consideration, nor of informed opinion, but of resentment and prejudice. It is expressed in the form of comments on papal extortion, avarice, simony, rapine, gluttony, licentiousness and temporal ambition, which occur so frequently as to become purely conventional; as well as in the form of mere abusive language. As with the king, so with the pope, almost every piece of governmental activity is interpreted as an attempt at extortion. Gregory IX's decretal that illegitimate priests must get a papal dispensation to hold a benefice, the absolution of would-be crusaders from their vows, and the dispatch of papal legates and others to England are all regarded as mere devices for raising money.[1] Matthew was always ready to report adverse rumours about the papacy, and to retail any scandalous stories which he heard. He reports that many people believed that the Cahorsin money-lenders were supported by the pope;[2] and he tells a story, in the form of a sermon by one of the cardinals to the citizens of Lyons, to the effect that the papal court had done a great deal of good while it was in Lyons, for it had converted the three or four brothels in the town when it first arrived there into one large brothel stretching right across it.[3] It is interesting to note that, in spite of all his disparagement of the papacy, Matthew on one occasion, when he is describing the schismatical Greek church (as we shall see, the Greeks were one of his *bêtes noires*), becomes a staunch supporter of papal supremacy, with only one slight qualification:[4] 'But that pillar of the church, the lord pope, the true successor—though not quite the perfect imitator—of St Peter, remained firm.'

Although many of Matthew's prejudices were evidently due to his monastic status, his nationality also played an important part in moulding his attitude.[5] His hatred of authority, for

---

[1] *CM.* III, pp. 328 and 374; IV, pp. 84 and 284–5.
[2] *CM.* III, p. 331.   [3] *CM.* V, p. 237.   [4] *CM.* III, p. 519.
[5] I use the word nationality in its widest sense, for it is not certain that Matthew was English by blood.

instance, is a typically English prejudice rather than a Benedictine one. 'England', he says in his genealogical chronicle,[1]
'is the queen of all islands.' The English are considered superior
to all other peoples, and foreigners are treated with a characteristically English contempt. Among them, the especial objects
of Matthew's dislike are the French, Poitevins, Welsh, Greeks,
and Flemings. He refers to the 'habitual insolence' of the
Greeks;[2] those 'wily traitors' the Poitevins;[3] the pride and envy
of the French;[4] and the 'filthy ignoble Flemings'.[5] At first[6]
the Welsh are described with opprobrium, and are called savage
and faithless; but later their resistance to the English is admired:
'Like the Trojans, from whom they are descended, they fought
firmly for their ancestral laws and liberties.'[7] For the queen's
relatives, Poitevins, Provençals, and Savoyards, who came over
to England after Henry's marriage in 1236, Matthew has feelings
of hatred and disgust which seem to have increased in intensity
as he grew older. Thus, in the part of the *Chronica Majora*
before the annal for 1252, they are accused of coming to England
to fatten themselves at the expense of the natives;[8] of bringing
over their female relatives for the purpose of making advan-
tageous marriages with the English nobility;[9] and, in one case,
of borrowing some horses from the abbot of Faversham and
omitting to return them.[10] Later they are called 'the scum of a
terrible rabble',[11] and we are told that they swarmed all over the
city of London in company with other foreigners, 'committing
adulteries, fornicating, brawling, wounding, and murdering'.[12]
Other typically English prejudices of Matthew Paris are against
civil servants, lawyers, and theologians. Lawyers are said to
rise to fame much too quickly for the good of their souls;
students are denigrated because they study law with an eye to
future emoluments; and theologians are criticized for daring to
inquire into the impenetrable secrets of the Almighty.[13] Matthew's healthy dislike of civil servants is reflected in a passage
where he complains severely about the *satellites regis*, and concludes his diatribe against them with the remark that there were

[1] *A*, f. ivb.　　[2] *CM*. iii, p. 386.　　[3] *CM*. iv, p. 205.
[4] *CM*. v, p. 76.　　[5] *HA*. ii, p. 170.　　[6] *CM*. iii, p. 385.
[7] *CM*. v, p. 639.　　[8] iii, p. 388.　　[9] iv, p. 598.
[10] v, pp. 204–5.　　[11] v, p. 597.　　[12] v, p. 531.
[13] *CM*. v, p. 428, and iv, pp. 280–1.

so many of these petty tyrants in England that the country seemed to have reverted to Anglo-Saxon times![1] Although he was prejudiced against the Cahorsin money-lenders[2] in spite of the fact that, on occasion, he made use of their services,[3] Matthew, to his credit, had no very deep-seated prejudices against the Jews, perhaps because of his sympathy for them as victims of royal extortion.[4]

The significance of the various prejudices which we have enumerated lies in the light they throw on Matthew's whole outlook. This, it becomes clear, was limited, deep-rooted, and thoroughly partisan. Matthew was a bigot: he not only allows his own opinions to colour his historical writings, but introduces them on every possible occasion. Moreover, since he was endowed with a vigorous imagination and had a developed appreciation of the value of 'news', the *Chronica Majora* is a colourful subjective account of current events rather than a sober history. We may perhaps be generous enough, in consequence, to extend to him the licence usually accorded to journalists, instead of judging him with the criteria normally applied to historians, but we must never forget, when we use the *Chronica Majora* as a historical source, that it can by no means be relied on for an accurate description of events. What it does tell us is what Matthew thought happened, or, more often, what Matthew wants us to think happened.

The character and content of Matthew's chronicle, then, are determined, and in many ways restricted, by his prejudiced outlook. But although he looked at things in a very limited way, he looked at almost everything; and his manifold interests and passionate curiosity have made the *Chronica Majora* a kind of chronological encyclopedia of almost universal scope. Matthew made no attempt to organize his chronicle, as, for instance, did William of Malmesbury, in the form of a coherent narrative covering a period of years: instead, he collected all the information he could obtain, and recorded it in rough chronological order. It has been said of him that the centre of his world was his own house of St Albans, but, if this be taken to imply narrow parochialism, then we must deny the statement. It is true that

---

[1] *CM.* v, p. 595.   [2] *CM.* iii, pp. 328–9.   [3] See above, p. 4.
[4] See *CM.* iii, p. 543, and iv, p. 260.

his usual metaphor for superiority is the relationship of St Albans to the other English abbeys, that his outlook on life was moulded by his monastic status, and that events at St Albans were more important to him than those, say, in France; but, by and large, he takes a wider view of things than we should expect of a monk. His interest in and knowledge of foreign affairs, for instance, has frequently been pointed out as exceptional.[1] Some of the great variety of subjects treated in the *Chronica Majora* coincide, as we should expect, with Matthew's prejudices, and much of it is consequently taken up with accounts of 'parliaments'; of the relation of king and barons; of royal demands for money, whether from the barons, the bishops, or the citizens of London; and of the doings of royal emissaries, wicked sheriffs, and the like. Much, too, is concerned with the struggle of empire and papacy; with papal interference in England and other countries; and with episcopal elections and royal interference in them. Again, Matthew takes especial care to record Benedictine 'news', such as quarrels of abbots with their monks; quarrels among monks in Benedictine houses; and statutes of provincial chapters. He concerns himself, too, with his own house of St Albans, and much of the *Chronica Majora* is consequently taken up with accounts of domestic events.[2] Some of Matthew's interests, however, seem to run contrary to his prejudices. It is to his credit, for instance, that, in spite of his dislike of foreigners, he was curious about the beliefs and way of life of non-Christians. He included in his chronicle a lengthy description of the Mohammedans, excerpted from some literary source;[3] and he collected a great deal of information about the Mongols, or, as he calls them, Tartars.[4] Much space is, of course, devoted to the usual medieval phenomena, such as freaks, prodigies, portents, comets and marine monsters. The weather receives a good deal of attention, and each annal is usually concluded with a meteorological summary. Heavy falls of snow, hard frosts, thunderstorms, floods, and droughts are all described, often in considerable detail. Many curious pieces of information, the result of Matthew's catholic interests and

---

[1] For instance, by Gairdner, *Early Chroniclers of Europe*, pp. 244 and 253.
[2] On this, see below, p. 185.   [3] *CM.* III, pp. 343–61.
[4] See *CM.* IV, pp. 76–8, 270–7, 386–9, etc.

great curiosity, are to be found in his *Chronica Majora*. There is, for instance, an account of the blood-drinking alliance of the Galloway chieftains,[1] and of the introduction of Greek numerals into England;[2] and the discovery of tin in Germany is mentioned.[3] Matthew was evidently fascinated by etymologies, and many of these—often, in the best medieval tradition, highly improbable—occur in the *Chronica Majora*. The word 'Cahorsin', for instance, is derived from *causantes* (cheating) or *capientes* (taking), and *ursini* (bearish); and Athens from *a-thanatos* (without death).[4]

The *Chronica Majora* betrays, on the part of its author, a rather mercenary outlook on life. Sums of money are mentioned on every possible occasion, and marginal notices about them are common there, as well as in the *Liber Additamentorum*. In the *Chronica*, for instance, we are informed of the amount paid by Henry III to various Poitevins in 1243;[5] of the annual sum paid to Italians from English benefices;[6] of the sum of the convent of Westminster's debts on the death of its abbot in 1246;[7] and of the amount of Louis IX's ransom in 1250.[8] Matthew's mercenary attitude seems to be reflected in his account of the provincial chapter of the Benedictines in 1249,[9] for he records the decision of the chapter to order a daily collect to be said on behalf of the king and queen in all Benedictine houses, and adds: 'though he [the king] made no allowance to them for this purpose'. This monetary interest is of great value to the historian, for it led to the recording, on nine or ten occasions in the *Chronica Majora*, of the price of bread, as well as, on one occasion, the price of wine.[10] There are some remarkable notices about trade in the *Chronica Majora*. We learn, for instance, how, for fear of the Mongols, the merchants of Gothland and Frisia did not make their annual journey, in 1238, to Yarmouth, for the herring fishery;[11] and of Frederick II's merchants sailing as far as India.[12] Merchants returning from Boston to London must have proved useful contacts, for on two occasions they gave Matthew information about floods in Frisia and further

[1] III, p. 365.   [2] V, pp. 285–6.   [3] IV, p. 151.
[4] III, p. 331, and V, p. 286.   [5] IV, p. 254.
[6] IV, p. 419.   [7] IV, p. 586.   [8] V, p. 309.
[9] *CM*. V, p. 81.   [10] V, p. 46.   [11] III, p. 488.
[12] V, p. 217.

east.[1] He notes, too, the effect of war on the Gascon wine trade,[2] and on the Cistercian wool exports.[3]

Of the leading men of his day, both in England and on the Continent, Matthew has much to say, and his vigorous likes and dislikes are often expressed in the form of praise and blame. He also permits himself to pass judgement on historical figures like Harold and William the Conqueror; the former being a perfidious traitor and a proud tyrant, and the latter a pious, just and magnificent conqueror, though he too is accused of tyrannical practices.[4] Matthew's views about King John are well known: he is greedy and libidinous, wicked, cruel and tyrannical.[5] Indeed, for Matthew, he is a personification of all the vices. Henry III receives only slightly better treatment, and it is a remarkable fact that, though Matthew knew him personally, and was honoured and befriended by him more than once,[6] his ideas about Henry remained inimical and offensive. No doubt much of the opprobrium which he heaps on Henry is an inevitable result of his political prejudices: any king who tried to govern at all would be bound to incur Matthew's wrath, for he strongly disapproved of all the activities of government except that of hanging thieves.

Henry, according to Matthew, was avaricious in the extreme, tyrannical, weak-minded, and perfidious; he enjoyed flattery and practised favouritism; he was contemptible in his subservience to the pope and in his military expeditions to Gascony; he was an enemy and plunderer of the English Church, who preferred his queen's foreign relatives to his own natural counsellors. This picture of Henry III will not bear close examination. Take, for instance, his supposed avarice. Matthew calls him 'a vigilant and indefatigable searcher after money',[7] and a new Crassus,[8] and is constantly inveighing against his greed. But he goes too far when he claims that it was avarice (as well as the devil) which prompted Henry to dispatch letters of credit to the pope to enlist his aid in the acquisition of the kingdom of Sicily for his son Edmund;[9] and that it was avarice which inspired him to cut

---

[1] *CM.* IV, p. 240, and V, p. 453.   [2] *CM.* V, p. 277.   [3] *CM.* V, p. 439.
[4] For Harold, see *HA.* I, pp. 5–6 and 8; and for William, *HA.* I, pp. 7, 8, and 12–13.   [5] See e.g. *FH.* II, pp. 136–7.
[6] See above, pp. 3–4.   [7] *CM.* V, p. 55.   [8] *CM.* V, p. 274.
[9] *CM.* V, pp. 458–9.

down his court expenses![1] In the annal for 1254 Matthew describes how the king, stranded in Gascony, sent home for assistance;[2] and the chapter is given the absurd heading: 'A crafty injunction for extorting money.' Matthew, like many of his contemporaries, had no idea of the expenses of government. Henry III may well have been avaricious, but an examination of Matthew's statements alone would never lead us to this conclusion. We might just as well argue that, because someone denounces the tax-collectors as a greedy set of rascals, the government is avaricious. We are more likely to conclude that the criticism is extremely superficial; which is certainly true of Matthew's criticism of Henry III. Even when this has some foundation in fact, it is impossible to assess its value, for Matthew's strictures are repeated so often that they become stereotyped and conventional. He frequently accuses the king of plundering vacant bishoprics and abbeys, and this no doubt happened on occasions, but what significance can we attach to his description of Henry 'laying his greedy hands' on the properties of the see of Bath, and carrying off what plunder he could?[3] Or to his account of how Henry deliberately prolonged the vacancy in the archbishopric of York in order to extract the maximum amount of money from the see?[4] It is evident that these detractions are a product of Matthew's grudge against the king rather than of a critical examination of his actions. The absurdity of many of his remarks about the king is illustrated by his comment on the occasion when Henry sent Simon Passelewe round to some of the larger Benedictine abbeys to try to borrow money on his behalf:[5] 'It was clear, from this, how eagerly the king desired to damage the Church irretrievably.' On the whole, Matthew's picture of Henry is a vicious, spiteful caricature, and not the least spiteful remark made about him is the comment that, had he not redeemed his evil deeds by constant and liberal almsgiving, his soul would have been seriously endangered.[6]

Matthew seems to have been fascinated by the character and career of the Emperor Frederick II. Although he criticizes him

[1] *CM.* v, p. 114.　　[2] *CM.* v, pp. 423–4.
[3] *CM.* v, p. 3.　　[4] *CM.* v, p. 516.
[5] *CM.* v, p. 683.　　[6] *CM.* III, pp. 522–3.

for his cruelty, tyranny, and pride,[1] he has much sympathy and even admiration for him. With evident relish, he tells the story of the French priest whose conscience would not allow him to obey the papal injunction to excommunicate the emperor, and who consequently excommunicated whichever of them was the offending party; and Matthew is pleased to be able to record that, while the pope punished him for his 'scurrilous levity', the emperor sent him some valuable gifts.[2] His enthusiasm for Frederick was not based on ideological considerations—Matthew never thought out the implications of the imperial-papal struggle—but it seems to have been due to the fact that he thought of Frederick as, like himself, a victim of, or at least a sufferer from, the activities of the papacy. After 1245, however, Matthew's enthusiasm waned rapidly, mainly, as A. L. Smith pointed out,[3] because Frederick published, in that year, his plans for the expropriation of the church: a direct threat to Matthew's material interests as a monk. It is interesting to find that, after Frederick's death, he became a staunch supporter of Conrad, and he describes how the hostility, threats, and insults of the pope, as well as poison, contributed to his death.[4] According to A. L. Smith, Matthew contributed a great deal to the growth of the legend of Frederick II as an appalling, mysterious, and romantic figure.[5] It is true that this is the impression we get in reading the *Chronica Majora*, but it is not so much due to Matthew himself, as to the reports and rumours about Frederick which he records, and which show that the legend of Frederick had already begun to develop. Rather than accuse Matthew of deliberate falsification, we ought to admit that here, at least, he is a useful guide to contemporary feeling.

Towards Earl Richard of Cornwall, Henry III's brother, he is reasonably well disposed, though he criticizes him for raising money by means of the redemption of crusaders' vows,[6] and for being on rather too friendly terms with the pope.[7]

[1] *CM.* III, p. 496; and IV, pp. 353–4 and 648.
[2] *CM.* IV, pp. 406–7.
[3] Smith, *Church and State in the Middle Ages*, pp. 176–7.
[4] *CM.* V, p. 460.
[5] Smith, *Church and State in the Middle Ages*, p. 169.
[6] *CM.* IV, pp. 133–4 and 629–30; V, pp. 73–4 and 146.
[7] *CM.* IV, pp. 561 and 577–8; V, p. 112.

Of Simon de Montfort he has little to say, but he regards him as a *naturalis* and not an *alienigena*, and sympathizes with him in his quarrels with Henry III.[1] He admired Bishop Grosseteste and revered him as a saint;[2] approving of his criticism of the papacy, though he strongly disapproved of his harsh methods of visitation. On several occasions he uses Grosseteste as a mouthpiece for airing his own prejudices, especially against the papacy, and in one place against the friars.[3] Matthew has much praise and sympathy for Hubert de Burgh; and he admired, among others, Edmund Rich and John Blund; Richard Fishacre and Robert Bacon; and Blanche, queen of France. His especial *bêtes noires* were Boniface of Savoy, archbishop of Canterbury and a foreigner; Fawkes de Breauté, an enemy of St Albans described as a 'bloody traitor';[4] and King Henry III.

It is worth noting that Matthew uses the word 'martyr' in a very loose sense. Thus William FitzOsbert, the leader of the London revolt of 1196, who was caught and hanged, was, according to Matthew, a martyr to the cause of truth and the poor; the Winchester monks imprisoned by the royal 'satellites' in 1241 obtained thereby the 'palm of martyrdom'; and the unfortunate messengers who first arrived in France with news of Louis IX's defeat and capture in 1250, and who were put to death as rumourmongers, were also, according to Matthew Paris, martyrs.[5] His awards of martyrdom are often useful as a guide to his sympathies: Archbishop Sewal of York, for instance, is said to have earned martyrdom on account of his persecution by the pope.[6]

In his highly developed prejudices, and in the lively picture he gives us of contemporary persons and events, Matthew is exceptional among medieval chroniclers; but his view of history

---

[1] *CM.* v, pp. 289–90.

[2] At any rate after his death. *CM.* v, pp. 490–1.

[3] For Matthew's view of Grosseteste, see especially *CM.* v, p. 389 note 1, where he calls the famous letter complaining of papal abuses 'optima epistola'; v, pp. 226–7, where Matthew deplores his tyrannical visitation of Ramsey; and v, pp. 400–9, where he puts his prejudices against the pope and friars into Grosseteste's mouth. Jourdain, in *Excursions historiques,* pp. 155 and 169–71, wrongly supposed that some of the passages about Grosseteste in the *Chronica Majora* were not due to Matthew Paris himself, but were later interpolations. [4] *CM.* v, p. 323.

[5] *CM.* ii, p. 419; iv, p. 160; and v, p. 169.   [6] *CM.* v, pp. 678–9.

and his understanding of the significance of events are typical
of them. He was a firm believer in the miraculous and in the
validity of portents. Earthquakes and thunder were a presage
of future events and a sure sign of Divine wrath and the
approach of the end of the world.[1] The disturbed state of the
elements is constantly connected with the turbulent state of
human affairs.[2] Of the latter Matthew takes a pessimistic view:
the world, he thought, was in a chaotic state, and England was
no exception.[3] Like most medieval chroniclers, he tends always
to take a moral view of history, attributing the bad state of
affairs to the vices and failings of human beings: 'Neither the
threats of the Bible nor the chaos of the elements affect the greed
and ambition of miserable mortals.'[4] Events are explained in
the usual manner of medieval chroniclers: the tragic failure of
Louis IX's crusade in Egypt was due, Matthew believed, to
God's exasperation with the pride of Louis's brother, Robert of
Artois, or with the pope and the crusading leaders for financing
the project with money extorted from the poor.[5] Floods,
Matthew surmises, were probably due to God's anger with the
pope.[6] On the rare occasions when God is left out of Matthew's
explanation of events, some human personality, often the king
or the pope, is introduced in his place. Matthew frequently
fails to understand the motives of those concerned in events, and
his occasional guesses at what was going on are often absurdly
far from the truth: he supposes, for instance, that the object of
the Castilian embassy in 1255 was to extract money from the
king of England, though in fact it was the arrangement of a
marriage alliance.[7]

Matthew's naïve and ingenuous view of events is especially
apparent in the annual summaries with which he concludes
his account of each year. These are stereotyped and conventional,
the effect of the year on the different countries being described
with one or two adjectives only. Here is a typical example of one
of these annual summaries, describing the year 1244:[8] 'And so
the year passed...most inimical to the Holy Land, turbulent

---

[1] *CM.* v, pp. 187 and 198–9. *CM.* IV, p. 603, and v, p. 47.
[2] *CM.* IV, pp. 85, 568, 603, etc.   [3] *CM.* v, p. 625.   [4] *AC.* p. 299.
[5] *CM.* v, pp. 134 and 165; 170–2.   [6] *CM.* v, pp. 175–7.
[7] *CM.* v, p. 509, and note 1.   [8] *CM.* IV, p. 402.

in England, dangerous for the kingdom of France, causing suspicion in the Church and confusion among the Italians.' For no ascertainable reason, we find that, in the *Historia Anglorum*,[1] the year is said also to have been 'pecuniae emunctivus' in England. The adjectives applied to each country in these summaries are nearly always chosen from among the following: 'inimicus', 'suspectus', 'hostilis', 'infamis', 'cruentus', 'nocivus', 'turbulentus' and 'periculosus'. With one exception— 1245 is said to have been 'augmentativus' for France,[2] presumably because of its acquisition of Macon and Provence in that year—they are adverse and deprecatory, and they reflect Matthew's pessimistic outlook on the world, as well as his inability to grasp the real significance of events.

Few principles guided Matthew in his choice of what to include in his history and what to omit: reticence, though often expressed, is seldom practised. He refuses, however, out of reverence for the Holy Church (he assures us), to expatiate on the rapacity of the papal nuncio Martin;[3] and he declines to describe the crimes of Robert Bugre and the charges against Gilbert Marshal in 1240[4]—probably because he did not know what they were, rather than, as he tells us, because he considered it better not to enumerate them. Matthew's object in writing history was largely didactic and monitory, as is the case with the great majority of medieval chroniclers. He tells us in one place that he has included a story about a wicked sheriff in his chronicle in order to demonstrate God's disapproval of tyranny,[5] and elsewhere he says:[6]

It is indeed an excellent thing to perpetuate notable events in writing, for the praise of God and in order that posterity should be instructed by reading, how to avoid those things which deserve punishment, and how to engage in the good things which are rewarded by God.

Posterity, in fact, has been tricked, rather than instructed, by Matthew Paris; tricked by the scope of his writings and by sententious platitudes such as these into accepting the thirteenth

---

[1] II, p. 498.
[2] *CM.* IV, p. 503.
[3] *CM.* IV, p. 416.
[4] *CM.* III, p. 520, and IV, p. 4.
[5] *CM.* V, pp. 580–1.
[6] *AC.* p. 319.

century as he saw it, and into regarding him as the greatest historian of his age, instead of the quidnunc that he was. But how has posterity treated Matthew Paris? And what was his influence on succeeding medieval chroniclers? The history of the St Albans historical school has been admirably surveyed by Professor Galbraith,[1] and a few remarks will suffice here. The *Gesta Abbatum*, Matthew's autograph manuscript of which remained for more than a hundred years the standard, if not the only, work on the subject,[2] was copied, abridged, and continued, at the end of the fourteenth century. His *Chronica Majora*, as Galbraith showed, was continued almost without break well into the fifteenth century, and served as a model and inspiration for Thomas Walsingham, the other great St Albans historian, who used it in the compilation of his *Ypodigma Neustriae*.[3] St Albans was unique, among English Benedictine houses, in producing a historical school which lasted until nearly the end of the Middle Ages, long after the tradition of historical writing in other houses had died away; and this was largely due to Matthew's commanding influence on succeeding generations of St Albans monks.

Outside his own house, Matthew exercised considerable influence through one work: the *Flores Historiarum*. This was copied and recopied, and continually brought up to date. It was a minor work, derived from the *Chronica Majora*, but incorporating a considerable amount of new material. It rapidly became one of the most popular history books of the age, and copies were soon circulating throughout England. Luard notices nineteen manuscripts in the introduction to his edition of the *Flores Historiarum*, nearly all of the fourteenth century; and more can be added to his list, especially if we include abridgements such as that in British Museum Harley MS. 5418, ff. 17–76 b. The *Flores Historiarum* was the basis of a number of

[1] *St Albans Chronicle*, pp. xxvii–lxxi.
[2] His *Liber Additamentorum* was referred to as the *Liber de Gestis Abbatum* as late as *c.* 1400: see above, p. 78.
[3] Ed. Riley; see, for instance, pp. 133 and 136. Madden, *HA.* 1, p. xxxviii, mistakenly derives these passages from the *Historia Anglorum*. It is worth noting that a compilation from the *Historia Anglorum* and *Chronica Majora* was made at St Albans in *c.* 1420–30: the MS. is described by Madden, *HA.* 1, pp. lxvi–lxix.

later chronicles, such as the *Annales Londonienses* and *Paulini*; and it was used, for instance, by Richard of Cirencester in his *Speculum Historiale*, and by the compiler of the *Liber de Hyda*. Only the latter mentions Matthew by name in connexion with his extracts from the *Flores Historiarum*,[1] and Matthew's influence on later medieval writers was exercised either anonymously, or else under the pseudonym 'Matthew of Westminster'— the fictitious author to whom his *Flores Historiarum* was soon attributed, and under whose name it went until the last century.

The *Chronica Majora* never seems to have passed into general circulation, and, though two copies of the section up to 1188 were made after Matthew's death, only one copy (*C*) is known of the second part of his chronicle, made in his lifetime, and extending only to the annal for 1250.[2] The *Chronica Majora* seems to have been used, towards the end of the thirteenth century, by the Bury St Edmunds chronicler John Taxster, and it was certainly used by Thomas Wykes and the Osney chronicler at about the same time. Wykes acknowledges his debt to Matthew, among others.[3] In his edition of the *Flores Historiarum*, Luard printed some extracts from 'the chronicles of Reginald of Wroxham' which he found in one of the manuscripts of the *Flores*, and which, since they contained some passages also in Matthew Paris, and were apparently written by a parson of Wroxham who died in 1235, Luard thought might be a hitherto unknown source of Matthew Paris.[4] In fact, however, collation shows that these extracts have been taken from Matthew Paris's writings, and not vice versa, so that the parson Reginald and the chronicler must have been two different persons. Whoever he was, the chronicler Reginald of Wroxham wrote before 1304, and he seems to have been the only medieval chronicler outside St Albans to use both the *Chronica Majora* and the *Historia Anglorum*. The latter was also used, in the fifteenth century, by the author of the *Breviarium Chronicorum*, probably the Winchester monk Thomas Rudbourne;[5] and it was

[1] See above, pp. 40–1.
[2] The two copies of the first part of the *Chronica* are B.M. Cotton MS. Nero D v, Part I, and B.M. Harley MS. 1620, both written late in the thirteenth century.   [3] See p. 20 above.
[4] *FH.* I, pp. xxiii and liii–lvii.   [5] *HA.* I, p. xxxix, and note 1.

extensively drawn on, and annotated by, the sixteenth-century historian, Polydore Vergil.[1] The authors of two chronicles published in the Rolls Series are said by their editors to have used Matthew Paris's writings: Luard thought that Bartholomew Cotton had used both Roger Wendover and Matthew,[2] and Sir Henry Ellis supposed that John of Oxenedes was well acquainted with the writings of Matthew Paris.[3] Actually both Cotton and Oxenedes used a chronicle written by John of Wallingford, Infirmarius of St Albans and a friend of Matthew Paris, which was almost entirely abridged from Matthew's *Chronica Majora* and *Historia Anglorum*, and there is no evidence that either of them knew Matthew's works at first hand. The *Flores Historiarum*, then, was the only one of Matthew's writings to be well known and widely used in medieval times. Only a handful of later writers knew anything of his other works, and it is indeed extraordinary that the *Chronica Majora*, the fullest and most detailed of all medieval English chronicles, was virtually unknown outside St Albans during the latter part of the Middle Ages.

A hundred years after the invention of printing, the first editions of Matthew Paris's historical works were published by Archbishop Matthew Parker. In 1567, he edited the *Flores Historiarum* under the name 'Matthew of Westminster', and, in 1570, having discovered another manuscript in the meanwhile, he brought out a second edition. A year later, he published his edition of the *Chronica Majora*, which was reprinted at Zürich in 1589, and again in 1606. Although these editions are inaccurate, and entirely inadequate by modern standards,[4] it was a great achievement of Parker's to make Matthew Paris's chronicle available to the reading public, even in the corrupt form in which he printed it. The new edition of the *Chronica Majora* which appeared in 1640 was evidently a direct result of

[1] See *HA*. I, p. xli.   [2] *Historia Anglicana*, p. xxxvii.
[3] *Chronica Johannis de Oxenedes*, p. ix.
[4] Loyalty to my college, of which Matthew Parker was a former Master, would make it painful for me to expatiate on the liberties he took with the texts of his manuscripts; but this is happily unnecessary, since it has already been done by Madden, *HA*. I, pp. xxxiii–xxxvii; Luard, *CM*. II, pp. xxii–xxviii and *FH*. I, pp. xliii–xlviii; and Hardy, *Descriptive Catalogue*, III, pp. 399–414.

Parker's work. Indeed it was originally intended to be a mere reprint of Parker's edition, and its editor, Dr William Wats, who was chaplain to Prince Rupert, did not begin work on it until the text up to the annal for 1188 had been printed off. Wats's edition, though far from perfect, was a definite advance on Parker's. It was reissued twice (Paris, 1644; London, 1684), and was not superseded until Luard undertook in 1869 to re-edit the whole of the *Chronica Majora* for the Rolls Series. Archbishop Parker had intended to publish Matthew Paris's *Historia Anglorum*, but (fortunately, Madden thought!) never proceeded further than a transcript,[1] and the *Historia Anglorum* was not printed until 1866–9, when Sir Frederick Madden edited it in three volumes for the Rolls Series, adding also the *Abbreviatio Chronicorum*. This edition was an important landmark in medieval studies, for it is one of the finest of all those published in the Rolls Series, and it set a standard of careful accuracy and profound scholarship which has seldom been equalled since. The last work of Matthew Paris to be critically edited was the *Flores Historiarum*, which, though not attributed to Matthew Paris, was published by Luard in 1890, also for the Rolls Series. To these two scholars, Madden and Luard, all succeeding students and users of Matthew Paris must acknowledge a debt of gratitude.

The gratitude of many a student of Matthew Paris, including myself, is also due to the two translators of the *Chronica Majora*. It is a remarkable fact that, by the middle of the last century, Matthew's *Chronica Majora* had been translated into both French and English; and even more remarkable, perhaps, that it was the French translation which appeared first. This fine work, entitled *Grand Chronique de Matthieu Paris*, was carried out by A. Huillard-Bréholles in 1840–1.[2] The English translation was undertaken by J. A. Giles, and appeared in 1852 in Bohn's Antiquarian Library; the publishers of which also produced, in 1853, a translation of the *Flores Historiarum* by C. D. Yonge.

[1] *HA*. I, p. xxxvii.
[2] It is perhaps worthy of remark that Baudelaire had read this edition of Matthew Paris, and one of his poems is based on a story related in the *Chronica Majora*, see P.-L. Faye, 'Baudelaire and Matthew Paris', *French Review*, XXIV (1950) pp. 80–1.

It is as a chronicler that Matthew Paris has chiefly excited the interest of scholars, and this chapter would be incomplete without at least a brief survey of recent Matthew Paris studies. These were inaugurated by Sir Frederick Madden in the prefaces to Volumes I and III of his edition of the *Historia Anglorum*. Until the appearance of this work, knowledge of Matthew Paris had been hazy and inexact: Giles, for instance, thought that Matthew died *c.* 1273, and he was even able to print the text of Matthew's chronicle up to that year![1] Although many of Madden's views were not accepted by later scholars, my studies have led me to conclude that, in the main, and especially on the question of Matthew's handwriting, Madden was right.[2] He collected together all the ascertainable facts about Matthew Paris, and produced an excellent account of his historical and other activities, which has remained the basis for all later studies of Matthew Paris. Madden also identified the handwriting of Matthew Paris; described the autograph manuscripts, some of which he himself discovered; and was the first modern scholar to attribute the *Flores Historiarum* to Matthew Paris. Within a few years of the publication of the *Historia Anglorum*, Sir Thomas Duffus Hardy published the third volume of his catalogue of English historical sources, in which he dissented entirely from Madden on the question of Matthew's handwriting, and denied the attribution of the *Flores Historiarum* to Matthew Paris. It is curious that later scholars have in general accepted Hardy's conclusions rather than Madden's, for, while Hardy was primarily an archivist, and spent most of his active life in the Record Office, of which for many years he was head, Madden's interest had always been in manuscript books, and, after nine years as Assistant Keeper at the British Museum, he served as Keeper of Manuscripts for thirty years. His knowledge of manuscripts has seldom, if ever, been rivalled; yet Luard, whose prefaces to the different volumes of the *Chronica Majora* were published between 1872 and 1883, agreed with Hardy on the identification of Matthew's handwriting, and the denial of Matthew's authorship of the *Flores Historiarum*. Luard's prefaces marked a great advance in Matthew Paris studies, for he gave an excellent account of the character of the

[1] Giles, *Matthew Paris's English History*, I, p. vi. [2] See p. 35 above.

Chronica Majora, and of Matthew's historical methods; of the sources used by both Roger Wendover and Matthew; and of the relationship of these two writers, whose chronicles he for the first time clearly distinguished by the use of two different types.

The appearance of Madden's and Luard's editions of Matthew Paris made possible a much more full and accurate estimate of Matthew Paris as a chronicler, and, during the next half century or so, the emphasis of Matthew Paris studies shifted from the critical investigation of manuscript and related problems to more general accounts of Matthew himself, and of his position in medieval historiography. The first of these was that of James Gairdner, published in 1879.[1] His account, though short, was scholarly and penetrating, unlike that which Augustus Jessopp contributed to the *Quarterly Review* in 1886, which was neither.[2] 'We have in Matthew Paris', wrote Jessopp, 'an instance of a born historian, one who never consented to be a mere advocate, taking a side and seeing only half the truth of anything: but a man gifted with the judicial faculty.' The article on Matthew Paris in the *Dictionary of National Biography*, written by W. Hunt, which appeared in 1895, is an excellent and balanced account, based largely on the work of Madden and Luard. In his Ford Lectures, published in 1913, A. L. Smith broke new ground with a stimulating and lively account of Matthew Paris the chronicler, in which he exposed some of Matthew's failings, and described how his record of events was coloured by his own feelings and prejudices. Meanwhile, Matthew Paris had excited the interest of German scholars, and Felix Liebermann included a detailed study of him and his writings in the introduction to his excerpts from the *Chronica Majora* relating to Germany, published in 1888.[3] Like Hardy and Luard, he disputed Madden's identification of Matthew's handwriting and his attribution of the *Flores Historiarum* to Matthew. In spite of his careful researches, Liebermann added very little to the work of Madden and Luard; but a great advance was made by H. Plehn, who, in 1897, published an important work entitled *Der politische*

---

[1] *Early Chroniclers of Europe*, pp. 243 ff.
[2] Reprinted in *Studies by a Recluse*, pp. 1–65; my excerpt is from p. 53.
[3] These excerpts were translated into German by Grandaur and Wattenbach, in the series, 'Geschichtschreiber der deutschen Vorzeit', 1890.

Charakter von Matheus Parisiensis, in which he put Luard's edition of the *Chronica Majora* to excellent use in giving an account, albeit a little too methodical and coherent, of Matthew's political outlook.

Matthew Paris received little notice from English scholars after the work of Smith at the beginning of the century, until in 1927 Professor Claude Jenkins published his vivacious and entertaining little book on the early St Albans chroniclers, in which, incidentally, he struck a nice compromise between Madden and Hardy on the question of Matthew's handwriting. In recent years the controversy between Madden and Hardy has been paralleled by a controversy between Powicke and Galbraith. In a paper contributed to *Modern Philology* in 1941 Sir Maurice Powicke suggested that Matthew Paris may have lived on after 1259, and inaugurated an entirely new line of study by attempting to outline the relationship and chronology of Matthew's historical manuscripts. This paper was severely handled by Professor Galbraith,[1] who maintained that Matthew Paris did die in 1259, and contested Powicke's belief that the *Historia Anglorum* was written before manuscripts *A* and *B* of the *Chronica Majora*. Galbraith made a penetrating comparison of Roger Wendover and Matthew Paris, and, against Hardy, Liebermann, Luard, and the rest, resuscitated Madden's belief that Matthew was the author of the *Flores Historiarum*, supporting his view with convincing evidence. Apart from two short papers contributed to the *English Historical Review*, in which Denholm-Young maintained that Matthew Paris had inserted an important constitutional document in the wrong place in his chronicle, and Professor Cheney (rightly, I think) maintained that he had not,[2] no critical studies of Matthew Paris have appeared since the second World War. Professor Knowles, however, gave an excellent short account of Matthew Paris in his book *The Religious Orders in England*.[3]

All these studies of different aspects of Matthew Paris have been of inestimable value in the writing of this book, and if I have been lucky enough to see slightly further than my predecessors, I have done this, as Bernard of Chartres and his contemporaries did, only by clambering on to their broad shoulders.

---

[1] *Roger Wendover and Matthew Paris*, published in 1944. For more on this controversy, see p. 50 above.   [2] See p. 136 above.   [3] Published in 1948.

CHAPTER IX

MATTHEW PARIS THE HAGIOLOGIST

So far we have been concerned with Matthew Paris's historical works, but he was active also in the field of hagiology. His saints' lives fall into two groups: those written in Latin, and those written in Anglo-Norman verse. So far as is known, he wrote only two Latin biographies, those of the archbishops Stephen Langton and Edmund Rich. Only a part of his life of Langton has survived, in the form of three separate fragments. Sir Frederick Madden pointed out that one of these was preserved on the verso of a leaf attached to the end of British Museum Cotton MS. Vespasian B xiii.[1] Later Liebermann identified, in the *Liber Additamentorum*, the two other fragments of this life, one of which contained some of the text immediately preceding that of the Vespasian fragment, and the other the rest of a paragraph left unfinished at the end of the Vespasian fragment.[2] Liebermann prefaced his edition of these fragments with an excellent discussion, but he thought that none of them was in Matthew's hand. I cannot agree with him about this, for a careful examination of the handwriting of these fragments has convinced me that all three were written out by Matthew himself. This is not true, however, of the matter on the recto of the Vespasian fragment (a letter of the abbots of Waltham and Bury St Edmunds dated 12 November 1253) and on the verso of f. 196 of the *Liber Additamentorum* (a document of 1252), none of which is written by Matthew. Neither Madden nor Liebermann discussed the question of the authorship of this Life of Langton in any detail; but there can be no doubt that they were right in attributing it to Matthew Paris. The style is his, and several of his characteristic phrases appear, such as: 'quasi inter duas contritus molas' (pp. 323–4); 'frendens denti-

---

[1] F. 133b: see *HA.* III, p. lii, note 6.
[2] F. 196a, and a separate leaf attached to f. 196b. Liebermann (ed.), *Ungedruckte anglo-norm. Geschichtsquellen*, p. 318; he prints the text on pp. 323–9. The references in parentheses which follow are to this edition.

bus' (p. 324); 'patulis rictibus' (p. 326); and 'que speciales exigunt tractatus' (p. 328). The *Liber Additamentorum* is referred to in Matthew's usual way: '[qui] legere desiderat, librum Additamentorum annalium, que apud Sanctum Albanum sunt, adeat inspecturus' (p. 328); and, as Liebermann pointed out, both the *Chronica Majora* and the *Historia Anglorum* have been used in the life. Matthew's authorship is confirmed by the mention of Gervase of Melkeley as a source of information (pp. 326–7), for Matthew used some of Gervase's verses, and cites him by name, in his *Chronica Majora*;[1] and by the marginal comment, so characteristic of Matthew: 'Nota piam decepcionem' (p. 326).

Matthew's Life of Langton is hagiographical rather than biographical, though it was evidently not written with the object of securing papal canonization.[2] The surviving fragments (which fit together into a continuous whole) describe an incident on Langton's journey to Rome, when he cured a maniac of his madness; his visit to Innocent III and the cardinals in Rome; his preaching in various parts on his return journey; and the translation of St Thomas Becket in 1220. The whole extends over only five printed pages, but, even in this small fragment, the general character of the work is revealed. As Liebermann noticed, Matthew here puts to good effect the use of dialogue, personal anecdote, and hyperbole: three literary devices which are effectively employed in his historical writings. Although Matthew cites Gervase of Melkeley as a source, and Powicke thought that he might have been one of Langton's clerks,[3] and therefore a reliable informant, he has made no attempt, in his Life of Langton, to adhere to the historical facts, even in the version of them already given in his *Chronica Majora*. Thus, in the Life, Langton is said to have incurred the wrath of Innocent III by refusing to pay the tribute to Rome, whereas neither in the *Chronica Majora* nor in the *Historia Anglorum* is there any mention of this; and the *Chronica Majora*'s explanation of the origin of the dispute between Langton and Innocent, in the encroachment by the papal legate upon the rights of Canterbury,

---

[1] *CM.* IV, p. 493; and *HA.* II, p. 232.
[2] Liebermann (ed.), *Ungedruckte a.-n. Geschichtsquellen*, p. 323.
[3] Powicke, *Stephen Langton*, p. 103.

is not mentioned in the life.[1] Again, whereas in the Life Langton is said to have been summoned to Rome 'sub terribili comminacione', on account of his opposition to the tribute, in the *Chronica Majora* and the *Historia Anglorum* he is said to have gone to Rome of his own accord, to defend his refusal to ban the Magna Carta barons. Langton's relationship with the pope is further falsified in the Life by the attribution to Innocent of an inveterate hatred for him; and history is also disregarded when Langton is said to have been allowed to return at once to England from Rome, for in the *Chronica Majora* Matthew states that his suspension was confirmed while he was there, and that he was not allowed to return to England until peace was made between the barons and the king.

In this biography Matthew portrays Stephen Langton as a staunch representative of the kingdom of England, firmly opposing the payment of tribute to Rome, and standing out against foreign influence. He is made to enshrine and represent that national feeling against Rome which seems to have been a more real sentiment in England in the forties and fifties of the thirteenth century than in Langton's time, and which was shared, as we have seen, by Matthew himself. Besides his relationship with the papacy, Langton's piety and holiness and his skill as a preacher and theologian are revealed in the surviving fragment of Matthew's life; and to the description of Langton's preaching after his visit to Rome Matthew adds the remark that he was the equal, in theology, of Augustine, Gregory, and Ambrose (p. 328). It is a pity that more of Matthew's Life of Stephen Langton has not survived, but fortunately his Latin hagiography can be studied in his Life of Langton's successor, Edmund Rich, which has come down to us in its entirety; and to this we may now turn.

Matthew refers, in his *Chronica Majora*, to a Life of St Edmund written by himself. He says:[2]

On the strength of the statements of this man [Richard Wych, bishop of Chichester], and of the friar, Master Roger Bacon, O.P., Dom Matthew Paris, monk of St Albans, wrote the Life of the

---

[1] Liebermann (ed.), *Ungedruckte a.-n. Geschichtsquellen*, pp. 319–20, where this and what follows is discussed.

[2] v, pp. 369–70.

above-mentioned St Edmund...which he who desires to see can find at St Albans....

Shortly after this, in the *Chronica Majora*, Matthew mentions this Life again,[1] and says that it contained also the miracles of Richard Wych. The identity of this Life of St Edmund has, however, only recently been established. In his biography of St Edmund, published in 1893,[2] the Reverend W. Wallace printed as an appendix three Lives of Edmund, one of which, from British Museum Cotton MS. Julius D vi (ff. 123–156b, written in the fourteenth century), he attributed to a Canterbury monk, Eustace. He thought that Matthew's Life was no longer in existence. Five years after the appearance of Wallace's book, the Baroness Paravicini published a biography of Edmund, in the introduction to which she claimed that the Life in Cotton MS. Julius D vi, printed by Wallace but attributed by him to Eustace, was in fact that of Matthew Paris. Davis, Baker, Legge and Lawrence have all accepted her attribution.[3]

Wallace's attribution of the Julius Life of Edmund to Eustace of Canterbury was based on conjecture, for the only fact he discovered which seemed to make Matthew's authorship unlikely was the occurrence of the first person in the description of events at which Matthew Paris was certainly not present.[4] This objection to Matthew's authorship of the Julius Life was removed by Paravicini and Baker, who pointed out that the first person could easily have been incorporated into Matthew's Life from some Canterbury source he was following.[5] The positive evidence for Matthew's authorship is entirely convincing. Paravicini noticed the general similarity of style and treatment in the Julius Life and the *Chronica Majora*. The vigorous dialogue and vivid, lively narrative of the Julius Life is indeed characteristic of Matthew Paris; and Paravicini showed

---

[1] v, p. 384.   [2] *The Life of St Edmund of Canterbury*.

[3] Davis, 'An unpublished Life of Edmund Rich', *EHR.* XXII (1907), p. 91; Baker, 'La Vie de S. Edmond', *Romania*, LV (1929), pp. 336–41; Legge, *Anglo-Norman in the Cloisters* (1950), p. 27; Lawrence, 'Robert of Abingdon and Matthew Paris', *EHR.* LXIX (1954), p. 410.

[4] Wallace, *Life of St Edmund*, pp. 8–9; see pp. 558, 580, etc., for the occurrence of the first person.

[5] Baker (ed.), 'Vie de S. Edmond', *loc. cit.* p. 338; for the references to Paravicini which follow, see the introduction to her *St Edmund of Abingdon*.

that the sources used in it include those which Matthew tells us he used for his Life of St Edmund. She printed two passages from the Julius Life in her introduction and compared them with similar passages in the *Historia Anglorum*, and she likewise compared a passage from the Julius Life concerning Edmund's private seal with Matthew's very similar description of it in his *Liber Additamentorum*. Furthermore, she found that two quotations from Ovid occur both in the Julius Life and in Matthew's *Chronica Majora*, and that one of them is introduced, in the Julius Life, with the same words as in the *Chronica Majora*, and the other in very similar words.[1] The second of these quotations actually occurs three times in the *Chronica Majora* and twice in the *Historia Anglorum*; indeed it is one of Matthew's favourites.[2] Paravicini also noticed that the author of the Julius Life had the same habit of playing on words as Matthew Paris, and she might have gone on to cite some of Matthew's typical pairs of similar words which are to be found in the Julius Life, such as 'dura' and 'dira', 'leviter' and 'leniter', 'valuit' and 'voluit', and 'ponens' and 'exponens'.[3] Paravicini's evidence of stylistic similarities can be further amplified: compare, for instance, the phrase in the Life, 'nec est fraudatus a desiderio suo', with the phrase from the *Abbreviatio Chronicorum*, 'nec est a suo desiderio fraudatus';[4] or 'ad instar fluvii qui ex torrentibus pluvialibus suscipit incrementum' of the Julius Life with 'ad instar fluminis quod ex torrentibus suscipit incrementum' of the *Chronica Majora*.[5] Again, many of the phrases characteristically employed by Matthew Paris in his historical writings occur also in the Julius Life; for instance: 'ab alto (*or* immo) trahens (*or* ducens) suspiria';[6] 'Haec idcirco scripserim';[7] 'felix suscepit incrementum';[8] 'luce clarius';[9] 'sicut sequens sermo declarabit';[10] and 'speciales tractatus

---

[1] Paravicini, *St Edmund of Abingdon*, p. xxxviii.
[2] Ovid, *Remed. Amor.* 119: *CM.* III, p. 483; IV, p. 158; V, p. 662; *HA.* II, pp. 396 and 405.
[3] See above, pp. 38–40; 46–7; and 127.
[4] Wallace, *Life of St Edmund*, p. 550; *AC.* p. 281.
[5] Wallace, *ibid.* p. 578; *CM.* V, p. 17.
[6] Wallace, *ibid.* pp. 566, 573.
[7] *Ibid.* p. 543. [8] *Ibid.* p. 546.
[9] *Ibid.* p. 550. [10] *Ibid.* pp. 555, 573.

exigerent'.[1] We can thus be quite sure that the Life of Edmund in Cotton MS. Julius D vi is a copy of the one written by Matthew Paris.

C. H. Lawrence has recently shown that Matthew's Life was based on a collection of materials made at Pontigny and extracted from the letters and documents of the canonization process. He shows, too, how Matthew has added to and altered his source in his characteristic way; and he gives a list of the longer passages which Matthew did not derive from his source.[2] These include a certain amount of documentary material, such as a long statement by Robert Bacon; a letter and a sermon of St Edmund; a letter of Richard Wych; and the bull of canonization. Others are probably based on information given to Matthew by Robert Bacon and Richard Wych, and Lawrence conjectures that the additional information about Edmund's family and childhood was given to Matthew by Robert of Abingdon, Edmund's brother. Though documents and personal information account for a number of Matthew's additions to his source, others have been taken from his own historical works. The description of Edmund's consecration in the Life is very close to that in the *Chronica Majora*, and an addition of Matthew's to Roger Wendover's chronicle is incorporated into the text of the Life,[3] so that it seems very likely that the *Chronica Majora* was used in its composition. On the other hand, in the course of the account in the Life of the quarrel between the archbishop and his monks, there are some very close parallels with the *Historia Anglorum*.[4] If we compare the passages concerning Edmund in the *Chronica Majora* and the *Historia Anglorum* with the corresponding passages in the Life, we find that, when the *Historia Anglorum* differs from the *Chronica Majora*, it is invariably closer to the Life. Now since the *Historia Anglorum* is for the most part derived directly from the *Chronica Majora*, it is probable that these divergences of the *Historia Anglorum* from its exemplar are due to the fact that the Life of Edmund

---

[1] Wallace, *Life of St Edmund*, p. 556; see also above, pp. 39, 40, and 126–7.
[2] Lawrence, 'Robert of Abingdon and Matthew Paris', *EHR.* LXIX (1954), pp. 413–15. For the source of Matthew's Life, see pp. 410–12, and for the probable connexion between Robert of Abingdon and Matthew, pp. 416–17.
[3] Wallace, *Life of St Edmund*, p. 555; *CM.* III, pp. 272 and 244.
[4] Wallace, *ibid.* p. 565; *HA.* II, p. 411.

was written after the *Chronica Majora*, but before the *Historia Anglorum* was abridged from it. Had the Life been written after the *Historia Anglorum*, it would be difficult to explain why the text of the *Historia*, normally close to that of the *Chronica Majora*, varies from it where St Edmund is mentioned, and comes, at these points, very close to the text of the Life.

Paravicini pointed out that since Matthew's Life of Edmund includes a letter of Richard Wych describing the translation of St Edmund on 9 June 1247, it must have been written after then;[1] and Lawrence noted that, since Blanche of Castile is referred to as still living, it must have been written before her death in 1253.[2] Paravicini noticed, further, that in the *Historia Anglorum* Matthew referred to the bull of canonization as being 'in libro Additamentorum', but that this was later altered to 'in libro de vita ipsius': Lawrence concluded from this that the Life was not written until after this part of the *Historia Anglorum*.[3] The bull of canonization thus referred to is still in the *Liber Additamentorum*, and we cannot therefore argue that the reference was altered because the document was removed thence into the Life, and the first reference thus made inaccurate. Furthermore, there are many references in the *Historia Anglorum* which have been altered in a similar way to this one; and we have seen that Matthew evidently worked through the text systematically, altering the explicit references to actual manuscripts at St Albans into vague general ones.[4] The alteration of this reference in the *Historia Anglorum* cannot therefore be used as evidence for the date of the Life, and we must fall back on the evidence noted above, and conclude that it was written between 1247 and 1253, and probably nearer 1247 than 1253, since, as we have seen, it seems to have been written before the *Historia Anglorum*. The only other hint as to its date is the fact that Matthew tells us that it was written with the help of Richard Wych and Robert Bacon, and his words suggest that information was supplied

[1] Paravicini, *St Edmund of Abingdon*, p. xxxii; see Wallace, *Life of St Edmund*, p. 583.
[2] Lawrence, 'Robert of Abingdon and Matthew Paris', *EHR.* LXIX (1954), p. 417, note 4; see Wallace, *Life of St Edmund*, p. 571.
[3] *HA.* III, p. 13, note 4; Paravicini, *St Edmund of Abingdon*, pp. xxxviii–xxxix; Lawrence, 'Robert of Abingdon and Matthew Paris', *loc. cit.* p. 417.
[4] See pp. 72–3 above.

verbally to him by these two.[1] If this was so, he must have been collecting material for his Life of Edmund before Bacon's death in 1248,[2] which adds to the probability of an early date, nearer 1247 than 1253.

In his Life of Edmund, Matthew treats his source in much the same way as, in his *Chronica Majora*, he treated the text of Roger Wendover's chronicle. Many small alterations of a stylistic kind are made, as well as short additions reflecting Matthew's opinions and attitude of mind.[3] In his longer interpolations, too, Matthew expresses his characteristic feelings, sometimes more forcibly than in the *Chronica Majora*. In describing the baptism of Henry III's son Edward, for instance, Matthew says in the *Chronica Majora* that he was baptized by the papal legate Otho, 'though he was not a priest', and 'though the archbishop was present'.[4] In the Life, Matthew's resentment that the heir to the throne should be baptized by a mere papal legate is expatiated upon, and a sharp contrast is drawn between the Englishman and the foreigner:[5]

When the king's son and heir was baptized, Otho, then legate, was chosen to baptize him: a deacon and a foreigner, of poor character and inadequate theological knowledge; instead of the archbishop of Canterbury and primate of all England, who was present: a priest and an Englishman, of excellent character and even sanctity, and a celebrated teacher and scholar....

Characteristic of Matthew, too, is his statement in the Life that Edmund was only elected archbishop 'after many royal and papal vexations'; and the insertion of a piece of direct speech, in which Edmund is warned that, if he does not accept the archbishopric, the king will intrude some unworthy alien.[6] Whereas in the *Chronica Majora* Matthew tends to take the side of the monks in their quarrel with Edmund,[7] in the *Historia Anglorum* and the Life he remains neutral, or even sympathizes with the archbishop. There are other differences between the

---

[1] See pp. 161–2 above.   [2] Which he records at *CM*. v, p. 16.
[3] See Lawrence, 'Robert of Abingdon and Matthew Paris', *EHR*. LXIX (1954), pp. 413–14.   [4] *CM*. III, pp. 539 and 540.
[5] Wallace, *Life of St Edmund*, p. 569.
[6] *Ibid*. p. 554; see also p. 139 above.
[7] See especially III, p. 527.

account of Edmund in the *Chronica Majora* and that in the Life, the most striking of which is in Matthew's treatment of the legate Otho. Although he is described in one place as an adversary of Edmund,[1] on the whole Matthew takes a fairly favourable view of Otho in the *Chronica Majora*. In the Life, however, he is systematically hostile: Otho is said to have annulled Edmund's acts in an intolerable manner,[2] and the reader is given to understand that it was the persecution of the legate and others which drove Edmund into exile, whereas in the *Chronica Majora*[3] his departure is construed as a protest against papal exactions.

The Life, of course, is a purely hagiological work, designed to praise St Edmund and demonstrate his sanctity, whereas the *Chronica Majora* gives a more factual account of him, with the emphasis on his part in politics rather than on his personal sanctity. Extravagant praise of Edmund is, however, a noticeable feature of the minor historical works written after 1250, especially of the *Flores Historiarum*, where he is referred to as 'a man of wonderful sanctity and gentleness' whose fame after his death spread through the whole of cisalpine Europe.[4] The *Flores Historiarum*, like the *Historia Anglorum*, seems to have been written after the Life, and it is interesting to find in it an account of the curing of the pope's illness by the archbishop shortly before he was canonized,[5] which is not in the Life, and which Matthew perhaps only heard about after the Life had been written. He did not attempt, in the Life, to collect all the available material about St Edmund, though he has added to his source a considerable amount of historical information already recorded in the *Chronica Majora*. On the whole, the Life lacks the bitter attacks on king and pope which are so common in the *Chronica*; and it is by no means the political biography we might have expected from the pen of Matthew Paris. Controversial issues are for the most part avoided, and though Edmund is represented as a much persecuted man, Matthew is careful not to enlarge on these persecutions, nor to attack the persecutors. So far as the Life is concerned, he is not

---

[1] IV, p. 72; the statement at III, p. 480 is in the margin and was no doubt added later; see note 4.   [2] Wallace, *Life of St Edmund*, p. 568.
[3] IV, p. 32.   [4] *FH*. II, pp. 213 and 274.   [5] II, pp. 314–15.

being hypocritical when, speaking of the archbishop's tribulations, he says that they were caused by some of the great men of the kingdom, and adds: 'Whom I do not think, on account of reverence for the pope and king, it would be decent or safe to contradict by name.'[1] Matthew's Life of Edmund is probably the fullest and most reliable of the contemporary lives, and Wallace was undoubtedly right in basing his own biography on it. For the most part it is a balanced and accurate, though rather fragmentary, account; in which Matthew's political passions, as well as his prejudices, are subdued in the interests of the central theme, the sanctity of St Edmund.

There exists a group of saints' Lives in Anglo-Norman verse, which have been attributed to Matthew Paris; and Dr Legge, in her book *Anglo-Norman in the Cloisters*,[2] devotes a chapter to 'Matthew Paris and his Fellows' in which she accepts them as Matthew's work, though without any detailed discussion of the evidence for his authorship of them. This I shall attempt to supply here, both for the sake of completeness, and because no coherent discussion of the authorship of all these Lives has yet been undertaken. The Lives in question are four in number:

(1) *Alban*: St Alban, including also St Amphibalus; in Trinity College, Dublin, MS. E i 40, ff. 29–50. The text and the illustrations which accompany it are executed by Matthew Paris.

(2) *Edward*: St Edward the Confessor; in Cambridge University Library MS. Ee iii 59. Written and illustrated (not by Matthew Paris) about the middle of the thirteenth century.

(3) *Thomas*: St Thomas Becket, a fragment. Text and illustrations as *Edward*.

(4) *Edmund*: St Edmund Rich; in the Welbeck Abbey MS., ff. 85 b–100; written in the second half of the thirteenth century.

Professor R. Atkinson published an edition of *Alban* in 1876. He thought that the poem was written in Matthew's own hand, and that it was probably also composed by Matthew. Some

[1] Wallace, *Life of St Edmund*, p. 570.
[2] Dr Legge has admirably discussed the place of these poems in Anglo-Norman literature as a whole, as well as their general character and significance; and I have, in consequence, limited the present discussion to topics not fully discussed by her.

of the inadequacies of Atkinson's edition were pointed out by Gaston Paris in a review contributed to *Romania* in the same year,[1] and many more in an elaborate study of the language and versification of the poem by Suchier, which also appeared in 1876.[2] Suchier thought that it would never be possible to establish whether or not *Alban* was Matthew's own work; and Uhlemann, in his study of the phonology and morphology of the poem,[3] contributed nothing to the question of its authorship, except for the suggestion that the legends to the pictures were probably not written by the author of the text. Matthew's authorship of *Alban* was doubted by Menger,[4] but M. R. James came to the conclusion that it was not only composed by Matthew, but also written by him, thus upholding the opinion of the editor of the poem, Atkinson. His theory about the authorship of *Alban* was linked to that concerning another of the Lives, *Edward*, and it appeared in his introductions to the facsimile editions of the manuscripts containing these two Lives, published in 1924 and 1920 respectively.[5] Until the appearance of James's facsimile edition of the manuscript, no one had thought of attributing *Edward* to Matthew Paris. Its editor, Luard,[6] believed that it had been written by a Westminster monk; and this theory was elaborated in a dissertation published by R. Fritz in 1910.[7] To *Alban* and *Edward* James added a third Life which he attributed to Matthew Paris, *Thomas*. A fragment of this had been found and published by Paul Meyer in 1885.[8] Meyer was uncertain of its authorship, but he compared it with *Edward*, and thought the illustrations similar to those of *Alban*. James was thus able, in 1920, to put forward a coherent theory for Matthew's authorship of *Alban*, *Edward*, and *Thomas*, but he thought that *Edmund* was irretrievably lost, for the copy of it which apparently once existed in British

[1] *Romania*, v (1876), pp. 384–9.
[2] Suchier, *Über die Matthaeus Paris zugeschriebene 'Vie de Seint Auban'*.
[3] In *Romanische Studien*, iv (1880), pp. 543–626.
[4] *Anglo-Norman Dialect* (1904), p. 27.
[5] Lowe and Jacob (edd.), *Illustrations to the Life of St Alban*; James (ed.), *La Estoire de Seint Aedward le Rei*.
[6] Luard (ed.), *Lives of Edward the Confessor*, i, pp. 1–315.
[7] Fritz, *Über Verfasser und Quellen der altfranzösischen Estoire de Seint Aedward le Rei*, pp. 13–20.
[8] With facsimiles (Société des Anciens Textes Français, 1885).

Museum Cotton MS. Vitellius D viii had been destroyed in the
Cottonian fire in 1731.[1] Fortunately, however, Professor Baker
discovered a copy of this Life at Welbeck Abbey, which he
edited in 1929.[2]

James's attribution of *Alban, Edward,* and *Thomas* to Matthew
Paris was partly based on the statement of Thomas Walsingham
which we have already had occasion to quote:[3] '...Matthew
Paris...who wrote and most elegantly illustrated the Lives of
Saints Alban and Amphibalus, and of the archbishops of
Canterbury Thomas and Edmund....' The phrase 'the Lives
of Saints Alban and Amphibalus' no doubt refers to our *Alban*
in Trinity College, Dublin, MS. E i 40, for the poem is called
by Matthew 'l'estoire de seint Auban...e de seint Amphibal'
(f. 50a), and includes a full account of Amphibalus. James
thought that the text was in Matthew's hand, and he was in-
clined to the belief that the illustrations were his work. In both
these opinions my own studies have fully borne him out.[4] On
the second fly-leaf of this manuscript are some notes in the
handwriting of Matthew Paris which James translates as follows:[5]

(1) If you please, you can keep this book until Easter.

(2) G., send, please, to the lady Countess of Arundel, Isabel, that
she is to send you the book about St Thomas the Martyr and
St Edward which I translated and illustrated, and which the lady
Countess of Cornwall may keep until Whitsuntide.

(3) In the Countess of Winchester's book let there be a pair of
images on each page, thus:....

The essentially private nature of these notes shows that the
manuscript in which they were written was Matthew's own.
The third note is in reference to a series of verses, arranged down
the page in pairs, on twelve different saints, and the images were
perhaps designed to preface a psalter.[6] The second note is more

[1] James (ed.), *Estoire de St Aedward le Rei,* p. 18.
[2] In *Romania,* LV (1929), pp. 332–81.
[3] Above, p. 19.
[4] See Vaughan, 'Handwriting of M. Paris', *Trans. Camb. Bibliog. Soc.*
I (1953), and below, p. 221.
[5] James in *Illustrations to the Life of St Alban,* pp. 15–16.
[6] See, for instance, British Museum Royal MS. 2 B vi, a psalter which is
prefixed with a series of pictures arranged in pairs, which include a number
of saints, executed at St Albans in Matthew's lifetime. See below, p. 224.

interesting, for it shows that Matthew had translated and illustrated the Lives of SS. Thomas and Edward, apparently in one book. 'Translated' means, of course, turned from Latin into Anglo-Norman.

It cannot be mere coincidence that the manuscripts of *Alban*, *Edward* and *Thomas* are so similar in date, size, format and style of illumination. *Alban*, however, which is Matthew's autograph, differs from the other two in a number of ways. The surviving leaves of *Thomas* are larger than those of *Edward*, and the scribes are different in the two manuscripts, and neither of them is Matthew himself. It is thus most unlikely that either *Edward* or *Thomas* ever formed part of the single volume mentioned by Matthew in his fly-leaf note in *Alban*. On the other hand they are, to judge from the script and the style of illumination, very close copies of Matthew's original, and obvious products of the scriptorium of St Albans during his lifetime.[1]

James was by no means content with the evidence so far discussed, and he went on to examine the textual similarities between the Lives he knew: *Alban*, *Edward*, and *Thomas*.[2] He pointed out that each is a close rendering of a Latin original; he pointed out, too, that *Edward* and *Thomas* are both written in octosyllabic couplets, usually with three columns on each page, though sometimes with only two; and that *Alban* and *Thomas* have Latin legends to the pictures as well as those in Anglo-Norman which *Edward* also has. James discovered seventy-five marked coincidences of vocabulary between *Edward* and *Thomas*, and 585 between *Edward* and *Alban*. The verbal parallels between these poems (including the newly discovered *Edmund*) certainly help to demonstrate their common authorship, though not enough of *Thomas* has survived to provide useful material in this respect. Here are some of the more striking parallels:

Edmund, l. 905: ke parveue et estuee
Edward, l. 3276: Li fu purveue e estuee
Edmund, l. 330: Ne prisa vaillant une pume (see also l. 1280)
Edward, l. 559: Ne...vailant une pume (see also l. 4470)
Edmund, l. 874: a chief de tur

---

[1] For the illustrations of these manuscripts see below, pp. 221–2.
[2] For what follows see James (ed.), *Estoire de St Aedward le Rei*, p. 26.

Edward, l. 398: au chef de tur (see also l. 4090)
Alban, l. 562: au chef de tur
Edmund, ll. 718–20: espanir...cum fet rosee en matinee
Edward, l. 141: u de lis e rose espanie
Alban, l. 1070: beus ke...n'est lis espani (see also l. 1721)
Edward, l. 561: Ne preisent vailant un bittun
Alban, l. 334: Ne prise mes vallant un butun
Edward, l. 719: Pur trestut l'or k'est a Damas
Alban, l. 1497: pur tut l'or de Damas
Edward, l. 2154: De quor entent e ben escute
Alban, l. 104: Auban ben l'escute e entent i de quor (see also l. 175)
Edward, l. 3502: Plus clers ke solailz de midiz
Alban, l. 1060: ke plus ert clers ke solailz de midi

The verbal parallels between these poems are not limited to phrases and metaphors. There is, for instance, a passage in *Alban* mentioning various illnesses, which is very similar to passages in *Edward* and *Edmund*;[1] and there is one parallel between *Edmund* and *Edward* which might by itself be considered to afford sufficient evidence of their common authorship:

Edmund	Sa char, le mund (et) l'enemi	(l. 14)
	Sa char...par chasteté	(ll. 15–16)
	Le mund par humilité	(l. 17)
	E si descunfist le diable	(l. 19)
	Par son penser espiritable	(l. 20)
	Bien dei de lui escrivre estoire	(l. 23)
	E son nun mettre en memoire	(l. 24)
Edward	ki lur char, diable e mund	(l. 21)
	venquirent...	(l. 22)
	Sa char venquis par chastete	(l. 29)
	Le mund par humilite	(l. 30)
	E diable par ses vertuz	(l. 31)
	Dunt vus escrif e vus translat	(l. 35)
	Pur refreschir sa memoire	(l. 38)

So far our argument may be summarized as follows. We know, from his own statements, as well as those of Walsingham, that Matthew Paris illustrated and wrote in Anglo-Norman the Lives of Alban and Amphibalus, Edward, Thomas, and Edmund. We have identified his original manuscript of *Alban* in the library of Trinity College, Dublin; and we have seen that our

[1] Cf. *Alban*, ll. 148 ff.; *Edward*, ll. 4426 ff.; and *Edmund*, ll. 1946 ff.

manuscripts of *Edward* and *Thomas* were probably produced at St Albans in Matthew's lifetime. They are both, it seems, 'first copies' of Matthew's original. Furthermore, we have shown that there are a number of textual similarities between the poems, which points to their common authorship. On the strength of this evidence alone we might well attribute *Alban*, *Edward*, *Thomas* and *Edmund* to Matthew Paris. In the case of *Edmund*, however, there is further convincing evidence pointing to Matthew Paris. Professor Baker noted the following significant facts about this poem:[1]

(1) It is dedicated to Isabel, countess of Arundel (who had borrowed from Matthew his copy of *Thomas* and *Edward*, see p. 170 above).

(2) The author had written the Life of Edmund in two languages, and the source of *Edmund* is Matthew's Latin Life of St Edmund.

(3) The author's name was Matthew (l. 1692: 'Faz ge Maheu en livre mettre').

The question of the authorship of *Edward* requires some further discussion, for Luard, followed by Fritz, maintained that it was written by a Westminster monk. Luard suggested this because the author in one place calls St Peter (l. 2022) 'le suen seigneur e le nostre';[2] and Fritz developed the theory with an elaborate and curious series of arguments. He did not, however, accept Luard's single piece of evidence, for he thought that the word 'nostre' might easily have been used in a vague general sense.[3] Fritz pointed out that the centre of interest of the poem is Westminster Abbey, of which the author clearly had a detailed knowledge, for he adds to his source a long description of it (ll. 2290–323). In the course of his account of the legend of the fisherman who rowed St Peter across the Thames for the dedication of the abbey church, the author of the poem says that the fisherman caught *salmon* in his nets, though his source mentioned only *fish*. From this Fritz deduced that the author of the poem knew the legend in more detail than was to

[1] Baker (ed.), 'Vie de S. Edmond', *Romania*, LV (1929), pp. 336–41.
[2] Luard (ed.), *Lives of Edward the Confessor*, I, pp. x–xi.
[3] Fritz, *Über Verfasser und Quellen der altfranzösischen Estoire de Seint Aedward le Rei*, p. 19, note 1; for what follows, see pp. 15–19.

be found in his source, and that he must therefore have been a monk of Westminster. Again, Fritz claimed that the author of the poem, since he says in one place, when copying from a document, that the original is before him in two languages, must have been writing in the scriptorium at Westminster, where the document in question, which concerns Westminster, would have been preserved.[1] Finally, Fritz noted that the author talks about the 'Beus maneres, terres e bois' of the monastery, while the source mentions only 'possessiones'; and he cited this as additional evidence that he was a monk of Westminster.

None of these arguments is convincing. Matthew Paris knew Westminster well and had been there at least once;[2] and his mention of the ruined hall of William Rufus at Westminster[3] demonstrates his personal knowledge of the place. He is, too, just the man to improve on his source by altering the word 'fish' into something a little more exciting. The undoubted fact that the poem was written in connexion with an important event at Westminster (it is dedicated to the queen) could adequately account for the interest in, and glorification of, that house, which is so apparent in the poem. Furthermore, we should bear in mind the fact that Matthew Paris wrote a version of his chronicle, the Chetham manuscript of the *Flores Historiarum*, especially for Westminster, and took the trouble to insert into it a number of passages of Westminster interest only.[4]

I think it can be proved conclusively that *Edward* was written at St Albans. Although most of it is translated from Aelred of Rievaulx's Latin Life of Edward the Confessor, some passages have been taken from a historical source which Fritz identified as the 'St Albans compilation'. But in fact this historical source was Matthew's own *Flores Historiarum*. In this Matthew adds to the text of the 'St Albans compilation' in *A* the metaphor 'quarum [hastarum] multitudo ad instar hiberni grandinis volando', which occurs, slightly altered, in *Edward*, where it is said that arrows, stones and darts flew 'Espessement cum gresle en Marz'.[5] Again, in the *Flores Historiarum*, Matthew

---

[1] Fritz, *op. cit.* p. 17; *Edward*, ll. 2342–5. [2] See above, p. 3.
[3] *HA.* I, p. 165. [4] Above, p. 100.
[5] *FH.* I, p. 596, and *Edward*, l. 4568; both are in reference to the battle of Hastings.

says that when William counter-attacked at the battle of Hastings, he charged into the English 'quasi prora navis fluctus procellosos penetrando', while in *Edward* the same metaphor is applied to the English when they attacked the Normans: 'Cum fait dromunz wage en und Quant curt siglant en mer parfund.'[1] The significance of William's fall on the beach, too, is elaborated in a similar way in the *Flores Historiarum* and in *Edward*.[2] There seem to be only two possible explanations of these parallels: either the *Flores Historiarum* and *Edward* were written by the same author, that is, Matthew Paris; or the *Flores Historiarum* was used in the composition of *Edward*. The former, in view of the nature of the parallels, which are not due to straightforward copying, is the more likely explanation; but, even if we only accept the latter, we are forced to conclude that *Edward* was written at St Albans, for we know that the *Flores Historiarum* was not sent to Westminster until after 1265, and that *Edward* was already written before then.[3]

There is some internal evidence that Matthew was the author of *Edward*, for remarks characteristic of him frequently occur in it. We find, for instance, a dig at Stigand which is typical of him: 'li simoniaus culvertz, Stigantz' (ll. 3706–7);[4] as well as sentiments identical with those expressed in the *Chronica Majora* on the subject of Englishmen and foreigners in the government of the country; for in one place Edward is praised for handing over responsibility to his own subjects, of whose loyalty he could be quite certain, and not to 'stranges aliens'.[5] Elsewhere the author of *Edward* tells us something about himself which can surely only apply to Matthew Paris:[6]

> Now I pray you, gentle King Edward,
> To have regard to me a sinner,
> Who have translated from the Latin,
> According to my knowledge and genius,
> Your history into French,
> That memory of thee may spread;

[1] *FH.* I, p. 595, and *Edward*, l. 4557.
[2] Cf. *FH.* I, p. 591, and *Edward*, ll. 4529 ff.
[3] *FH.* I, p. xiii, and Fritz, *op. cit.* pp. 11–12.
[4] Cf. *HA.* I, p. 13.   [5] *Edward*, ll. 2496 ff.
[6] *Edward*, ll. 3855–966; I have used Luard's translation, *Lives of Edward the Confessor*, I, p. 290.

And for lay people who letters
Know not, in portraiture
Have I clearly figured it
In this present book....

It is scarcely likely that two different people translated and themselves illustrated a Life of St Edward towards the middle of the thirteenth century, and we may be certain, therefore, that this Life of Edward is the same as that referred to by Matthew in his fly-leaf note in the Dublin manuscript;[1] and that Matthew Paris was indeed the author of our four Anglo-Norman saints' Lives: *Alban, Edward, Thomas*, and *Edmund*.

There is plenty of evidence, in Matthew's historical manuscripts, of his concern with hagiology, and with these four saints in particular. We shall discuss his interest in St Alban in the next chapter, and we have already discussed in detail his Latin Life of Edmund. His interest in St Edward the Confessor is well shown in the *Abbreviatio Chronicorum* (p. 167), where he mentions several legends about the saint which are described in *Edward*; as well as in a note on the penultimate fly-leaf of *A*, which reads: 'Here one should consider carefully the exposition of the parable of Blessed King Edward when he was dying. Read [it] at the end of his history.' This remark, made in connexion with the genealogical chronicle on this page, refers to Edward's explanation of a vision, which is described in detail in *Edward*. It is worth noting, too, in connexion with Matthew's interest in St Edward, that there is a marginal note of his in the *Gesta Abbatum*[2] to the effect that, in the time of Abbot Robert of St Albans, Abbot Lawrence of Westminster caused the Life of Edward the Confessor to be written, as a result of a request of Henry II's. This is the Life by Aelred of Rievaulx—the very one which was used as a basis for our *Edward*. Of St Thomas we read a great deal in the *Chronica Majora*, and Matthew has added some long passages about him to Roger Wendover's account.[3] Moreover, in his manuscript of the poems of Henry of Avranches Matthew has himself written out Henry's Latin verse Life of Thomas.[4]

---

[1] See p. 170 above.
[2] Wats, p. 82.   [3] *CM.* ii, pp. 261, 278, etc.
[4] University Library, Cambridge, MS. Dd xi 78, ff. 1b–29a.

Matthew Paris, as we should expect, knew Anglo-Norman perfectly well and frequently used it. Thus nearly all the geographical and other notes on his maps and itineraries are in Anglo-Norman, as are some of his rough notes in the *Liber Additamentorum*. Sometimes a document is transcribed in Anglo-Norman, and in one place in the *Liber Additamentorum* Matthew writes out a heading in it.[1] Furthermore, there is some evidence that he was acquainted with French epic literature in general. René Louis surmised that Matthew may have known something of the poem *Girart de Roussillon*, since he marks Roussillon on his itinerary from London to Apulia, and is the earliest writer to localize this name.[2] In the *Gesta Abbatum* Matthew says of Roger de Thony that he was descended from those famous knights 'qui a Cigni nomine intitulantur';[3] a remark which seems to imply some knowledge of the epic literature concerning *Le Chevalier au Cygne*. In the Anglo-Norman poems themselves there is more evidence of Matthew's knowledge of literature, but it is interesting to find that, even without reference to them, Matthew appears to have been perfectly capable of writing in Anglo-Norman verse.

The problem of finding a date for the writing and illustration of Matthew's Anglo-Norman saints' Lives is a difficult one, especially when we consider how busy he must have been, towards the end of his life, with his historical writing. It seems probable that *Alban* was written first, for the handwriting is tidy and controlled, and the illustrations seem to be earlier than the others attributed to Matthew Paris.[4] The handwriting is in fact considerably neater than anything in the historical manuscripts, and there seems to be no reason why *Alban* should not have been written and illustrated in the third, or even the second, decade of the thirteenth century. If *Alban* was the first of Matthew's Anglo-Norman poems, *Edmund* was probably the last, for it is based on his Latin Life of Edmund, and must

---

[1] *CM.* vi, p. 165.

[2] Louis, *De l'Histoire à la Légende*, iii, p. 173. For Matthew's possible knowledge of the *Roman de Renaud de Montauban*, see Bédier, *Les Légendes épiques*, iv, p. 244, note 1.   [3] Wats, p. 46.

[4] See, for instance, Rickert, *Painting in Britain*, p. 119; see also below, pp. 227–8. Legge, *Anglo-Norman in the Cloisters*, pp. 21–3, argues that *Alban* is the earliest of the four poems.

therefore have been written after 1247.[1] Indeed there is some
evidence that it was not written until after 1253, for the reference
to Queen Blanche in the Latin Life—'quam constat esse muli-
erem consilii magni'—is altered in the Anglo-Norman life to
'ke seinte fu et sage et franche', as if the queen's death had
occurred in the meanwhile.[2] *Thomas* and *Edward* seem to have
been written at about the same time, for they were originally in
the same manuscript.[3] Both Luard and James thought that
Edward was especially written to be presented to Queen Eleanor
in connexion with some great Westminster event: soon after
1241, thought James; and Luard favoured 1245.[4] We shall
therefore perhaps not be far wrong if we date *Alban* before 1240;
Thomas and *Edward* fairly soon after 1240; and *Edmund* after
1250, or even perhaps after 1253.

The sources of these poems are in every case easily identifiable.
Alban has been taken, often word for word, from William of
St Albans's Latin Life of St Alban, the text of which, written out
in Matthew's own hand, precedes the Anglo-Norman poem in
the Dublin manuscript. Suchier showed that, in *Alban*, the
Latin was frequently very closely followed, even sometimes in
the order of words;[5] and this is true of the other poems. Meyer
pointed out that the source of *Thomas* was the well-known
Quadrilogus, and he made a detailed comparison between it and
the text of *Thomas*.[6] *Edward* is based on Aelred of Rievaulx's
Latin Life of Edward the Confessor, but Matthew's *Flores
Historiarum*, as well as, in one place, Henry of Huntingdon,
were also probably used.[7] *Edmund* is a literal translation from
Matthew's own Latin Life of St Edmund. Thus in each of these
poems (with the partial exception of *Edward*) a single Latin
source is followed more or less closely, though with minor
additions and alterations of the type usual with Matthew Paris,
and with occasional longer additions. These additions are some-

---

[1] See above, p. 165.
[2] Wallace, *Life of St Edmund*, p. 571; *Edmund*, l. 1408. Queen Blanche
died in 1253.　　　　[3] See p. 170 above.
[4] James (ed.), *Estoire de St Aedward*, p. 17; Luard, *Lives of Edward the
Confessor*, I, p. xi. Fritz agreed with Luard, *Über Verfasser der Estoire de
Seint Aedward*, p. 12.　　　[5] Suchier, *Über die Vie de Seint Auban*, pp. 8–9.
[6] Meyer (ed.), *Vie de Saint Thomas*, pp. viii–xxvi.
[7] See pp. 174–5 above, and Fritz, *Über Verfasser der Estoire de Seint
Aedward*, pp. 21 ff.

times lyrical passages;[1] sometimes explanatory;[2] and sometimes political.[3] Frequently a metaphor or a proverb is added to the source, and direct speech is introduced as a literary device to increase the dramatic intensity. The occasional slight variations between *Edmund* and its Latin source are of interest because both were written by Matthew. In *Edmund*, the papal legate Otho's hostility to Edmund is expatiated upon at greater length than in the Latin Life, and the archbishop's flight is linked more closely with Otho's machinations.[4] Furthermore, the Canterbury monks are explicitly exonerated from their part in the quarrel with Edmund, and are said to have been deceived by malicious advisers, or, as Matthew calls them, 'legistres faus'.[5]

In all these poems certain proverbs, phrases, and allusions occur, which show, I think, that Matthew's Anglo-Norman poetry was influenced by the epic conventions of his day; and that he knew something of contemporary vernacular literature. Thus, in *Thomas*, two well-known proverbs are added to the source:[6]

leaf 4, ll. 59–60: De dous mals doit hom le mendre Eslire...
  ll. 60–1: meuz nus vaut atendre Ke d'estre hastifs e engrès

Another proverb occurs in *Alban* (l. 1314): 'cist se fert ki ne veit'. Of the stock literary phrases, 'au chef du tur' is the commonest,[7] and many others occur. In *Alban*, for instance, we find the following:

l. 69: n'a pl(ace ne liu)s ci k'a l'euue de Rin
l. 1264: ...de ci k'a Burdele
l. 1825: pur tut l'or Costentin
l. 1497: pur tut l'or de Damas[8]
l. 734: ki par autres est garniz, cist beu se chastie

Literary allusions, too, are not uncommon in these poems. Thus, in *Edward*, Harold is criticized, and it is said of him that:

  ll. 4497–8: D'el hestoires n'enquert, n'en ot
      Ne d'ancienne geste un mot

---

[1] E.g. *Alban*, ll. 104–6; *Edmund*, ll. 229–32, etc.
[2] E.g. *Edmund*, ll. 1976–7; *Edward*, ll. 3955–74.
[3] E.g. *Edmund*, ll. 1355–80; *Edward*, ll. 2496 ff.
[4] *Edmund*, ll. 1355–80.   [5] *Edmund*, ll. 1191 and 1199–1200.
[6] Meyer (ed.), *Vie de Saint Thomas*, p. xxiv, and note 1.
[7] See pp. 171–2 above.   [8] See p. 172 above.

A similar remark is made in *Edmund*, though this time in praise of its subject:

ll. 331–2: Romanz d'Oger u (de) Charlemeine
Ne preisa il une chasteine

There seem to be three allusions, in these poems, to a Brut of some kind:

Alban, l. 1836: en l'eille ke cunquist Brutus e Cornelin
l. 1832: passerai Mun Giu, le roiste munt alpin
Edward, ll. 786–7: Venant en la cumpanie
Brut e la chere hardie

Matthew had evidently read something of the epic literature concerning Duke Richard of Normandy, and probably also the *Roman de Rou*; as may be seen from the following passage in *Edward* (ll. 4577–83):

Reis Rou, ki as coups de lance
Descumfist le rei de France
E la mata enmi sa terre
Par force de bataille e guerre.
E ducs Richard k'apres li vint
Ki li diable ateint e tint
E le venquit e le lia....

It is interesting to note some of the historical and mythical figures introduced into these poems. In *Alban* we find Apollo, Phoebus, Diana, Neptune, Pallas, Jupiter, Tetim (Tethys?), and Pluto; and in *Edward*, Priam, Menelaus, and Julius Caesar. In *Edmund* (ll. 521–3) Matthew tells us that, when the saint gave up secular studies, he abandoned Plato and Ptolemy— a remark which perhaps tells us more of Matthew's ignorance of secular studies than of his 'stock-in-trade' of literary characters.

The language and versification of these poems are characteristic of thirteenth-century Anglo-Norman verse. In *Thomas*, for instance, which, like *Edmund* and *Edward*, was written in octosyllabic rhyming couplets, there are many lines of seven or nine syllables, and the same variation occurs in the other two poems. In these three poems, the same rhyme is frequently used for four or even six lines in succession—another common feature of thirteenth-century Anglo-Norman verse. *Alban* is unlike the other poems, for it is written in *laisses*. Alexandrines are here the norm, but Matthew often uses ten- and even fourteensyllabled lines, usually for literary effect and to avoid monotony. It is curious that he should have used the old epic metre for *Alban*, and the new romance metre for the other three poems; but this is perhaps explicable on the assumption that *Alban* was the first of Matthew's ventures into Anglo-Norman verse.[1] He was bound by few rules of grammar and syntax, and he often confuses subject and object, or fails to distinguish between the singular and plural of the second person of the personal pronoun. It is interesting to note that Meyer made a careful study of the phonology of *Thomas*, and came to the conclusion that the author was certainly born in England.[2]

There is nothing beautiful or stylish about Matthew's Anglo-Norman verse: it is the characteristic doggerel of his day. Nor does he seem to have taken very much trouble with the texts of these poems, for even in the autograph *Alban* careless errors abound. On the other hand, the illustration of the manuscripts was evidently carefully and systematically executed. As Dr Legge pointed out, they were designed (except perhaps for *Alban*) for the laity,[3] and so the pictures were of paramount importance, and their subject-matter is explained by means of rhymed legends. These poems are closely related to Matthew's historical writings, and they fit into our general picture of his interests and activities; but they also show us a new aspect of him, as the successful producer of illustrated hagiological literature designed for his friends among the lay aristocracy. *Alban* seems to have been produced for Matthew's own house; *Edward*, however, is dedicated to Queen Eleanor; and *Edmund* to Isabel of Arundel. Unfortunately the dedication of *Thomas* is lost. It appears from his fly-leaf notes in *Alban*[4] that Matthew ran a kind of circulating library among his aristocratic friends—all of whom were apparently women—which specialized in illustrated, vernacular hagiology. New light is thus thrown on Matthew Paris, for we find that the pessimistic enemy of the world revealed in the historical writings is quite capable, not only of mixing with the secular aristocracy of his day, but also of making a contribution to its rather specialized culture.

[1] See p. 177 above.
[2] Meyer (ed.), *Vie de Saint Thomas*, pp. xxvii–xxviii.
[3] Legge, *Anglo-Norman in the Cloisters*, p. 29.   [4] See p. 170 above.

CHAPTER X

MATTHEW PARIS THE DOMESTIC HISTORIAN

I. THE 'GESTA ABBATUM'

ATTHEW'S most important contribution to the domestic history of St Albans is his *Gesta Abbatum*, the autograph text of which, written in two parts, survives in his *Liber Additamentorum*.[1] This was printed by Wats in 1639, though with numerous errors, without distinguishing the marginalia from the text, and with no attempt to describe the sources used. Another edition of the *Gesta Abbatum* was carried out by H. T. Riley for the Rolls Series in 1867–9; but this was printed from Thomas Walsingham's manuscript, written *c.* 1394, with little reference to the text of Matthew's manuscript, with an incomplete and inaccurate collation of Wats's text, and, again, with no attempt to describe the sources.

In the upper margin of the first leaf of Matthew's text of the *Gesta Abbatum* is a note in his own hand which reads:[2] 'According to (*secundum*) the ancient roll of Bartholomew the clerk, who for a long time had been servant to Adam the Cellarer, and who kept this roll for himself from among his writings (*scriptis suis*), choosing this one alone.' The implication of this note seems to be that Matthew Paris based at any rate the earlier part of his *Gesta Abbatum* on an 'ancient roll' written by Bartholomew the clerk, which had probably either been in the possession of Adam the Cellarer, or had been dictated by him to Bartholomew; and it is only natural that the roll in question should have been attributed to Adam the Cellarer, a well-known twelfth-century monk of St Albans. There is no record, however, of a clerk, Bartholomew, connected with Adam the Cellarer; but a 'Bartholomeus clericus' signs a number of charters between 1230 and 1247 immediately after Adam de Belvoir, the *praepositus*.

---

[1] See above, pp. 48 and 82 ff.
[2] B.M. Cotton MS. Nero D i, f. 30 a, printed in *GA.* I, p. xiv.

It is possible that the *praepositus* was the same official as the extern cellarer or *cellerarius curiae*, and that this Adam and Bartholomew, contemporaries of Matthew Paris, are the ones mentioned in his note. Adam the Cellarer, however, has a much stronger claim to be the author of the 'ancient roll'. He began his career as cellarer on his return from Croyland, where he had been sent in 1138 to help his uncle Geoffrey, another St Albans monk, who became abbot of Croyland, in the reformation of that house,[1] and he held the office of cellarer at St Albans from *c.* 1140 until his death, which probably took place between 1167 and 1176.[2] His career is reflected in a striking manner in the text of Matthew's *Gesta Abbatum*. We know that he was engaged in litigation on behalf of the convent, and that he played an especially important part in the territorial transactions of the middle years of the twelfth century. Up to the end of the account of Robert's abbacy (1151–66), the whole emphasis of the *Gesta Abbatum* is on territorial acquisitions and litigation concerning them, and the long description of Abbot Robert's rule is almost entirely devoted to detailed, and often, it seems, eyewitness, accounts of lawsuits concerning land, in which Adam the Cellarer is a central figure. After the description of Robert's rule the character of the *Gesta Abbatum* alters radically. Although Simon, who succeeded Robert, was actively engaged in various territorial transactions,[3] not one of these is mentioned in the *Gesta*, and, in the rest of it, territorial transactions and litigation take their place beside many other topics. We find, too, that whereas the account of Abbot Robert, who ruled for fifteen years, occupies twenty-five printed pages, that of Simon, who ruled for sixteen, takes up only three. This change in the

[1] See Dugdale, *Monasticon anglicanum*, II, p. 101, and Wats, p. 69.

[2] Adam signs one undated charter of Abbot Simon (1167–83. B.M. Cotton MS. Otho D iii, f. 73 col. 2), but the absence of his signature from several other of Simon's charters (for instance B.M. Cotton MS. Otho D iii, f. 115, of 1179, and Chatsworth cartulary, f. 64b, of 1180), as well as the charter of 1176 disposing of the lands acquired by him (Chatsworth cartulary, ff. 10a–b, printed in Dugdale, *Monasticon*, II, pp. 228–9; see Eyton, *Court, Household and Itinerary of King Henry II*, p. 204), points to his death during the first half of Simon's abbacy. Abbot Warin (1183–95) instituted his anniversary (Wats, p. 98).

[3] See, for instance, B.M. Cotton MS. Otho D iii, ff. 29b, 30a, 73a–74a, 115a, 167b and 177a; Chatsworth cartulary, f. 64b; and B.M. Cotton MS. Julius D iii, f. 75b.

content of the *Gesta Abbatum* coincides with a change in authorship, for throughout the account of Simon's rule there are unmistakable signs of Matthew's style, which, up to this point, appear only in a few passages evidently interpolated by him into the text of his source. We may surely conclude from this that the 'ancient roll', which Matthew used for the early part of his *Gesta*, was closely connected with Adam the Cellarer, and was probably compiled under his auspices.

Matthew seems to have used some other source besides the roll of Adam the Cellarer, for his text contains a considerable amount of repetition, and, in the course of the description of Abbot Ralph's rule, he has added in the margin another version of a passage in the text, and headed it: *Additum de alio rotulo*.[1] There are a number of other marginal additions in the early part of Matthew's *Gesta Abbatum*, some of which were no doubt taken from this 'other roll'. Fortunately for us, the passages which Matthew has added to the text of Adam's roll are usually readily identified, for they frequently include some of his favourite phrases and expressions, and they often interrupt Adam's narrative because they are carelessly inserted into it, sometimes in the wrong place. A good example is the story of Adrian IV's appointment of three bishops to examine into the claims of the convent of Ely to possess the relics of St Alban, which is inserted near the end of the account of Abbot Robert's rule, although the event it describes must have occurred (if it ever did occur) soon after Robert's accession.[2] Again, the description of the reformation of Croyland by St Albans monks[3] is inserted into the account of Abbot Robert (1151–66), although it actually occurred in 1138. In copying his source, Matthew has made many alterations and additions of the sort we have noticed when discussing his treatment of sources in his other works. Thus he sometimes adds a quotation or an allusion;[4] or introduces one of his usual phrases or characteristic comments.[5] He adds, for instance, to Adam's account of Abbot

---

[1] Wats, p. 65, omits the heading. The passage begins 'Iste quoque Radulphus', and ends 'et creatus est'.

[2] Wats, pp. 88–9; see also below, p. 201.   [3] Wats, p. 69.

[4] E.g. Wats, pp. 36 (Virgil, *Aen.* II, 646) and 47 (Terence, *Andr.* v, iv, 38).

[5] E.g. Wats, pp. 42 ('novit Ille qui nihil ignorat') and 53 ('felix suscepit incrementum').

Robert's gifts to various people when he was leaving Rome the words: 'sciens ipsos Romanos esse insatiabiles sanguissugae filios, pecuniae sitibundos'.[1] Of Matthew's longer additions to his source, apart from those concerning the relics of St Alban, which we shall examine later, the most noteworthy are one or two excerpts from Diceto;[2] accounts of Anselm's vision of William Rufus's death and the foundation of the nunnery of Sopwell;[3] some additional information about Nicholas Breakspear;[4] and the account of the reformation of Croyland already mentioned.

From the account of Abbot Simon's rule (1167–83) up to nearly the end of that of Abbot John of Hertford (1235–63), the *Gesta Abbatum* seems to be an original composition of Matthew Paris. His description of Abbot Simon's rule is brief, but that of Warin's (1183–95) is fuller, and is especially interesting for the account it contains of Warin's statutes, many of which Matthew transcribes in full. Of John de Cella (1195–1214) we have a most interesting account, and the picture of William of Trumpington's abbacy (1214–35) is detailed and fascinating. Matthew goes on to give us a very full account of the election of the next abbot, John of Hertford, in 1235. Soon after this, however, his *Gesta Abbatum* shrinks to a series of laconic entries which peter out *c.* 1255. But although Matthew tells us very little, in the *Gesta*, of Abbot John of Hertford's rule, he included a detailed record of contemporary domestic history in his *Chronica Majora*, which, from *c.* 1240 on, seems to have claimed most of his attention. Fortunately, too, he took the trouble to transcribe documents of domestic import into his *Liber Additamentorum*, so that Thomas Walsingham, who continued the *Gesta Abbatum*, was able to amplify his narrative of the abbacy of John of Hertford with transcripts of these documents, as well as with long and numerous extracts from the *Chronica Majora*.

The sources of Matthew's section of the *Gesta Abbatum* need not detain us long, for he relied to a very large extent on his own experience and memory, and on the personal information provided by the older members of his community. His description, for instance, of the artistic work carried on at St Albans in the

[1] Wats, p. 71.　　　　　　　　　　[2] Wats, pp. 50 and 74.
[3] Wats, pp. 53 and 58–9.　　　　[4] Wats, p. 66.

time of Abbot Simon no doubt derives from information given him by Master John, one of the goldsmiths concerned, whom Matthew knew personally.[1] Written sources were also used; for, in the course of the account of Abbot William, Matthew in one place excerpts from a document which, he tells us, was written out by Abbot William himself;[2] and some of the marginalia in this part of the *Gesta Abbatum*[3] were taken from the St Albans manuscript of Diceto's history, which contains a number of additional annals written at St Albans and also used by Roger Wendover.

Matthew's contribution to the *Gesta Abbatum* is notable for the variety of subjects treated. He tells us a great deal, for instance, about the improvements and alterations to the monastic buildings carried out by the abbots John de Cella and William of Trumpington. He describes how Abbot William installed oak beds in the dorter; restored the tower of the abbey church and roofed it with lead; repaired the aisle roofs; whitewashed the inside walls of the church; finished the new bays at the west end of the nave begun by his predecessor; and built new cloisters connecting the various convent buildings. Matthew's section of the *Gesta Abbatum* is remarkable, too, for its notices of the chief local artists of the time and their works. Cups, chalices, copes, ornamental crosses and reliquaries are all noticed, and Matthew gives us a detailed description of the altar-pieces existing in the abbey in John de Cella's time (*c.* 1200), as well as the names of some of their artists. The most important of these were a small group from Colchester: Walter the Painter, his brother Simon, and Simon's son Richard. Among other things, Walter executed a magnificent rood-screen supporting a carving of the Crucifixion, with figures of SS. Mary and John. Richard painted the interior of Abbot John of Hertford's new guest-hall.[4] Books, too, are noted, often with valuable detail. Matthew tells us that Abbot Simon's books were kept in a painted cupboard near the tomb of Roger the Hermit, and that the documents concerning Abbot William's rule were kept in

---

[1] *GA.* I, p. 19. [2] Wats, p. 128.

[3] For instance the dedications etc., Wats, p. 119. The annals are printed, Liebermann (ed.), *Ungedruckte a.-n. Geschichtsquellen*, pp. 167–72.

[4] Wats, pp. 108, 122 and 142.

an oaken casket inside the big chest of charters.[1] He describes two Bibles executed in John de Cella's time,[2] one of which was prefixed with a painting of Christ in Majesty surrounded by the Four Evangelists by Walter of Colchester; and the other with a painting of the Crucifixion. One of the books which he mentions particularly, a copy of the *Historia Scholastica* acquired in the early years of the century by Prior Raymond, still exists, and includes some matter added by Matthew himself.[3]

Matthew's *Gesta Abbatum* is strongly coloured by his zealous devotion to St Albans. Litigation is seen as persecution of his house, and the temporal affairs of the house are measured in terms of acquisitions and losses. Richard Marsh, bishop of Durham, is described as 'an inexorable exactor of money', 'drunk with the poison of satan', because he had demanded a sum of a hundred marks from the abbey on behalf of the king.[4] Robert FitzWalter, involved in litigation with St Albans over the wood of Northaw, is likewise bitterly attacked;[5] and the sudden deaths in sordid circumstances of persecutors of the abbey, such as Falkes de Breauté and Ralph Cheinduit, are gloated over with relish, and regarded as personal triumphs of the avenging St Alban himself.[6] Innocent III's fourth Lateran Council, one of the most important councils of the Middle Ages, is criticized by Matthew because some of its provisions infringed the privileges of St Albans.[7] Matthew's 'constitutionalism' is a conspicuous feature of the *Gesta Abbatum*, and he invariably supports the convent against its abbot. During the years his history covers, a very real constitutional struggle was going on at St Albans over the question of the abbot's right to banish any monk he pleased to a distant cell; and Matthew gives us a very partisan description of this struggle. Of Abbot Warin, for instance, he says:[8]

He [Warin], together with his brother Matthew, the distrustful prior, in order that he might enjoy unquestioned authority, persecuted, dispersed, and followed with inexorable hate the whole

---

[1] Wats, pp. 91 and 128.   [2] Wats, p. 108.
[3] B.M. Royal MS. 4 D vii; see Wats, p. 108.
[4] Wats, p. 110.   [5] Wats, pp. 104–5.
[6] Wats, pp. 119 and 144.   [7] Wats, p. 141.
[8] Wats, p. 102.

nobility of venerable persons in the convent; so that juniors of five years' standing held the foremost positions, and those [of the seniors] who had remained dared not mutter against his tyranny.

A very similar tale is told of Abbot John de Cella, who, Matthew feared, would have to answer for his dictatorial conduct at the Last Judgement.[1] The account of his rule includes an interesting and detailed description of the attempt made by some of the monks to impose on the next abbot a signed agreement not to send monks away from St Albans against their wishes.[2] This in fact came to nothing, since the new abbot, William, although he had been foremost among the 'constitutionalists' during the vacancy, went back on his word; and in this he was supported by the papal legate, who appeared in chapter to remind the monks of the duty of canonical obedience to their abbot, and tore up the offending document in front of them.[3] If his sympathy with the monks against their abbot has led Matthew to describe this struggle in such fascinating detail, his constitutional feelings also led him to record with unusual care the various abbatial elections of this period, and this interest in elections is another noteworthy feature of his section of the *Gesta Abbatum*. Concerning Warin's election in 1183 Matthew notes that he was opposed by William Martel, the sacrist, who complained that Warin (who in fact suffered only from a squint) was completely blind; but he goes on to state the good constitutional principle that 'the opinions of one could not affect the fixed intention of the many'.[4] William of Trumpington's election in 1214 prompted Matthew to record in detail a conversation held afterwards among some of the monks, from which it was clear that the king had put pressure on the electors: 'it was not only the will of God that was at work in this election', comments Matthew meaningly.[5] The importance he attached to elections is most apparent in that of John of Hertford in 1235, for he gives a long and detailed account of it, supported with a group of some twenty documents relating to it.[6]

[1] Wats, p. 113. [2] Wats, pp. 111–12. [3] Wats, p. 115.
[4] Wats, p. 94. [5] Wats, p. 114.
[6] Wats, pp. 133–41; for more on Matthew's interest in abbatial elections, see Vaughan, 'Election of abbots at St Albans in the thirteenth and fourteenth centuries', *Proc. Camb. Antiq. Soc.* XLVII (1954), pp. 1–12.

Many of the characteristic features of Matthew's historical writings are apparent in the *Gesta Abbatum*. Besides the usual phrases,[1] play on words,[2] and quotations,[3] we find him airing his usual prejudices: Richard Marsh, Matthew says, was not elected to the bishopric of Durham, but intruded by the king;[4] the pope's ministers and servants are described as hanging about 'waiting for gifts with gaping mouths';[5] and King John is said to have been the greatest tyrant born of woman.[6] Matthew's rather cynical, embittered attitude towards the papacy is well reflected in his remarks about the damage done to the tower of the abbey church by lightning. He says:[7] '...twice the abbey church was struck by lightning and set on fire.... And just as it is useless to rely on privileges and indulgences of the saints, so the impression of the papal seal...which was fixed to the summit of the tower, was useless against the lightning....'

In sum, Matthew's *Gesta Abbatum*, though very short in comparison with his *Chronica Majora*, is an important and fascinating work, characteristic of him, and full of human interest, which served as a model and inspiration to his successors, who continued it up to the first half of the fifteenth century.

II. THE 'VITAE OFFARUM'

We have already shown that the *Vitae Offarum* is an authentic work of Matthew Paris, and that it was probably written *c.* 1250.[8] I have included it here, among Matthew's contributions to the history of St Albans, because it is, in essence, a work of domestic interest. The Lives of the two Offas, Offa of Angel and Offa of Mercia, are linked together by the promise of Offa I to found a monastery, and the eventual fulfilment of this promise by Offa II, in the foundation of St Albans. The real object of the *Vitae Offarum* is to describe and account for the foundation of

---

[1] Wats, p. 91, 'ab alto trahens suspirium'; p. 103, 'libra rationis trutinare' (cf. p. 112, 'rationis trutina'); p. 115, 'Ne prospera in huius mundi fluctibus impermixta eveniant' (cf. p. 40 above); etc.

[2] Wats, p. 113, 'nec volo nec valeo'; pp. 121, 129, 'misertus ac miseratus', etc.

[3] E.g. at Wats, pp. 92, 107 and 117, all of which occur elsewhere in Matthew's writings.

[4] Wats, p. 110.

[5] Wats, p. 138.

[6] Wats, p. 128.

[7] Wats, p. 142.

[8] See above, pp. 41–8; and 89–90.

St Albans; to emphasize its antiquity and connexion with royalty; and to whitewash the character of the founder, Offa of Mercia.

Although Offa I is described as king of England, the account of him shows that Offa of Angel is really meant. Matthew describes how Warmund, king of the West Angles, had an only son, Offa, who was at first blind and dumb, but whose faculties were later miraculously restored to him, so that he was able to lead an army to defeat the rebels who had conspired to seize his rightful throne. So far Matthew's account of Offa I agrees, in the main, with the accounts of Offa of Angel given by Saxo Grammaticus and Sweyn Aageson, and alluded to in Widsith and Beowulf.[1] The rest of Matthew's account is taken up with the story of Offa's marriage to the daughter of the king of York; of the loss of his wife and children through trickery; and of his subsequent recovery of them. This seems to be derived from a folk-lore theme having no connexion with either Offa.[2] Matthew closes his Life of Offa I with a paragraph describing his vow to found a monastery, which remained unfulfilled for many generations.

The early part of the Life of Offa II is very similar to the early part of Matthew's account of his ancestor. Tuinfreth and Marcellina have a son, Pinefred, who is blind and deaf from birth. Remembering the story of Offa I, they pray for his cure, promising, on his behalf, that, if cured, he will found the monastery which Offa I had neglected to found. He is cured, and, having defeated the rebel tyrant Beornred who had expelled his father from the kingdom, he rules over Mercia with the name of Offa II; his father Tuinfreth having resigned the kingdom to him. Offa then marries the wicked Drida, who had been exiled from France, and, after a series of campaigns which he fought against rival English kings and against Marmodius, king of Wales, he makes peace with Charlemagne, who had been supporting his enemies in England. Offa then settles down to rule England; transfers the archiepiscopal see to Lichfield; and drives off the first Danish invaders of the country. Matthew then describes in detail the murder of Aethelbert, king of East Anglia, by Offa's wicked queen Drida; her death and the burial

[1] Chambers, *Beowulf*, pp. 31–40; and Wilson, *Lost Literature of Medieval England*, p. 10.   [2] Wilson, *Lost Literature*, p. 12.

of Aethelbert; and the Council of Chelsea. He then goes on to describe Offa's miraculous invention of St Alban; his journey to Rome in quest of privileges for the new house, and its foundation and endowment on his return; and he concludes with an account of the burial of Offa by the river Ouse near Bedford.

The historical or quasi-historical matter used in the *Vitae Offarum* seems to derive entirely from Roger Wendover. It might be supposed that the matter common to the *Vitae Offarum* and Roger Wendover was derived independently in each of them from the same source, and that this source was a tract on the foundation of St Albans by Offa of Mercia. That such a tract existed seems probable from passages in William of Malmesbury and Henry of Huntingdon; for the former mentions some of the details of the invention of St Alban by Offa, and the latter his gift of St Peter's Pence to Rome.[1] But the matter common to the *Vitae Offarum* and Roger Wendover includes more than just the account of the invention of St Alban and the foundation of St Albans. It includes, for instance, a description of the transference of the archiepiscopal see from Canterbury to Lichfield, the martyrdom of Aethelbert, the Council of Chelsea, the area ruled over by Offa, and the death and burial of Offa. It is not difficult to show that it was Roger Wendover who laboriously gathered together this material from various different sources, to incorporate it into his *Flores Historiarum*; and that Matthew Paris, when he came to use it in the *Vitae Offarum*, took it directly from Roger's chronicle.[2] Compare, for instance, the following passages from the source, Roger Wendover's *Flores Historiarum* and Matthew Paris's *Vitae Offarum*:

The source, Henry of Huntingdon's 'Historia Anglorum'.[3]

Adrianus papa misit legatos in Brittanniam ad renovandam fidem quam praedicaverat Augustinus. Ipsi vero honorifice a regibus et populis suscepti, super fundamentum stabile aedificaverunt, pulchre Christi misericordia cooperante. Tenuerunt autem concilium apud Cealchide, ubi Iambert dimisit partem episcopatus sui.

---

[1] Hamilton (ed.), *Gesta pontificum*, p. 316; Arnold (ed.), *Historia Anglorum*, pp. 123–4.
[2] Theopold, *Kritische Untersuchungen über die Quellen zur angelsächsischen Geschichte des achten Jahrhunderts*, pp. 117 ff., provides detailed evidence in support of this conclusion.   [3] Ed. T. Arnold, p. 128.

191

Roger Wendover.[1]

Adrianus papa legatos misit in Britanniam ad fidem, quam Augustinus praedicaverat, renovandam. Ipsi vero a regibus cum clero et populo honorifice suscepti super stabile fidei fundamentum pulchre aedificaverunt, Christi gratia cooperante. Tenuerunt autem concilium apud Chalchuthe, ubi Lambertus, archiepiscopus Cantuariensis, partem sui episcopatus archiepiscopo Lichesfeldensi resignavit. . . .

Matthew Paris, 'Vitae Offarum'.[2]

Adrianus papa[3] legatos misit in Britanniam, ad fidem quam Augustinus episcopus praedicaverat, renovandam et confirmandam, qui et verbis et operibus sanctae doctrinae et virtutum, populos adhuc rudes salubriter informarent. Ipsi igitur a rege et clero honorifice ac reverenter suscepti, super stabile fidei catholicae fundamentum, sane ac prudenter, Christi cooperante gratia, aedificaverunt. Ut hoc autem sapientius, rite prosequerentur, tenuerunt consilium apud Chalcuthe, ubi etiam Lambertus archiepiscopus Cantuariensis, partem sui episcopatus archiepiscopo Lichfeldensi, sponte quam postulaverat, resignavit.

A comparison of these three extracts shows that Roger's account is taken, almost word for word, from Henry's, while Matthew, enlarging and embroidering in his usual way, has taken his account from Roger, not from Henry. A more detailed examination of the manuscripts enables us to discover which manuscript of Roger's *Flores Historiarum* Matthew used for the writing of the *Vitae Offarum*: it was his own text of the *Chronica Majora*, in *A*. In one place, for instance, Luard points out that *A* has 'totis' wrongly for 'toto'. The manuscripts of Roger Wendover and the source, William of Malmesbury's *Gesta pontificum*, have 'toto' correctly, but 'totis' is also the reading of the *Vitae Offarum*, though this is not pointed out by the editor of the *Vitae*, Wats, who has corrected it to 'toto' without giving us the reading of his manuscript.[4] Elsewhere, too, Matthew copies into the *Vitae Offarum A*'s erroneous reading of 'dominus' for 'dictis' of the other manuscripts.[5]

The only considerable piece of historical matter in the *Vitae Offarum* which is not from Roger Wendover is the account of

---

[1] *CM.* I, p. 352.   [2] Wats, p. 25.

[3] 'papa': erased in the manuscript and consequently not in Wats's text.

[4] *CM.* I, p. 345, note 3; Wats, p. 22; and Hamilton (ed.), *Gesta pontificum*, p. 16.   [5] *CM.* I, p. 357, note 1; and Wats, p. 27.

Offa's campaign against Marmodius, and of the building of his famous dyke.[1] We can only speculate on the nature of the source of this account. Rickert has shown that the Marmodius of the *Vitae Offarum* was probably the Maredudd of the Welsh sources, whose death is recorded in 796;[2] and the existence of Offa's dyke shows that Matthew's story of Offa's Welsh campaigns has some basis in history. A written source was probably used, and Rickert thought that this was a border tradition of some kind, perhaps a ballad. The story of Offa II's early life has evidently been adapted from that of Offa I; and the account of Offa II's wicked queen, Drida, as well as her name, appears to have been transferred from Offa I, whose legendary wife was the valkyrie Thryth. Just as a folk tale was used in the account of Offa I's queen, so, in the case of Offa II, a folk tale was used to explain the origins of Drida, who is discovered set adrift in an open boat on account of her crimes in France. The most important legendary source used by Matthew in the *Vitae Offarum* was evidently an account of Offa I which may have been an Old English epic whose text actually survived at St Albans, or only a floating mass of verbal tradition. The source material is so skilfully woven together in the *Vitae Offarum* that it is impossible to unravel it in detail, but it seems that, besides the historical material he derived from Roger Wendover, Matthew used a number of rather shadowy sources which included an epic poem about Offa I (which he used, too, in his Life of Offa II), a border tradition concerning Offa and Marmodius, and two popular folk tales.

The writing of the *Vitae Offarum* marks the last and most important stage in the development of the story of the foundation of St Albans, and later writers were content to copy it without further amplification.[3] Of the development of the story before the writing of the *Vitae Offarum* little can be ascertained; but, as we have seen, its core was very probably a tract describing Offa's miraculous discovery of the tomb of St Alban, and his subsequent foundation of a monastery on the spot. The next

---

[1] Wats, pp. 16–19.

[2] Rickert, 'Old English Offa Saga', *Modern Philol.* II (1904–5), p. 324; see her paper, too, for what follows.

[3] In part only, in B.M. Cotton MS. Vitellius A xx, ff. 67–70; in full in Bute MS. 3, ff. 50–91, and B.M. Cotton MS. Claudius E iv, ff. 84–97.

stage is marked by the anonymous author of the chronicle attributed to John of Wallingford. He knows more about Offa than was recorded in the tract on the foundation of St Albans, and he says: 'I have heard many other things worthy of record about this man [Offa], which, when their veracity is sufficiently ascertained, I hope, with God's help, to explain elsewhere....'[1] He does not, however, know 'the truth' about the murder of Aethelbert, a deed which he, in common with other chroniclers, attributes to Offa. In Roger Wendover's *Flores Historiarum* we have a more developed stage in the legend, for here Offa is explicitly exonerated from 'the only stain on his glory',[2] and the murder is attributed to his wicked queen Drida. Finally, in the *Vitae Offarum*, Matthew systematically converts the story of Offa of Mercia into an eulogy of 'pius fundator noster'. He is made the hero of the first battle against the marauding Danes;[3] he is praised for his humility, piety, and munificence;[4] and he is represented as making good the defaults of his ancestor in restoring the kingdom to its former extent and fulfilling the vow made by Offa I. The merits of the first Offa as a military leader and as the subject of a remarkable miracle are attributed also to the second Offa; while the faults of the second Offa are attributed either to his ancestor or to his queen. The skill with which Matthew has used the contrasts and parallels between the two Offas is noteworthy, and the way in which he has built up his story and linked its various elements in a common glorification of St Albans and its celebrated founder also reflects considerable literary talent. Matthew was not especially interested in historical research (he much preferred to concentrate on the recording of contemporary events), but his imagination seems to have been fired by the career of Offa, and his curiosity, spurred on, no doubt, by the design of glorifying his house, led him to piece together all the information he could obtain, both legendary and historical. The result is a largely fictitious work of value both for the legendary matter preserved in it and for the light it throws on Matthew's skill as a story-teller.[5]

---

[1] Gale (ed.), *Scriptores XV*, p. 530.
[2] *Ibid.*   [3] Wats, p. 22.   [4] Wats, p. 19.
[5] A brief glance at the *Vitae Offarum* suffices to demonstrate Matthew's very slight knowledge of history; one of its many blunders is noticed above, p. 125.

III. DOMESTIC HAGIOLOGY

Matthew's hagiological activities have been described in a previous chapter, but something remains to be said about his work on the hagiology of his own house. By his time the legend of SS. Alban and Amphibalus was already fully developed: William of St Albans had written the definitive prose *Passio* before the end of the twelfth century,[1] and Ralph of Dunstable had followed with a verse rendering of this. Matthew, however, was keenly interested in domestic hagiology. It was he, as we have seen, who finally wrote up the story of the foundation of St Albans by Offa of Mercia, and turned William's Life of St Alban into Anglo-Norman verse. In the *Chronica Majora* and the *Gesta Abbatum* his concern with domestic hagiology is very apparent: he amplified the existing account of Abbot Geoffrey's translation of St Alban in 1129; he amplified Roger Wendover's account of the invention of St Amphibalus in 1178; and he gave a detailed description of the discovery of St Alban's original tomb in 1257.[2] But his pursuit of the subject is best reflected in his own collection of material concerning SS. Alban and Amphibalus, which is now manuscript E i 40 in the library of Trinity College, Dublin. This book contains Ralph Dunstable's verse Life of St Alban (ff. 3–20); William's prose Life (ff. 20–28 b); Matthew's own Anglo-Norman verse Life (ff. 29–50); eight lessons for the feast of the invention and translation of St Alban (ff. 50 b–52 b); a tract on the invention and translation of St Alban (ff. 53–62 b and 68 b–69 b); part of a tract on the miracles wrought by the relics of St Amphibalus (ff. 73–7); copies of the St Albans foundation charters (ff. 63–8); and other fragments. The Lives of Ralph and William, Matthew's Anglo-Norman poem, and the tract on the miracles of Amphibalus are all written out by Matthew himself, in a neat, early hand, and seem to be the earliest surviving examples of his handwriting.

Matthew has provided marginal rubrics for the texts of Ralph's and William's Lives, and he has also added, in the margins or between the lines of Ralph's verse Life, a number of

---

[1] *Acta SS. Boll. June*, IV, pp. 149 ff.
[2] Wats, pp. 59–61; *CM.* II, pp. 301–7; and v, p. 608.

alternative readings in his characteristic manner. Thus, where
Ralph has the words 'Dulcis amor', Matthew writes, above the
word 'amor', 'vel honor'; and elsewhere he writes 'vel futu-
rabant' in the margin with reference to the line: 'Ista figurabant
scemate quodque suo.'[1] This is typical of him, and his treatment
of William's prose Life is equally characteristic. Besides the
addition of many marginal comments, often in red with a blue
paragraph marker, he makes one or two explanatory comments
in the margins in his usual manner. One of the more curious of
his marginalia is on f. 22, where we read in a later hand con-
trasting strangely with the young man's hand of the text: 'Hoc
de libro Johannis Mansel: Erat [i.e. St Alban] nanque [sic] dux
et magister militie tocius Britannie.' What this book was I have
not been able to ascertain; but John Mansel was a leading
councillor of Henry III, who figures prominently in the *Chronica
Majora*, and whom Matthew probably knew personally. Another
curious marginal note, reflecting Matthew's interest in etymologies, occurs on f. 25b: 'Hoc apud Lichefeld euenit. Inde
Lichfeld dicitur quasi campus cadauerum. Lich enim Anglice
cadauer siue corpus mortui dicitur.'

Matthew evidently took some trouble to furnish himself with
a corpus of hagiographical material relating to his own house,
and he was interested enough to work over his material and to
suggest alternative readings, to add something here and there or
to explain some obscurity, and even to correct his own text; for
on f. 25b he provides in the margin a line which he had at first
carelessly omitted. It is worth noting, however, that he does not
tamper with his source material as he does in his historical
writings, for his text of William's life is copied accurately and
preserved intact, the suggestions and comments being relegated
to the margins. It seems that this is not to be explained on the
assumption that he had more respect for his hagiological sources
than for his historical ones, but rather because he wrote these
lives while still a comparatively young man, and before he had
developed his itch for alteration and improvement.

One of the tracts in this manuscript, also written by Matthew
himself, describes the miracles wrought by the relics of St
Amphibalus after their translation by Abbot William of Trump-

[1] T.C.D. MS. E i 40 ff. 10 and 4.

ington in 1220.[1] This must have been written after Abbot William's death in 1235, since he is referred to in the prologue as 'venerabilis memorie'. There is every reason to suppose that Matthew was the author, as well as the scribe, of this little tract. In the first place, there are some striking parallels between its prologue and the account of the translation of St Amphibalus in the *Gesta Abbatum*, this part of which we know to have been written by Matthew Paris. For instance, in the tract the feretory is said to have been moved (f. 73) 'de loco ubi antea collocatum fuerat, scilicet juxta magnum altare sancti Albani, ad locum ubi nunc positum est in medio videlicet ecclesie...', while according to the *Gesta Abbatum*[2] it was moved 'a loco ubi prius collocatum fuerat, videlicet secus majus altare juxta feretrum sancti Albani, a parte aquilonari usque ad locum qui in medio ecclesie includitur'. Secondly, a number of phrases commonly used by Matthew Paris in his historical writings are to be found in this tract. For instance:

f. 73: dignum duximus commendare
f. 74: temporis...evoluto curriculo
      misertus ac miseratus
f. 74b: torvo vultu
f. 75b: dignum memoria censemus recolendum

The fact that this tract was probably composed, as well as written, by Matthew Paris throws further light on his interests. It seems that, in his early years, Matthew was much concerned with domestic hagiology, and we may surmise that the compilation of this manuscript, perhaps mainly in the years before *c.* 1235–40, reflects his early absorption in domestic matters. It was not till later, it seems, that Matthew embarked on a general history of his house, and on the recording of events in the world at large.

Of the other tracts in Trinity College, Dublin, manuscript E i 40, the most noteworthy is that on the invention and translation of St Alban, for this contains a long interpolation about King Offa written by Matthew himself, apparently fairly late in his life. The first part of the text of this tract, together with the

[1] Ff. 73–7; imperfect at the end: the only known copy.
[2] Wats, p. 122.

interpolation, is written out by Matthew in his *Liber Addita-mentorum*, and it has been copied thence into the Dublin manuscript by the scribe whom Matthew employed to write those parts of it not written by himself.[1] This interpolation, though based on the account of King Offa in the *Chronica Majora*, contains a reference to the *Vitae Offarum*: 'prout plenius in historia de Offa rege scripta continetur'.[2] Though Matthew evidently hoped to incorporate this interpolation into the 'official' text of the tract on the foundation of St Albans, it is not in fact to be found in either of the later copies which survive.[3] It is noteworthy, both in connexion with his known interest in King Offa, and as showing that, later in life at any rate,[4] he was quite prepared to interpolate passages written by himself into his source material, even when this consisted of a venerable and quasi-official account of the foundation of his own house.

IV. THE RELICS OF ST ALBAN

In the course of the early part of the *Gesta Abbatum* there are a number of passages concerning the relics of St Alban which seem to have been interpolated into the text of Adam the Cellarer's roll by Matthew Paris, for they interrupt the narrative, and contain phrases or quotations typical of Matthew. The clumsiest of these interpolations[5] describes the pious fraud of Abbot Alfric of St Albans, who, fearing that the precious relics of St Alban might fall a prey to the marauding Danes, walled them up under the altar of St Nicholas, and, to 'make assurance double sure', sent the bones of a certain 'holy monk' to Ely for safe keeping, giving out that they were the genuine relics of St Alban. The threatened invasion, however, never took place, owing to the drowning of the Danish king—which was miraculously revealed to King Edward the Confessor as he was attending mass one day at Westminster. As soon as the danger

---

[1] Ff. 27b–29b of the *Liber Additamentorum*; ff. 53–62b and 68b–69b of the Dublin manuscript. The scribe left Matthew to fill in the proper names.
[2] Dublin manuscript, f. 58b.
[3] Bute MS. 3, ff. 34 ff.; B.M. Cotton MS. Claudius E iv, ff. 40 ff.
[4] It refers to the *Vitae Offarum* which was probably written *c.* 1250; and it is written, in the *Liber Additamentorum*, in an untidy, straggly, and therefore probably late, hand.　　　　[5] Wats, pp. 43–4.

was over, Alfric sent to Ely to demand the return of the relics, which had been there almost a year. The monks of Ely, however, determined to keep so precious a treasure, returned, not the bones which they had been sent, but another set. Alfric, when he received them, realized at once that the Ely monks were trying to catch him in just the pious trap he had so successfully set for them; but, to avoid scandal, he pretended to accept these bones as the genuine relics of the saint, while secretly recovering the real relics from the altar of St Nicholas, and placing them in a shrine in the centre of the church. The Ely monks kept their set of bones, firmly believing them to be those of St Alban. The story ends with the statement that King Edward was furious when he heard of the pretences of the Ely monks, but that he died before he had time to take action.

Abbot Alfric of St Albans actually ruled from *c.* 970 until 990, when he became bishop of Ramsbury. In 995 he was made archbishop of Canterbury, and he died in 1005. His brother, Leofric, succeeded him as abbot of St Albans in 990, and ruled at least until 1007. According to the *Gesta Abbatum*, Leofric was succeeded by Leofstan, who died in 1066. In Matthew's autograph copy of the *Gesta Abbatum* the names *Alfric* and *Leofric* in the headings to the section of text concerning each abbot have been transposed, so that the account of Alfric's abbacy is headed *Leofric*, and that of Leofric's is headed *Alfric*. Owing to this error, Leofric was recorded as later becoming archbishop of Canterbury. Now Matthew knew quite well that it was Alfric and not Leofric who became archbishop, but, presumably because the names of the abbots did not occur in the accounts of their respective abbacies (except in the opening sentence), he was unaware of the mistaken transposition of their names. He therefore tried to put matters right by erasing the statement, under *Leofric*, to the effect that this abbot later became archbishop of Canterbury, and substituting a remark to the effect that Leofric, elected archbishop of Canterbury, refused to accept the honour, asserting that his brother Alfric was more worthy of it.[1] In the course of the story of Abbot Alfric and the relics of St Alban, which is added to the account of Leofric's abbacy, wrongly headed *Alfric*, the abbot's name, Alfric, is mentioned

[1] Wats, p. 42; see the *Liber Additamentorum*, f. 32a.

several times, a fact which proves that this story was interpolated by someone who did not suspect the error of the transposition of the abbots' names. It is found in Matthew's autograph manuscript, and we know that Matthew did not suspect
the error of transposition. It is therefore highly probable that
it was Matthew who inserted the story of Alfric and the relics
into the text of the *Gesta Abbatum*. It is worth noting, in this
connexion, that a quotation occurs in the course of this story
which is also used in the *Chronica Majora*,[1] and that Matthew
describes, in his *Edward*, the king's vision during mass mentioned
in this story.

This story of the pretended transference of the relics from
St Albans to Ely has many absurd features: indeed it seems to
be a mere clumsy fabrication. Matthew evidently knew that it
referred to an Abbot Alfric, and therefore inserted it under
Alfric; and he must have invented the references to Edward the
Confessor in an attempt to give the story some kind of historical
context. There can be little doubt that the Ely claims to possess
the relics of St Alban did originate in the actions of an Abbot
Alfric of St Albans; but the Ely story is very different from
Matthew's. According to the *Liber Eliensis*, this part of which
was written about the middle of the twelfth century, an Abbot
Egfrid of St Albans, who was a nominee of Stigand, fled to Ely
from St Albans on the deposition of his patron in 1070, taking
with him some of the relics of St Alban.[2] John of Tynemouth,
in the first half of the fourteenth century, repeats this story,
which he says he took from a book he found at Ely; but he calls
the abbot in question Alfric, and adds that when the new abbot of
St Albans, Paul, supported by William the Conqueror, demanded
the return of the relics, the Ely monks sent back a false set.[3]

There is, of course, no difficulty in deciding on the relative
merits of these two stories. The Ely account—and the version
recorded by John of Tynemouth is fuller and evidently more
accurate than that in the *Liber Eliensis*—is far more credible;
and it seems clear that the St Albans story of Alfric's trick has

[1] Ovid, *Metam.* III, 5, and IX, 408; *CM.* III, p. 249.
[2] Stewart (ed.), *Liber Eliensis*, p. 227.
[3] Horstmann (ed.), *Nova Legenda Anglie*, I, p. 36. This story is also found
in B.M. Cotton MS. Claudius E iv, f. 45b, in a St Albans tract on the 'false
opinions' of the Ely monks, written at the end of the fourteenth century.

been fabricated as a counter to the more authentic Ely story. Other passages seem to have been interpolated by Matthew in the *Gesta Abbatum* with a similar end in view. He inserts, for instance, into Adam the Cellarer's account of Abbot Robert's rule,[1] a description of how, while he was in Rome, Abbot Robert induced his old friend Nicholas Breakspear, then pope, to appoint a panel of bishops to inquire into the Ely monks' claim to possess the genuine relics of St Alban. This commission is said to have taken evidence on oath from twelve senior Ely monks, who admitted that they did not possess the relics. There is little doubt that this story has been invented, no doubt in an attempt to meet the claims of Ely to possess the relics. Two documents of Adrian IV, dating from 1156, mention the fact that St Alban's bones were at St Albans, as if this was generally known and undisputed;[2] there is no evidence, apart from this account, that the investigation ever took place; and it seems most unlikely that the Ely monks would have admitted that their claims were false, even under oath.

We must now interrupt our discussion in order to describe another incident in the curious history of the relics of St Alban, this time quite certainly recorded by Matthew Paris.[3] According to this story, a party of Danes, at the time of their invasions of England, carried off the bones of St Alban and took them to the Benedictine monastery of Odense. The bones were, however, later recovered by an enterprising monk of St Albans called Egwin. He entered the monastery of Odense, was made a monk there, and, after several years, was at last promoted to the post at which he had been aiming, that of sacristan. As sacristan he had charge of the relics, and it was a comparatively simple matter for him to choose a dark night, creep down to the feretory, and bore a hole through it. He removed the bones of the saint through this hole, and covered up his traces by filling it in carefully. He then put the bones in a box especially prepared for the purpose, and kept them under his bed until he found a merchant who agreed to convey what Egwin ingenuously

---

[1] See above, p. 184.

[2] Holtzmann (ed.), *Papsturkunden in England*, III, nos. 100 and 102.

[3] He tells us so himself. The story is described on ff. 25b–26b of the *Liber Additamentorum*, and printed in *GA.* I, pp. 12 ff.

described as 'a parcel of books' to the abbey of St Albans. The chest was joyfully received by the abbot and brethren, and the merchant presently returned to Denmark with news of its safe delivery. Once Egwin knew that his task at Odense was accomplished, he went to the abbot and complained of homesickness, brought on by advancing age. The unsuspecting abbot, taking pity on the English sacrist, who, after years of faithful service, wished once more to see his native land, gave him leave to return. Matthew ends his account with a list of his informants— a group of St Albans men who had been in the service of the king of Denmark.

Although this story is not to be found in the text of the *Gesta Abbatum*, a marginal reference shows that Matthew meant it to be inserted into the account of Wlnoth's abbacy during the middle years of the ninth century. In spite of Matthew's blunder over its date, the story has a core of truth behind it. The *Vita et Passio S. Canuti*, written early in the twelfth century by the Englishman Aelnoth, describes how Cnut removed some of the relics of St Alban from England, and deposited them in the newly founded monastery of Odense in Denmark.[1] There is early evidence for the dedication of the church at Odense to St Alban, since the *Chronicon Roskildense* records the martyrdom of Cnut in the church of St Alban there;[2] and the cult of St Alban even survived into the present century, for W. R. L. Lowe found a 'St Albans Mineral Water Manufactory', a pleasure steamer called 'St Alban', and a 'St Albans Market' there.[3] Cnut was in England in 1070 and 1075, but in 1075 he achieved only a fleeting pillage of York minster. In 1070 he was actually at Ely, and took part in the sack of the neighbouring monastery of Peterborough. Cnut, in fact, almost certainly removed some relics of St Alban from England in 1070, and the house whence he removed them was evidently not St Albans, but Ely. Matthew's story of the recovery of the relics by Egwin is probably due to a confusion with Hugo Candidus's account of the recovery by Ywar, the sacrist of Peterborough, of the

---

[1] Langebek (ed.), *Scriptores rerum Danicarum*, III, pp. 368–72.

[2] *Chronicon Roskildense* (ed. M. C. Gertz) in *Scriptores minores historiae Danicae*, I, p. 24; see also Jørgensen, *Helgendyrkelse i Danmark*, pp. 17 ff.

[3] Lowe, 'The cult of St. Alban abroad', *Hertfordshire Post*, 13 July 1910.

relics of St Oswald,[1] which had been removed from Peter-borough by Cnut in 1070, and likewise taken to Odense.[2] No doubt Matthew's informants assumed that the monastery con-cerned was St Albans, because the relics, or some of them at any rate, were those of St Alban.

There is no sign, in the *Gesta Abbatum*, of the Ely story of an abbot of St Albans called Alfric (or Egfrid) fleeing to Ely in 1070 with the precious relics of St Alban. Instead Matthew Paris describes the flight of the first post-Conquest abbot, Fretheric, to Ely in 1077, as a result of his enmity with William the Con-queror, and explicitly states that he went by leave of his convent with only a few books, some clothing, and other necessaries[3]— a remark which shows that this part of the account of Abbot Fretheric was written with the express design of combating the Ely claims to possess the relics. The story of Abbot Fretheric's flight to Ely is almost as absurd as that of Abbot Alfric's pious fraud, for it is most unlikely that an abbot of St Albans would, were he really hostile to William the Conqueror, have remained abbot until as late as 1077, and then fled to Ely. On the other hand, we have already seen that there is much to be said for the Ely account of what happened. The reason there given for the flight of the abbot of St Albans to Ely, that he was a nominee of Stigand, seems to be the true one, for we know that, among other benefices, Stigand held the abbey of St Albans on the eve of the Conquest.[4] Furthermore, Domesday Book records that, at the time of the Conquest, Stigand was in control of at least two of the abbot of St Albans's manors.[5] The truth seems to have been that Leofstan, who died in 1065, was succeeded as abbot of St Albans by a nominee of Stigand's called Alfric; that this Alfric left St Albans for the safe recesses of Ely on the deposition of his patron in 1069 or 1070; and that he was succeeded at St Albans by Fretheric. It seems clear that Alfric did take some of the relics of St Alban with him to Ely, and that some of these were soon afterwards removed by Cnut to Denmark.

[1] Mellows (ed.), *Chronicle of Hugo Candidus*, p. 82.
[2] In later times the church at Odense claimed to possess relics of St Oswald as well as of St Alban; Lowe, 'Cult of St Alban abroad', *loc. cit.*
[3] Wats, p. 49.
[4] Stewart (ed.), *Liber Eliensis*, p. 219.
[5] *Victoria County History, Herts.* IV, p. 372, note 61.

We cannot perhaps be sure that Matthew Paris alone was responsible for the various stories devised at St Albans to explain away, and demonstrate the falsity of, Ely's claims to possess the relics of St Alban. Nor can we always distinguish between what is due to deliberate falsification, and what to ignorance. It is clear, however, that there *was* a certain amount of conscious fabrication, and that much of it was the work of Matthew Paris. He seems to have suppressed altogether from the history of his house the offending Abbot Alfric, and to have tried to account for the Ely story of the flight of an abbot of St Albans to their house, by making out that it was another abbot, Fretheric, who had fled, some years later, and for a quite different reason, to Ely, and without taking any relics with him. But it was not enough merely to account for the story of the flight of an abbot to Ely: the existence of the Ely monks' claims had still to be explained. And so, it seems, Matthew fabricated the story of the pious fraud of Abbot Alfric, which had the merit of explaining how the Ely claims had originated, and yet showing them to be false. The story related by Matthew, of the recovery of the relics from Denmark by Egwin, was probably not the result of deliberate falsification on his part, for it seems likely that he was ignorant of Cnut's removal of St Alban's and other relics from Ely, and that he merely recorded the story as it was told him by his informants, and guessed that it referred to the first period of Danish invasion in England, the ninth century. His treatment of the history of St Alban's relics seems to have been inspired far more by devotion to his house than by any regard for historical accuracy, and we need not be surprised to find that he was prepared to use his literary skill and fertile imagination in order to substantiate the claims of his own house to possess the relics of its patron saint, at the expense of historical truth and even to the extent of deliberately inventing 'facts' and of suppressing one abbot entirely from the records.

CHAPTER XI

MATTHEW PARIS THE ARTIST

SIR Frederick Madden was one of the first to draw attention to Matthew Paris's artistic work. He attributed the drawings in the historical manuscripts to Matthew, as well as some of those in British Museum Cotton MS. Julius D vii and Royal MS. 2 B vi.[1] Sir Thomas Duffus Hardy, however, supposed that the drawings enumerated by Madden were the work of several different hands, one of which might have been Matthew's, and he remarked, in particular, that the drawings of the elephant, made in or soon after 1255, were much too vigorous in execution to be the work of Matthew Paris, who must by then have been an old man.[2] It is curious that, whereas in the controversy over the identification of Matthew's handwriting later scholars followed the sceptical Hardy rather than Madden, on the problem of the identification of his drawings and paintings they have tended to follow Madden. Thus both Harry Fett and A. Lindblom accepted Madden's attribution of the drawings in the historical manuscripts to Matthew. Fett also attributed the paintings in Cambridge University Library MS. Ee iii 59 (*Edward*) to Matthew, but Lindblom disagreed about this, though he thought that the illustrated Apocalypse in Trinity College, Cambridge, as well as some of the paintings in British Museum Royal MS. 2 A xxii, might have been executed by Matthew.[3] These two scholars engaged in a controversy over Matthew's position in the development of Norwegian art in the Middle Ages. Both agreed that a panel painting of St Peter formerly at Faaberg was very closely connected with Matthew Paris, and was perhaps his own work, but Fett thought that a number of other paintings in Norway showed the influence of Matthew Paris, and regarded him as the father of medieval art

---

[1] *HA.* iii, pp. xlviii–xlix, especially p. xlviii, notes 3 and 4.

[2] Hardy, *Descriptive Catalogue*, iii, pp. lxx–lxxii; for one of the drawings, see below, Plate xxi (*a*).

[3] Lindblom, *Peinture gothique en Suède et en Norvège*, pp. 128–32 and 184. He sums up the controversy between himself and Fett, with references.

in Norway. Lindblom contested this strongly, and maintained that Matthew's influence was only apparent in the Faaberg St Peter, and that in any case this was not important for the subsequent development of painting in Norway. He made some interesting remarks about Matthew's style, which he thought rather conservative, especially in the treatment of drapery by means of short, rather stylized folds. In 1916 and 1917 W. R. Lethaby contributed a series of articles on 'English Primitives' to the *Burlington Magazine*. He too followed Madden in attributing the marginal and other drawings in the historical manuscripts to Matthew himself, and he thought that the Faaberg St Peter was very likely a painting executed by Matthew and taken over to Norway by him. He noticed that the drapery in this painting is decorated with groups of three red dots characteristic of Matthew, and that the parallel lines across the sleeves, so typical of Matthew's drawings, occurred in it.[1]

A great advance was made in the study of Matthew's artistic works during the years after the Great War. In 1920 the Roxburghe Club brought out a facsimile edition of Cambridge University Library MS. Ee iii 59 (*Edward*), the paintings in which are similar in some respects to those attributed by Madden to Matthew Paris. In 1924, Lowe and Jacob published a facsimile of Matthew's illustrated autograph *Alban* in Trinity College, Dublin, MS. E i 40; and finally, in 1926, the Walpole Society published excellent collotype reproductions of nearly all the important drawings and paintings attributed to Matthew Paris and not already published. The presiding genius behind this work was M. R. James, for it was he who wrote the introductions to all three of these important facsimile editions. Although he nowhere committed himself to a definite statement, James made it clear that he thought the drawings in the manuscripts of the *Chronica Majora* and the *Historia Anglorum* (*A*, *B*, and *R*), a number of those in the *Liber Additamentorum*, as well as those in the Trinity College, Dublin, manuscript of *Alban*, had a very strong claim to be the work of Matthew himself; and he thought that the paintings in British Museum MS. Royal 2 A xxii, and the Faaberg St Peter, were at any rate very closely connected with him. He attributed two of the drawings

[1] Lethaby in *Burlington Magazine*, XXXI (1917), p. 193.

in British Museum MS. Cotton Julius D vii to Matthew Paris or his school, and also those in the surviving leaves of the illustrated copy of Matthew's *Thomas*. He believed that Matthew had perhaps designed the illustrations in the Cambridge *Edward*, but did not himself execute them; nor did he think that Madden was right in attributing the paintings in British Museum Royal MS. 2 B vi to Matthew Paris.[1]

Subsequent historians of art have usually based their discussion of Matthew Paris on the work of James. Millar, for instance, followed James, and so did Borenius and Tristram.[2] The latter pointed out that the Faaberg St Peter is painted on oak, whereas indigenous Norwegian paintings of similar date are invariably on pine: an additional reason for believing that this painting was taken over to Norway by Matthew Paris. Saunders thought that Matthew probably had several monks working under or with him, and that many of the drawings attributed to Matthew were not actually his.[3] Hermannsson, in his book on medieval Icelandic manuscripts published in 1935, pointed out that certain thirteenth-century drawings in Icelandic manuscripts may well have been influenced by Matthew Paris via Norway;[4] but this seems to be doubtful, for thirteenth-century line drawings from different countries are apt to be similar in style —Lethaby, for instance, drew attention to the similarity between Matthew's drawings and those of Villard of Honne-court.[5] The only important addition to the corpus of artistic material attributed to Matthew Paris by James was made by Professor Wormald in 1943.[6] He discovered that Bodleian MS. Ashmole 304, a collection of fortune-telling tracts which will demand our attention in the next chapter, contained a number of drawings, as well as some diagrams of spheres containing

---

[1] See James, 'Drawings of Matthew Paris', *Walpole Society*, XIV (1925–6), pp. 1–3; *Illustrations to the Life of St Alban*, p. 18; and *Estoire de St Aedward le Rei*, pp. 32–4.

[2] Millar, *English Illuminated Manuscripts*, pp. 56–60; and Borenius and Tristram, *English Medieval Painting*, pp. 9 and 13, who reproduce the Faaberg painting, Plate 26.   [3] Saunders, *English Illumination*, I, p. 75.

[4] Hermannsson, *Icelandic Illuminated Manuscripts of the Middle Ages*, p. 10.

[5] Lethaby in *Burlington Magazine*, XXXI, p. 234; see also Kurth, 'M. Paris and Villard de Honnecourt', *ibid.* LXXXI (1942), pp. 227–8.

[6] Wormald, 'More M. Paris drawings', *Walpole Soc.* XXXI (1942–3), pp. 109 ff.

animals etc., which were identical in style with the drawings attributed to Matthew Paris, and he concluded that these drawings, as well as those in the nine manuscripts mentioned by James, 'can be with good reason ascribed to his [Matthew's] hand'.[1] Wormald put forward a tentative chronology of Matthew's paintings: he thought that the Offa illustrations in the *Liber Additamentorum* may have been executed before the drawings in the Ashmole manuscript, and that the *Alban* illustrations in the Trinity College, Dublin, manuscript were probably later. In 1944 Hollaender published a detailed account of the illustrations in the Chetham Library manuscript of the *Flores Historiarum*, together with reproductions of them all. He thought that occasionally Matthew himself personally collaborated in the designing of this series of pictures depicting the coronations of English kings.[2]

The most recent discussion of Matthew Paris as an artist appeared in 1954, in Miss Rickert's book on medieval English painting.[3] As a result of a 'careful stylistic analysis' (which was unfortunately not included in her book), based on the famous painting of the Virgin and Child which prefaces British Museum Royal MS. 14 C vii (*R*), she attributed the following paintings and drawings to Matthew Paris himself:

(1) British Museum Royal MS. 14 C vii: Virgin and Child.

(2) Heads on p. 283 of *A*.[4]

(3) Head of Christ on f. 49b of *B*.

(4) All the drawings and some of the tinting in the Dublin *Alban* ('perhaps Matthew Paris's earliest work').

(5) 'Some original sketches for marginal drawings' in *A* and *B*.

Rickert also described the work of two assistants of Matthew Paris. The first of these, she claimed, executed 'at least a part' of the drawings in the Cambridge *Edward*, and the five tinted drawings in British Museum Royal MS. 2 A xxii. According to Rickert, this artist has 'richer decorative detail, more pains-

[1] Wormald, 'More Matthew Paris drawings', *loc. cit.* p. 109; see also p. 112.

[2] Hollaender, 'Pictorial work in the *Flores Historiarum*', *Bulletin of the John Rylands Library*, xxviii (1944), p. 378.

[3] Rickert, *Painting in Britain*, pp. 119–20.

[4] 'Fol. 281', Rickert, *Painting in Britain*, p. 119, in error. She is doubtful of this attribution; p. 134, note 63.

taking execution, and less convincing figure modelling' than Matthew Paris. The second of these assistants, thought Rickert, executed the marginal paintings in *A* and *B*, 'which, with their text, may have been added later than the original writing'. Rickert described this artist's style as very close to Matthew's, and went on to say that he used a 'linear formula which gives the pictures a monotonous sameness in figure types'. She thought that some of the marginal drawings in *A* and *B* were 'certainly' by the Franciscan, Brother William.

Not one of these studies can be accepted as definitive, for each scholar has voiced his or her opinion on the subject of Matthew's artistic works without publishing the detailed stylistic analysis on which such opinions must be based. Moreover, as we have seen, there is a very large measure of disagreement among scholars as to the works actually executed by Matthew Paris. I hope, therefore, that the reader will forgive my examining in detail the evidence for the authorship of these paintings and drawings, and forgive, too, a rather detailed but, as I think, necessary attempt to describe the salient features of Matthew's artistic style.

It is quite certain that Matthew Paris was an artist, for we have both his own and Thomas Walsingham's word for this. Walsingham tells us that Matthew 'wrote and most elegantly illustrated the Lives of SS. Alban and Amphibalus, and of Thomas and Edmund, archbishops of Canterbury';[1] and that he 'provided many books [for the monastery] written in his own and other hands, in which his excellence in both learning and painting is clear enough'.[2] Matthew himself rcfcrs to 'the book about St Thomas the Martyr and St Edward which I translated and illustrated'.[3] We have already noticed his keen interest in artistic matters in connexion with the *Gesta Abbatum*, and it only remains to add here that in the *Liber Additamentorum* he has inserted a treatise written and illustrated by himself on the rings and gems of his house,[4] and a list of the paintings and other works of art executed by Richard the Painter during the

---

[1] Above, p. 19.
[2] B.M. Cotton MS. Nero D vii, f. 51 a.   [3] Above, p. 170.
[4] Oman, 'Jewels of St Albans Abbey', *Burlington Magazine*, LVII (1930), pp. 81–2, where it is reproduced in facsimile.

years 1241–50.[1] These are valuable both in themselves and for the light they throw on Matthew's artistic interests.

Some, at any rate, of the books which Matthew himself provided for his house still contain an inscription in his own hand recording the gift. Since these are the books on which, in later times, his reputation at St Albans as an artist evidently in a large measure depended, we may begin our discussion with them. Of the four manuscripts whose inscriptions survive, one, Cambridge University Library MS. Dd xi 78, contains no drawings or illustrations of any kind, and may therefore be omitted from the present discussion. The others are:[2]

(1) The *Liber Additamentorum*, B.M. Cotton MS. Nero D i.
(2) *R*, B.M. Royal MS. 14 C vii.
(3) *B*, Corpus Christi College, Cambridge, MS. 16.

A fourth illustrated manuscript ought undoubtedly to be added to these: Corpus Christi College, Cambridge, MS. 26 (*A*). Although no inscription survives in this book, it was, as we have seen, at first written as part of *B*. Furthermore, in *R* Matthew refers to the last part of the text of his *Chronica Majora* (1254–9) as 'the third volume',[3] which shows that he thought of it as divided between three separate volumes, *A*, *B* and *R*. Now it is hardly likely that he would have given Volumes II and III to St Albans, and not Volume I; and I conclude, therefore, that *A* was among the manuscripts provided by him for his house, and that it formerly had an inscription similar to those in *B*, *R*, and the *Liber Additamentorum*. It seems, then, that the books to which Walsingham refers as provided by Matthew for his house, and 'written in his own and other hands', included *A*, *B*, *R*, and the *Liber Additamentorum*, as well as perhaps some others either lost or unidentified. Three of these books are almost entirely autograph, and were presumably regarded as Matthew's private property until he handed them over to his house; and if we take into account his known artistic skill, there is a strong *prima facie* case for supposing that Matthew was also responsible for the artistic work in these manuscripts.

---

[1] *CM.* VI, pp. 202–3.
[2] The inscriptions are reproduced in Vaughan, 'Handwriting of M. Paris', *Trans. Camb. Bibl. Soc.* I (1953), Plate XIX.
[3] *CM.* V, p. 483, note 3; p. 544, note 1; p. 604, note 1; and p. 675, note 2.

The aesthetic features of these four manuscripts support this conclusion. In all of them the same sense of colour in decorative detail is apparent. Blue paragraph markers and rubric lettering are skilfully employed in the margins to give the whole page a colourful effect, and marginalia are frequently enclosed with coloured lines, to which a narrow strip of green or brown tint is often added. Even the quire numbers are beautifully executed in red and blue. All this, to judge from the writing, is the work of Matthew himself; and the system of reference signs, too, which is used in these manuscripts, is due to him.[1] Sometimes these *signa* take a pictorial form such as we should expect from an artist: we find in one place a fish, in another a stag's head.[2] Elsewhere the two halves of an animal's body are used, the reader being referred, at a point in the manuscript where the hind half of the body is drawn, to another leaf, where the fore half is to be found.[3] It is but a short step from these reference signs to the conventional pictorial signs which Matthew freely uses in the margins of his historical manuscripts. These conventional signs are so closely related to the text of the chronicle that it would be difficult to attribute them to a hand other than Matthew's. The commonest of them are shields, often inserted reversed to mark the death of the bearer; mitres and croziers to mark the death and accession of bishops; crowns; and documents with a pendent seal. But we find also hands, crossbows, swords, heads, a bell, and so on, each figure symbolizing or representing an event described in the text. In one place two hands clasped together in the margin represent a wedding; and in another a hand reaching down from Heaven to a crowned head represents Henry III's narrow escape from an assassin at Woodstock.[4] No hard and fast line can be drawn between these pictorial representations and the more complex ones which might properly be called 'marginal illustrations'; and a number of the drawings in the margins of these manuscripts reproduced by James are really only symbolical representations of events rather than actual drawings of them. We may draw attention,

---

[1] See above, pp. 65 ff.

[2] *Liber Additamentorum*, f. 63 b and *B*, f. 186 (James, 'Drawings of M. Paris', *Walpole Soc.* XIV (1925–6), no. 95).

[3] *Liber Additamentorum*, ff. 30 b and 25 b.   [4] *R*, ff. 109 and 128.

in this connexion, to the bell with the rope thrown over the gudgeon, to represent the Interdict; the two kings embracing each other, to represent the peace signed between Louis and Henry III in 1217; and the peasant threshing with a flail, to represent the plundering of the barns of a papal official.[1] Like these pictorial representations, the straightforward drawings of events are intimately related to the text of the chronicle, and all this artistic work seems to represent the aesthetic feelings and expression of one man only. It must surely have been Matthew Paris who conceived of the idea of illustrating his manuscripts in this way, and who carried out this coherent scheme of illustration, from the simplest reference sign to the complicated battle scenes in the margins of the *Chronica Majora*. It seems to me most unlikely that he would have called in an assistant to carry out this task, which as we know he himself was perfectly well equipped to undertake. The marginal pictures, as well as the other pictorial and decorative work, form an integral part of the historical manuscripts, and the illustrations are provided with detailed legends invariably written by Matthew himself. I think that he would by no means have *allowed* another monk to interfere in the writing and illustration of these manuscripts, which were, after all, his own. In one case, where a drawing by another hand has found its way into the *Liber Additamentorum*, Matthew tells us explicitly that this was executed by his Franciscan friend, Brother William.[2]

So far we have done little more than put forward a reasonable hypothesis. We have pointed out that the historical manuscripts *A, B, R*, and the *Liber Additamentorum* were Matthew's own books, composed and written by him, that he himself wrote the legends to the illustrations which form, together with the other artistic work, an integral part of the manuscripts, and that Matthew Paris was an artist; and we have concluded that the illustrations in these manuscripts were executed by him. But we can, and must, go further than this. What the art historians have never done, in forming their opinions as to the authorship of these marginal illustrations, is to take into account the palaeo-

[1] James, 'Drawings of M. Paris', *Walpole Soc.* XIV (1925–6), nos. 31, 39, and 56.
[2] *Liber Additamentorum*, f. 155.

graphical evidence. When this is done, a very significant co-incidence is found between the frequency of, and changes of style in, the illustrations, and our knowledge of the writing of these manuscripts. Let us look, first, at the marginal pictures in the three volumes of the *Chronica Majora*: *A*, *B* and the second part of *R*. There are twenty-four reasonably important marginal drawings in *A* (Volume I, –1188); sixty-five in *B* (Volume II, 1189–1253); and not one in Volume III of the *Chronica Majora* in *R* (1254–9). From about f. 183 onwards in *B*, at a point in the annal for 1244, the execution of the drawings becomes cruder and often clumsy, and their frequency markedly declines until they peter out altogether during the annal for 1247 (f. 215). There are some twenty drawings of importance in the *Historia Anglorum* (the first part of *R*), and these are consistently inferior in execution and detail to those in *A* and the early part of *B* (up to *c*. f. 183). It may be remarked further that in the *Abbreviatio Chronicorum* (British Museum Cotton MS. Claudius D vi), as in Volume III of the *Chronica Majora*, there are very few pictorial representations of any kind, and no drawings worth the name.

If we bear in mind the evidence about the writing of *B* put forward in Chapter IV above, and examine the marginal drawings in this manuscript with care, some interesting facts are revealed. Thus on f. 64b we find that a drawing in the upper margin, representing the death of Fawkes de Breauté, has interfered with Matthew's rubric lettering across the page to the extent of causing him to omit the letters '-pore' from the words 'De tempore regis Henrici III'.[1] The drawing, in fact, must have been executed *before* the rubric headings—and we have shown that the latter were carried out in or soon after 1250.[2] Again, on f. 138b of *B*, a drawing in the lower margin, of the treaty between Earl Richard and the Saracens, was clearly executed before Matthew's quire number XI; for this is placed near the lower edge of the leaf, instead of in the usual place higher up, obviously in order to avoid the picture.[3] This quire number is one of the second series written into *B*, and was

---

[1] James, 'Drawings of M. Paris', *Walpole Soc.* XIV (1925–6), no. 49; see also fig. 4 above, p. 57.   [2] Above, p. 57.
[3] See Plate XIV (*b*). For the quire numbers in *B*, see pp. 56–7 above.

probably executed *c.* 1250–1. On f. 186b is an even more significant piece of evidence, for here the remains of the *original* quire number, as well as the one replacing it (xiiii), can be seen tucked away at the side of the leaf to avoid the picture, instead of in the usual place in the centre of the lower margin.[1] This, I think, proves conclusively that the picture was drawn before the first set of quire numbers were written into *AB*, that is, in or before 1250.

I think it permissible to deduce from this evidence that the illustration of *A* and *B* was carried out more or less contemporaneously with the writing of the text. In one place at least this is certainly the case, for on f. 126 of *B* the *text* has had to make room for the drawing of the imperial seal in the lower margin, so that the drawing must have been executed before Matthew had finished writing the text on this page.

What is the significance of all this? We know that Matthew had the writing of *AB* well in hand by the year 1245, and he probably worked at it more or less continuously up to 1250, apart from the interruption in 1248–9 caused by his visit to Norway. By February, 1251, *AB* had been completed to 1250, and Matthew was already busy with the *Historia Anglorum*. During the years which followed 1250 he must have been extremely busy coping with the continuation of the *Chronica Majora*, as well as with the writing of the *Historia Anglorum* and the *Flores Historiarum*, and, later, the *Abbreviatio Chronicorum*. Moreover we must remember that by this time he was well past his prime. Now the decline, both in quantity and quality, of the marginal illustrations in the historical manuscripts, from about the annal for 1244 in *B*, which we have noted, fits in exactly with our knowledge of the writing of these manuscripts, but only if we assume that Matthew was their artist. Had the illustrations been carried out by an assistant, we should not expect their number and quality to fall off during the very years when Matthew Paris was becoming ever older and busier. On the contrary, we should expect the work to be even throughout. The marked decline in the numbers of the illustrations is most easily explained on the grounds that Matthew found it impossible to find time, amidst his other activities, to continue with the

[1] James, 'Drawings of M. Paris', *Walpole Soc.* xiv (1925–6), no. 94.

lavish illustration of his historical manuscripts; and their very obvious deterioration in quality seems to be due partly to this and partly to his increasing age. The later illustrations, especially those in the *Historia Anglorum*, which we know were executed after 1250, show definite signs of hurried, and sometimes careless, execution, as well as a loss in technical skill. None of this would be apparent, I think, had Matthew been employing an assistant, and if it should be maintained that the assistant, as well as Matthew Paris, was getting older and busier and therefore less skilled and prolific, I would point out that there were plenty of skilled artists available at St Albans at this time, whose help Matthew could have called in had he so desired. I conclude that he had no desire for assistance in carrying out the intimate task of illustrating his historical manuscripts, and that, in consequence, the changes in the style and number of the illustrations directly reflect his growing age and his increasing preoccupation with the texts of his historical manuscripts, which themselves increased in number after *c.* 1250.

When, at the end of his life, probably during his last few months, Matthew found it impossible to continue writing, he handed over his pen to an assistant, whose hand is easily recognized on the closing leaves of the *Chronica Majora*, the *Historia Anglorum*, and the *Abbreviatio Chronicorum*, as well as in the colophon at the end of the *Chronica Majora*.[1] A brief glance at the manuscripts is sufficient to show that an assistant also took over the decorative and minor pictorial work on these pages. We notice at once, for instance, that the paragraph markers, shields, mitres, croziers and initial letter, on the last eight leaves of the *Chronica Majora*, written by Matthew's scribe, are quite different from those on the earlier pages written by Matthew himself, and of much less artistic merit. Some of this work is illustrated in Plate IV, where it can be compared with some shields and crowns of Matthew's reproduced in Plate V.[2] I think it safe to conclude from this that Matthew himself executed the minor pictorial representations of shields and the like, as well as the large-scale drawings, for we can

---

[1] See p. 7 above, and Plate I.

[2] For Matthew's heraldic work, see below, pp. 250–3 and Plates XVIII and XIX.

hardly assume that, at a certain point in three different books when he began to employ a scribe, Matthew also changed or abandoned his artistic assistant. There can have been no such assistant, and clearly what happened was that Matthew called in a helper who wrote the text and executed as best he could the pictorial work which had formerly been done by Matthew.

I hope, now, that I have convinced the reader that the large-scale drawings and the pictorial representations or symbols in *A*, *B* and *R* were executed by Matthew himself. I shall have to discuss later some of the earliest drawings in *A*, which seem to be, at any rate partly, the work of another hand;[1] but there is one other matter connected with these drawings in the historical manuscripts, which ought to be discussed here. Miss Rickert, in her recent book,[2] attributed only a small fraction of the pictorial matter in these manuscripts to Matthew Paris: she allowed him the Virgin and Child which prefaces *R* (reproduced as the frontispiece above); and some drawings of heads and 'original sketches for marginal drawings' in *A* and *B*. She attributed the Virgin and Child to him on the grounds that it was signed; and the heads and faces presumably because they approach the Virgin and Child closely in style and treatment;[3] but I do not know why she attributed the 'original sketches' to Matthew, rather than the drawings themselves. What are these 'original sketches'? One of those mentioned by Rickert is on p. 66 of *A*, where a detailed plummet sketch has been made, and only part of it 'worked up' in ink.[4] The other is said by Rickert to be on f. 215 of *B*, but I have not been able to find it there, though there is a rather crudely executed ink drawing,[5] which is in fact the last considerable drawing in the *Chronica Majora*, referring to part of the annal for 1247.

It seems to me that almost all the marginal drawings in *A* and *B* have been 'worked up' from pencil sketches, and signs of

---

[1] See p. 223 below.

[2] *Painting in Britain*, p. 119; for the 'signature' below the Virgin and Child painting, see Vaughan, 'Handwriting of M. Paris', *Trans. Camb. Bibl. Soc.* I (1953), p. 380.

[3] It is perhaps worth pointing out that these drawings (James, 'Drawings of M. Paris', *Walpole Soc.* XIV (1925–6), nos. 25 and 140) are on separate pieces of parchment attached to the manuscripts.

[4] *Ibid.* no. 10. [5] *Ibid.* no. 96.

pencil work are still clearly visible in a number of them. I have been able to discover only three pencil sketches which have not been 'worked up' in ink: a crucifix on f. 259b of *B*; the death of Queen Blanche on f. 268b; and a boat on f. 279.[1] All of them, we note, are after the last proper drawing in the *Chronica Majora*, in that part of it which Matthew seems never to have found time to illustrate. If we suppose that Matthew himself designed the illustrations in the *Chronica Majora*, and left the 'working up' to an assistant, then it follows that, at just the point when Matthew's artistic powers were declining, and his time becoming more and more taken up with other things, his assistant, too, was becoming incapable of carrying out his work properly; and we have to assume, too, that Matthew was unable to find another assistant to replace him. All this is most unlikely, and I venture to suggest that Matthew habitually sketched out his illustrations in pencil, and later worked them up in ink; and that the 'original pencil sketches' in *B* are merely unfinished illustrations of Matthew's which he never managed to 'work up' finally in ink.

I propose now to try to describe the salient features of Matthew's artistic style, basing my analysis on the marginal illustrations in *A*, *B*, and *R*, two of which are reproduced in Plates VI and VII. The drawings in these manuscripts are all of the same basic type, either line alone, or line and wash. The chief colours are pale green, pale yellowish, and pale brown, and these tints are very effectively used in the shading of drapery. On the whole these drawings are executed with remarkable skill. There is a boldness of line, a confidence, which gives the impression that they are the work of a skilled artist working accurately with a rapid, sure touch. The proportions are usually good, and the human figures especially are lifelike and well drawn. Economy of line is a notable feature of all the drawings: there is nothing useless, no unnecessary detail. Hands and feet, for instance, are usually sketched impressionistically with a few deft lines, instead of being drawn in detail. No harshness or angularity mars the softness and roundness of the lines. There is no idea of perspective, and architectural features are therefore often badly distorted; but the way in which things are put together or worn

---

[1] There is another in the *Historia Anglorum*, *R*, f. 42.

is usually very well shown. Crowns and mitres, for instance, fit neatly on to the head, and ships' sails to the masts.

All this constitutes a recognizable, individual style, which may be further defined by describing some of its most characteristic details. Crowns, for instance, are usually divided into three, are well-drawn and balanced in shape, and are usually decorated with dots or circlets. There is invariably a double line at the base, which allows a curl of hair to protrude characteristically at the side of the face. Certain types of hat recur in these drawings, including a floppy, conical one, often used for pagans, and a curious, flat, round one. Hats are usually carefully and artistically fitted on to the head. Mitres are very often decorated with two circlets, or crosses. Drapery is realistic and often beautifully drawn and shaped. Its outlines are usually soft and rounded, and the edges of pieces of drapery, and the folds, are represented by slightly stylized, curved, parallel lines. A fold across the chest and a series of parallel lines across the sleeve near the hand are characteristic; and the upper part of the dress is often tucked neatly into the girdle on either side. Patterns on drapery are very characteristic, the commonest being a sprinkling of small dots (usually red) in triangular groups of three. Sprinklings of circlets, small crosses, and dots with a semicircular line half enclosing them are also frequent. Hair is usually represented with a few well-defined parallel curves with shading between them, and a lock usually shows behind a hat or crown. Faces in profile often have a pronounced indentation above the nose, and a protuberance above that: they are often rather uncouth and striking. A feature common to many faces is a single decurved line to represent the mouth, with a dot below it. Full faces usually have the hair neatly arranged on either side of the head, and the line of the nose is connected to that of one of the eyebrows. Heads, or heads and shoulders, are frequently added behind a figure or group of figures in order to give an impression of number without adding too much detail to the drawing. Feet are drawn in a rather peculiar and characteristic way, and often seem to be bent backwards. Sometimes they are coloured black, save for a central white line. The toes are normally only roughly sketched in with a number of parallel lines, though the big toe is usually drawn more completely; fingers, too, are usually hinted at with parallel lines, except, often, for the thumb. The separate lines of feet, hands, and drapery are often not joined together, for the artist is skilled enough to convey his meaning without elaborate and accurate linear detail. In a hand praying, or held out for some reason, the thumb is nearly always held away from the fingers in a curious manner. The ground is invariably depicted in a characteristic way, with a wavy line. Architectural details, as can be seen from Plates XIV and XV, are stereotyped and very individual: spires are drawn in a characteristic manner, and walls are decorated with quatrefoils, groups of two or three narrow lights, and small circlets. Many more equally characteristic details could be described, but it would be tedious to enumerate them all here.

I have examined all the drawings that appear in any way to be connected with Matthew Paris, or have been previously attributed to him, and conclude that the following can be definitely attributed to him, since, in all of them, I have found identical details of style and execution:

A: Corpus Christi College, Cambridge, MS. 26; Volume I of the *Chronica Majora*. All the drawings and pictorial material except perhaps for three of the marginal drawings (for which see p. 223 below).

B: Corpus Christi College, Cambridge, MS. 16; Volume II of the *Chronica Majora*. The pictorial material on the preliminary leaves, and all the marginal illustrations, including shields, mitres, etc.

R: British Museum Royal MS. 14 C vii; the *Historia Anglorum* and Volume III of the *Chronica Majora*. All the pictorial material except for the shields etc. on ff. 210–18 and the drawing on f. 218b.

British Museum Cotton MS. Nero D i; the *Liber Additamentorum*. All the pictorial material except for the drawings on ff. 5a–25a and f. 155.

British Museum Cotton MS. Claudius D vi; the *Abbreviatio Chronicorum*. Drawings of kings of England on ff. 2–5b, but helped by another hand; medallion drawings in the genealogical chronicle, ff. 6b–8; and pictorial representations on ff. 16b, 36b, and 29b.

Trinity College, Dublin, MS. E i 40; *Vie de S. Auban etc.* All the illustrations.

Bodleian Library, Oxford, Ashmole MS. 304; fortune-telling tracts and verses. All the pictorial matter.

British Museum Cotton MS. Julius D vii; miscellaneous historical material collected by John of Wallingford. Two tinted drawings, ff. 42 b and 60 b.

Corpus Christi College, Cambridge, MS. 385, Part II; *Dragmaticon Philosophiae*. A series of twenty-three diagrams, some of which have pictorial detail.

Chetham Library, Manchester, MS. 6712; the *Flores Historiarum*. Four shields.[1]

Although by no means all Matthew's illustrations have been reproduced, most of the more important drawings attributed to him are available in facsimile: the marginal illustrations in the historical manuscripts, as well as the drawings in the *Liber Additamentorum* and Cotton MS. Julius D vii, in volume XIV of the Walpole Society's publications; the drawings in Bodleian Ashmole MS. 304 in volume XXXI of the same society; and the *Alban* drawings in Lowe and Jacob's facsimile edition, entitled: *Illustrations to the Life of St. Alban in Trinity College, Dublin, MS. E i 40.*

There is one further point which must be taken into account in connexion with Matthew's artistic work. In every one of the manuscripts which I have listed here as containing drawings by Matthew Paris there is a close connexion between the illustrations and his handwriting; for nearly all the drawings, including even the diagrams in the *Dragmaticon Philosophiae* and one of the paintings in Cotton MS. Julius D vii, are furnished with legends written by Matthew himself. I am not of course arguing that, because any given drawing has legends in Matthew's hand, the drawing must have been executed by him; but I do suggest, since almost all the drawings attributable to him on stylistic and other grounds are in fact provided with such legends, that one of Matthew's peculiarities as an artist is the provision of these explanatory legends in his own hand, and that their presence or absence must be taken into account when drawings of doubtful authorship are under consideration.

[1] Described in *FH.* II, p. 304, note 2; p. 305, note 2; p. 308, note 1; and p. 312, note 8.

We have already discussed the illustrations in the historical manuscripts which were among those presented by Matthew to his house and noticed later by Walsingham; but Walsingham tells us of other manuscripts written and illustrated by Matthew Paris: Lives of SS. Alban and Amphibalus, and of Thomas and Edmund.[1] The reader will remember that we came to the conclusion in Chapter IX[2] that the Trinity College, Dublin, manuscript is Matthew's original autograph manuscript of his Life of SS. Alban and Amphibalus, to which Walsingham refers. Even Rickert was prepared to allow that Matthew was responsible for the drawing in this manuscript, though she evidently thought that much of the colour had been applied by another hand.[3] The illustrations, two of which are reproduced in Plate VIII, consist of a series of fifty-four line and wash drawings enclosed in frames, depicting the Life of SS. Alban and Amphibalus; the visit of SS. Germanus and Lupus to England in the fifth century; and the invention and translation of St Alban and the foundation of St Albans by Offa of Mercia. In style they are very similar to the earlier drawings in *A* and *B*, and in my opinion are wholly the work of Matthew Paris.

We have seen that Matthew himself refers to 'the book about SS. Thomas and Edward' which he translated and illustrated,[4] and that neither of the existing illustrated manuscripts of *Thomas* and *Edward* can have formed part of this book.[5] They are, however, very similar, especially in size and format, to Matthew's original manuscript of *Alban*, and it seems, therefore, that each is a close copy of part of Matthew's original book containing both lives. This is fully borne out by an examination of their illustrations. Many of the characteristic details of style and execution, which we noted above as peculiar to Matthew's artistic work, occur in the illustrations of University Library, Cambridge, MS. Ee iii 59 (*Edward*), but their general appearance is quite different from the authentic drawings of Matthew Paris in *Alban* and the historical manuscripts. One of these drawings is reproduced in Plate IX (*b*). The execution is painstaking and has none of Matthew's dash and vigour; and the elaborate and

---

[1] Above, p. 209.   [2] Above, p. 170.
[3] Rickert, *Painting in Britain*, p. 119.
[4] Above, p. 209.   [5] Above, p. 171.

minute detail is wholly unlike Matthew's rapid, deft strokes. The individual lines are weakly drawn and often overlap each other, a fault that is seldom, if ever, found in Matthew's drawings. Certain tricks of style appear which are common in Matthew's work, such as the rather angular, almost twisted, feet, and the addition of heads alone behind other figures; but these stylistic peculiarities are stiff and unreal in the *Edward* illustrations, and they are often exaggerated unnaturally. All this shows, I think, that the artist of *Edward* was closely copying a series of drawings of Matthew's; and we need not therefore be surprised to find parts of pictures sometimes unaccountably missing, as, for instance, part of a boat on f. 14a. James supposed that these pictures were perhaps designed by Matthew Paris and executed by an assistant,[1] but I think it more likely that Matthew had no hand in them at all, and that the similarities between them and Matthew's own drawings are simply due to the fact that their artist was copying from Matthew's drawings. I agree with Rickert's identification of the work of this assistant of Matthew's, and with her attribution to him of the five tinted drawings in British Museum Royal MS. 2 A xxii, ff. 219b–221b.[2] These psalter illustrations are much too detailed and ornate, too laboriously executed, to be the work of Matthew himself; but many features of them closely approach the work of the artist of *Edward*, and there are some close parallels in detail: the very ornate helm, for instance, figured on f. 220a of the psalter, is almost identical with the helms in some of the *Edward* illustrations.[3] Of the *Thomas* manuscript too little remains for a detailed analysis of the illustrations to be made. However, they do not appear to be by Matthew Paris, but, to judge from the collotype reproductions (I have not been able to see the original), they seem to be close to the work of the *Edward* artist.[4]

Matthew's style is a distinctive one, and Rickert's contention, that some of the marginal drawings in the historical manuscripts were executed by Brother William, a Franciscan friend of Matthew's, seems to me to be entirely without founda-

[1] James (ed.), *Estoire de St Aedward le Rei*, p. 32.

[2] Rickert, *Painting in Britain*, p. 120.

[3] Cf. James, 'Drawings of M. Paris', *Walpole Soc.* XIV (1925–6), no. 137; and James (ed.), *St Aedward le Rei*, especially p. 64 of the facsimiles.

[4] For these, see Meyer (ed.), *Vie de Saint Thomas*.

tion.[1] The whole-page painting of Christ on f. 155 of the *Liber Additamentorum*, which Matthew states was the work of Brother William, is quite different in style from any of the chronicle illustrations. The hair, for instance, is drawn in with a large number of very fine lines, whereas Matthew invariably depicts hair with a small number of thickish lines. The drapery, too, is treated quite differently, for Brother William's stylized, angular folds are very unlike Matthew's more rounded and less rigid drapery patterns.

There are a few drawings about whose attribution to Matthew Paris I feel rather doubtful. These are the figures of seated kings in the *Abbreviatio Chronicorum*, and the drawings on pp. 28, 30 and 35 of *A*.[2] The figures of kings in the *Abbreviatio* are much inferior to Matthew's other drawings, especially in execution, and in the proportions of the figures. Some of the faces seem to have been drawn in by another hand, and the colouring, too, owing to the crude way in which it has been applied, could hardly have been done by Matthew Paris. On the other hand, the subject of each picture has been written on the edge of the leaf by Matthew himself, and much of the drawing seems to be his. The figure of King Richard, for instance, reproduced in Plate x (*a*), seems to be wholly Matthew's work, except perhaps for the lines round the mouth. This manuscript was almost certainly his last historical production, and it seems possible that he left these drawings to be finished by an assistant. The doubtful drawings near the beginning of *A* present a rather different problem. Their general style is very like Matthew's, but some of the drawing is more finnicky and detailed than that in the other illustrations in this book. Part of the drawing, for instance, of the seated king illustrated in Plate x (*b*), particularly the face and hair, seems to be too fine to be Matthew's. It is perhaps permissible to conjecture that these were the first illustrations to be inserted into this book, and that they are partly the work of another monk, who perhaps instructed

---

[1] Rickert, *Painting in Britain*, p. 120. She states, in error, that Brother William's painting of Christ is signed by him. It is reproduced in Little, 'Brother William of England', *Franciscan Papers, Lists and Documents*, Plate IV.

[2] British Museum Cotton MS. Claudius D vi, ff. 2a–5b; and James, 'Drawings of M. Paris', *Walpole Soc.* XIV (1925–6), nos. 4, 5 and 7.

Matthew in the art of drawing, and lent a helping hand to his first artistic ventures.

Madden attributed to Matthew Paris a series of tinted drawings in British Museum Royal MS. 2 B vi;[1] but not so James, who thought that they were definitely inferior in artistic merit (Plate IX (a)). They are very similar to Matthew's own drawings, and it is only when a detailed comparison reveals certain tricks of style absent in Matthew's work that they can be distinguished from it. I would point out, in particular, the presence of lines on the knees and elbows of the figures, which I have not found in Matthew's drawings; the lack of a sense of proportion; and the elaboration of detail, especially of hair. These paintings were certainly executed at St Albans in Matthew's lifetime, and an inscription on f. 2a records the gift of the book to St Albans by John de Dalling, a monk of the house.[2]

There are a number of other paintings and drawings which were executed by Matthew's contemporaries at St Albans. The most famous of these, which accompanies the colophon at the end of the *Chronica Majora* (see Plate I), depicts the chronicler reclining on his death-bed, with his book of chronicles lying open by him. A superficial glance might give the impression that this drawing was indistinguishable from those attributed to Matthew Paris, but a closer inspection reveals numerous differences. The face and hair, for instance, are unlike anything in Matthew's drawings, and the hands and fingers, too, are drawn in with a detail which is quite unlike Matthew's impressionistic treatment of this subject. Some other paintings executed at St Albans in Matthew's lifetime may be seen in the Chetham Library manuscript of his *Flores Historiarum* (*Ch*). These are a series of nine illustrations of the coronations of English kings, which are different in style from, and inferior in merit to, Matthew's drawings. Hollaender thought that Matthew might occasionally have helped this artist;[3] but this seems to me

---

[1] Ff. 8a–12b. Madden, *HA*. III, p. xlviii, note 4; and James (ed.), *Estoire de St Aedward le Rei*, p. 34.

[2] The unfinished drawings in *C* (B.M. Cotton MS. Nero D v, Part II, ff. 208, 213b, and 214) have been attributed by Madden to Matthew Paris (*HA*. I, p. lxii), but I cannot myself see any grounds for this.

[3] Hollaender, 'Pictorial work in the *Flores Historiarum*', *Bull. of J. Rylands Lib.* XXVIII (1944), p. 378. He reproduces all the drawings.

unlikely, although the four shields in the margins of the section of text written by Matthew are certainly his work, for they are identical with those in the historical manuscripts already discussed. In the coronation drawings the figures are tall and slender, and tend to be out of proportion in consequence; the drawing is often rough and clumsy, and the general style of the drapery and other details quite different from Matthew's. The artist is not so skilled as the artist of the *Edward* illustrations, and his style is different from that of the artist of Royal MS. 2 B vi. He must have worked in close collaboration with Matthew, for this manuscript was certainly produced under Matthew's supervision.

Another book illustrated with line drawings in medallions in a style similar to that of Matthew Paris is the extended version of Peter of Poitiers's *Compendium historiae in genealogia Christi* in the library of Eton College.[1] The text of this brief universal chronicle extends to the year 1245, and the last events mentioned are the Council of Lyons and the deposition of the Emperor Frederick II. The accession of Innocent IV is recorded, but the original hand has not inserted the number of years he reigned, so we may assume that the book was written while Innocent was still alive, that is, before 1254. This manuscript has all the appearance of having been written and illustrated at St Albans, and, indeed, it seems to be associated to some extent with Matthew Paris, for some of the last entries in it mention events described in detail in the *Chronica Majora*: the invasion of Tartars in 1241, the story of St Edmund Rich, and the Council of Lyons. The illustrations are chiefly heads enclosed in medallions, but there are some tinted drawings rather like those of Matthew, though cruder and less finished than his. None of them seem to be by any of the artists so far discussed.

While we are on the subject of manuscripts illustrated in the 'Matthew Paris style', but not by him, mention ought to be made of the illustrated Apocalypses which began to appear in England during the middle years of the century. James and other students of medieval art have attributed a number of the finest and earliest of these to St Albans: Trinity College, Cambridge, MS. R 16 2; Bibliothèque Nationale, MS. Fr. 403;

---

[1] MS. 96. See Moore, *Works of Peter of Poitiers*, pp. 97–117.

Bodleian Library, MS. Auct. D 4 17; Pierrepont Morgan MS. 524, a replica of Bibliothèque Nationale MS. Fr. 403; British Museum Additional MS. 35, 166; and Dyson-Perrins MS. 10.[1] There is no trace, in any of these manuscripts, of Matthew's hand, either in the text or the illustrations, but the latter are often very close to his general style, though usually superior in artistic merit. All these books seem to have been produced at St Albans in Matthew's lifetime, and there are some very striking parallels, for instance, between the artist of the *Edward* illustrations and those of the Bibliothèque Nationale and Dyson-Perrins MSS. mentioned above. These manuscripts represent, it appears, the finest artistic work which the St Albans scriptorium could produce at this time, and Matthew may well have picked up some tricks of style from, or even have been taught to paint by, one or more of the artists who illustrated these magnificent books. Rickert thought that the scriptorium at St Albans was 'under the tutelage of Matthew Paris',[2] but it seems to me that these Apocalypse artists were his masters rather than his pupils, and I cannot believe that he was responsible for the style and technique which they brought to such perfection.

A critic who does not accept the corpus of illustrations here attributed to Matthew Paris would no doubt maintain that these drawings are the work of a school or group of artists working with Matthew Paris. But the force of this argument is surely somewhat weakened by the separate identification of the work of several other artists working at the same time and in the same place as Matthew, and sometimes in very close collaboration with him. We have discussed the work of several such artists: the artist of the *Edward* manuscript and Royal MS. 2 A xxii; the artist of Royal MS. 2 B vi; the artist of the coronation pictures in the Chetham manuscript of the *Flores Historiarum*; not to mention the Eton medallion pictures, the picture of Matthew on his death-bed, the shields and marginal illustrations of his assistant scribe, and the manuscripts of the Apocalypses just mentioned. It seems to me that our separate identification of the

---

[1] For references to facsimiles of these MSS., see Rickert, *Painting in Britain*, p. 134.

[2] *Ibid.* p. 122.

work of many of these artists adds considerably to the probability that those drawings which we have attributed to Matthew really are the work of one man, and not that of a group of artists painting in the same general style.

The chronology of Matthew Paris's drawings and paintings is difficult to determine with any degree of certainty. I have tried to work it out on the basis of the drawings in the historical manuscripts, which are the only ones that can be dated more or less reliably. We know that the *Chronica Majora* in *A* and *B* was written during the years before 1251, and that it was begun some time before 1245. Originally, it was written as one volume, *AB*, which was finished up to the annal for 1250 early in 1251. Here Matthew at first intended to close his historical labours, and he put the finishing touches to his single volume: rubric page headings and quire numbers. Now we have seen that some, at any rate, of the marginal illustrations in *B* were executed before these rubric headings and quire numbers, and I think it reasonable to suppose that this is true of them all, and that the single manuscript *AB* was completed, and illustrated, by 1251. (Actually there are no illustrations of importance after the annal for 1247.) The deterioration which they exhibit towards the end and the appearance of a helping hand in some of those near the beginning of *A* show that these marginal illustrations were executed over a period of years, beginning, perhaps, as early as *c.* 1240 or even before.[1] The *Historia Anglorum* was begun in 1250, and probably not finished until 1255 or after. Stylistically, the illustrations in it seem to be late: they are on a far less elaborate scale than those in *A* and *B*; they are fewer in number; and they are much inferior in execution and technique. How late they are we do not know, but it seems unlikely that they were done much later than the text, and we may date them with some confidence to the years 1250–5.

We have to rely almost entirely on stylistic evidence for the dating of Matthew's other important surviving group of paintings in the Trinity College, Dublin, manuscript containing his *Alban*, though the appearance of the hand-writing of *Alban* seems to indicate that it was written before

---

[1] For the evidence lying behind these statements, see above, pp. 52–61, 213–15, and 223. For the *Historia Anglorum*, see p. 61 above.

1240,[1] and there is no reason to suppose that the illustrations were not done at the same time. The fifty-four paintings in this book are very carefully executed in considerable detail (Plate VIII), and Matthew evidently spent a great deal of time and trouble over them. Minute details such as the nails in the horses' hoofs and the spurs are meticulously drawn in, and the hands and fingers are more carefully delineated than in the chronicle illustrations. On f. 48a there is a rather *macabre* battle-scene, similar to those in the early part of *B*. All this seems to point to an early date, and we may agree with Rickert in attributing the illustrations in Trinity College, Dublin, MS. E i 40 to Matthew's early period,[2] and probably to the years before 1240.

The marginal drawings in *A*, *B* and *R*, and the illustrations in the Dublin manuscript, are the two most important surviving groups of Matthew's drawings: indeed together they form the bulk of what has come down to us. The rest of his artistic work may be conveniently grouped as follows:

(1) A page of monumental drawings of faces (one of the Virgin and Child and two of Christ) at the end of *A*; a vernicle on f. 49b of *B*; and the famous Virgin and Child which prefaces *R*.[3] To them we may add the panel painting of St Peter formerly at Faaberg in Norway, and now in the Oslo Museum.[4]

(2) Two tinted drawings in British Museum Cotton MS. Julius D vii.[5]

(3) An unfinished series of drawings in the *Liber Additamentorum* illustrating the *Vitae Offarum*.[6]

(4) Two sets of tinted drawings of seated kings, one prefacing *R* (ff. 8b–9a), the other the *Abbreviatio Chronicorum* (ff. 2–5b).

---

[1] Vaughan, 'Handwriting of M. Paris', *Trans. Camb. Bibl. Soc.* I (1953), pp. 388–9.

[2] Rickert, *Painting in Britain*, p. 119.

[3] Reproduced in James (ed.), 'Drawings of M. Paris', *Walpole Soc.* XIV (1925–6), nos. 25 and 140; and in the frontispiece above.

[4] Reproduced in Lindblom, *Peinture gothique*, Plate VII; and in Borenius and Tristram, *English Medieval Painting*, Plate XXVI.

[5] Reproduced in James (ed.), 'Drawings of M. Paris', *Walpole Soc.* XIV (1925–6), nos. 142 and 143.

[6] Reproduced in James (ed.), 'Drawings of M. Paris', *Walpole Soc.* XIV (1925–6), nos. 125–30.

(5) Half-length drawings of English kings enclosed in medallions, illustrating the genealogical chronicles in the historical manuscripts.[1]

(6) The pictorial matter in the maps and itineraries.[2]

(7) The drawings and diagrams in Bodleian Library, Ashmole MS. 304.[3]

(8) A series of twenty-three diagrams in Corpus Christi College, Cambridge, MS. 385.[4]

Items (6) and (8) will demand our attention in the next chapter, and I need only point out here that the illustration of the maps and itineraries seems to date from after 1252, and that I am unable to suggest a date for the diagrams of the Corpus Christi manuscript which in any case are of no importance from the artistic point of view. The work mentioned in item (1) seems to be fairly early. I have no hesitation at all in attributing the Faaberg St Peter to Matthew Paris: it was certainly painted in his lifetime; the style seems to be identical with his; and, unlike the contemporary Norwegian panel paintings, it is on oak. Moreover we know that Matthew was in Norway in 1248, and it seems very likely that he took this painting with him as a gift either to his friend King Haakon, or to the monks of St Benet Holm. The drawings of faces in *A* and *B*, and the Virgin and Child in *R*, exhibit a monumental style more akin to large-scale painting than to manuscript illustration, and it is reasonable to suppose that they were executed at about the same time as the Faaberg St Peter, that is, in or before 1248.

The two tinted drawings in the Cotton MS. Julius D vii have been inserted into a miscellaneous collection of historical material almost entirely copied or abridged from Matthew's manuscripts by his friend John of Wallingford, the infirmarer of St Albans: one is a Christ in Majesty, the other a drawing of John of Wallingford, above which Matthew has written: 'Frater Johannes de Walingeford quandoque Infirmarius'. If these words mean 'John of Wallingford, onetime infirmarer', then the drawing presumably dates from after 1253, for John was still

---

[1] See p. 116 above.   [2] See below, pp. 235 ff.

[3] The most important of these are reproduced by Wormald in *Walpole Soc.* XXXI (1942–3), Plates XXVII, XXVIII.

[4] See below, pp. 254–5.

infirmarer in that year.[1] The three drawings of philosophers
in Ashmole MS. 304 are rather similar to those in John of
Wallingford's book. Plato and Socrates share one drawing,
Euclid and Hermann another, and Pythagoras has the third to
himself. The fourth drawing reproduced by Wormald depicts
the heads of the twelve Patriarchs, and exhibits the characteristic
features of Matthew's treatment of the human face. Besides
these, there are a number of rather poor outline drawings of
birds, and some spherical figures which include a certain
amount of well executed pictorial detail (Plate XXI (*b*)). Both
the birds and the spheres seem to me certainly Matthew's
work.[2] I have found no evidence for the date of these illustrations in Ashmole MS. 304, but much of the handwriting in it is
Matthew's, and appears to date from between 1240 and 1250,
for it is less neat and controlled than that of *Alban*, but less
'twisted' and ragged than that dating from after 1250. Although
it is little more than a guess, then, I would ascribe the illustration of this manuscript, with its text, to the decade 1240–50.

I would agree with James in attributing the first six of a series
of outline drawings in the *Liber Additamentorum*, illustrating the
Vitae Offarum and completed some time after his death, to
Matthew Paris.[3] Most of the characteristic features of his style
are apparent here, including in particular the very characteristic
architectural details,[4] treatment of drapery, and the impressionistic drawing of hands. The helms are identical with many
of those in the chronicle illustrations, and two of the drawings
depict a battle, and share many of the features of the battle-
scenes in *B*.[5] The sixth drawing has been completed by another
—and, as I think, much later—hand, and only the central
figures are Matthew's.[6] The *Vitae Offarum*, as he planned it,
was evidently to be a book on the lines of his *Alban*, with a

---

[1] See *GA*. I, pp. 330–8.

[2] The birds are on ff. 43b–52; the spheres, ff. 32b–38b. Wormald, 'More
M. Paris drawings', *Walpole Soc.* XXXI (1942–3), p. 109, says that the spheres
are by the same hand as the drawings of philosophers.

[3] 'Drawings of M. Paris', *Walpole Soc.* XIV (1925–6), p. 21. Rickert,
Painting in Britain, p. 134, note 69, disagrees.

[4] See Plate XIV (*d*).

[5] James, 'Drawings of M. Paris', *Walpole Soc.* XIV (1925–6), nos. 128 and
129.

[6] *Ibid.* no. 130.

framed picture at the top of each page, for spaces were left by Matthew on each page, and legends for each picture have been written by him on the lower margins.[1] But although this was his intention at first, he must have abandoned his plan some time before his death, for on f. 20 he has added a lengthy passage to the original text in the space left for a picture. Moreover, none of the drawings executed by him is completed: they all lack tinting; only the first two have detailed legends; and the frame of the sixth was only roughly sketched in. There is some reason to suppose that the text of the *Vitae Offarum* was written in 1250,[2] and I think it likely that these drawings were executed at about the same time, and that it was other commitments, rather than death, which interrupted Matthew's work on them.

Matthew's drawings of seated kings, prefacing *R* and the *Abbreviatio Chronicorum*, have scarcely been noticed by students of his artistic work. Madden attributed them to Matthew, but James felt uncertain about this.[3] I have no hesitation in ascribing those in *R* to Matthew, and, as I have already pointed out,[4] those in the *Abbreviatio Chronicorum* seem to have been, at least in part, executed by him: either he was helped with them, or they were left unfinished at his death and completed afterwards. In *R* there are two pages, one of which is reproduced in Plate XI, each containing four kings, enthroned and crowned, and fitted into an ornamental frame. These pictures are well drawn and tinted, and exhibit the usual features of Matthew's style, especially in the architectural details, crowns, fcct, and hands. The drapery, too, is characteristic of Matthew, particularly the patterns of dots and circlets, which can be exactly paralleled in *Alban* and the chronicle illustrations. The legends to these pictures are all in Matthew's hand. A much more ambitious programme was envisaged in the *Abbreviatio Chronicorum*, where four leaves are devoted to a series of thirty-two drawings of enthroned kings, four to a page (Plate X (*a*)). But the work is less fine than that in

---

[1] Many have been cut off by the binder.
[2] See pp. 89–90 above.
[3] *HA.* I, p. xlviii, and James, 'Drawings of M. Paris', *Walpole Soc.* XIV (1925–6), p. 18.
[4] Above, p. 223.

R: indeed it is for the most part crudely executed, and the frames are no longer ornamental, nor are the pictures provided with proper legends, though most of the kings' names have been written into the margin by Matthew. The date of both these sets of drawings is hard to determine, but the *Historia Anglorum*, forming the first part of *R*, was begun in 1250, and the kings prefacing it may be presumed to date from about that time. Those prefacing the *Abbreviatio Chronicorum* must be considerably later, and are probably the latest surviving examples of Matthew's artistry.

Finally, we come to the drawings of kings in the genealogical chronicles in *A*, *B* and the *Abbreviatio Chronicorum* (Plate XVIII (*d*)). These are half-length figures, or mere faces, of Alfred, William the Conqueror, Cnut, St Edward the Confessor, and Richard I.[1] They are of little artistic importance, and were probably executed after 1250. They seem to be Matthew's own work, for, although the execution is crude, many of his tricks of style occur in them. I have not here enumerated all Matthew's artistic work, for there are some drawings in the *Liber Additamentorum*, in particular the tiny portraits of the abbots of St Albans illustrating the *Gesta Abbatum*, which seem certainly to be his, and I feel sure, too, that the decorative work and the initials, one of which includes figures,[2] in the historical manuscripts are also his.

With the exception of the Faaberg St Peter and, perhaps, the page of monumental faces now at the end of *A*, Matthew's surviving artistic work consists entirely of book illustration. Although he was certainly a competent, if not highly skilled, craftsman, it is perhaps difficult to claim him as a great artist, for his work has few signs of originality, and seldom conveys any real depth of feeling. His *Alban* shows that he could produce a book in the tradition of the best illustrated Apocalypses of his day, though artistically inferior to them; but even if all his illustrated saints' Lives had survived, it is doubtful if his fame as an artist would have been much enhanced. These books, after all, were typical products of his age, and his fame really

[1] *B*, f. iiia–b; medallions of Alfred and William. *A*, f. ivb; medallion of Alfred. *Abbreviatio*, ff. 6b–8a; medallions of Alfred, Cnut, Edward, William, and Richard.   [2] *B*, f. 167b.

depends on the more original use to which he put his talents in the historical manuscripts. Here, and particularly in the margins of the first two volumes of the *Chronica Majora*, Matthew is primarily, perhaps, a cartoonist: certainly he illustrates secular subjects in a way unusual in thirteenth-century England, and with remarkable skill. As can be seen in Plate VI he excels especially in depicting the human figure in action. Both the large-scale drawings of events recorded in the chronicle, and the extensive use of pictorial symbols, are foreign to the traditional book illustration of Matthew's time. Among the former, battle-scenes are prominent, and the care with which Matthew draws in the dismembered corpses, as well as the liberality with which he sprinkles them with blood, reveal a slightly *macabre*, perhaps rather sordid, element in his art: he can be relied upon to make the most of the martyrdom of a saint (Plate VIII (*a*)); and he seems to have enjoyed depicting the cannibalistic orgies of the Tartars.[1] Above all else, however, Matthew the artist is a careful observer, and his drawings are unusually accurate in the representation of details: we note, particularly, his ships, clothing, drinking vessels, weapons, armour, bells, and various mechanical details. In the work of many a medieval artist we can recognize animals of various shapes and sizes but of no identifiable species: Matthew has left us lifelike and easily recognizable drawings of a cat, elephant, goat, tortoise, deer, camels, horses, lions, oxen and boars. It is a pity that he did not illustrate a bestiary.

Of Matthew's influence on later artists, and of his place in the history of art as a whole, I can say but little. Though individual in style, and original in his illustration of a secular subject like history, his art remains in most respects a characteristic product of his age; and if it is true to say that the *Chronica Majora* was the first illustrated record of contemporary events to be produced in medieval England, it is also true that Matthew's work is in many ways typical of twelfth- and thirteenth-century monastic art. His influence on subsequent developments appears to have been slight, for the only artistic production of his which

---

[1] For battles, see James (ed.), 'Drawings of M. Paris', *Walpole Soc.* XIV (1925–6), nos. 24, 41 and 89. For the Tartars, see no. 86; see also Matthew's detailed drawings of people being tortured (no. 34), and dying of the plague (no. 84).

seems to have been copied and widely diffused was the illustrated genealogical chronicle.[1] At St Albans he inherited the
artistic tradition and aptitude of men such as Walter of Colchester,
Richard the Painter, and the artists of the illustrated Apocalypses;
and he seems to have been the last great member of that
flourishing school of monk artists.

[1] Above, pp. 116–17.

CHAPTER XII

OTHER INTERESTS

I. CARTOGRAPHY

A LTHOUGH Richard Gough, in 1780, had published descriptions and engravings of three maps of England from manuscripts of Matthew Paris,[1] it was Madden who, in his preface to volume three of the *Historia Anglorum*, first claimed for Matthew an important place in the history of cartography:[2] he believed that the maps and itineraries in Matthew's historical manuscripts were the work of Matthew himself. Hardy, however, repudiated Madden's belief, for he thought that Matthew could never have found time to produce this cartographical material as well as his histories.[3] Hardy's objections seem to have influenced later scholars. Thus Michelant and Raynaud thought that Matthew was the author, though not perhaps the scribe or artist, of the maps of Palestine, or at least their legends.[4] These two scholars produced an excellent edition of the legends on three of the maps of Palestine,[5] but they confused these maps with the itineraries from London to Apulia which precede them in the manuscripts, and consequently believed that they were printing the text of the eastern half of an itinerary from London to Jerusalem, instead of only the legends of a map of Palestine. This mistake was pointed out by Konrad Miller, who included a full study of Matthew Paris's cartographical work in his important book on medieval world-maps.[6] He gave the first accurate and full account of Matthew's maps and itineraries, and thought that Matthew was probably the author of all this material, but the scribe only of two of the maps of England. Another German scholar, Friedrich Ludwig, made a detailed study of Matthew's itinerary from London to Apulia, in which

[1] *British Topography*, I, pp. 61–71 and Plates II–IV.
[2] *HA.* III, pp. l–lii; see also I, p. xlvii, and note 2.
[3] Hardy, *Descriptive Catalogue*, III, pp. lxxii–lxxiv.
[4] *Itinéraires à Jérusalem*, p. xxiii.   [5] In *A, B,* and *R.*
[6] *Mappae Mundi. Die ältesten Weltkarten*, III, pp. 68–94.

235

he analysed the length of each day's journey, and pointed out a number of errors.[1] As a cartographer, Matthew Paris was first introduced to English readers in the second volume of C. R. Beazley's *The Dawn of Modern Geography*.[2] Beazley gave an account of Matthew's cartographical work, based, apparently, on Miller's, and accompanied it with reproductions of some of the maps and itineraries. He assumed that Matthew was the author of this material, and supposed that the maps of England, at least, were autograph. A great advance in the study of Matthew's cartographical work was made in 1928, with the publication in colour facsimile by the British Museum of the four maps of England and Scotland previously attributed to him. The Reverend H. Poole compiled a list of all the place-names occurring in these maps, and he and J. P. Gilson together wrote a short introduction to the facsimiles. On the important question of the authorship of the maps, Gilson stated that they were certainly executed under Matthew's supervision, and he went on to say: 'It seems, in fact, possible that all four maps are the work of the same hand, and also possible, though to me by no means certain, that this is the hand of Matthew Paris himself.'[3] The publication of these maps in facsimile must have eased the task of Miss Mitchell, who published a detailed study of them in the *Geographical Journal* for 1933, in which she discussed at length their geography, construction, and place-names.[4] She did not, however, come to any definite conclusion as to their relationship, nor as to the identity of their scribe or scribes. She calls these maps 'the work of what may probably be regarded as the earliest English school of cartography'.[5]

Before we can embark on a description of this corpus of carto-graphical material or an appraisement of Matthew's carto-graphical work, we must decide whether or not it is correctly attributed to him, and in what sense. Was he the author only, and were the maps and itineraries executed by a skilled assistant? Or was he merely a copyist? I have no hesitation in agreeing with Madden that Matthew was at once author and artist. These maps

---

[1] See below, p. 249. [2] See pp. 584–90 and 638–41.

[3] *Four Maps of Great Britain*, p. 3.

[4] 'Early maps of Great Britain, I. The Matthew Paris maps', *Geog. Jour.* LXXXI (1933), pp. 27 ff. [5] Mitchell, *ibid.* p. 27.

and itineraries are only found in manuscripts closely associated with him, and they form a prominent part of the preliminary material which prefaces his historical manuscripts. Furthermore, though there are four separate versions of the map of England and Scotland, three of the map of Palestine, and four of the Apulian itinerary, not one of these can be shown to be slavishly copied from another. All appear to be the work of one person who, while he repeats these three works on a number of occasions, introduces, on each occasion, variations, improvements and alterations. No wonder that Miss Mitchell found it hard to establish the relationship of the four maps of England and Scotland. If the reader glances at the British Museum facsimile edition of these maps, he will see that, though map D is clearly an unfinished rough sketch, it contains a group of Yorkshire place-names not on the other maps. He will note, too, that while on map C Salisbury is placed south of St Albans, in A it is due north; and that maps A and B, in spite of their general similarities, each contain features not found in the other. The same phenomenon occurs in the Palestine maps and the itineraries. In the latter, the architectural details are quite distinct in each itinerary (cf. Plates XII and XIII) and the treatment of Italy varies from one itinerary to another. From this variation we may surely conclude that all this material is the work of a single scribe-artist who was enough of a cartographer to find it impossible to copy slavishly his own productions.[1]

All these maps and itineraries are illustrated in a manner identical in style and technique with that employed in the drawings and paintings we have attributed to Matthew Paris: the same artist is clearly at work in both. The architectural details, for instance, as can be seen from Plates XIV and XV, are identical with those found in Matthew's drawings; and the same is true of the animals, birds, boats, and such-like, which are found in the Palestine maps and the itineraries. Moreover the same use of colour, in writing and decoration, is found in the cartographical

---

[1] *Copies* of some of Matthew's cartographical productions have survived (see below, p. 241). They differ strikingly in handwriting, style and technique from Matthew's own maps and itineraries, yet their *matter* is closer to that of their exemplars than that of Matthew's maps and itineraries to each other.

productions and in Matthew's manuscripts generally: we find the same use of rubric, the same characteristic blue paragraph markers, the same trick of enclosing inscriptions and notes with a coloured rectangular line, often wavy, or looped at the corners.[1] Even more important is the fact that the handwriting on all the maps and itineraries is undoubtedly that of Matthew Paris, and contrasts strikingly with that of other scribes. The names, for instance, which John of Wallingford added to the map of England and Scotland given to him by Matthew Paris,[2] can be distinguished at a glance from those written on to the same map by Matthew Paris. I think that there can be no question that the whole of this cartographical material is the work of Matthew, as author, artist, and scribe. Such a combination of talents in one person need occasion no surprise, for we know that Matthew was a competent scribe, an author, and an excellent artist.

To what extent Matthew really was the effective author of these maps and itineraries must unfortunately remain in doubt, for no source survives of any of them, and we are free to speculate to what degree he relied on existing material, and to what extent he based his work on information collected by himself. There is, however, some evidence to guide our speculation on this important point. We know, for instance, that Matthew's world-map is a reduced copy of an existing one, for he tells us this himself.[3] On the other hand, in the maps of England and Scotland, the outline varies so much from map to map that it seems more likely that Matthew drew each map more or less 'out of his head', so to speak, than that he based them on an existing map. All of them, however, are evidently based on the same itinerary from Dover to Newcastle,[4] which seems to have been the only written cartographical source which Matthew used. If this is so, the England maps are almost entirely his own work. There is less evidence as to the extent of Matthew's authorship in the case of the itineraries and maps of Palestine, but again it seems that he made an original contribution of his own of some importance. The obvious connexion

[1] See Vaughan, 'Handwriting of M. Paris', *Trans. Camb. Bibl. Soc.* (1953), p. 383.
[2] See below, p. 243.
[3] See p. 247 below.　　　　　[4] See p. 244 below.

between both of these and the *Chronica Majora* makes this clear. The itinerary, for instance, is evidently connected with the pope's offer of the Sicilian crown to Richard of Cornwall, which is described in the *Chronica Majora*,[1] for one of the versions of it has a legend describing this; and Richard's landing at Trapani in 1241, which is mentioned in the itinerary, is also mentioned in the *Chronica Majora*.[2] The information about the Tartars in the legends of the Palestine map seems to be derived from that given by Matthew in his *Chronica Majora*;[3] and a legend on one of the maps mentions the ruler of Morocco—'l'amiral Murmelin'—who is the subject of a long addition by Matthew to the text of Roger Wendover's chronicle.[4] Two of the legends of the Palestine map give information about Noah's Ark.[5] According to one of these, Noah's Ark was in Armenia, where Joseph Cartaphila, the Wandering Jew, lived, who had been baptized by Ananias, who also baptized St Paul. The other also states that Noah's Ark was in Armenia, among wild inaccessible mountains, surrounded by a desert full of serpents, and adds that Armenia marches with India. Now information identical with this is found in two different places in the *Chronica Majora*: in the annal for 1228 it is said that Ananias baptized St Paul and Cartaphila, the latter of whom then lived in Armenia; and in the annal for 1252 Matthew records the visit of some Armenians to St Albans, who gave him the rest of the information given in these two legends.[6] The only possible conclusion from this seems to be that much, at any rate, of the information given in the legends on the Palestine maps was gathered by Matthew Paris himself.

There is a certain amount of evidence to show that Matthew was interested in cartography, and that his maps are not mere slavish copies of existing ones. In the margin of a St Albans historical manuscript, for instance, next to an account of the size of England and its bishoprics, he notes:[7] 'Hic est discordia

---

[1] v, pp. 346–7. [2] IV, pp. 144 and 145.
[3] *Itinéraires à Jérusalem*, edd. Michelant and Raynaud, pp. 125–6; *CM.* IV, p. 77, and v, p. 341.
[4] *Itinéraires à Jérusalem*, p. 138; and *CM.* II, pp. 559 ff.
[5] *Itinéraires à Jérusalem*, p. 126.
[6] *CM.* III, p. 163; and v, p. 341.
[7] British Museum Royal MS. 13 D v, f. 152 a.

inter hoc et Gildam de dimensione Anglie. Respice in principio Gilde.' In his map of England and Scotland Matthew follows this account in preference to Gildas, and copies out the part of it describing the size of Great Britain to give his map a rough scale.[1] His interest in cartography is shown, too, in some notes on the last fly-leaf of *A*, which James deciphered thus:[2]

> Circa Carleolum patria est dicta Aluedele.
> Hic versus austrum Cocormue villa patria complem. [*sic*]
> Aqua Dorecte et currit (?) per Cocormue.

Other notes, in part illegible, have been written by Matthew on a fly-leaf of Corpus Christi College, Oxford, MS. 2, on the same leaf as his map of Palestine.[3] They seem to show him in the very act of collecting cartographical material, and, since they have never been published, I give them here, in so far as I have been able to decipher them:

> Messana propinquior est terre sancte quam Brundusium. Navigantibus a Massilia in terram sanctam est Messana media [ui]a. Marsilia est contermina Hyspanie.
> Siciliam, Apuliam, Calabriam, ...que ducat usque ad Alpes, Campaniam, Romam cum Romania, Vallem [Spoleti?], Vallem Anconie, Venetiam, Dalmatiam.
> In Arabia est Ydumea ubi crescit...balsam. [S]aba [flumen?] Sabea patria. ...media contermine sunt Indie. Parthia, id est Tur[c]hia.
> Pamfir[i]a⎫ Idem.
> Armenia ⎭
> Rex Aragonie adeptus est super sarracenos [in] hispania xxx dietas. Katalonia est patria contermina prouincie Vallis Moriane. Sabaudia.
> Tharsus est archiepiscopatus prope Antiochiam ubi natus est sanctus Paulus, et est in cilia Armenie minoris. In parte boreali est Ruscia et [R]umania et B..lakania, et superius uersus Anthiokiam est Yconium.
> [Caba?] est [insula?] prope Januam ubi optimi sunt ancipitres.
> Inter Ciprim et Acon comp...per mare ccc leuce.

No one of Matthew's cartographical productions is identical with another, and for this reason it seems worth while to give here

---

[1] He copied this memorandum out again on one of the preliminary leaves of the *Abbreviatio Chronicorum*, f. 1 b.
[2] James, *Catalogue of C.C.C.C. MSS.* I, p. 53.
[3] See pp. 245–7 below for this map.

a complete list of them all. In this list I have prefixed each map with the letter used for it in previous editions.

(1) *Maps of England and Scotland.*[1]

A. British Museum, Cotton MS. Claudius D vi (*AC*), f. 8b (now bound separately).

B. Corpus Christi College, Cambridge, MS. 16 (*B*), f. vb (incomplete).

C. British Museum Cotton MS. Julius D vii, ff. 50b–53 (now bound separately with map A).

D. British Museum Royal MS. 14 C vii (*R*), f. 5b.

To these we should add the *Scema Britannie* on f. 186b of British Museum Cotton MS. Nero D i (*LA*), a sketch-map of the main Roman roads.[2]

(2) *Maps of Palestine.*[3]

A. British Museum Royal MS. 14 C vii (*R*), ff. 4b–5a.

C. Corpus Christi College, Cambridge, MS. 16 (*B*), ff. iib and va (incomplete).

D. Corpus Christi College, Cambridge, MS. 26 (*A*), ff. iiib–iva.

B, of Michelant, is a post-medieval copy of A. Another copy exists in British Museum Cotton MS. Tiberius E vi, ff. 3b–4a, badly damaged by fire, and probably copied from D.

To these we must add the map of Palestine in Corpus Christi College, Oxford, MS. 2, ff. 2b–1a.[4]

(3) *World-map.*

Corpus Christi College, Cambridge, MS. 26, p. 284.[5]

A medieval copy of this map exists in British Museum Cotton MS. Nero D v, f. 1b.[6]

---

[1] Excellently reproduced in colour in *Four Maps of Great Britain*, edited by J. P. Gilson.

[2] Engraved by Miller, *Mappae Mundi. Die ältesten Weltkarten*, III, p. 83.

[3] The legends of these maps are printed in *Itinéraires à Jérusalem*, pp. 125 ff. Map A is reproduced in Beazley, *Dawn of Modern Geography*, II, facing p. 590; part of C (f. iib) in James, 'Drawings of M. Paris', *Walpole Soc.* XIV (1925–6), no. 26; and D is reproduced below as Plate XVI.

[4] Reproduced below for the first time as Plate XVII.

[5] Reproduced in Miller, *Mappae Mundi. Die ältesten Weltkarten*, III, p. 71.

[6] Reproduced in Beazley, *Dawn of Modern Geography*, II, facing p. 586.

(4) *Itineraries from London to Apulia.*[1]

1. British Museum Royal MS. 14 C vii (*R*), ff. 2a–4a.
2. British Museum Cotton MS. Nero D i (*LA*), ff. 182b–183a.
3. Corpus Christi College, Cambridge, MS. 26 (*A*), ff. ia–iiia.
4. Corpus Christi College, Cambridge, MS. 16 (*B*), f. iia (incomplete).

This mass of material is for the most part arranged systematically, each volume of the *Chronica Majora* having been originally prefaced with, among other preliminary matter, a copy of the itinerary, the map of Palestine, and the map of England and Scotland, in that order. The present arrangement of the cartographical material in these manuscripts is as follows:

		Itinerary	Palestine	England
Chronica	Vol. i (*A*)	i–iiia	iiib–iva	none
Majora	Vol. ii (*B*)	iia (fragm.)	iib–va	vb
	Vol. iii (*R*)	2a–4a	4b–5a	5b

Little need be said here about Matthew's four maps of England and Scotland, for they have been reproduced admirably in facsimile, and discussed at length by Miss Mitchell.[2] They are the earliest detailed maps of England in existence. Of their date nothing certain can be ascertained, though the handwriting shows that they were executed fairly late in Matthew's life, probably after *c.* 1245. The best of these maps is that prefacing the *Abbreviatio Chronicorum* (A). That in *B* (B) is also excellent, but unfortunately only about half of it survives. In both these maps the sea is coloured green and the rivers blue, and many of the legends are written in red, with blue paragraph markers. Map A is drawn in an oblong frame, round the outside of which inscriptions indicate the nearest land lying opposite each quarter of the map. The map in *R* (D) is only an outline sketch, though the sea has been coloured in, and is much less accurate in shape than maps A and B. It seems to have been either an early attempt soon abandoned, or else a late, very

---

[1] The only good modern reproduction of any of these seems to be that of f. 4a of no. 1 in Beazley, *Dawn of Modern Geography*, II, facing p. 588. The first pages of nos. 1 and 3 are reproduced below, Plates XII and XIII. The text is printed in Miller, *Mappae Mundi. Die ältesten Weltkarten*, III, pp. 85–90.

[2] See above, p. 236.

rough copy, which was never completed. It has few close similarities with the other maps, all of which resemble each other more or less closely. The map in British Museum Cotton MS. Julius D vii (c) is rather similar to map B, and, since it was never finished by Matthew Paris, may have been a first draft which he later abandoned. The main route to the north is displaced to the east, as in map B; but, whereas in map C the space thus provided is left blank, in map B it is filled with a legend describing the size of England, evidently intended to serve as a rough scale. Map C has recently been taken out of the manuscript in which it was bound, and preserved in a separate cover with map A. Its early history is interesting. British Museum Cotton MS. Julius D vii is a small manuscript containing the historical collections of John of Wallingford, infirmarer of St Albans, and a friend of Matthew Paris. Matthew must have given map C to John of Wallingford while it was still unfinished, unless John rescued it from the scriptorium wastepaper-basket, for many of the names on it have been written by John and not by Matthew. Although this map is on a folio-size leaf, John decided to incorporate it into his little historical volume, which unfortunately entailed folding it into four and cutting through two of the folds. Later John filled in the four pages provided by the blank verso of the map with some miscellaneous material of his own.[1]

Matthew's maps of England and Scotland are outstanding among early medieval attempts at cartography, in that they represent a genuine attempt at a map, rather than a mere diagrammatical representation. They are orientated with north at the top, unlike most early medieval maps, and the four points of the compass were written in at the sides, top and bottom.[2] We have seen that one of them has been provided with an attempt at a scale. That Matthew was conscious of the importance of scale is shown by a note on map D, to the effect that, if the page allowed it, the whole map should have been longer.[3] In these maps, too, we find examples of the use of conventional signs for mountains, trees and towns, which seem to be among the earliest known. Matthew, of course, was perfectly well

---

[1] See Vaughan, 'Handwriting of M. Paris', *Trans. Camb. Bibl. Soc.* I (1953), p. 382, note 9.   [2] Not all of these survive.

[3] 'Si pagina pateretur, hec totalis insula longior esse deberet.'

acquainted with this idea, for, as we have seen, he used a number of conventional signs in the margins of his chronicles. All four maps of England and Scotland are based on an itinerary from Dover to Newcastle, which runs through Canterbury, Rochester, London, St Albans, Dunstable, Northampton, Leicester, Belvoir, Newark, Blyth, Doncaster, Pontefract, Boroughbridge, North-allerton and Durham, and which, on all the maps, runs north–south, so that Dover, Canterbury and Rochester are marked due south of London. This is the one major error in the maps, and it has caused a serious displacement of much of the south of England. Norfolk and Suffolk fill up the south-east corner of the map; Kent is displaced due south of London; Sussex south-west of London; Essex due west; and, in map A, Wiltshire is inserted north of London, and even of Northampton. In map C John of Wallingford has shown more sense, for he marks Wiltshire roughly in the right place, south-west of London. Of the relative positions of Devon, Somerset and Dorset Matthew evidently knew little, but Cornwall is correctly marked in the south-western extremity of the island. Some idea of the amount of detail in these maps is afforded by the 250 names listed in the British Museum edition. As we should expect, St Albans is placed conspicuously on all four maps, in a central position due north of London. The abbey's five chief cells are also marked: Tynemouth, Belvoir, Binham, Wymondham and Wallingford.

The *Scema Britannie* in the *Liber Additamentorum* need not detain us long. It is a rough outline sketch of England and Scotland showing the four main Roman roads, quite wrongly intersecting at Dunstable. They are Icknield Street, the Fosse Way, Ermine Street and Watling Street. This map is orientated with west at the top, and Matthew has given the rough bearings of each of the four roads. Thus, Icknield Street is said to lead 'ab oriente in occidentem'; the Fosse Way, 'a zephiro australi in eurum septentrionalem', and so on.

Three of Matthew's maps of Palestine are very similar, and their legends have been printed in full.[1] Each takes up an opening in one of the three volumes of the *Chronica Majora*. That in *B*, besides surviving only in part, is on the whole rougher

[1] See above, p. 241 note 3.

and less full than either of the others, both of which are more carefully executed and ornamented in colour. The map in *A* is reproduced below as Plate XVI. The editors of the legends of these maps thought that the map in *R* represented an early version, and those in *A* and *B* a later one. None of these maps is copied directly from another, and, as with the maps of England, each displays some features peculiar to itself. Evidence of their date is scanty, but one of the legends of the map in *A* gives some information which Matthew obtained from the Armenians who visited St Albans in 1252, which shows that it was executed in or after that year;[1] and the other two maps were probably executed at about the same time. From the cartographical point of view, the map of Palestine represented in these three versions is of little interest. It seems to have been based on the traditional world-maps, and, like them, lacks any true sense of proportion or scale. An inordinate amount of space is taken up with descriptive legends of little or no carto-graphical importance, and with drawings of boats, cities, animals, and so on. In accordance with traditional usage, the map is orientated with east at the top. Only twenty-seven towns are marked, and natural features are represented only by the Dead Sea, the rivers Jordan and Farfar, the Caspian mountains, and the mountains of Lebanon. Although the proportion of the map has been ruined by the large-scale plan of Acre, this is an interesting feature in itself, since a number of the more im-portant buildings are individually marked.

Besides these three maps of Palestine, notable mainly for their descriptive legends and artistic features, Matthew executed a fourth map quite different from them, and of much greater cartographical interest, which is reproduced here for the first time as Plate XVII. It occupies part of one side of a parchment bifolium bound at the beginning of Corpus Christi College, Oxford, MS. 2, a St Albans Bible partly executed by Matthew Paris.[2] This map is not very carefully finished, and some of it is sketched in very roughly. The only colouring consists in a few

[1] See p. 239 above.
[2] See Vaughan, 'Handwriting of M. Paris', *Trans. Camb. Bibliog. Soc.* 1 (1953), p. 391, where I have wrongly attributed only a part of the map of Palestine to Matthew.

words written in rubric. The writing is rough and cursive, and the carefully executed drawings of towns which form so conspicuous a feature of the itineraries and other maps of Palestine are almost entirely lacking. In its general character, this map is more similar to the maps of England and Scotland than to the other maps of Palestine. North is placed at the top of the page, and an attempt at a correct representation of proportion has been made, in contrast to the more diagrammatic approach of the other Palestine maps. There are no long descriptive legends or elaborate drawings to spoil the cartographical qualities of this map. The coast, marked by a wavy black line on the extreme left of the page, extends from Antioch and its port, St Symeon, at the top, to Alexandria and Cairo at the bottom. The different territories are clearly marked with letters spaced out across the page: 'Terra Antiochie', 'Armenia', 'Terra Senis de Monte', 'Terra Sirie', 'Terra Egypti', and 'Terra Soldani Babilonie'. A number of natural features are marked, such as mountains, rivers, lakes, and springs. The Nile is wrongly called the Tigris, and is made to flow east–west, but the relative positions of the Sea of Galilee and the Dead Sea are roughly correct, and the Jordan is shown joining them. Other natural features recorded are palm trees, forests, and a plain, the 'planicies Fabe'; and it is interesting to find that the crocodiles of the Nile, the salt of the Dead Sea, and the lions of the 'foresta de Arches' are all noted. A number of biblical features, too, are marked, such as the tomb of Abraham, Isaac, and Jacob, the ditch where Adam was created, and the place where the wood of the Cross grew. The most valuable feature of this map, however, is the large number of inhabited places marked on it. There are nearly sixty in all, and in nearly every case something of the nature of the settlement is indicated by the word *episcopatus, civitas, monasterium,* or *castrum* (usually the single letter *C*). To this mass of information Matthew has added the distances in days' journeys between many of the coastal settlements; and the route to Jerusalem is also marked. Finally, a number of notes give additional information about the relative positions of various places, and sometimes even correct the map. Thus, whereas on the map Damascus is placed on the river Jordan, due north of the Sea of Galilee, a note correctly states that in fact Damascus is not on the Jordan, and that the headwaters of that river are much nearer the coast than Damascus.[1] Although this map contains a number of errors and has many shortcomings, it is probably the most detailed and important of all the earlier medieval maps of Palestine, though it seems to have entirely escaped the notice of historians of cartography; and, even if Matthew's share of responsibility in it must remain in doubt, we can at least be thankful to him for preserving it for us.

Matthew's world-map is the least interesting of his carto-graphical productions. It is traditional in form, and it makes no advance on the many earlier medieval world-maps. On it, however, Matthew has written an inscription of great interest, which reads as follows:[2] 'This is a reduced copy of the world-maps of Master Robert Melkeley and Waltham [Abbey]. The king's world-map, which is in his chamber at Westminster, is most accurately copied in Matthew Paris's Ordinal.' Unfortunately Matthew's Ordinal is not now known to exist. He does not seem to have thought very highly of the existing world-map, for it is not executed with especial care, and part of the page on which it is drawn has been used for his rough notes.

The last of Matthew's cartographical productions is the famous itinerary from London to Apulia, of which four autograph copies are known to exist. I have listed these on p. 242 above, and shall use the numbers used there in reference to them. This work was formerly thought to be an itinerary from London to Jerusalem, but Miller showed that in fact it extended only to the south of Italy, and that the map of Palestine, showing Jerusalem, which follows it in three of the manuscripts, is a separate work.[3] The word 'Apulia' has been rather loosely used in reference to this work, for the itinerary proper seems to have ended at Rome. The existing versions, however, vary so much towards the end that no single title can accurately describe them all. These variations may be summarized as follows:

(1) The itinerary proper ends with Rome—'terminus itineris multorum'—which is followed by a diagram or map of southern

---

[1] 'Istud propinquius est mari, nec contingit Damascum fluuius [*sc.* Jordanus].'

[2] *HA.* III, p. li, note 1.

[3] Miller, *Mappae Mundi. Die ältesten Weltkarten*, III, p. 84.

Italy, called by Matthew Apulia. To this are added (*a*) a diagram of Sicily, and (*b*) a plan of Rome; (*a*) and (*b*) are on separate slips of parchment stuck to the edges of the leaf.

(2) The itinerary ends at Rome, but the diagram of Apulia which follows has been rearranged in a single column as if it formed part of the itinerary.

(3) The itinerary proper ends with Siena, and this is followed by a group of towns in central Italy arranged roughly in two columns: Arezzo, Viterbo, Sutri; and Perugia, Assisi, Spoleto. After these comes the diagram of Apulia, and then the plans of Sicily and Rome fixed to the edges of the leaf.

(4) A simplified version of no. 1 which has lost its plans of Sicily and Rome.

I have already mentioned the fact that this itinerary seems to be connected with the papal offer of the Sicilian crown to Richard of Cornwall in 1252.[1] No. 1 has the inscription:[2] 'Earl Richard, brother of the king of England, was offered the crown of all this country [that is, Apulia].... This was in the time of Pope Innocent IV, who made him the offer in the year of grace 1253.' This proposal is described in the *Chronica Majora*, and it does seem likely that the itinerary was made in connexion with it. The words of the inscription, 'This was in the time of Pope Innocent IV', seem to show that itinerary no. 1, at any rate, was executed after Innocent's death in 1254; and it seems probable that both the itineraries and the maps of Palestine which follow them date from after *c.* 1252. The striking variations between the four versions of this itinerary bear out the theory outlined above, that Matthew himself was a cartographer, and that they are not mere copies of an existing work. We are, unfortunately, entirely ignorant as to the nature of their source material, but it does not seem unreasonable to suggest that Matthew compiled them from information provided by contemporary travellers to Rome, of whom we know there were many among his acquaintances.

The two most detailed and finished versions of Matthew's Apulian itinerary are nos. 1 and 3 of our list, and the first page of each is illustrated in Plates XII and XIII. No. 2 seems to

[1] Above, p. 239.
[2] Printed in Miller, *Mappae Mundi. Die ältesten Weltkarten*, III, p. 89.

derive from these, for in it Matthew has tried to convert the diagram of Apulia into a continuation of the itinerary beyond Rome. The German scholar, Ludwig, made a detailed study of Matthew's itinerary, and compiled a useful table giving the towns on the main route with the distances between them, as well as Matthew's distances in days' journeys.[1] He showed that, while Matthew's distances between the places on the main route are mostly correct, those of the side-routes, several of which are marked, are often wildly wrong. He found that the average day's journey was 35 km., but that days' journeys of up to 60 km. occurred occasionally. He pointed out that a number of quite serious mistakes occur in the itinerary: the river Po, for instance, is in the wrong place, and Valence is wrongly marked between Lyons and Vienne. For the most part, Matthew's itinerary is a list of names of towns in French, with the word 'Jurnee' written vertically between them. They are arranged in vertical columns, and the itinerary begins in the bottom left-hand corner of the first page, and runs up each column. In the strict sense of the word, it is not an itinerary at all, for, especially in Italy and in no. 3, Matthew seems to have included all the towns he knew of, without any reference to an actual itinerary. The towns are indicated by thumbnail sketches of architectural features in Matthew's characteristic fashion, showing a piece of wall and a tower or two, and perhaps a spire. Sometimes there is more information than this. Thus, the gates and some of the chief buildings of London are marked. Occasionally, minute drawings are to be found. At Pontremoli, for instance, two pine trees are drawn in, and marked 'pin'; and a carefully drawn tortoise is labelled 'tortue'. At Sutri, in no. 1, a stork sits on a tower, and, in no. 3, excellent little drawings of a man with a mule, and a goat, decorate the neighbourhood of Arezzo.

The map of southern Italy which follows, or forms part of, the itinerary is of no cartographical importance, and Matthew's information was evidently too scanty for him to do more than make a diagram, in which most of the important towns are marked with little or no relation to their true position. Southern Italy itself is wrongly placed in relation to the itinerary; for,

[1] Ludwig, *Untersuchungen über die Reise- und Marschgeschwindigkeit im XII. und XIII. Jahrhundert*, pp. 122–9.

whereas in the itinerary south is at the top of the page and north at the bottom, in the map of southern Italy the west coast, with Naples and Salerno on it, is placed at the top. Moreover, Barletta, Trani, Bari, Brindisi and Otranto are shown along a coastline vertical to the page and down the left-hand side of the map, at right angles to the west coast along the top of the page. Both coastlines are shown more or less straight, and no idea is given of the outline of southern Italy. The same is true of the map or diagram of Sicily, which shows the island in the form of a triangle lying, apparently, more or less opposite Naples.

Matthew's interest in cartography and his skill at drawing maps are linked closely to his historical and artistic activities, and to his avid desire to collect and record information of every kind. It is not therefore surprising that a man of his talents and curiosity should have added this body of cartographical and geographical material to his historical manuscripts. His maps of England and Scotland and the Oxford map of Palestine are landmarks of the first importance in the history of cartography; and the itinerary, too, is interesting and valuable. As we have seen, it is not possible to ascertain exactly the extent of Matthew's own contribution to this material, but, even if, as seems unlikely, this was small, we owe its preservation to him, and for this alone he deserves an important place in the history of medieval cartography.

II. HERALDRY

When, in the text of Matthew's chronicles, mention is made of a battle or other event, the shields of the persons concerned are often painted in the margin of the manuscript; and when the death of a knight is recorded, his shield is inserted reversed. There are ninety-five shields in the margins of R; seventy-eight in B; fourteen in A; six in the *Abbreviatio Chronicorum*; and four in the Chetham manuscript of the *Flores Historiarum*. Moreover, in the *Liber Additamentorum* there is a leaf with some fifty shields painted in colour, as well as twenty-five uncoloured; and another page in the same manuscript has twenty-seven shields roughly tricked and blazoned. Sir Frederick Madden thought that all these shields were the work of Matthew Paris, and he included a knowledge of heraldry among Matthew's attainments.[1] Hardy, however, doubted if the shields were drawn by Matthew; and Luard thought it possible that they were designed by another hand.[2] I have already put forward evidence to show that Matthew himself executed the shields in the margins of the historical manuscripts;[3] and the reader can corroborate this by examining Plate XVIII,[4] where he will see that the heraldic animals of these shields are identical with those in the drawings and paintings attributed to Matthew Paris. Madden, then, was right in attributing the shields to Matthew Paris, but was he also right in attributing to him a knowledge of heraldry? That Matthew was not a mere artist carrying out someone else's instructions seems to be indicated by the fact that nearly all the shields in the *Liber Additamentorum*, including those only drawn in trick, are blazoned in his own handwriting, for this shows that he understood and used heraldic terminology. The same thing is found in the *Chronica Majora*. On f. 144b of *B*, for instance, Matthew's own plummet notes survive, describing the shields painted in the margin; and this, I think, shows that he painted these shields on the basis of his own descriptions, and not directly from some roll of arms. His statements, too, sometimes reflect his interest in heraldry. In the *Historia Anglorum*, for instance, he says in the margin of one leaf that 'many other French nobles fell, whose names and shields are unknown to me [*nobis*]';[5] and in the margin of another he explains that half of Otto's shield bore the imperial arms, and the other half those of the kings of England.[6] The very scope and variety, too, of Matthew's heraldic work indicates his interest in the subject, and makes it clear that he knew something about it, and was more than a mere heraldic copyist.

The relationship of the different sets of shields in Matthew's manuscripts is very hard to determine. On f. 170b of the *Liber Additamentorum* (Plate XIX) there are forty-two shields in full colour arranged in rows of six, with the names of their owners and the blazons written above each shield. Three other shields have been added in the margins, two of which are in

---

[1] *HA.* III, pp. xlix–l.
[2] Hardy, *Descriptive Catalogue*, III, p. lxxii; and *CM.* VI, p. 469.
[3] Above, pp. 211–16 and Plates IV and V.
[4] Cf. also Plate X (*a*).
[5] *HA.* III, p. 84 note 1. [6] *HA.* II, p. 65.

colour.[1] These shields were probably copied by Matthew from a roll of arms, since they are arranged in a definite order: King Henry III comes first, followed by his brother the earl of Cornwall, the other earls, and then a number of knights. On the recto of this leaf the shields are arranged in rows of five in no particular order, and only the first four are completed, the rest being left either partly coloured, or entirely blank. Five partly coloured shields have been added in the margin of the leaf, and the three shields in the lower margin are also later additions.[1] There is good reason to believe that these shields were executed in 1244, and, if this is so, the same is no doubt true of the shields on the verso. The shields drawn in trick and blazoned on f. 198 are mostly repeated on f. 170, but they are not directly copied thence. These shields in the *Liber Additamentorum* do not form a collection designed to provide exemplars for the heraldic illustration in the historical manuscripts, for, while thirty-five of the shields in the *Liber Additamentorum* do not occur in the other manuscripts, there are thirty-five shields in the *Chronica Majora* which are not in the *Liber Additamentorum*. Nor have the shields in the *Historia Anglorum* been directly copied from those in the *Chronica*, for seventeen of them are peculiar to the *Historia Anglorum*. On the other hand, all these shields must derive from a common source, whether this was a roll of arms in Matthew's possession, or one which he borrowed, or a collection of paintings and blazons made by himself at different times.

Matthew's love of heraldry seems to have been partly artistic —he evidently appreciated the pictorial value of coloured shields —and partly historical. He collected shields in much the same way as he collected documents, and, just as he tampered with his documentary material, so he seems to have tampered with his heraldic material, for he provides or invents coats of arms for William the Conqueror and Cnut.[2] Apart from occasional errors his shields are accurate, and are usually ascribed to individuals rather than to families. In the history of heraldry Matthew's work is of the utmost importance, for he was a

[1] For these shields, see von Pusikan (O. Göschen), 'Wappen aus den Werken des Matthias von Paris', *Vierteljahrschrift für Heraldik, Sphragistik und Genealogie*, II, where they are described and reproduced.

[2] See James, 'Drawings of M. Paris', *Walpole Soc.* XIV (1925–6), no. 16; and Plate XVIII (d) below.

pioneer in the subject, and his shields take the first place in A. R. Wagner's *Catalogue of English Medieval Rolls of Arms.* The earliest actual roll of arms catalogued by Wagner is Glover's roll, the lost original of which is thought to have been executed *c.* 1255, at a time when the bulk of Matthew's shields had already been painted. Glover's roll probably contained 214 shields: Matthew gives us some 130, including a number of Continental shields, the presence of which reflects the breadth of his interests, and makes him important as a source for Continental, as well as English, heraldry. In any estimate of him, then, his heraldic work must be given a place of importance, both on account of its utility and significance for historians, and because of its originality, for Matthew seems to have been one of the first to conceive the idea of making a collection of coats of arms.

The identification and cataloguing of Matthew's shields was undertaken by that careful scholar, H. R. Luard, and he printed a complete list of all the shields occurring in Matthew's manuscripts, with the exception of the four in the *Flores Historiarum,* as an appendix to the sixth volume of his edition of the *Chronica Majora.* A year before the appearance of this, in 1881, Major Göschen, writing under the pseudonym von Pusikan, published a detailed account of the shields on f. 170 of the *Liber Additamentorum,* accompanied by a colour reproduction of this leaf. The only other detailed study of Matthew's shields was published in 1909 by F. Hauptmann, who carefully described all the shields in the *Historia Anglorum* and the *Abbreviatio Chronicorum,* and discussed them at length.[1] It is to be hoped that, some day, this remarkable collection of shields will be reproduced in full colour and with an adequate commentary, so as to collect them together in one volume and do full justice to their artistic and heraldic merit.

III. NATURAL SCIENCE

We have already discussed Matthew's concern with natural history and natural phenomena of all kinds in connexion with the *Chronica Majora,*[2] but certain aspects of his interest in these

---

[1] Hauptmann, 'Die Wappen in der *Historia Minor* des M. Parisiensis', *Jahrbuch der K.K. Heraldischen Gesellschaft,* XIX (1909).

[2] See above, pp. 144–5; see also *HA.* III, pp. xlvi–xlvii.

and similar things merit separate discussion here. I use the word 'science' in a very loose sense, which includes, for the purposes of this chapter, both astrology and fortune-telling. To begin, however, with the more authentic sciences, we ought to note that Matthew's interest in meteorology is by no means limited to the pages of his chronicles. In the *Liber Additamentorum* the greater part of a page (f. 185a) is devoted to an elaborate drawing, with many annotations, of a parhelion seen in the sky on 8 April 1233. Matthew tells us that an eyewitness made a drawing of it while it was still visible, and his drawing is evidently based on this one. Although the drawing and notes leave no doubt as to the kind of phenomenon observed, neither is in fact accurate, and either the observer or Matthew seems to have been confused by the number and relationship of the suns and their haloes. It is interesting to find that the points of the compass are marked on this drawing, east being placed at the top of the page.

On two occasions Matthew inserts a diagram of an eclipse of the sun in the margins of his chronicles; in one of these the earth, moon and sun are shown in a straight line; and, in the other, the moon is shown superimposed on the sun.[1] These diagrams are similar to some of those executed by Matthew in a manuscript which affords further proof of his interest in these matters. This is Part II of manuscript no. 385 in the library of Corpus Christi College, Cambridge, a copy of William of Conches's *Dragmaticon Philosophiae* which Matthew illustrated with a series of twenty-three diagrams, some of which are reproduced in Plate xx.[2] William of Conches (1080–1145) was a well-known philosopher and teacher at Chartres, and this work takes the form of a dialogue on 'natural substances', during the

---

[1] *B*, f. 75b, and *R*, f. 181a.

[2] See also Plate xiv (*e*). When I first examined this manuscript, I attributed these diagrams to Matthew Paris on grounds of style and handwriting alone, but there is some more convincing evidence which connects it very closely with Matthew. For instance, on p. 111 the couplet from Henry of Avranches's poem on the dedication of Salisbury Cathedral, written in the lower margin (not by Matthew himself), is misquoted in the same words as by Matthew in the *Chronica Majora*, III, pp. 189–90 (and see p. 189, note 5). Some verses on the winds, too, are written in the lower margin of p. 151 as well as by Matthew himself in *LA* (*CM*. VI, p. 465). See Vaughan, 'Handwriting of M. Paris', *Trans. Camb. Bibliog. Soc.* I (1953), pp. 382–3.

course of which various subjects, such as demons, angels, the four elements, the world, astronomy, creation, animal life, the seasons, meteorology, and human biology, are discussed; and it was illustrated with a number of figures.[1] Many illustrated manuscripts of this work have survived, and Matthew's differs in no important respect from the others, though his diagrams are of much more artistic merit. Those reproduced in Plate xx illustrate (a) the solar system, (b) the phases of the moon, (c) an eclipse of the moon, (d) the twelve winds; (e) is a schematic world-map. The diagram reproduced as Plate xiv (e) shows the path of the sun. Matthew Paris was not a professional artist, and his illustration of this manuscript is therefore important for the light it throws on his scientific interests. The fact that one of the diagrams in it is a wind rose is significant, for his manuscripts contain several of these drawn by himself. Professor Taylor made a special study of the two wind roses drawn by Matthew in the *Liber Additamentorum*.[2] One of these is the traditional twelve-ray rose represented in Plate xx (d), which came down to the Middle Ages from classical antiquity. It is headed by Matthew with the words, 'Secundum magistrum Elyam de Derham', which show that it is a copy of a wind rose designed by Elias of Dereham, the canon of Salisbury who died in 1245. It is very like another twelve-ray diagram copied by John of Wallingford into his manuscript of miscellaneous matter with the heading:[3] 'Secundum Robertum Grosseteste episcopum Lincolniensem'. Taylor noticed that the other wind rose in the *Liber Additamentorum* was very different from these, and of much greater interest, for in it the circle is divided into sixteen rays instead of twelve, in accordance with the practice of the seamen of Matthew's day.[4] This rose is certainly Matthew's own work, and below it he has written out some mnemonic verses on the winds composed by himself. He made two other versions of this sixteen-ray wind rose, which are to be found among the preliminary matter of the first two volumes of the *Chronica*

---

[1] It was edited by W. Gratarolus in 1567. For the MSS., see Wilmart, 'Analecta reginensia', *Studi e Testi*, LIX (1933), p. 263, note 2.

[2] 'The *De ventis* of Matthew Paris', *Imago Mundi*, II (1937), pp. 23–6. They are on f. 184a and b of the *Liber Additamentorum*.

[3] British Museum Cotton MS. Julius D vii, f. 51b.

[4] Taylor, 'The *De ventis* of Matthew Paris', *loc. cit.* p. 23.

Majora;[1] and in each of them Matthew has added, to the Latin names of the sixteen wind directions, the vernacular equivalents which are still in use today. Although he himself was probably not responsible for first bringing the classical twelve-ray wind rose up to date by dividing the horizon into sixteen parts, his diagram seems to be the earliest surviving example of this important modification.

Besides astronomy and meteorology, Matthew interested himself in natural history, and, in particular, in the natural history of the elephant. In February 1255[2] Louis IX presented an elephant to Henry III. This animal was brought across the Channel by John Gouch, and was housed at the Tower in a special elephant-house, forty feet long and twenty feet broad. Matthew records this gift in his *Chronica Majora*, and he wrote a short tract on the elephant to accompany the drawings which he made from life ('ipso elephante exemplariter assistente'), and which he inserted into two of his manuscripts.[3] The accuracy of these drawings can be judged from Plate XXI (*a*), where one of them is reproduced. The rather wooden appearance of the beast seems partly due to Matthew's belief, expressed in the tract accompanying the drawings and shared by his contemporaries, that elephants had no joints in their legs. In the drawing reproduced here the *magister bestie* has been drawn in, standing under the animal's head, in order to give an idea of its size, for Matthew says: 'From the size of the man drawn here one can get an idea of the size of the beast.' The short tract on the elephant written by Matthew, which accompanies these drawings, is incomplete in each of the manuscripts, and the two versions of it differ considerably. There is also a third version which was copied from that in the *Liber Additamentorum* by John of Wallingford, who also made a rather poor copy of Matthew's drawing.[4] This particular elephant is described as being ten years old, and ten feet high, and Matthew goes on to explain, presumably on the basis of his own observations, that

[1] *A*, f. vb, and *B*, f. ib.
[2] For what follows, see also Madden's article in Brayley, *Graphic and Historical Illustrator*, pp. 335–6.
[3] *CM*. v, p. 489. For the tract and drawings, see *B*, ff. iva–vb and the *Liber Additamentorum*, f. 168b and attached slip.
[4] British Museum Cotton MS. Julius D vii, ff. 114a–115a.

the elephant is greyish-black in colour and, unlike other animals, has no fur; that it is ponderous and robust, and indeed an altogether prodigious and monstrous animal. It uses its trunk for obtaining food and drink; has small eyes in the upper part of its head; and its skin is rough and very hard. So much for observation: the rest of the tract is compiled from the Bible, Bernard Sylvester, Virgil, Horace, and the medieval bestiary. From the latter Matthew took his account of the method of trapping elephants. Since they have no joints in their legs, they cannot get up once they have fallen to the ground, and are forced therefore to sleep reclining against a tree. All the huntsman has to do is to saw partly through the trunks of the trees used by the elephants for this purpose, and then kill them as they lie helpless on the ground![1] On the whole, this little tract is a characteristic example of medieval natural-history studies, and its significance lies in its demonstration of Matthew's interest in them rather than in any inherent merit.

Matthew's belief in portents and prognostics is well attested in the *Chronica Majora*,[2] and his curiosity about natural phenomena is at any rate partly due to this belief. It was only, however, when Professor Wormald identified the illustrations in Bodleian Library Ashmole MS. 304 as the work of Matthew Paris that this well-known collection of fortune-telling tracts was linked with him.[3] Matthew himself wrote out a large part of the text of this book,[4] and was no doubt responsible for the whole of it. It contains a number of different works designed to tell the fortune of the inquiring reader.[5] Thus in the first work in the book, the *Experimentarius* of Bernard of Chartres, four preliminary tables direct the reader to a line of verse which forms part of the responses of twenty-five 'judges', and which tells him his 'fate'. The next work in the collection is the *Pronosticon Socratis Basilei*. This is a rather more complicated

---

[1] Caesar tells a similar tale of the elk, *De Bello Gallico*, VI, 27.

[2] Above, p. 150.

[3] Wormald, 'More Matthew Paris drawings', *Walpole Soc.* XXXI (1942–3), pp. 109–12.

[4] See Vaughan, 'Handwriting of M. Paris', *Trans. Camb. Bibliog. Soc.* I (1953), pp. 390–1.

[5] For what follows see also Black, *Catalogue of Ashmolean MSS.*, pp. 214–15; and Lynn Thorndike, *History of Magic*, II, pp. 113–18.

method of fortune-telling, in which certain definite questions, such as whether or no it is safe to leave the house, are answered by reference to a series of circular diagrams which direct the reader to one of the responses of the sixteen kings, giving the answer to his question.[1] One of the diagrams forming part of this tract is illustrated here, in Plate XXI (*b*). Following this in the manuscript is the *Pronostica Pitagorice Considerationis*, in which any one of thirty-six questions is answered by means of a number obtained by chance, which refers the reader to one line of verse among thirty-six different groups of twelve lines, arranged opposite each of thirty-six different birds. Other geomancies follow, in which a similar method obtains, but the answers are given by the twelve patriarchs, the twelve signs of the zodiac, and so on.[2] This little manuscript fits into our general picture of Matthew's scientific interests, although it is a rather curious example of them.

Matthew made no important contribution to medieval science, but his scientific leanings, especially as revealed by the *Dragmaticon Philosophiae* diagrams, the tract on the elephant, and the Ashmole fortune-telling manuscript, were evidently very real, and formed an important element in his outlook. It is true that his interest in scientific matters was only the result of curiosity; but, after all, scientific progress and knowledge is still based on this elementary motive, and we need not deny Matthew a small share of the authentic scientific approach: he wanted to find out about things, and, what is more important for us, he recorded his findings.

IV. VERSE

We have already discussed Matthew's Anglo-Norman verse Lives of SS. Alban, Edward, Edmund and Thomas.[3] They show that he was adept at composing the vernacular verse current in his day. Matthew also tried his hand at writing Latin verse, though only one or two short pieces are certainly his. The following lines on the winds, for instance, are written into the

[1] To Lynn Thorndike's list of MSS. of this work, *History of Magic*, II, p. 117, note 1, should be added Eton College MS. 132, ff. 188b–190b.

[2] Some of them are printed by Brandin, 'Prognostica du MS. Ashmole 304', in *Miscellany of Studies in Romance Languages*, pp. 59–67.

[3] In Chapter IX above.

Liber Additamentorum in his own hand, and prefixed with the words: 'Frater Mathaeus de Ventis':[1]

> Sunt Subsolano socii Wlturnus et Eurus.
> Austro junguntur Nothus, Affricus, associati.
> Flant Zephiro, Chorus, hinc inde, Favonius imo.
> Circius et Boreas Aquilonem concomitantur.

We can be sure, too, that the verses with which he originally terminated his chronicle were composed by himself;[2] as well as the couplets added in his hand at the foot of many of the leaves of his Anglo-Norman *Alban*. Here is a characteristic example:[3]

> Nocte reuelatur Albano uisio grandis
> Quomodo dampnatur Saluans pro saluificandis.

The verses on King Offa of Mercia, too, which Matthew wrote into the margin of his *Chronica Majora*,[4] may well have been composed by himself.

Matthew's interest in, and appreciation of, verse and poetry led him to quote freely from the classical poets, and to enliven his chronicle with occasional apposite fragments of contemporary verse. Many of these fragments are epitaphs, such as those of William Marshal written by Gervase of Melkeley, and of Simon de Montfort the Elder, written by Roger de Insula.[5] Others refer to some contemporary event, for instance, the leonine hexameter put into Innocent IV's mouth on his receipt of the news of Frederick's defeat at Victoria, or that on Richard of Cornwall's election as king of the Romans in 1257.[6] These fragments are valuable examples of the current satiric verse of the day, and we owe their preservation to Matthew Paris. Two longer pieces of contemporary verse are preserved in the *Liber Additamentorum*: one a characteristic goliardic piece, the other some lines on Abbot William of St Albans by Henry of Avranches.[7] This poet was writing in England for various

---

[1] *CM.* vi, p. 465.   [2] *CM.* v, pp. 197–8.
[3] Trinity College, Dublin, MS. E i 40, f. 30b.
[4] *CM.* i, p. 348; they have also been written by Matthew into the margin of f. 65 of British Museum Royal MS. 13 D v.
[5] *CM.* iii, pp. 43 and 57. See also *HA.* ii, pp. 232 and 240.
[6] *CM.* v, pp. 15 and 603.   [7] *CM.* vi, p. 520, note 2, and pp. 62–3.

patrons between 1244 and 1262, and Matthew seems to have taken a special interest in him. In the margin of a leaf of the *Chronica Majora* he has written an epitaph of William Marshal, and has added the words:[1] 'There are more epitaphs written about him in the book of Henry of Avranches's verses which Brother Matthew Paris has.'

The volume here referred to has fortunately survived: it is now MS. Dd xi 78 in the University Library, Cambridge. It is a small but thick volume of poetry, much of which is in Matthew's handwriting, and on f. 1b is the characteristic inscription in red (partly cut off by the binder) recording his gift of the book to God and St Albans. This is one of the most important surviving collections of contemporary Latin verse, and much of it is explicitly attributed by Matthew to Henry of Avranches. A full description of it, together with an edition of part of it, was published by J. C. Russell and J. P. Heironimus in 1935.[2] Besides Henry's poems, it contains some excerpts from the *Doctrinale* of Alexander of Ville-Dieu; a poem by Michael of Cornwall describing Henry III's speech to the surgeons attending John Mansel in 1243; a poem in French probably by Rutebeuf; a well-known poem on the heart and the eye, probably by Philip de Grève, and some miscellaneous epigrams and short verses. From the list of contents in Matthew's hand on f. 1, we find that some of the manuscript has been lost, for the epitaphs of William Marshal and a poem by Paulin Piper, listed there, are no longer to be found. The manuscript contains ample evidence of Matthew's interest in poetry, for there are corrections and alternative readings in his own hand throughout it, as well as a number of notes and reference marks. Once again, we are indebted to Matthew Paris for the preservation of an important collection of material relating to the intellectual activities of his age, and it is true to say that, without this collection of verse, our knowledge of the Latin verse of the first half of the thirteenth century would be considerably diminished.

---

[1] *CM.* III, pp. 43–4.
[2] *The Shorter Latin Poems of Master Henry of Avranches.*

EPILOGUE

WHAT sort of a person was Matthew Paris? It might be supposed that the eighteen manuscripts containing his handwriting which still survive would provide us with ample material to answer this question. Certainly they do provide us with much useful evidence about him, though they cannot completely bridge the gap of 700 years which separates him from us. The very fact that he lived in so different a world vitiates our picture of Matthew Paris, making the details blurred and out of focus. Our almost entire lack of information about the facts of his life forces us to rely on his writings for evidence of his personality—and this in itself is bound to give us a one-sided picture. Another very real difficulty—at any rate for most of us—is the language in which he wrote, for his Latin is an artificial medium which places him at once at a distance from us. A greater difficulty attending any attempt to describe and understand his personality lies in the fact that up to now there has been little agreement among scholars upon the identity of Matthew's handwriting, and upon the authorship of some of the books and paintings attributed to him. Much of this book has in consequence been taken up with rather technical discussions of manuscript relationships, authorship, and so on. If this study proves of any value, I think that it will lie in the solution of these problems, and in the consequent definition and description of the material evidence about Matthew Paris. As to his personality, I propose now to try to integrate and augment the rather fragmentary picture which has, I hope, gradually taken shape in the preceding pages. I am only too conscious of the difficulties outlined above, and it is with some diffidence that I offer the reader, by way of epilogue, an attempt at a rough sketch of Matthew Paris as a person.

The brilliant sketch of Matthew Paris which A. L. Smith included in his Ford Lectures on *Church and State in the Middle Ages*, and which underlined, in particular, his quaintness and prejudice, and his feelings about the papacy, is in some respects incomplete. In particular, since he was concerned only with

Matthew as a chronicler, his picture is the picture of Matthew Paris as an old man, though not quite, perhaps, in his dotage. Can we not recognize, in the pages of the *Chronica Majora*, something of the asperity, the conservatism, the fixed ways of thought, the cantankerousness, of middle and old age? So far as we know, the surviving manuscript of Matthew's own section of the *Chronica* was written after 1245—and Matthew was as old as the century. It is perhaps a little unfair that we can watch him sinking to his grave, but cannot observe him in his youth and prime. We see him clearly, in the last decade of his life, developing a sort of mania for writing, an itch to use the quill. He becomes rather decrepit; he fiddles about with his material, rewriting, abridging, correcting, revising. He traverses the same ground over and over again; he tries with little success to reduce his vast collection of historical material to some kind of literary coherence and order. As death approaches, he is forced to give up writing with his own hand, and to employ a scribe. At the last, he takes to expurgation, in an effort to tone down or expunge the worst of his earlier extravagances. Although the *Chronica Majora* itself shows no falling-off in these years—it remains lively and colourful to the end—it seems clear that, after his expedition to Norway in 1248-9, Matthew became more and more engrossed in his books, and it is his character in these last years of his life which is revealed in the *Chronica*. Perhaps he had always been like this, rather crusty and embittered; perhaps he went sour only in this last period of his life; we cannot tell, and we are forced to take him as we find him, already well advanced in years.

Matthew's greatest virtue is that he is readable. He belongs to the handful of medieval writers whose works can still be appreciated and enjoyed today. He was a gifted writer. His narrative is vivid, animated and dramatic; his description is colourful; his characters are lifelike. Direct speech is put to excellent and skilful use to heighten the literary effect of his narrative. His excellence as a writer tells in his favour: we enjoy him, and we enjoy, too, his intensely personal way of looking at things. Actually, there is only one point of view in the *Chronica Majora*: Matthew's own. He is an egoist: he exaggerates the importance of his mission to Norway; he boasts of his acquaintance with the king; and was it not the streak of vanity in him which prompted him to suppress the name of his predecessor and mentor, Roger Wendover, whose chronicle he took over and made his own? Matthew's egoism, however, is of the sort that appeals, for it is, in the main, the egoism of the man in the street with an excessive regard for liberty and a high idea of his own importance. Another quality of Matthew's is his unashamed dislike of the abstract. He is always down to earth, and never afraid to reveal his dislike of things intellectual. Invariably, he is unreasonable and prejudiced, and he is proud of his attitude. He takes every opportunity to air his prejudices unabashed, and it is partly because of this that his writing has that naïve freshness and vigour which makes him one of the most readable of English medieval chroniclers.

It is high time that the ghost of Matthew's anti-papalism was laid. He did not understand politics, though he was keenly interested in them, and his anti-papalism is by no means ideological. He never thought about the theory of papal power: he merely had a grudge against authority. He resented all attempts at interference with his own material interests, and the king suffers just as much from his tirades as does the pope. His so-called 'constitutionalism' has no connexion with political theory—it springs from his zealous defence of the resources and privileges of his house and order, and from his characteristically English hatred of authority. But Matthew was a humbug and a hypocrite. He deplored the splendours of the world, yet he revelled in them; he played the toady to Abbot William, though, according to his usual sentiments, he should have despised his tyranny; he took good care to be on friendly terms with the king, yet he never ceased to slander him; he showered abuse on the *satellites regis*, though he numbered many of them among his friends. It is possible that this hypocrisy has something to do with the sort of double life that Matthew led. He was a cloister monk, yet a man of the world with a flair for business and courtly aspirations. In spite of his crudities he was polished enough to mix with contemporary high society: he rubbed shoulders with the aristocracy and even mixed with the ladies. Although he was by no means averse to picking up and recording what the servant overheard, he preferred to have his information straight from the horse's mouth, and he took care to know the right people. He, in his turn, was certainly considered a man to know.

The *Chronica Majora* reveals a kindly, human element in Matthew's character. He must have been, we feel, a friendly, sympathetic person, with a robust sense of humour sometimes bordering on the burlesque. Often we cannot tell whether or not he wrote with laughter in his eyes. Was it in fun that he took care to insert the drooping eyelid into his drawing of Henry III among the other kings of England? His language is often picturesque and amusing. He was an excellent raconteur, and his gossip is often inspired even when it is worthless and malicious. As for malicious gossip, we cannot deny that Matthew was an accomplished scandalmonger. His dislikes often take the form of slanderous remarks or stories which make us feel bound to attribute to him something of the vicious and spiteful.

Matthew was endowed with an extremely inquisitive mind, and his curiosity about everything around him is one of his most valuable qualities, for it led him to record much of interest besides the usual medieval 'natural' curiosities such as hermaphrodites and other freaks. A great collector of information, albeit on a rather superficial level, he engaged in some of those quasi-intellectual pursuits which are of vital importance to a small mind, but mere relaxation to a great one: heraldry, cartography, Latin verse; the medieval equivalents, perhaps, of philately, tourism, or crosswords. To these we should add art and hagiology, for Matthew was a man of talents as well as of wide interests. He evidently knew something of vernacular culture and was quite at home when writing in Anglo-Norman. Of art and architecture he seems to have had a genuine and deep appreciation, and, though not himself one of the great artists of his time, he was thoroughly competent, and interested enough to leave us much detailed information about the artistic works of his contemporaries and precursors at St Albans.

When all is said and done, the name of Matthew Paris deserves to be remembered, not for any inherent greatness, but for his enshrinement of the foibles and prejudices of the ordinary man in the street, and, perhaps, because he is the first recognizable personification of John Bull. The value of the *Chronica Majora* lies just as much in the personality it reveals as in the events it records, and, indeed, Matthew is in many ways much more interesting as a person than he is useful as a chronicler. As a mirror of his age he is in some measure a failure, for he reflects only the surface. He was, too, extremely conservative, and found it impossible to move with the times. By the middle of the thirteenth century, if not before, he was a venerable but antiquated figure. He deplored all novelties: like a true Tory, he was against all change. The great movements and high ideals of his time all passed him by. The friars, church reform, scholasticism meant nothing to him—indeed the friars were a particular object of his opprobrium, and he takes a hostile view of church reformers and theologians, whom he regards with suspicion and distrust. The fuss he makes about the introduction of a knowledge of Greek numerals into Western Europe is a sign of his superficiality, for he quite fails to understand that this was merely accidental to the discovery and assimilation of Greek philosophy which was going on during his lifetime. There is nothing profound or noble about Matthew Paris, and even among chroniclers the Middle Ages can boast many superior to him. He was a jack-of-all-trades, a story-teller, a crusty old gossip; but his stolid, earthy, kindly, prejudiced figure deserves a place, though a very subordinate one, among the great personalities of the age. St Francis, Albert the Great, St Thomas Aquinas, and many others stand out as representatives of its nobler ideals and aspirations: Matthew Paris shows us its seamier side and its trivialities, but, with all his quaintness, he is a likeable person, who, for his vivid and colourful chronological encyclopedia, the *Chronica Majora*, well deserves the gratitude of posterity.

BIBLIOGRAPHY

LIST OF MANUSCRIPTS CITED

Bute, Marquis of:
  MS. 3, *Gesta Abbatum* etc.; see p. 8, note 3.
Cambridge, Corpus Christi College:
  MSS. 26 and 16 (*A* and *B*), *Chronica Majora* to 1253; see especially pp. 30–1 and 49 ff.
  MS. 264, containing excerpts from Roger Wendover's *Flores Historiarum*; see p. 21, note 2.
  MS. 385, Part II, William of Conches's *Dragmaticon Philosophiae* with Matthew Paris's diagrams; see pp. 254–5.
Cambridge, University Library:
  MS. Dd xi 78, verses of Henry of Avranches etc.; see p. 260.
  MS. Ee iii 39, copy of Matthew Paris's *Edward*; see pp. 168 ff., and 221–2.
Chatsworth, Duke of Devonshire MS.:
  St Albans cartulary; cited on p. 183.
Dublin, Trinity College:
  MS. E i 40, Matthew's collection of domestic hagiographical material, including his illustrated *Alban*; see pp. 168 ff., 195 ff., and 227–8.
Eton College:
  MS. 96, version of Peter of Poitou's universal chronicle; see pp. 116 and 225.
  MS. 123 (*E*), *Flores Historiarum*; see pp. 92 ff.
  MS. 132, containing a copy of the *Pronosticon Socratis Basilei*; see p. 258, note 1.
London, British Museum:
  Cotton MS. Julius D iii, St Albans cartulary; cited on p. 183.
  Cotton MS. Julius D vi, containing a copy of Matthew Paris's Latin Life of St Edmund; see pp. 162 ff.
  Cotton MS. Julius D vii, miscellaneous material collected by John of Wallingford, mostly copied from Matthew Paris's MSS.; see pp. 22, 229 and 243.
  Cotton MS. Tiberius E vi, *Liber Memorandorum* of St Albans; mentioned on p. 78.
  Cotton MS. Claudius D vi, containing Matthew Paris's *Abbreviatio Chronicorum*; see p. 36 etc.
  Cotton MS. Claudius E iv, *Gesta Abbatum*, etc., by T. Walsingham; cited, p. 19, note 3, p. 193, note 3, and p. 200, note 3.

London, British Museum (*cont.*)

Cotton MS. Nero D i (*LA*), Matthew Paris's *Liber Additamentorum*; see especially pp. 78 ff.

Cotton MS. Nero D v, Part II (*C*), fair copy of Matthew's *Chronica Majora*, 1189–1250; see especially p. 110. For Part I of this MS., see p. 153, note 2.

Cotton MS. Nero D vii, *Book of Benefactors of St Albans*; see pp. 18–19.

Cotton MS. Otho B v (*O*), *Flores Historiarum* of Roger Wendover; see pp. 21 ff.

Cotton MS. Otho D iii, St Albans cartulary; cited on p. 183.

Cotton MS. Vitellius A xx (*V*), containing a short chronicle *Excerpta a cronicis magnis S. Albani*; see especially pp. 115 ff.

Cotton MS. Vitellius D viii, formerly containing Lives of SS. Edmund and Alban; see pp. 169–70.

Cotton MS. Vespasian B xiii, containing a fragment of Matthew Paris's Life of Stephen Langton; see p. 159.

Cotton MS. Faustina A viii, containing the *Southwark Annals*; see pp. 104 ff.

Harley MS. 1620, copy of the *Chronica Majora* to 1188; see p. 153, note 2.

Harley MS. 5418, containing an abridgement of the *Flores Historiarum*; see p. 152.

Royal MS. 2 A xxii, Psalter; see p. 222.

Royal MS. 2 B vi, Psalter; see p. 224.

Royal MS. 4 D vii, *Historia Scholastica*, etc.; see pp. 15, 129, note 3, and p. 187.

Royal MS. 13 D v, William of Malmesbury, etc.; see p. 129, note 2, and pp. 239–40.

Royal MS. 13 E vi, Ralph de Diceto, etc.; see pp. 24, 129, note 2, and 186.

Royal MS. 14 C vii (*R*), containing Matthew Paris's *Historia Anglorum* and the last part of his *Chronica Majora*, 1254–9; see pp. 21, 36, etc.

London, Record Office:

MS. E 164/2, the *Red Book of the Exchequer*; see pp. 17–18 and 132, note 4.

Manchester, Chetham's Library:

MS. 6712 (*Ch*), *Flores Historiarum* of Matthew Paris; see pp. 92 ff. and 224–5.

Oxford, Bodleian Library:

Ashmole MS. 304, fortune-telling tracts; see pp. 207–8, 230 and 257–8.

Oxford, Bodleian Library (*cont.*)
Douce MS. 207 (*W*), *Flores Historiarum* of Roger Wendover; see
pp. 21 ff.
Oxford, Corpus Christi College:
MS. 2, Bible, containing Matthew Paris's map of Palestine; see
pp. 245–6.
Welbeck Abbey, Duke of Portland MS.:
Containing a copy of Matthew Paris's *Edmund*; see p. 168.

PRINTED SOURCES AND FACSIMILES

Acta Sanctorum Bollandiana June, IV (Antwerp, 1707).
*Aelnothi monachi Historia ortus, vitae, et passionis S. Canuti regis
Daniae*, ed. J. Langebek in *Scriptores rerum Danicarum medii
aevi*, III (Copenhagen, 1774).
Amundesham, John of. *Annales*, ed. H. T. Riley, 2 vols. (Rolls
Series, 1870–1).
Avranches, Henry of. *Shorter Latin Poems*, ed. J. C. Russell and
J. P. Heironimus (Cambridge, Mass., 1935).
Calendar of Patent Rolls, 1258–1266, V (1910).
Candidus, Hugh. *Chronicle*, ed. W. T. Mellows (Oxford, 1949).
Chronicon Roskildense, ed. M. C. Gertz in *Scriptores minores historiae
Danicae medii aevi*, I (Copenhagen, 1917–18).
Conches, William of. *Dragmaticon Philosophiae*, ed. W. Gratarolus
under the title *Dialogus de substantiis physicis*...(Strassburg,
1567).
Cotton, Bartholomew. *Historia Anglicana*, ed. H. R. Luard (Rolls
Series, 1859).
Foedera etc., I, ed. T. Rymer (Record Commission, 1816).
Huntingdon, Henry of. *Historia Anglorum*, ed. T. Arnold (Rolls
Series, 1879).
Lanfranc. *Monastic Constitutions*, ed. and transl. M. D. Knowles
(London, 1951).
Liber Eliensis ad fidem codicum variorum, ed. D. J. Stewart (Anglia
Christiana Society, 1848).
Liber monasterii de Hyda, ed. E. Edwards (Rolls Series, 1866).
Malmesbury, William of. *Gesta pontificum*, ed. N. E. S. A. Hamilton
(Rolls Series, 1870).
Monmouth, Geoffrey of. *Historia regum Britanniae*, ed. A. Griscom
(London, 1929).
Nova Legenda Anglie, I, ed. C. Horstmann (Oxford, 1901).
Oxenedes, John of. *Chronica*, ed. Sir H. Ellis (Rolls Series, 1859).
Papsturkunden in England, III, ed. W. Holtzmann (Berlin, 1952).

Paris, Matthew. *Chronica Majora* from 1066 onwards, ed. M. Parker under the title *Matthaei Paris monachi Albanensis Historia Major*...(London, 1571).

Chronica Majora from 1066 onwards, ed. W. Wats under the title *Matthaei Paris monachi Albanensis angli Historia Major*... (London, 1640).

Chronica Majora (*CM.*), ed. H. R. Luard, 7 vols. (Rolls Series, 1872–84).

Excerpts from the *Chronica Majora*, *Flores Historiarum*, etc., ed. F. Liebermann in *Ex rerum Anglicarum scriptoribus saeculi XIII*, *MGH,SS.* xxviii (Hanover, 1888).

Chronica Majora, transl. by J. A. Giles under the title *Matthew Paris's English History*, 3 vols. (London, 1852–4).

Chronica Majora, transl. into French by A. Huillard-Bréholles under the title *Grand Chronique de Matthieu Paris*, 9 vols. (Paris, 1840–1).

Excerpts from the *Chronica Majora*, transl. into German by G. Grandaur and W. Wattenbach, under the title, *Auszüge aus der grösseren Chronik des Matthäus von Paris* (Leipzig, 1890).

Flores Historiarum, ed. M. Parker under the title *Flores Historiarum Matthaei Westmonasteriensis monachi*...(London, 1567).

Flores Historiarum (*FH.*), ed. H. R. Luard, 3 vols. (Rolls Series, 1890).

Flores Historiarum, transl. by C. D. Yonge under the title *Matthew of Westminster's Flowers of History*, 2 vols. (London, 1853).

Historia Anglorum (*HA.*) and *Abbreviatio Chronicorum* (*AC.*), ed. Sir F. Madden, 3 vols. (Rolls Series, 1866–9).

Vitae duorum Offarum and *Gesta Abbatum* (Wats), ed. W. Wats under the title *Vitae duorum Offarum*...*et viginti trium abbatum Sancti Albani*...(London, 1639).

Vie de Seint Auban, ed. R. Atkinson (London, 1876).

Illustrations to the Life of St Alban in Trinity College, Dublin, MS. E i 40, ed. in facsimile, W. R. L. Lowe and E. F. Jacob, with an introduction by M. R. James (Oxford, 1924).

Estoire de Seint Aedward le Rei, ed. H. R. Luard in *Lives of Edward the Confessor* (Rolls Series, 1858).

Estoire de Seint Aedward le Rei, ed. in facsimile, M. R. James (Roxburghe Club, 1920).

'Vie de S. Edmond', ed. A. T. Baker, in *Romania*, lv (1929).

Vie de Saint Thomas de Cantorbéry, fragments, ed. with facsimiles, P. Meyer (Société des Anciens Textes Français, 1885).

'The drawings of Matthew Paris', ed. in facsimile, M. R. James, in *Walpole Society*, xiv (1925–6).

Paris, Matthew (*cont.*)

'More Matthew Paris drawings' reproduced by F .Wormald in *Walpole Society*, XXXI (1942–3).

Legends on the maps of Palestine, ed. H. Michelant and G. Raynaud, in *Itinéraires à Jérusalem* (Société de l'Orient Latin, 1882).

Four Maps of Great Britain, ed. in facsimile, J. P. Gilson (London, 1928).

'Prognostica du MS. Ashmole 304 de la Bodléienne', ed. L. Brandin in *A Miscellany of Studies in Romance Languages and Literatures*, presented to L. E. Kastner (Cambridge, 1932).

Red Book of the Exchequer, ed. H. Hall, 3 parts (Rolls Series, 1897).

Rishanger, William de. *Chronicle*, ed. J. O. Halliwell (Camden Society, 1840).

Saga of Hacon, ed. G. W. Dasent (Rolls Series, 1894).

St Albans Chronicle, 1406–1420, ed. V. H. Galbraith (Oxford, 1937).

Stapleton, Bishop, *Calendar*. Ed. Sir F. Palgrave in *Ancient Kalendars and Inventories of the Treasury of H.M. Exchequer*, 3 vols. (Record Commission, 1836).

'Two Lives of St Aethelbert, King and Martyr', ed. M. R. James, in *EHR*. XXXII (1917).

Ungedruckte anglo-normannische Geschichtsquellen, ed. F. Liebermann (Strassburg, 1879).

Wallingford, John of. *Chronica* attributed to, ed. T. Gale in *Historiae ...Scriptores XV* (Oxford, 1691).

Walsingham, Thomas. *Gesta Abbatum (GA)*, ed. H. T. Riley, 3 vols. (Rolls Series, 1867).

Ypodigma Neustriae, ed. H. T. Riley (Rolls Series, 1876).

Wendover, Roger. *Flores Historiarum* from 447 onwards, ed. H. O. Coxe under the title *Rogeri de Wendover Chronica sive Flores Historiarum*, 5 vols. (English Historical Society, 1841–4).

Flores Historiarum ed. H. G. Hewlett under the title *The Flowers of History by Roger de Wendover from the year of Our Lord 1154...*, 3 vols. (Rolls Series, 1886–9).

Excerpts from the *Flores Historiarum*, ed. F. Liebermann in *Ex rerum Anglicarum scriptoribus saeculi XIII, MGH,SS.* XXVIII (Hanover, 1888).

Worcester, Florence of. *Chronicon ex chronicis*, ed. B. Thorpe, 2 vols. (English Historical Society, 1848–9).

Wykes, Thomas. *Chronicon*, ed. H. R. Luard in *Annales monastici*, IV (Rolls Series, 1869).

MODERN WORKS

BEAZLEY, C. R. *The Dawn of Modern Geography*, 3 vols. (London, 1897–1906).

BÉDIER, J. *Les Légendes épiques*, IV (Paris, 1913).

BLACK, W. H. *A Descriptive Catalogue of the MSS. bequeathed unto the University of Oxford by Elias Ashmole* (Oxford, 1845).

BORENIUS, T. and TRISTRAM, E. W. *English Medieval Painting* (Cambridge, 1927).

BROWNE, R. A. *British Latin Selections. A.D. 500–1400* (Oxford, 1954).

CHAMBERS, R. W. *Beowulf* (2nd. ed., Cambridge, 1932).

CHENEY, C. R. 'The Paper Constitution preserved by Matthew Paris', *EHR.* LXV (1950).

COLLINS, A. J. 'The documents of the Great Charter', *Proceedings of the British Academy*, XXXIV (1948).

COULTON, G. G. *Five Centuries of Religion*, 4 vols. (Cambridge, 1923–50).

DAVIS, H. W. C. 'An unpublished Life of Edmund Rich', *EHR.* XXII (1907).

DENHOLM-YOUNG, N. *Handwriting in England and Wales* (Cardiff, 1954).

'The Paper Constitution of 1244', *EHR.* LVIII (1943).

DUGDALE, SIR W. *Monasticon anglicanum*; new enlarged edition by J. Caley etc., 6 vols. (London, 1817–30).

EYTON, R. W. *Court, Household and Itinerary of King Henry II* (London, 1878).

FAYE, PAUL-LOUIS. 'Baudelaire and Matthew Paris', *French Review*, XXIV (1950).

FELTEN, J. *Papst Gregor IX* (Freiburg, 1886).

FRITZ, R. *Über Verfasser und Quellen der altfranzösischen Estoire de Seint Aedward le Rei* (Heidelberg, 1910).

GAIRDNER, J. *Early Chroniclers of Europe: England* (London, 1879).

GALBRAITH, V. H. *Roger Wendover and Matthew Paris* (Glasgow, 1944).

GEROULD, G. H. 'A text of Merlin's prophecies', *Speculum*, XXIII (1948).

GIBBS, M. and LANG, J. *Bishops and Reform, 1215–1272* (Oxford, 1934).

GÖSCHEN, O. (writing under the name 'Von Pusikan'), 'Wappen aus den Werken des Matthias von Paris', *Vierteljahrschrift für Heraldik, Sphragistik und Genealogie*, II (Berlin, 1881).

GOUGH, R. *British Topography*, 2 vols. (London, 1780).

HARDY, SIR T. D. *A Descriptive Catalogue of Materials relating to the History of Great Britain and Ireland*, 3 vols. (Rolls Series, 1862–71).

HAUPTMANN, F. 'Die Wappen in der *Historia Minor* des Matthäus Parisiensis', *Jahrbuch der K.K. Heraldischen Gesellschaft*, XIX (1909).

HERMANNSSON, H. *Icelandic Illuminated Manuscripts of the Middle Ages* (Copenhagen, 1935).

HOLLAENDER, A. 'The pictorial work in the *Flores Historiarum*', *Bulletin of the John Rylands Library*, XXVIII (1944).

HUNT, W. 'Matthew Paris', *Dictionary of National Biography*, XV (1895).

JAMES, M. R. *A Descriptive Catalogue of the Manuscripts in the Library of Corpus Christi College, Cambridge*, 2 vols. (Cambridge, 1912).

JENKINS, CLAUDE. *The Monastic Chronicler and the Early School of St Albans* (London, 1922).

JESSOPP, A. 'St Albans and her historian', in *Studies by a Recluse* (London, 1893); reprinted from the *Quarterly Review*, April 1886.

JØRGENSEN, E. *Helgendyrkelse i Danmark* (Copenhagen, 1909).

JOURDAIN, C. 'Doutes sur l'authenticité de quelques écrits contre la cour de Rome attribués à Robert Grossetête', in *Excursions historiques et philosophiques à travers le moyen âge* (Paris, 1888); reprinted from the *Bulletin de l'Académie des inscriptions et belles-lettres* (1868).

KEMPF, J. *Geschichte des deutschen Reiches während des grossen Interregnums* (Würzburg, 1893).

KNOWLES, M. D. *The Religious Orders in England*, I (Cambridge, 1948).

KURTH, B. 'Matthew Paris and Villard de Honnecourt', *Burlington Magazine*, LXXXI (1942).

LAWRENCE, C. H. 'Robert of Abingdon and Matthew Paris', *EHR.* LXIX (1954).

LEACH, H. G. *Angevin Britain and Scandinavia* (Cambridge, Mass., 1921).

LEGGE, M. D. *Anglo-Norman in the Cloisters* (Edinburgh, 1950).

LETHABY, W. R. 'English Primitives, V and VI', *Burlington Magazine*, XXXI (1917).

LIEBERMANN, F. 'Bericht über Arbeiten in England während des Sommers 1877', *Neues Archiv der Gesellschaft für ältere deutsche Geschichtskunde*, IV (1879).

LINDBLOM, A. *La Peinture gothique en Suède et en Norvège* (Stockholm, 1916).

LITTLE, A. G. 'Brother William of England', in *Franciscan Papers, Lists and Documents* (Manchester, 1943).

LOUIS, R. *De l'Histoire à la Légende*, III (Auxerre, 1947).

LOWE, W. R. L. 'The Cult of St Alban abroad', *Hertfordshire Post*, 13 July 1910.

LUDWIG, F. F. A. *Untersuchungen über die Reise- und Marschgeschwindigkeit im XII. und XIII. Jahrhundert* (Berlin, 1897).

MADDEN, SIR F. 'On the knowledge possessed by Europeans of the elephant in the thirteenth century', in *The Graphic and Historical Illustrator*, ed. E. W. Brayley (London, 1834).

MARSHALL, M. H. 'Thirteenth-century culture as illustrated by Matthew Paris', *Speculum*, XIV (1939).

MENGER, L. E. *The Anglo-Norman Dialect* (New York, 1904).

MILLAR, E. G. *English Illuminated Manuscripts from the Xth to the XIIIth Century* (Paris, 1926).

MILLER, K. *Mappae Mundi. Die ältesten Weltkarten*, III (Stuttgart, 1895).

MITCHELL, J. B. 'Early maps of Great Britain. I. The Matthew Paris maps', *Geographical Journal*, LXXXI (1933).

MOORE, P. S. *The Works of Peter of Poitiers* (Notre Dame, Ind., 1936).

OMAN, C. C. 'The goldsmiths at St Albans Abbey during the twelfth and thirteenth centuries', *Transactions of the St Albans and Hertfordshire Architectural and Archaeological Society* (1932). 'The jewels of St Albans Abbey', *Burlington Magazine*, LVII (1930).

PAGE, W., and REDDAN, M. 'St Albans Abbey', in *Victoria County History: Hertfordshire*, IV (London, 1914).

PARAVICINI, F. DE. *St Edmund of Abingdon* (London, 1898).

PARIS, G. Review of Atkinson's *Vie de Seint Auban*, in *Romania*, V (1876).

PLEHN, H. 'Der politische Charakter von Matheus Parisiensis', in *Staats- und socialwissenschaftliche Forschungen*, XIV, ed. G. Schmoller (1897).

POWICKE, F. M. *King Henry III and the Lord Edward*, 2 vols. (Oxford, 1947).
Stephen Langton (Oxford, 1928).
'The compilation of the *Chronica Majora* of Matthew Paris', *Proceedings of the British Academy*, XXX (1944); reprinted, with some revisions, from *Modern Philology*, XXXVIII (1940–1).
'Roger Wendover and the Coggeshall Chronicle', *EHR.* XXI (1906).
'The writ for enforcing watch and ward, 1242', *EHR.* LVII (1942).

RICKERT, E. 'The Old English Offa Saga', *Modern Philology*, II (1904–5).

RICKERT, M. *Painting in Britain: the Middle Ages* (London, 1954).

SAUNDERS, O. E. *English Illumination*, 2 vols. (Florence, 1928).

SMITH, A. L. *Church and State in the Middle Ages* (Oxford, 1913).

SUCHIER, H. *Über die Matthaeus Paris zugeschriebene 'Vie de Seint Auban'* (Halle a. S., 1876).

TAYLOR, E. G. R. 'The *De ventis* of Matthew Paris', *Imago Mundi*, II (1937).

THEOPOLD, L. *Kritische Untersuchungen über die Quellen zur angelsächsischen Geschichte des achten Jahrhunderts* (Lwoff, 1872).

THOMSON, S. H. *The Writings of Robert Grosseteste* (Cambridge, 1940).

THORNDIKE, LYNN. *A History of Magic and Experimental Science*, II (London, 1923).

TYSON, M. 'The Annals of Southwark and Merton', *Surrey Archaeological Collections*, XXXVI (1925).

UHLEMANN, E. 'Über die anglonormannische "Vie de Seint Auban" in Bezug auf Quelle, Lautverhältnisse und Flexion', *Romanische Studien*, ed. E. Boehmer, IV (1880).

VAUGHAN, R. 'The election of abbots at St Albans in the thirteenth and fourteenth centuries', *Proceedings of the Cambridge Antiquarian Society*, XLVII (1954).

'The handwriting of Matthew Paris', *Transactions of the Cambridge Bibliographical Society*, I (1953).

WAGNER, A. R. *A Catalogue of English Medieval Rolls of Arms* (Oxford, 1950).

WALLACE, W. *The Life of St Edmund of Canterbury* (London, 1893).

WILMART, A. 'Analecta reginensia', *Studi e Testi*, LIX (1933).

WILSON, R. M. *The Lost Literature of Medieval England* (London, 1952).

THE PLATES

PLATE I

Matthew Paris on his death-bed. B.M. Roy. MS. 14 C vii, f. 218 b.
(See pp. 7 ff.)

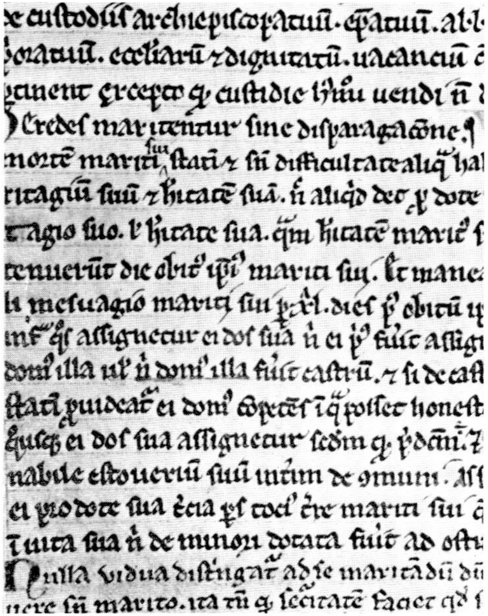

PLATE II

(a) Part of f. 38b.

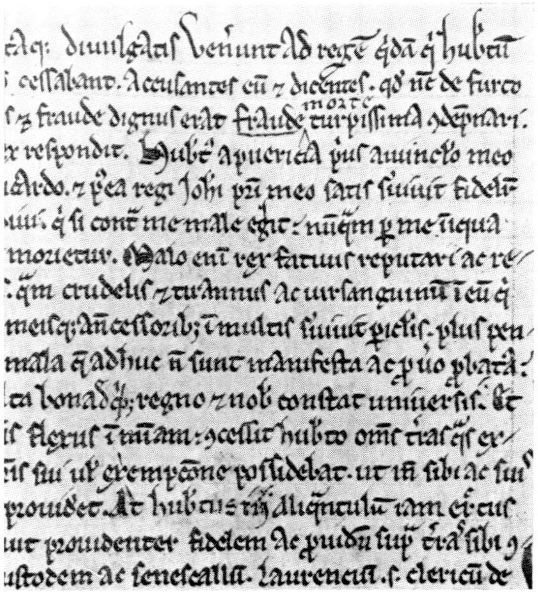

(b) Part of f. 82a.

Examples of Matthew Paris's handwriting in the early part of the *Chronica Majora* (actual size). C.C.C.C. MS. 16. (See pp. 50 ff.)

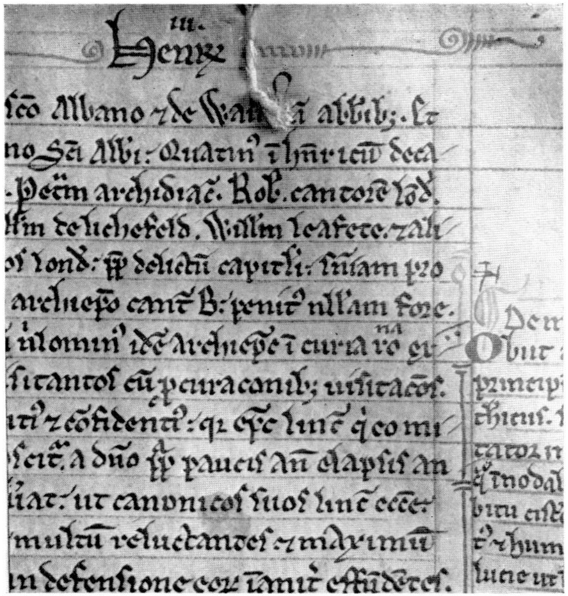

PLATE III

(a) Part of f. 242 a.

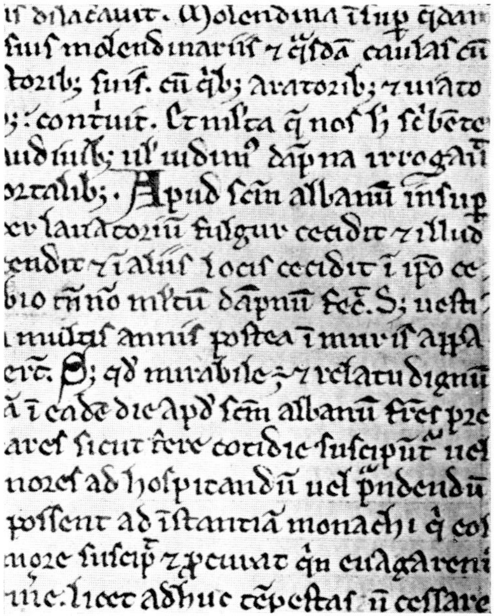

(b) Part of f. 253 b.

Examples of Matthew Paris's handwriting in the later part of the *Chronica Majora* (actual size). C.C.C.C. MS. 16. (See pp. 50 ff.)

PLATE IV

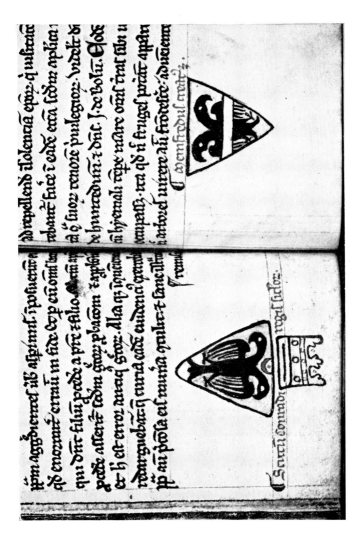

Shields in the lower margin of B.M. Cott. MS. Claud. D vi, ff. 91b–92a
(actual size). (See pp. 215–16.)

PLATE V

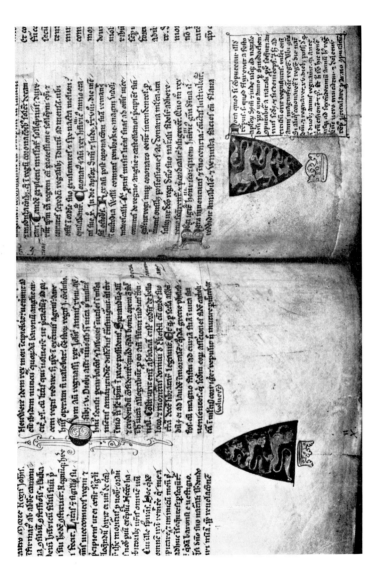

Shields in the lower margin of B.M. Roy. MS. 14 C vii, ff. 99b–100a (reduced).

(See pp. 215–16.)

PLATE VI

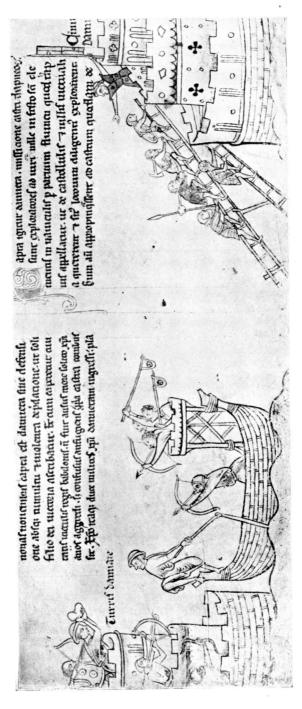

The siege of Damietta in 1219, from the margin of the *Chronica Majora*.
C.C.C.C. MS. 16, f. 55 b. (See pp. 217 ff.)

PLATE VII

The defeat of the French at Damascus in 1240, from the margin of the *Chronica Majora*.
C.C.C. MS. 16, f. 133 b. (See pp. 217 ff.)

PLATE VIII

(*a*) The martyrdom of St Alban, f. 38 a.

(*b*) The massacre of the converts, f. 41 b.

Two of Matthew Paris's illustrations of his *Vie de Seint Auban.*
T.C.D. MS. E i 40. (See p. 221.)

PLATE IX

(*a*) The Crucifixion. B.M. Roy. MS. 2 B vi, f. 9b. (See p. 224.)

(*b*) The landing of Edward in England. An illustration from the *Estoire de Seint Aedward*. U.L.C. MS. Ee iii 59, f. 9a. (See pp. 221–2.)

PLATE X

(*a*) Richard I. B.M. Cott. MS. Claud. D vi, f. 5 b.

(*b*) Cassibelaunus (?) C.C.C.C. MS. 26, p. 28.

Drawings of seated kings. (See p. 223.)

PLATE XI

Drawings of seated kings. B.M. Roy. MS. 14 C vii, f. 8b. (See p. 231.)

PLATE XII

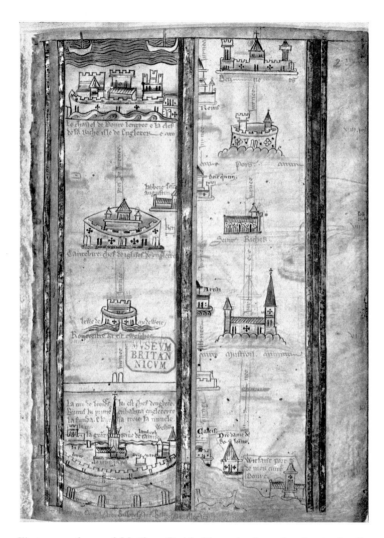

First page of one of Matthew Paris's itineraries from London to Apulia.
B.M. Roy. MS. 14 C vii, f. 2 a. (See pp. 237 and 247 ff.)

PLATE XIII

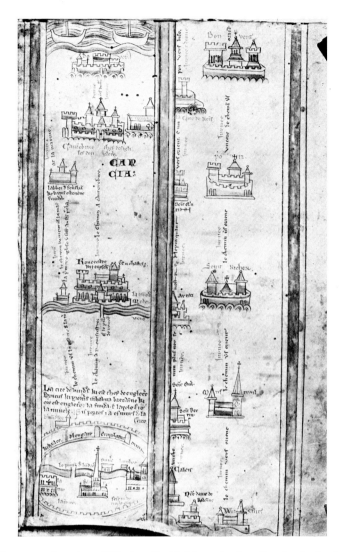

First page of another of Matthew Paris's itineraries from London to Apulia.
C.C.C.C. MS. 26, f. ia. (See pp. 237 and 247 ff.)

PLATE XIV

(b) *B*, f. 138 b.

(a) *A*, p. 220.

(c) *R*, f. 9 a.

(d) *LA*, f. 2 b.

(e) C.C.C.C., 385, p. 173.

(f) Bodl. Ashm., 304, f. 38 a.

Architectural details in Matthew Paris's drawings (see p. 237).
(a) and (b) are from the margins of the *Chronica Majora*.

PLATE XV

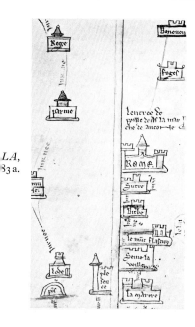

LA,
33 a.

(*b*) Claud.
D vi,
f. 8 b.

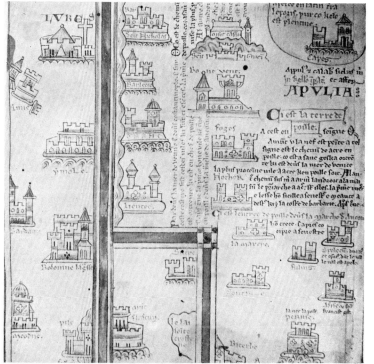

(*c*) *A,*
f. iii a.

Architectural details in Matthew Paris's itineraries ((*a*) and (*c*)) and
map of England and Scotland (*b*). (See p. 237.)

PLATE XVI

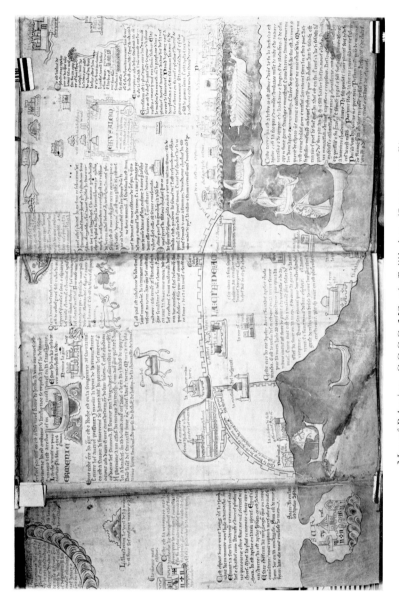

Map of Palestine. C.C.C.C. MS. 26, ff. iiib-iva. (See pp. 244 ff.)

PLATE XVII

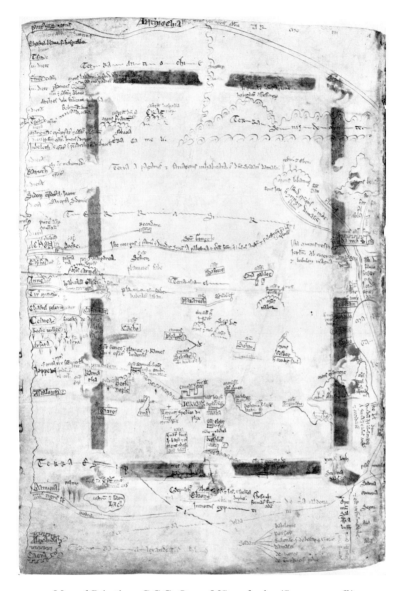

Map of Palestine. C.C.C. Oxon. MS. 2, f. 2b. (See pp. 245 ff.)

PLATE XVIII

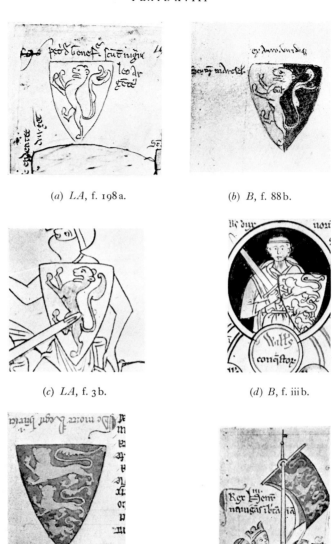

(a) *LA*, f. 198 a.

(b) *B*, f. 88 b.

(c) *LA*, f. 3 b.

(d) *B*, f. iii b.

(e) *A*, p. 225.

(f) *R*, f. 116 b.

Heraldic lions on some of Matthew Paris's shields. (See p. 251.)
(a) One of several shields roughly tricked on a leaf of the *Liber
Additamentorum*. (b) and (e) Shields in the margin of the *Chronica
Majora*. (c) and (f) Details from two of Matthew's drawings. (d) One
of the illustrations of Matthew's genealogical chronicle (see p. 232).

PLATE XIX

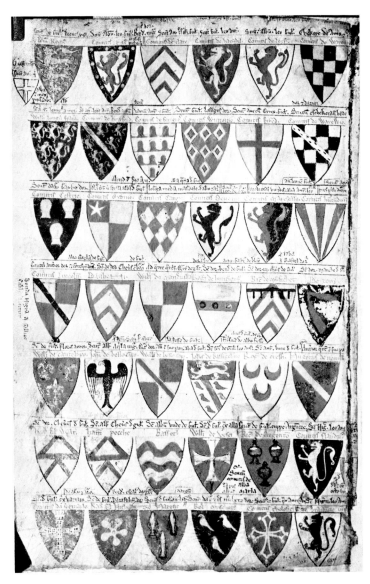

A page of coloured shields in the *Liber Additamentorum*. B.M. Cott.
MS. Nero D i, f. 170b. (See pp. 251–2.)

PLATE XX

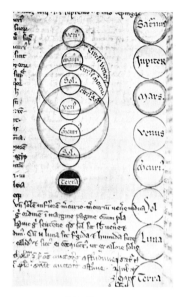

(a) P. 130.

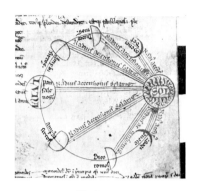

(b) P. 147.

(d) P. 152.

(c) P. 148.

(e) P. 178.

Some of Matthew Paris's diagrams illustrating the *Dragmaticon Philosophiae*. C.C.C.C. MS. 385, Part II. (See pp. 244–5.)

PLATE XXI

(*a*) Matthew Paris's drawing of an elephant in C.C.C.C. MS. 16, f. iv a. (See p. 256.)

(*b*) The *Sphera Bestiarum*. Bodl. Lib., Oxon., Ashm. MS. 304, f. 34 b. (See pp. 257–8.)

INDEX

Aageson, Sweyn, 190
Aaron, a Jew of York, 17
Abbreviatio Chronicorum of M. Paris, 36, 113–14, 123; authorship, 37–9; illustrations, 219, 223, 231–2
Abdias, apocryphal *Acta Apostolorum* of, 128
Abingdon, Robert of, brother of Edmund Rich, 164
Abraham, tomb of, 246
Acre, 240, 245
Adam, 246
Adam the Cellarer, 182–4, 198, 201
Adrian I, pope, 48, 191–2
Adrian IV, pope, 184, 185, 201
Aelnoth, *Vita et Passio S. Canuti*, 202
Aethelbert, St, king of East Anglia, 43–4, 46, 190–1, 194
Aigueblanche, Peter, bishop of Hereford, 131
Albert the Great, 265
Albigensian crusade, 112
Alexander IV, pope, 134
Alexander II, king of Scotland, 136
Alexander, papal collector, 12
Alexandria, 69, 246
Alfred, 232
Alfric, abbot of St Albans (*c.* 970–90), later bishop of Ramsbury and archbishop of Canterbury, 198–200, 203, 204
Alfric or Egfrid, abbot of St Albans (? *c.* 1066–70), 200, 203, 204
Alps, 240
Aluedele (? Allerdale), 240
Amadeus IV, count of Savoy, 13
Ananias, 239
Ancona (Vallis Anconie), 240
Anglo-Norman, 168–81
animals, drawings of, 233
Annales Londonienses, 153
Annales Paulini, 153
Annales Sancti Edmundi, 24
Anselm, archbishop of Canterbury, 185

Antioch, 240, 246
Antioch, prince of, probably Reginald of Chatillon, 15
Apocalypses, illustrated, 205, 225–6
Apollo, 180
Apulia, *see* itinerary, 240
Aqua Dorecte (? river Derwent), 240
Aquinas, St Thomas, 265
Arabia, 240
Aragon, king of, 240
'Arches, foresta de' (? forest of Arsur), 246
Ardfert, John bishop of, 15
Arezzo, 248, 249
Argenton, Richard of, 13
Armenia, 239, 240, 246
Armenia, archbishop of, 2–3, 12, 13
Armenians, certain, visit St Albans, 12, 239, 245
Arsur?, forest of ('Foresta de Arches'), 246
artists and artistic works, 185–7, 209–10
artists at St Albans in Matthew Paris's lifetime, 221–7
Artois, Robert of, 150
Arundel, William de Albini, earl of, 15
Assisi, 248
Assisi, St Francis of, 265
Athens, 145
Atkinson, R., 168
Augustinian canons, 138
Avignon, siege of, 112
Avranches, Henry of, 128; book of his verses, 129, 259–60; Life of Becket, 176; on Salisbury cathedral, 254 n.; on Abbot William of St Albans, 85, 259

'Babylon', 69; lands of the sultan of ('Terra Soldanis Babilonie'), 246
Bacon, Robert, 16, 149, 161, 164, 165–6
Baker, A. T., 162, 170, 173
Bangor, Richard, bishop of, 12, 15
Bardney, abbot of, 137

INDEX

Savoy, Boniface of, archbishop of
Canterbury, 119, 120, 124; M.
Paris on, 119, 120, 122, 138, 149;
visits St Albans, 12, 13
Savoy, Philip of, archbishop-elect of
Lyons, 17
Savoy, Thomas of, count of Flanders,
12
Scema Britannie 91, 241, 244
Scotland, *see* England and Scotland
'Senis de Monte, Terra', 246
Sicily, 240; diagram of, 248, 250;
kingdom of, 146, 239, 248
Siena, 248
Simon, abbot of St Albans (1167–83),
183–5
Smith, A. L., 133–4, 148, 157, 261–2
Socrates, 230
Somerset, 244
Sopwell, nunnery of, 185
Southwark Annals, the, 98, 104–6, 129
'Spelman MS.', the, of the *Gesta
Abbatum*, 8 n. 3
Spoleto, 240, 248
Stavensby, Alexander, bishop of
Coventry and Lichfield, 14
Stigand, archbishop of Canterbury,
Matthew Paris on, 175; and St
Albans, 200, 203
Suchier, H., 169, 178
Suffield, Walter, bishop of Norwich,
12
Suffolk, 244
Sussex, 244
Sutri, 248, 249
Swan, knights of the, 89, 177
Swereford, Alexander, 14, 17
Sylvester, Bernard, 257; *Cosmo-
graphia*, 128
Syria, 246

Tarsus, 240
Taxster, John, 24, 153
Templars, 138
Temple, the, master of in Scotland, 14
Terence, 39 n.
Tetim (Tethys?), 180
Thames, 173
Theobald I, count of Champagne
and king of Navarre, 37
Theopold, L., 42, 46
Thingferth (Tuinfreth), 190

Thomas, chaplain of Cardinal Ray-
nier Cappochi, 17
Thomas, monk of Sherborne, 4, 16
Thomson, S. H., 134
Thony, Roger de, 177
Thryth, legendary wife of Offa I, 193
Thurkelby, Roger, 14
'Tigris', in error for Nile, 246
tin, discovered in Germany, 145
trade, 145–6
Trani, 250
Tournay, Simon of, story of, 15, 34
Tower, the, 256
Trapani, 239
Trumpington, William of, abbot of
St Albans (1214–35), 85, 87,
185–8 *passim*, 196–7, 259, 263
Tuinfreth (Thingferth), 190
'Tur[c]hia', 240
Tynemouth, St Albans cell at, 244;
prior of, *see* Dunham
Tynemouth, John of, 200
Tyre, William of, on the marvels of
the East, 15, 129

Uhlemann, E., 169

Valence, 249
Valence, William de, 121; household
of, 12
'Vallis Anconie', 240
'Vallis Moriane' (Maurienne), 240
'Vallis Spoleti', 240
Venetia, 240
Vere, Baldwin de, 14
Vergil, Polydore, 154
verse, Anglo-Norman, 168–81; Latin,
129, 258–60
Vescy, Eustace de, 32–3
Victoria, 259
Vie de Saint Thomas (*Thomas*),
168 ff., date and sources, 178;
illustration, 207, 221–2
Vie de Seint Auban (*Alban*), 168 ff.,
195; autograph MS., 170, 221;
date and sources, 177–8; fac-
simile, 206, 220; illustration,
206, 208, 219–21, 227–8, Pl. VIII
Vie de Seint Edmond (*Edmund*),
168 ff., authorship, 173–6; date
and sources, 177–8
Vienne, 249

287